Pain and Injury in Sport

For elite athletes, pain and injury are standard. In a challenge to the orthodox medical model in which pain, injury and physical suffering are largely understood in terms of physiology alone, the text examines the influence of social and cultural processes on athletes' experiences of pain and injury, and goes on to raise important social and ethical questions about the culture of pain and 'playing hurt'.

The authors examine pain in sport from a range of theoretical perspectives including medical, psychological, philosophical, historical and sociological, and the text provides comprehensive discussion of key themes including:

- pain, injury and sports performance
- the deliberate infliction of pain
- management of pain and injury
- the role of sports coaches and medical staff
- the meaning of pain and injury.

Drawing on the contributions of leading international researchers, *Pain and Injury in Sport*'s multidisciplinary approach provides a uniquely broad basis for discussion. This is essential reading not just for students and those with a professional interest in managing injuries, but for all those who wish to understand more about the culture of sport and, in particular, about the culture of risk so integral to elite sport.

Sigmund Loland is Professor and Head of Section of Sport, Culture and Society at the Norwegian School of Sport Sciences, Oslo. **Berit Skirstad** is Associate Professor and responsible for Sport Management at the Norwegian School of Sport Sciences, Oslo. **Ivan Waddington** is Visiting Professor at the Norwegian School of Sport Sciences, Oslo; the Centre for Research into Sport and Society, University of Chester, UK; and the Centre for Sports Studies, University College Dublin, Ireland.

Ethics and Sport

Series Editors

Mike McNamee
University of Wales Swansea

Jim Parry
University of Leeds

The Ethics and Sport series aims to encourage critical reflection on the practice of sport, and to stimulate professional evaluation and development. Each volume explores new work relating to philosophical ethics and the social and cultural study of ethical issues. Each is different in scope, appeal, focus and treatment but a balance is sought between local and international focus, perennial and contemporary issues, level of audience, teaching and research application, and variety of practical concerns.

Also available in this series:

Pain and Injury in Sport
Social and ethical analysis

**Edited by Sigmund Loland,
Berit Skirstad and Ivan Waddington**

Routledge
Taylor & Francis Group

LONDON AND NEW YORK

First published 2006 by Routledge
2 Park Square, Milton Park, Abingdon, Oxon OX14 4RN

Simultaneously published in the USA and Canada
by Routledge
270 Madison Avenue, New York, NY 10016

Routledge is an imprint of the Taylor & Francis Group

© 2006 Selection and editorial matter, Sigmund Loland,
Berit Skirstad and Ivan Waddington;
individual chapters, the contributors

Typeset in Goudy by BC Typesetting Ltd, Bristol
Printed and bound in Great Britain by
The Cromwell Press Ltd, Trowbridge, Wiltshire

British Library Cataloguing in Publication Data
A catalogue record for this book is available from the British Library

Library of Congress Cataloging in Publication Data
A catalog record for this book has been requested

ISBN 10 0–415–35703–9 (hbk)
ISBN 10 0–415–35704–7 (pbk)
ISBN 13 978–0–415–35703–6 (hbk)
ISBN 13 978–0–415–35704–3 (pbk)

Contents

Contributors

John Bale is a teacher and researcher at the University of Aarhus, Denmark and Keele University, UK. He has been a visiting professor at the University of Jyvaskyla (Finland), the University of Western Ontario, and Queensland University. His main areas of research have focused on geographical dimensions of sports. Recent publications include *Imagined Olympians* (University of Minnesota Press) and *Running Cultures* (Routledge). Among his current projects is a study of sport and slowness.

Hannah Charlesworth gained her MA from the University of Leicester in 2000 and carried out her doctoral research into the sports-related pain and injury experiences of female university athletes at Loughborough University. She is currently employed by the Institute of Youth Sport at Loughborough University as a Research Associate. Her research interests include sports-related risk, injury, pain and gender. She was co-author, with Dr Kevin Young, of 'Why English Female University Athletes Play with Pain: Motivations and Rationalisations', a chapter published in *Sporting Bodies, Damaged Selves: Sociological Studies of Sports-related Injury* (Elsevier, 2004).

Dr Jeffrey P. Fry is an Assistant Professor in the Department of Philosophy and Religious Studies and Director of the Center for Sport, Ethics & Culture at Ball State University, Muncie, Indiana, USA. He has served on the Executive Council of the International Association for the Philosophy of Sport and is a member of the Editorial Board of the *Journal of the Philosophy of Sport*. He holds a double major PhD in Philosophy and Religious Studies from Indiana University. His recent publications have focused on ethical issues in sports, especially the ethics of coaching.

Matti Goksøyr, Cand. polit. in History 1982 at the University of Bergen, he completed his doctorate in 1991 at the Norwegian School of Sport Sciences, where he is now Professor of History. Goksøyr has published books and articles both nationally and internationally. Recent research topics include sport and national identity, sport and politics, polar history and football history. Recent publications include *Fotball! Norges Fotballforbund 100 år*. Oslo 2002 (co-written with Finn Olstad); 'Norway: Neighbourly Neutrality', in *The Nazi*

Olympics: Sports, Politics and Appeasement in the 1930s (eds. Arnd Krüger and Bill Murray), University of Illinois Press, Urbana and Chicago, 2003; 'Kappløp i gamle spor', in *Norsk Polarhistorie*, vol. 1 (eds. E. A. Drivenes and H. D. Jølle), Oslo 2004.

Dr P. David Howe is a medical anthropologist at the University of Brighton. His scholarly interests include, but are not limited to, the professionalization of sports medicine, particularly as this relates to issues of injury and risk. He is the author of *Sport, Professionalism and Pain: Ethnographies of Injury and Risk* (Routledge 2004). Equity related issues are central to his other research focus, the Paralympic Games. Currently he is completing a manuscript entitled *The Cultural Politics of the Paralympic Movement: Through the Anthropological Lens*.

Sigmund Loland is Professor and Head of Department of Cultural and Social Studies at The Norwegian School of Sport Sciences. His research interests include ethics in sport, epistemological issues, and sport and ecology. He has published extensively on these issues both nationally and internationally. His most recent book is *Fair Play: A Moral Norm System* (London: Routledge 2002).

Yotam Lurie is a Senior Lecturer in Philosophy and Ethics in the School of Management at the Ben-Gurion University of the Negev, Beer-Sheva, Israel. His degrees include a BA from Tel-Aviv University and an MA and PhD in Philosophy from the University of Illinois at Urbana-Champaign. His primary research interests are in applied ethics in general and business and professional ethics in particular. In addition, he does research and teaches in the fields of sport philosophy, ethical theory and social and political philosophy. His research has been published in a variety of journals.

Mike McNamee is Senior Lecturer in the Centre for Philosophy, Humanities and Law in Healthcare, at University of Wales Swansea, UK. He has broad interests in applied philosophy and particularly in ethics. His latest edited work is *Philosophy and the Sciences of Exercise, Health and Sport* (Routledge, 2005). He is the inaugural Chair of the British Philosophy of Sport Association and a former President of the International Association for the Philosophy of Sport. He co-edits the Ethics and Sports Series (Routledge).

Dominic Malcolm is Lecturer in the Sociology of Sport, Loughborough University. His research interests include cricket and race relations, cricket spectator and player violence, and the commercialization of sport. He has also recently published a number of journal articles stemming from his research with Ken Sheard on the management of injury in elite rugby union. His recent co-edited books include *Sport: Critical Concepts* (with Eric Dunning, Routledge 2003) and *Sport Histories: Figurational Studies in the Development of Sport* (with Eric Dunning and Ivan Waddington, Routledge 2004). He is currently writing *The Sage Dictionary of Sports Studies* for publication in 2007.

Dr Jim Parry is Senior Lecturer and former Head of the School of Philosophy at the University of Leeds, England, working in applied ethics and social and political philosophy as well as philosophy of sport. He is a qualified coach of basketball, soccer and rugby, and has also taught English and PE in secondary schools. He now enjoys undergraduate teaching of PE and sport students outside the University of Leeds, and is an external examiner with Leeds Metropolitan and Loughborough Universities. He is former chair of the British Universities PE Association, Founding Director of the British Olympic Academy, has been a collaborator of the International Olympic Academy for 20 years, and he held the International Chair in Olympic Studies at the Autonomous University of Barcelona for 2003.

Martin Roderick spent several years at the University of Leicester before moving to the University of Durham in 2004, where he is a Lecturer in Sociology. In 2003 he completed his PhD examining the careers of professional footballers. He has worked with Ivan Waddington on research focusing specifically on the management of injuries in professional football. His other research interests concern the sociology of emotions and sport, and the problems of participating in sport at elite levels.

Kirsten Kaya Roessler, PhD and MSc in Psychology and BA in Sport Science, is Associate Professor at the University of Southern Denmark. She is a former member of the Sport Research Council, a member of the Danish Forum of Sport Psychology and a co-editor of the Danish Journal *Sport & Psyke*. She has published in the areas of sport and health, sport and pain, movement and culture.

Ken Sheard has first-hand experience of pain and injury, having played rugby for over 30 years at various levels. This sporting interest found academic expression with research into the development of rugby football published, with Eric Dunning, as *Barbarians, Gentlemen and Players* (1979; 2005). His doctorate, *Boxing in the Civilizing Process* (1992), and subsequent publications, continued this interest in violent sports. Recently, with ex-colleagues at the Centre for Research into Sport and Society, University of Leicester, UK, he has published on the management of pain and injury in rugby football. He is former Research Director of the CRSS.

Associate Professor Berit Skirstad has been responsible for Sport Management Studies at the Norwegian School of Sport Sciences and at the EMDAPA in Leuwen for the past six years. She is the acting president of the European Association of Sport Management (EASM). Her books include *Hvem er hvem i norsk idrett* (1986), *Worldwide Trends in Youth Sport* (co-edited with P. DeKnop, L.-M. Engström and M. R. Weiss (1996) and *Idretten som del av tredje sektor* (co-edited with K. Felde and F. Thomassen). She has also contributed to K. Heinemann (ed.), *Sport Clubs in Various European Countries* (Hofmann Verlag, Stuttgart, 1999), to T. Tännsjö and C. Tamburrini, *Values in Sport* (Ethics and Sport series), (E. & F. N. Spon, London, 2000), and to Ø. Seippel (ed.), *Idrettens bevegelser: sosiologiske studier av idrett i et moderne samfunn*, (Novus forlag, Oslo, 2002).

Giselher Spitzer works as Privatdozent at Potsdam University and Humboldt University Berlin. Dr Spitzer is also a Visiting Professor at the University of Southern Denmark, Odense. He is a member of the Steering Committee of the International Network on Humanistic Doping Research, established in 2001 at the University of Southern Denmark. In 2003 he was awarded the Heidi Krieger Medal for his work against doping and assistance to victims of doping. His most recent books include *Doping in der DDR*, Sport und Buch Strauss, Cologne 1998 (2nd edition 2000, 3rd edition 2004); *Fussball und Triathlon. Sportentwicklungen in der DDR*, Aachen, Meyer & Meyer 2004; *Sicherungsvorgang Sport. Das Ministerium für Staatssicherheit und der DDR-Spitzensport*, Schorndorf, Hofmann Verlag, 2004; he is also a co-author of *Sport ohne Doping! Argumente und Entscheidungshilfen fuer junge Sportlerinnen und Sportler sowie in deren Umfeld*, 2004.

Ivan Waddington is Visiting Professor at the Norwegian School of Sport Sciences, Oslo; at the Chester Centre for Research into Sport and Society, University of Chester, UK; and at the Centre for Sports Studies, University College Dublin. His major research interests lie at the interface between the sociology of sport and the sociology of health. He is the author of *Sport, Health and Drugs* (Spon 2000) and a co-author of the British Medical Association report, *Drugs in Sport: the Pressure to Perform* (British Medical Journal Books, 2002). He has recently co-edited *Fighting Fans: Football Hooliganism as a World Phenomenon* (University College Dublin Press, 2002) and *Sport Histories: Figurational Studies of the Development of Modern Sports* (Routledge, 2004).

Kevin Young is Professor of Sociology at the University of Calgary in Canada. He has published on a variety of sports-related topics, including violence, gender and sub-cultural identity. His books include *Theory, Sport & Society* (Elsevier Press 2002) and *Sporting Bodies, Damaged Selves: Sociological Studies of Sports-related Injury* (Elsevier Press 2004). He has served on the editorial boards of several journals, including the *International Review for the Sociology of Sport, Sociology of Sport Journal, Soccer and Society* and *Avante*, as well as on the Executive Board of the North American Society for the Sociology of Sport. He is currently serving a second four-year, elected term as Vice President of the International Sociology of Sport Association.

Series editors' preface

The Ethics and Sport series aims to support and contribute to the development of the study of ethical issues in sport, and indeed to the establishing of Sports Ethics as a legitimate discipline in its own right. It does this by identifying issues of practical concern and exploring them systematically in extended discussion.

Given the logical basis of ethics at the heart of sport as a practical activity, every important and topical issue in sport necessarily has an ethical dimension – and often the ethical dimension is of overwhelming significance. The series addresses a variety of both perennial and contemporary issues in this rapidly expanding field, aiming to engage the community of teachers, researchers and professionals, as well as the general reader.

Philosophical ethics may be seen both as a theoretical academic discipline and as an ordinary everyday activity contributing to conversation, journalism and practical decision-making. The series aims to bridge that gap. Academic disciplines will be brought to bear on the practical issues of the day, illuminating them and exploring strategies for problem-solving. A philosophical interest in ethical issues may also be complemented and broadened by research within related disciplines, such as sociology and psychology.

The series aims to encourage critical reflection on the practice of sport, and to stimulate professional evaluation and development. Each volume explores new work relating to philosophical ethics and the social and cultural study of ethical issues. Each is different in scope, appeal, focus and treatment, but a balance is sought within the series between local and international focus, perennial and contemporary issues, level of audience, teaching and research application and variety of practical concern. Each volume is complete in itself, but also complements others in the series.

In the first two edited volumes of this series, a range of issues is explored, addressing issues central to the philosophical exploration of sports ethics as a discipline. Subsequent volumes were planned to develop individual themes in depth, as well as to pose general questions about the evolving significance of sport in contemporary society. Our aims are both to encourage and contribute to the debate and to sport's ethical development.

This volume is a prime example of what the series aims to achieve. Until very recently, the study of pain and injury had been almost exclusively the preserve of biomedical researchers. Only in the past 10–15 years has serious attention been given to the ethical and social significance of pain and injury in the context of sporting activity.

The editors of this volume have brought together discussions from a number of disciplines and perspectives, across a variety of sports and dealing with a wide range of issues and concerns. They present us with theoretical frameworks from philosophy, sociology and psychology, and case studies and examples from many different contexts. This, then, is a rich blend of state-of-the-art knowledge and expertise across the humanistic disciplines, and a rich resource for anyone interested in the outcomes of recent empirical studies of pain and injury in sport.

Specifically the book comprises philosophical enquiry into the meanings of pain and injury in sport, and the rationales and justifications for undergoing the associated risks and dangers, or for subjecting others to them; socio-political and ethical analysis of the deliberate infliction of pain, both on oneself and on others; psychological research into the self-perceptions of athletes; sociological accounts of the clinical management of pain; anthropological work with disabled athletes; and many detailed and illuminative case studies from various sports and perspectives.

Mike McNamee, University of Wales Swansea
Jim Parry, University of Leeds

Acknowledgements

This book is the outcome of a workshop on 'Pain and Injury in Sport' which was organized by Sigmund Loland, Berit Skirstad and Ivan Waddington and held in Oslo on 12–13 February 2004. Both the workshop and the preparation for publishing the book have been kindly supported by the Norwegian School of Sport Sciences. The authors have had the chance to work on their manuscript after the workshop and we gratefully acknowledge their contributions. Without their efforts and thoughtful work this book would not have been possible. Each author contributed her or his valuable expertise and experience to create a book which we hope provides useful insights in the field of pain and injury in sport. We are further grateful to PhD student Petter Kristiansen who helped in organizing the workshop and tracking the manuscripts. Anne Kristi Rimeslåtten has done an excellent job in formatting the manuscripts and checking the last details.

Introduction

Pain and injury in sport

Ivan Waddington, Sigmund Loland and Berit Skirstad

In recent years, researchers in the social and human sciences have begun to make a significant contribution to our understanding of the ways in which athletes experience pain and injury and the ways in which injuries are managed within the sporting context. Several authors in this volume have already made notable contributions to this area of study (see for example Howe 2001, 2004; Malcolm and Sheard 2002; Malcolm *et al.* 2004; Roderick 1998, 2004; Roderick *et al.* 2000; Waddington 2000, 2002, 2004; Waddington *et al.* 2001; Waddington and Roderick 2002; Young 1993, 2004; Young *et al.* 1994; Young and White, 1995). Prior to the1990s, however, issues associated with sports injuries seemed to be of little concern to social scientists for, as Roderick notes in his chapter in this volume, the study of sports injuries was considered to be the more or less exclusive domain of those involved in the bio-medical sciences, such as sports medicine specialists, physiotherapists and exercise physiologists.

In some respects, the fact that researchers in the social and human sciences have only entered this field in the past few years may not seem surprising and might not appear to merit any special comment; or, to put the issue another way, it is perhaps not surprising that the bio-medical model should have enjoyed for so long what amounted almost to a monopolistic position in terms of the explanation of pain and injury. In this regard it is important to note that, although social science researchers have in recent years become increasingly critical of a perspective which regards pain as – to use Roderick's words – merely 'a matter of nerves and neurotransmitters', it is also important to bear in mind that, as Loland points out in Chapter 3 of this volume, the bio-medical model has provided the basis for impressive advances in both the understanding and the treatment of injury (and also, of course, of illness more generally). There is little doubt that the – until recently – almost unquestioned dominance of the bio-medical model has been strongly underpinned by the very considerable therapeutic payoff which it has generated. However, and notwithstanding the therapeutic success and associated dominance of the bio-medical model, in some respects the relatively late entry of social scientists into this field is still worthy of comment not least because, outside the sporting context, social scientists have for more than half a century been involved in the study, and have made important contributions to our understanding, of the ways in which people respond to pain and other symptoms of illness. Let us explore these issues a little further.

As Armstrong (2003: 24) has noted:

> At the end of the eighteenth century a new explanatory model of illness emerged in Parisian hospitals . . . This new model replaced the constantly shifting symptoms of humoral medicine with the novel idea that illness was a product of a specific localized pathological lesion within the body.

The institutional basis of this development in medical science – that is, the development of the hospital system and the emergence within the hospitals of a structure of medical dominance – has been described elsewhere (Waddington 1973) and need not detain us here. What is important to note is that this new explanatory model of illness, which was further developed in the nineteenth century with the emergence of laboratory medicine (Jewson 1976), 'provided what must count as the most successful theory of health and illness, spreading over the last two centuries to become the major formal explanatory framework of illness in all countries of the world' (Armstrong 2003: 24). The success of the bio-medical model also provided the basis, in the twentieth century, for a process of medicalization involving the extension of medical intervention into more and more areas of life (Zola 1972), one aspect of which has been the medicalization of sport which was given its clearest institutional expression in the development of sports medicine (Waddington 1996).

Armstrong (2003: 24) has correctly noted that the 'phenomenal success of the biomedical theory of illness has constituted the essential backdrop for social theorizing about health and illness'. However, and notwithstanding the dominance of the bio-medical explanatory model, researchers in the sociology and anthropology of health and illness began from the very beginnings of those sub-disciplines to develop perspectives which at first supplemented, and later challenged, the bio-medical model. For example, in his classic paper, 'Cultural components in response to pain', published over half a century ago, Zborowski ([1952], 1958) investigated the ways in which hospital patients in the Bronx, New York, responded to pain. All the patients were suffering from a similar pathology, but Zborowski found significant, culturally patterned, differences in the ways in which members of three different ethnic groups – Italians, Jews and 'Old Americans' – responded to and coped with pain, and the ways in which they interpreted the meaning of their pain. Zborowski noted that the physiology of pain and the understanding of the biological function of pain do not explain other key aspects of 'the *pain experience*, which includes not only the pain sensation and certain automatic reactive responses but also certain "associated feeling states"'. In this regard, he noted that the bio-medical model would not explain, for example, the acceptance of intense pain in torture which is part of initiation rites in some simple societies, nor would it explain the strong emotional reactions of some people to the slight sting of a hypodermic needle. He suggested that 'the understanding of the significance and role of social and cultural patterns in human physiology is necessary to clarify those aspects of human experience which remain puzzling if studied only within the physiological frame of reference' (Zborowski [1952] 1958: 257).

Two years after the publication of Zborowski's study, another classic work in medical sociology, Earl Koos's *The Health of Regionsville* (1954) recorded that people from higher social classes were more likely than people from lower social classes to view themselves as ill when they had particular symptoms, and when they were questioned about specific symptoms, they reported more frequently than lower-class people that they would seek medical advice. Koos's study thus reinforced Zborowski's central finding that people with the same or similar symptoms can perceive, respond to and seek to manage those symptoms in very different ways; in other words, the way in which humans respond to symptoms, including pain and discomfort, is *not* just 'a matter of nerves and neurotransmitters'.

These findings were confirmed by many other early studies in medical sociology and anthropology. Largely because of its implications for health care, the finding by Koos and others that many people do not seek medical attention, even when they have clear symptoms of illness, ushered in a major body of investigations into what became known as 'illness behaviour', defined by Mechanic (1966: 12) as:

the study of attentiveness to pain and symptomatology, the examination of processes affecting how pain and symptoms are defined, accorded significance and socially labelled, and the consideration of the extent to which help is sought, changes in life regimen affected, and claims on others made.

It is interesting to note that this definition of illness behaviour, offered by Mechanic almost 40 years ago, continues to serve as an acceptable statement of the key issues in relation to pain and injury which have recently aroused the interests of sociologists of sport.

From this brief outline of the early development of the sociology and anthropology of health, it is clear that social scientists in these sub-disciplines were researching key aspects of the perception, response to and management of pain and other symptoms some three or four decades before researchers in the sociology of sport recognized this as an important area for study. To revisit our earlier question: how does one account for the fact that until relatively recently, researchers in the social and human sciences showed little interest in the study of pain and injury in sport?

One obvious reason why sociologists and other social scientists concerned with the analysis of sport began to study pain much later than did their colleagues working in the study of health more generally is that the sociology and anthropology of sport, as sub-disciplines, developed much later than did the sociology and anthropology of health. In the 1960s the sociology of sport hardly existed as a sub-discipline; indeed, as Dunning (1992: 224) has noted, there was among some sociologists at that time a 'contemptuous dismissal of sport as an area of

sociological enquiry'. In the United States there were at that time only a handful of sociologists working in the area, while in Britain, two short papers by Eric
Dunning, published in 1963 and 1964, were probably the very first published
pieces of research there to examine sport from a properly sociological perspective. In marked contrast, the sociology of health was already well established
at that time, both in Britain and in the United States. As we have noted,
there were in the 1950s several major studies in the United States which had
already laid the foundations for the study of illness behaviour. Moreover, medical sociology attracted the attention of some of the leading American social
theorists of that period. For example, Talcott Parsons, in his classic study of
modern medical practice in *The Social System* (1951), and Robert K. Merton
(1957) and Howard Becker *et al.* (1961) in their studies of medical education,
all made early and major contributions to the field. At about the same time,
the first edition of E. Gartley Jaco's *Patients, Physicians and Illness* (1958) sought
to bring together some key aspects of what Jaco (1958: 7) described as the
'many diversified and multitudinous efforts in behavioral science and medicine
[which] have been going on during the past few years'. In Britain, medical
sociologists had, by the mid-1960s, already made a sufficiently substantial
contribution to the study of health and illness for the Royal Commission on
Medical Education (1965–8) to recommend that the teaching of sociology
should be included in the curriculum of all medical schools. Thus while those
sociologists who studied sport were still involved in a struggle to establish the
legitimacy of their work, even within their parent discipline, the case for medical sociology had largely been established, not just within sociology but also
within the medical schools.

Not only was medical sociology firmly established as a sub-discipline long
before the sociology of sport enjoyed this status but, from the beginning, a central
focus – perhaps *the* central focus – of medical sociology and anthropology was on
illness behaviour. This was perhaps not surprising, for an understanding of why
patients reacted differently to pain and other symptoms of illness, and in particular why some patients did not consult a doctor even when they had clear
symptoms of illness, had obvious and important policy implications in relation
to the provision of medical care. In marked contrast, there were at that time
no obvious or compelling practical concerns which might have led social scientists who were interested in the study of sport to focus on the ways in which
athletes respond to and manage injury and pain, rather than on the many other
aspects of sport which, quite legitimately, claimed their interest. For example,
one of the earliest texts in the field, Eric Dunning's edited collection *The Sociology
of Sport* (1971), contained a section outlining some key concepts and theories in
the study of sport, followed by sections on the development of sports and games;
sports and socialization; class, race and sport; sport as an occupation; and conflict and social control in sport. There was nothing in the book on injuries in
sport, though at the time that would not have been seen as a significant omis-
sion from a text in the sociology of sport. Despite a very longstanding, widely
accepted and very powerful ideology linking sport and health, for example in

the provision of sport in schools (Waddington 2000), it was to be some years before sociologists and other social scientists became involved in the study of a key aspect of the relationship between sport and health, namely injuries in sport.

As we noted earlier, social scientists began to take an interest in pain and injury in sport from the 1980s and, more especially, from the 1990s. This may have been associated, in part, with a slowly growing awareness of the economic costs of sports injuries at both the mass and elite levels. For example, the growing awareness of the magnitude of the problems associated with sports injuries was graphically conveyed in the subtitle of one American text on sports injuries: 'The Unthwarted Epidemic' (Vinger and Hoerner 1982). In Britain, the economic costs of sports injuries were clearly brought out in a large-scale epidemiological study which was carried out by researchers at Sheffield University Medical School and which sought to ascertain the direct health care costs and benefits of participation in sport. The researchers came up with some surprising results. The health benefits of exercise (for example, avoidance of certain chronic illnesses such as cardiovascular disease and osteoporosis) were weighed against the costs of treatment of exercise-related injuries. It was found that, although there were clear economic benefits associated with exercise for adults aged 45 and over, for younger adults (aged 15–44), the costs avoided by the disease-prevention effects of exercise (less than £5 per person per year) were more than offset by the medical costs resulting from participation in sport and exercise (approximately £30 per person per year). In other words the study found that for every person aged 15–44 who regularly participates in sport and exercise, there is a net cost to the British taxpayer of £25 per year (Nicholl et al. 1994). It had for many years been taken for granted that participation in sport was part of the solution to public health problems, but the Sheffield research, which echoed similar findings in a Dutch study (Reijnen and Velthuijsen 1989, cited in Nicholl et al. 1994) suggested that sporting participation and the associated injuries were, at least in some respects, themselves part of a public health problem.

But perhaps of greater importance has been the growing recognition of the personal and social (including economic) costs of injuries at the elite level, for it has become increasingly clear that injuries are of much more than just clinical significance. The increasing recognition of the social and economic significance of injuries in elite sport has been associated with a number of processes, one of which is the growing competitiveness of modern sport. As Dunning (1986) has noted, the growing competitiveness of modern sport is a long-term trend which can be traced back over two or more centuries. This process has, however, been especially marked in recent years and has been associated with the increasing politicization and, especially, the commercialization of sport, both of which have had the effect of greatly increasing the importance of, and the rewards associated with, winning, while downgrading the traditional value associated with taking part (Waddington 2000: 123–7).

The increase in the competitiveness of modern sport has had two important consequences in relation to injuries. First, as Donohoe and Johnson (1986: 93) have noted, to 'succeed in modern sport, athletes are forced to train longer, harder, and earlier in life. They may be rewarded by faster times, better performances and increased fitness, but there is a price to pay for such intense training.' Part of the price of such intense training and of the readiness to continue training and competing even when injured, is unquestionably paid in the form of more stress injuries and more overuse and recurrent injuries, which now constitute a serious problem in sport. As Donohoe and Johnson (1986: 93) have noted, the 'long-term effects of overuse injuries are not known, but some concerned doctors have asked whether today's gold medallists could be crippled by arthritis by the age of 30' and they cite world-class competitors who have, in their words, 'been plagued by a succession of overuse injuries'. In this respect, the results from a study at Coventry University in England are very revealing. Of 284 former professional football (soccer) players who completed a questionnaire from the University's Psychosocial Rheumatology Research Centre, 49 per cent had been diagnosed with osteoarthritis, a percentage which is five times as high as that in males of a similar age in the general population. Fifteen per cent of all respondents were now registered disabled and one-third of ex-players had, since retiring from professional football, undergone surgery for football-related injuries (Hicks 1998).

If, as is almost certainly the case, the increasing competitiveness of modern sport has been associated with an increase in the incidence of injury, it has also been associated with an increase in the social and economic significance of injury for individual athletes and their careers. As we noted above, one of the key processes in the increased competitiveness of modern sport has been the increasing commercialization of sport. Particularly important in this regard has been the huge increase in sports sponsorship in recent years. Gratton and Taylor (2000: 163) have noted that 'sports sponsorship hardly existed as an economic activity before 1970 in Britain, yet by 1999 it was estimated to be worth £350 million'. They add that, globally, sports sponsorship is a massive industry estimated to be worth around $20 billion in 1999, having grown by over 300 per cent in the 1990s alone. This growth in sponsorship has been one of the key processes which has transformed the careers of elite athletes and, by implication, the significance of injuries. As Howe notes in Chapter 13 of this volume, an injury can deprive an elite competitor of the opportunity to compete in an Olympic competition for which he or she may have spent four years preparing. But for those athletes who are successful in events which attract major media coverage, and who are therefore able to secure major sponsorship deals, injury may lead not just to the loss of a medal, but also to the loss of a huge potential income, for in many countries Olympic gold medal winners and other sports stars can earn huge incomes not just from their sporting salaries but also from sponsorship, television commercials and product endorsement. The significance of sponsorship is indicated by the fact that in 1995, Michael Jordan's salary from the Chicago Bulls was a not inconsiderable $3.9 million, but this was dwarfed by his earnings from product endorsement, estimated to be in the region of $40 million (Armstrong 1996). To elite athletes, injuries can be *very* expensive.

If injuries have come to be of growing significance, in career terms, for individual athletes, they have also come to be of increasing significance for team performance and perhaps particularly for professional teams which have to compete in a world that is increasingly competitive not only in sporting, but also in commercial terms. Waddington (1998) has pointed to the significance of injuries in professional football (soccer) by using an analogy between the football industry and other industries. He writes:

> Imagine the following scenario. The board of directors of a large company decides that, in order to maintain a competitive edge over their major rivals, it is necessary for the company to embark on a major program of capital investment. With this in mind, much of the old equipment is dismantled and replaced with gleaming brand new, state-of-the-art machinery. Each of these new items of machinery costs several million pounds, but unfortunately the new machines continually break down and are out of use. At the end of the year, a review of the way in which the plant has been working indicates that only one or two of the machines have been working continuously; most of the machines have been out of action for several months of the year and some machines have broken down so frequently that they have hardly been used at all.

He adds:

> It is, of course, difficult to imagine how any company could compete effectively if it was run this way. There is however one industry – not, it should be noted, a single company, but a whole industry – which does appear to be run in this way: the football industry. Football fans will of course be familiar with the situation described above. Many fans will have experienced a sense of excitement and anticipation when their team signs an expensive striker, only to be followed very quickly by a sense of despair when, after just one or two games, the player sustains a serious injury which puts him out of the game for several weeks or perhaps even months.
>
> (Waddington 1998: 3)

The analogy is not based on an exaggeration of the risks of injury. As Young (1993: 373) has pointed out:

> By any measure, professional sport is a violent and hazardous workplace, replete with its own unique forms of 'industrial disease'. No other single milieu, including the risky and labor-intensive settings of miners, oil drillers, or construction site workers, can compare with the routine injuries of team sports such as football, ice-hockey, soccer, rugby and the like.

Just how high these injury risks are was indicated by an epidemiological study of injuries in English professional football, which found that the risk of injury to professional footballers is no less than 1,000 times the risk of injury in other occupations normally considered high risk, such as construction and mining (Hawkins and Fuller 1999). It is clear that the economic costs of injuries to the club are likely to be very substantial for, as Johnson (1998: 332) has pointed out, while the ground and other facilities of a football club are fixed assets which can be sold at any time, the players 'only have a book asset value while fit and playing in the first team'. Fuller (1998) notes that a risk assessment approach to the analysis of accidents and injuries in professional football suggests that typically players receive at least one injury each season that results in their non-availability for selection for, on average, 7–8 matches per season. Although it is difficult to calculate precisely the full economic costs to the club, Fuller notes that, in addition to the salary costs associated with this lost time, other potential costs to an English Premier League club include the costs of rehabili- tation arising from the injury, the purchase of replacement players, the reduced income from a lower final league placing, elimination from cup competitions and failure to qualify for European competition as a result of impaired team per- formance. In some situations – for example, where a club buys an expensive player who then almost immediately receives a career-ending injury – the costs would be substantially greater.

It is perhaps a reasonable hypothesis to suggest that the increased incidence of injuries associated with the increased competitiveness of modern sport, and the growing recognition of the increased social and economic significance of injuries, are among the processes which, to some extent, have underpinned the recent growth in the study of pain and injury in sport by researchers in the social and human sciences. This volume is, of course, part of that growth.

The volume is the result of a workshop on pain and injury, organized by Sigmund Loland, Berit Skirstad and Ivan Waddington and held at the Norwegian School of Sports Sciences (formerly the Norwegian University of Sport and Physical Education) Oslo, on 12 and 13 February 2004. It includes 16 chapters written by an international group of scholars and offers social and ethical per- spectives on pain and injury in sports. The chapters are organized thematically in five sections, each of which has a clear rationale.

Section I, Pain and Injury in Sports: Three Overviews, outlines three general theoretical frameworks for the study of pain and injury in sport. Martin Roderick provides a broad overview of the sociological literature on pain and injury in sport and identifies some key areas for further research. Writing from the perspective of a psychologist, Kirsten Kaya Roessler examines some general theoretical approaches to the study of pain before reporting an empirical study of the management of pain and injury by Danish athletes. She concludes her chapter by arguing for a more existentially oriented sports psychology. In the final chapter in this section, Sigmund Loland examines three rather different approaches to the study of pain in sport: the classical, medical approach; the approach which sees pain as socially and culturally constructed; and the approach which is inspired by phenomenology and which departs from the immediate and experiential qualities of pain. He concludes by reflecting upon the implications of these differing approaches for further research into pain in sport. It is hoped that this first section will not only provide some indication of the contributions which the social and human sciences can make to the study of pain and injury – and of the ways in which the contributions of the social and human sciences are distinctively different from the contributions of the biological sciences – but that it will also provide useful theoretical frameworks within which the more empirically based chapters in other sections can be located.

The next three sections all deal with more specific case studies. Section II: Pain, Injury and Performance, focuses on athletes' experience of and responses to pain. A key issue underlying the three chapters in this section is the acceptance by athletes that the search for improved performance will almost certainly require their acceptance of a significant degree of pain. There is, of course, the obvious risk of injury and the pain which is associated with injury and, given the fact that elite sport is a high-risk activity, it is almost inevitable that elite athletes will experience injury-related pain from time to time. But there are also, as John Bale and Matti Goksøyr point out in their chapters on running and on polar adventurers, other kinds of pain which are a central part of elite sport. There is, for example, what Bale calls the pain of 'non-injured' athletes – the muscular pain and exhaustion which is associated with pushing oneself very hard, whether in training or competition, and without which athletes are unlikely to reach the level of fitness required to succeed. As Bale notes in Chapter 4, such pain may be regarded by runners as 'the deposit, the investment, through which speed is extracted. Pain is a form of bodily or physical capital, a bearer of symbolic value.' In much the same way, the pain associated with drudgery, toil and exhaustion is accepted as a necessary price to be paid for success in the harsh world of polar exploration, as Goksøyr makes clear in Chapter 5. The final chapter in this section, by Hannah Charlesworth and Kevin Young, focuses on the pain associated with injury and offers new insights into this area of research by focusing on what has been a relatively under-researched area, namely the perception of pain and injury by female athletes.

Section III deals with the deliberate infliction of pain and injury and raises a number of issues which in some key respects are rather different, in social and ethical terms, from the issues raised in the previous section. As Bale notes in his chapter in the previous section, there is a sense in which one could say that in long-distance running, athletes 'choose to torture themselves'. The same could be said of athletes in many other sports, particularly perhaps in other endurance sports such as professional cycling (see, for example, Fry's discussion of seven-time Tour de France winner Lance Armstrong in the final chapter of this volume). But the infliction of pain described by Giselher Spitzer in Chapter 7 was not pain which athletes themselves more or less freely accepted as part of high-level sport, but rather pain which was inflicted on them, often without their knowledge or consent, as part of the institutionalized, state-sponsored mandatory doping programme of the former German Democratic

Republic. This clearly raises important socio-political questions, for example about the relationship between the state and its individual citizens, about the different patterns of drug use in sport which are associated with different socio-economic-political systems, and it also, of course, raises a number of very serious ethical questions.

Boxing, which is the subject of Ken Sheard's chapter in this section, also raises a number of ethical questions which do not apply to most other sports. Although people are always likely to suffer pain and injury while playing sport, the deliberate infliction of pain and injury on one's opponent is precisely the objective of boxing and the means by which victory is secured; in this respect, boxing raises ethical questions which most other sports do not raise. It has also, in the twentieth century, been the subject of much greater opposition from the medical profession than almost any other sport and Ken Sheard presents a very scholarly analysis of these medical debates about boxing. In the final chapter in this section, Jim Parry, writing from the perspective of a philosopher, considers, with particular reference to boxing, some of the ethical issues which are raised by sporting situations in which pain is deliberately inflicted on athletes.

Section IV is on the Management of Pain and Injury. Perhaps surprisingly, most researchers have paid only marginal attention to sports medicine clinicians. This section addresses this generally neglected area. Dominic Malcolm and Ivan Waddington focus, respectively, on the provision of medical care in professional rugby and in professional football in England, and both raise important questions about the quality of care. Malcolm concludes that, among other things, the 'skills and commitment of rugby club doctors can, at best, be described as variable, and may expose some players, even at leading clubs, to what many might consider unacceptable levels of risk', while Waddington focuses on some ethical issues in football and, in particular, on ethical issues surrounding questions of informed consent, return to play decisions following injury, and issues relating to medical confidentiality.

In Chapter 12, Yotam Lurie focuses on what he refers to as the ontology of sports injuries, which he uses as a basis for considering the ethics of sports medicine. More specifically, Lurie refers to four models of understanding pain and injury in sport: a medical model oriented towards health, a normative model for the professional athlete, a liberal model relevant to those who practise sport as part of a scheme of total well-being, and the phenomenological model in which the injury is understood as part of an individual's life world (*Lebenswelt*). Finally, P. David Howe concludes this section by looking at the management of injury among elite athletes with a disability and associated issues concerned with the systems which are used to classify disability within sport and how these help to shape the socio-political environment within the Paralympic movement.

The book ends, as it began, with a consideration of some more general issues. In the final section, The Meaning of Pain and Injury, Mike McNamee and Jeffrey Fry examine how pain and injury have been and are interpreted within various philosophical and religious contexts. Mike McNamee looks at the role of the emotions in relation to pain and injury. He first discusses some opposing philosophical understandings of the emotions and proceeds by discussing pain as distinctive of the deeper rooted and culturally contextualized suffering. This leads to a clearer and richer picture of the emotional aspects of suffering in sport than is traditionally found. In the final chapter of the book, Jeff Fry looks at conceptions of pain and suffering in sport and religion. To Fry, pain and suffering present an ambiguous picture. Both in sport and in religion, devotees attempt to avoid pain and suffering. On the other hand, positive appraisals of pain and suffering as empowering and deeply meaningful can be found in both sport and religion.

The book is structured so as to provide perspectives on pain and injury in sport both from the social sciences and the humanities, and from individual as well as institutional perspectives. The hope of the editors is that each chapter offers an in-depth analysis of specific research areas, and that the chapters together offer some of the width necessary to develop a better understanding of the complexity and diversity of pain and injury in sport as social and philosophical phenomena.

Bibliography

Armstrong, D. (2003) 'Social theorizing about health and illness', in G. L. Albrecht, R. Fitzpatrick and S. C. Scrimshaw (eds) *The Handbook of Social Studies in Health and Medicine*, London: Sage: 24–35.

Armstrong, E. A. (1996) 'The commodified 23, or, Michael Jordan as text', *Sociology of Sport Journal*, 13: 325–43.

Becker, H., Geer, B., Hughes, E. C. and Strauss, A. (1961) *Boys in White: Student Culture in Medical School*, Chicago: University of Chicago Press.

Donohoe, T. and Johnson, N. (1986) *Foul Play: Drug Abuse in Sports*, Oxford: Blackwell Scientific Publications.

Dunning, E. (1963) 'Football in its early stages', *History Today*, December.

Dunning, E. (1964) 'The evolution of football', *New Society*, 83, April.

Dunning, E. (1986) 'The dynamics of modern sport: notes on achievement-striving and the social significance of sport' in N. Elias and E. Dunning, *Quest for Excitement*, Oxford: Blackwell: 205–23.

Dunning, E. (1992) 'Figurational sociology and the sociology of sport: some concluding remarks' in E. Dunning and C. Rojek (eds) *Sport and Leisure in the Civilizing Process: Critique and Counter-Critique*, Basingstoke and London: Macmillan.

Dunning, E. (ed.) (1971) *The Sociology of Sport*, London: Cass.

Fuller, C. W. (1998) 'Professional footballers and risk management', *Sport and Medicine Today*, 1: 41–2.

Gratton, C. and Taylor, P. (2000) *Economics of Sport and Recreation*, London: E. and F. N. Spon.

Hawkins, R. D. and Fuller, C. W. (1999) 'A prospective epidemiological study of injuries in four English professional football clubs', *British Journal of Sports Medicine*, 33: 196–203.

Hicks, R. (1998) 'Arthritis and the professional footballer', *Football Decision*, December: 22–3.

Howe, P. D. (2001) 'An ethnography of pain and injury in professional rugby union: the case of Pontypridd RFC', *International Review for the Sociology of Sport*, 35, 3: 289–303.

Howe, P. D. (2004) *Sport, Pain and Professionalism: Ethnographies of Injury and Risk*, London: Routledge.

Jaco, E. G. (ed.) (1958) *Patients, Physicians and Illness*, New York: Free Press.

Jewson, N. (1976) 'The disappearance of the sick-man from medical cosmology 1770–1870', *Sociology*: 225–44.

Johnson, D. P. (1998) 'Costs of league soccer injuries', *British Journal of Sports Medicine*, 32: 326–32.

Koos, E. (1954) *The Health of Regionsville: What the People Thought and Did About It*, New York: Columbia University Press.

Malcolm, D. and Sheard, K. (2002) '"Pain in the assets": The effects of commercialization and professionalization on the management of injury in English rugby union', *Sociology of Sport Journal*, 19, 2: 149–69.

Malcolm, D., Sheard, K. and Smith, S. (2004) 'Protected research: Sports medicine and rugby injuries', *Culture, Sport, Society* 7, 1: 97–110.

Mechanic, D. (1966), 'Response factors in illness: the study of illness behavior', *Social Psychiatry*, 1: 11–20.

Merton, R. K. and Reader, G. G. (eds) (1957) *The Student Physician*, Cambridge, MA: Harvard University Press.

Nicholl, J. P., Coleman, P. and Brazier, J. E. (1994) 'Health and healthcare costs and benefits of exercise', *PharmacoEconomics*, 5, 2: 109–22.

Parsons, T. (1951) *The Social System*, New York: Free Press.

Roderick, M. J. (1998) 'The sociology of risk, pain and injury: A comment on the work of Howard L. Nixon II', *Sociology of Sport Journal*, 11: 175–94.

Roderick, M. J. (2004) 'English professional soccer players and the uncertainty of injury' in K. Young (ed.), *Sporting Bodies, Damaged Selves*, Oxford: Elsevier: 137–50.

Roderick, M., Waddington, I. and Parker, G. (2000) 'Playing hurt: Managing injuries in English professional football', *International Review for the Sociology of Sport*, 35, 2: 165–80.

Royal Commission on Medical Education 1965–8. *Report*. (Chairman: Lord Todd). London, HMSO, 1968. Cmnd 3569.

Vinger, P. F. and Hoerner, E. F. (eds) (1982) *Sports Injuries: The Unthwarted Epidemic*, Littleton, MA: PSG Publishing Co. Inc.

Waddington, I. (1973) 'The role of the hospital in the development of modern medicine', *Sociology*, 7: 211–24.

Waddington, I. (1996) 'The development of sports medicine', *Sociology of Sport Journal*, 13, 2: 176–96.

Waddington, I. (1998) 'No pain, no game' in P. Murphy (ed.) *Singer and Friedlander's Review 1997–98 Season*, London: Singer and Friedlander: 3–5.

Waddington, I. (2000) *Sport, Health and Drugs: A Critical Sociological Perspective*, London and New York: E. & F. N. Spon.

Waddington, I. (2002) 'Jobs for the boys? A study of the employment of club doctors and physiotherapists in English professional football', *Soccer and Society*, 3, 3: 51–64.

Waddington, I. (2004), 'Sport, health and public policy' in K. Young (ed.), *Sporting Bodies, Damaged Selves*, Oxford: Elsevier: 287–308.

Waddington, I. and Roderick, M. (2002) 'The management of medical confidentiality in English professional football clubs: some ethical problems and issues', *British Journal of Sports Medicine*, 36, 2: 118–23.

Waddington, I., Roderick, M. and Naik, R. (2001) 'Methods of appointment and quali-fications of club doctors and physiotherapists in English professional football: some problems and issues', *British Journal of Sports Medicine*, 35, 1: 48–53.

Young, K. (1993) 'Violence, risk and liability in male sports culture', *Sociology of Sport Journal*, 10, 4: 373–96.

Young, K. (ed.) (2004) *Sporting Bodies, Damaged Selves*, Oxford: Elsevier.

Young, K. and White, P. (1995) 'Sport, physical danger and injury: the experiences of elite women athletes', *Journal of Sport and Social Issues*, 19, 1: 45–61.

Young, K., White, P. and McTeer, W. (1994) 'Body talk: male athletes reflect on sport, injury and pain', *Sociology of Sport Journal*, 11, 2: 175–94.

Zborowski, M. [1952], (1958) 'Cultural components in responses to pain', *Journal of Social Issues*, 1952, 8: 16–30. Reprinted in E. G. Jaco (ed.) (1958) *Patients, Physicians and Illness*, New York: Free Press: 256–68.

Zola, I. (1972) 'Medicine as an institution of social control', *Sociological Review*, n.s., 20: 487–504.

Section I

Pain and injury in sports:
Three overviews

1 The sociology of pain and injury in sport

Main perspectives and problems

Martin Roderick

Since the early 1990s, an increasing number of qualitative sociological studies have examined the ways in which athletes experience pain and injury in the course of participating in sport. Prior to the 1990s, however, few sociologists had written about this problem, for the study of sports injuries was considered to be the domain of physiotherapists, exercise physiologists and sports medicine specialists. Yet through the 1970s and 1980s there were numerous biographical and journalistic accounts of professional and high-level athletes who continued to compete stoically when injured and in pain. For example, in his classic study of Tottenham Hotspur Football Club, *The Glory Game*, Hunter Davies ([1972], 1996) devoted an entire chapter to an injury sustained by former England international player, Alan Mullery. Writing in 1972, Davies recorded that:

> [Mullery had] been playing all season with stomach pains. He'd hoped he could play it out, that the pains would just fade away, but they hadn't. He'd been using a corset for some time . . . This had helped slightly at first, but then the pains had grown worse.
>
> (Davies 1996: 168)

Having finally admitted to a serious problem and therefore become unavailable for selection, Mullery, in conversation with Davies, goes on to make the following point:

> I didn't want to complain about it or moan, that's why I didn't tell the lads for a long time. I didn't really want to tell Bill [Nicholson, the club manager]. His first reaction was what I knew he'd say. He said Dave McKay had it and he played on till it [broke down completely].
>
> (Davies 1996: 169)

Davies did not focus on the physiological breakdown of Mullery's groin or the accuracy of the diagnosis; rather, he concentrated on the way Mullery managed his injury among team-mates, his club manager, the club medical personnel and his wife. Implicitly, Davies also examined the network of relationships in which Mullery was embedded. It would be inaccurate to suggest that incidents such as the one concerning Mullery are isolated, as for some time there has been sub-stantial evidence that, particularly at the higher levels, there are considerable pressures on athletes to compete when injured and in pain (Waddington 2000). However, despite the availability of a wealth of such anecdotal evidence, it was not until the 1990s that systematic sociological examinations of the social relations of managing pain and injury in sport commenced.

Until very recently, the study of pain has received scant sociological atten-tion, despite its significant positioning at the intersection between biology and culture (Bendelow 2000). Theoretical approaches to pain have tended to be dominated by bio-medicine, a perspective that considers pain to be a matter of nerves and neurotransmitters, both in diagnosis and in treatment. According to Bendelow (2000), scientific medicine stands accused of reducing the experi-ence of pain to an elaborate broadcasting system of signals, rather than seeing it as moulded and shaped both by individuals and by their socio-cultural context. It has been argued that a major impediment to a more adequate conceptualization of pain has been the manner in which it has been 'medicalized', resulting in an artificial split between body and mind, which is one of the prime characteristics of the bio-medical model (Williams and Bendelow 1998). Consequently, the dominant (biomedical) conceptualization of pain has focused upon sensation, as though it could be objectively measured. Yet, as well as being a 'medical' problem, pain is an everyday experience and, while the medical perspective is a valid one, other voices, especially those of living humans, are often lost in what Morris (1991: 3) calls 'the neglected encounter between pain and meaning'.

In this chapter I am not concerned with undermining medical approaches; rather, I argue that the contribution of the sociology of sport enhances our understanding of pain and that narrative accounts have their place alongside evidence-based medicine. To date, most sociologists who have examined the concept of injury have concerned themselves primarily with industrial work environments (Bellaby 1990; Nichols 1997; Tombs 1990). This pattern is a little odd given that being 'fit to work' is of paramount importance, in particular, for professional athletes who desire or need to remain 'active' participants in sporting competition. Involvement in sport, and especially involvement in elite sport, exposes all participants to the risk of pain and injury. Some injuries sustained while training for, and participating in, sport may lead to the termina-tion of a professional or amateur athletic 'career', and even permanent disability. The focus by sociologists of sport on the physical risks that athletes take has to some degree been influenced by a more general trend among social scientists to centralize 'the body' as a focus of their analysis (Howe 2004). Sparkes and Smith (2002) suggest that much of the early theorizing in this respect tended to be dis-tant and cerebral and lacking any direct connection to the *lived experiences* of the people – whom they term 'embodied beings' (p. 259) – under scrutiny. In short, what Leder (1990) has termed the 'lived body' has remained relatively marginalized in contemporary sociological and psychological literature. How-ever, much of the early literature discussed in this chapter makes it clear that many athletes learn to disregard the risk of physical harm and to normalize pain and injury as part of their sporting experience (Curry 1993; Young *et al.* 1994). For example, Howard Nixon's work considers the notion of 'a culture of risk' as a domain feature and Young *et al.* (1994) discuss the ways in which athletes talk about injuries, examining the coping strategies devised by athletes to deal with their experiences of pain. Research in this area, as will be demonstrated, has emphasized the point that while injuries occur naturally, their appearance is mediated by social relationships.

Discussions of pain by psychologists, philosophers, theologians and novelists (among others) abound with considerations of the nature and purpose of pain (Williams and Bendelow 1998). With such diverse traditions, the pleasure/ pain dichotomy is constantly inferred and emphasized. However, in contrast to the dominant (Western) biomedical model, sociologists have recently come to examine pain as a lived, embodied, physical and emotional experience (see, for example, the work of Leder 1990). Pain, in other words, can be used to describe not only physical agony but emotional turmoil and spiritual suffering (Leder 1990). Bendelow's (2000) research concerning pain and gender, for instance, indicates that while physical pain was frequently mentioned – by both men and women – all interviewees in her study acknowledged or made reference to the notion of 'emotional pain'. In sport, the picture is similarly complex. Howe, for example, refers to 'positive pain' (2004: 85) with respect to the structured hardships endured by athletes during training; Monaghan (2001: 94) likewise discusses the way bodybuilders 'learn to enjoy' non-injurious pain during their gym sessions. Monaghan argues that learning to convert non-injurious pain to pleasure contributes to the sustainability of bodybuilding and is wholly constructive. In their work on professional rugby union players, Malcolm and Sheard (2002) refer to the important conceptual distinction between pain and injury and the attributes of, and acceptance of, each by rugby players. Their research data concerning the management of injury in English rugby union indicate that: 'Players can be in pain, yet continue to play with little or no risk of (further) injury. This, almost universally, they are prepared to do' (p. 166). The anthropologist P. David Howe (2001, 2004) looked more closely at the concepts of pain and injury and suggested that, with respect to his own research: 'Pain is the marker of injury', while injury can be understood as 'a breakdown in the structure of the body . . . that may affect its functioning' (2004: 74). In its totality, much of the research discussed in this chapter explores the social practices by which injured bodies are 'disciplined' by medical arrangements, managed within the sports organization/team and represented within a community of athletes, coaches and sports medicine specialists.

In the light of these opening remarks, the objects of this chapter are twofold: first, to review briefly the early and more prominent attempts by a number of sociologists to examine the complex ways in which athletes learn to play while injured and the pressures on them to continue training and competing when in pain; second, to focus in more depth on a number of more recent studies that have attempted to build on, and address the limitations of, this earlier literature. At the outset it should be noted that there is one central caveat to bear in mind: the literature on which these remarks are based stems exclusively from research undertaken in high-level organized sport in North America and the UK.

Risk, pain and injury in sport

Joseph Kotarba was among the first sociologists to consider pain and injury as an aspect of the social context of high-level sport. In 1983 Kotarba published *Chronic Pain*, a study of the social dimensions of this subject, examining in part the dilemmas faced by many professional athletes in deciding whether or not to disclose 'their experiences of pain' – which he refers to as 'pain talk' – to potentially critical audiences. Kotarba suggests that for professional athletes the distinction between normal and chronic pain is unclear and he argues that the realities of occupational life for them direct attention to the inherently *irrational* aspects of participating at elite levels. Kotarba employs examples from 'big-time' American professional sport in order to examine the process of deciding when and how to talk about one's pain problem. People in bureaucratic and professional occupations, he argues, seek to eliminate pain from their existences as an aspect of their rational worldviews; yet, by contrast, professional athletes must actively confront pain in their chosen employment. In a similar fashion to Kotarba, Allen Guttmann (1988), in his critical essay on sport in America, describes the 'ironic destruction' of the human body by activities that supposedly contribute to its perfection. Hughes and Coakley (1991) examine what they call 'positive deviance' among athletes and suggest that risking one's health in the pursuit of sporting success is likely to occur where athletes have accepted wholeheartedly and uncritically the goals – in particular, the goal of winning – associated with sport. In their work, an emphasis is placed on the relationship between risk, pain and injury and the achievement of athletic identity. However, of all the authors to be cited in this chapter, American sociologist Howard L. Nixon II has published most regularly in the area of the sociology of risk, pain and injury in sport.

Nixon employs social network theory to organize and interpret his research findings. This approach, as Stephen Walk (1997) indicates, offers a more formal framework for an organizational analysis of risk, pain and injury. Nixon focuses upon the interrelationships within sports groups and attempts to identify and explain the patterns of personal links that athletes have with other people, for example other athletes, coaches and physiotherapists. Much of his research has focused on what he describes as a *risk–pain–injury* paradox. This paradox is indicative of a sporting culture – 'the culture of risk' – that rationalizes the risks of athletic participation and normalizes injuries and 'playing hurt' in order to continue competing. Specifically, the paradox identified by Nixon concerns athletes' continued efforts to gain success while injured or in pain, a situation in which their chances to perform well, and to achieve success, would appear to be reduced. This paradox is distinct from, although not unconnected with, the more obvious one which links sport and exercise with good health and enjoyment. For Nixon, the idea of participating in sport in which risk taking is expected and which may lead to chronic pain and long-term injury, conflicts with what he holds to be 'common sense' notions. But, as he demonstrates, this paradox represents a largely accurate picture of professional and elite-level sport.

Nixon attempts to analyse the many varied ways in which aspects of a sporting culture such as this are transmitted and he argues that athletes are exposed to 'biased social support' (Nixon 1994b) – what he termed a 'conspiratorial alliance' of coaches, administrators and physicians – that can influence and impose messages which normalize experiences of pain and injury. He uses the concept of 'sportsnets' to refer to webs of interaction that directly or indirectly link members of social networks in a particular sport-related setting. For Nixon, the structural characteristics of sportsnets foster the acceptance of pain and injury and insulate athletes from, and inhibit them from seeking, regular medical care. He suggests that sportsnets are more likely to 'entrap' athletes in a culture of risk when the sportsnet is large, dense, centralized, closed, undifferentiated, and stable, and where athletes are very accessible to coaches and others with authority or control within the sporting context (Nixon 1992). Nixon is not, however, the only academic to focus attention on the social dimensions of sports injuries. In this respect, Kevin Young has also made a significant contribution to the analysis of risk and injury in high-level sport.

Dangerous masculinities

Young's (1993) work draws attention to several key aspects of the management of risk and injury in sport. Focusing on the intersections between violence, risk and issues of liability in male sports cultures – and specifically on routine violence done both by and to professional athletes – Young makes the following general points:

(i)   in modern times, sports workplaces are simultaneously sites of medical mastery and extraordinary medical neglect;
(ii) tolerant attitudes to injury and other workplace hazards emerge in a process of masculinization that brings central meaning to the lives of many male athletes;
(iii) professional athletes receive 'official recognition' from significant others for playing through pain and carrying injuries. This recognition serves not only to enhance the status of the individual athlete involved but also to legitimize 'playing hurt' and to rationalize away the health risks associated with this course of action.

Young suggests that two important but separate bodies of literature have emerged which attempt to examine sociologically the issues of sports violence and sport-related occupational safety. The first arises out of the large body of work on white-collar crime and victimization which raises questions about corporate neglect and the social control of violence related to paid work, while he sees the second as developing out of feminist sports studies, where scholars have started to look at pain and injury in sport as a 'gendered and gendering practice' (1993: 374).

With respect to this earlier social-legal approach to understanding the connections between violence, law and masculinity, it is Kevin Young's collaboration with colleagues Philip White and William McTeer (Young and White 1995; Young, White and McTeer 1994) for which, in this field of study, he is arguably best known. Their 1994 paper, 'Body talk', had a significant impact when it was published and remains a widely acknowledged and referenced piece of work. Employing a conceptual framework that considers gendering experiences of sport and body awareness developed through sport – what they refer to as a pro-feminist approach – Young *et al.* examine the subjective experiences and meanings attached to sport injuries by men and explain how sports participation is valued by some young males in order to reinforce dominant notions of masculinity. Male athletes, they argue, are socialized via everyday dialogues into thinking and accepting that as *real men* they should conceal pain and ignore the pain and injuries of others. Young and his co-authors examine the risks of playing with pain and injury in terms of the way in which it leads to the validation – that is, the construction, reinforcement and maintenance – of masculine and athletic identities. At the heart of this research, Young and his colleagues identify four patterns in terms of the ways in which the athletes in their sample talked about their experiences of injury. Their data indicate that there are tendencies for athletes to deny the existence of pain; to develop an irreverent attitude towards their pain; to conceal pain from significant others; and to depersonalize pain, that is to refer to injured parts of their bodies as though they were not their own. They conclude by arguing that the adoption by male athletes of a generally unreflexive approach to past disablement and a relatively unquestioning posture towards the possibility of future injury is an extraordinary domain feature of contemporary sport.

A conceptual framework that considers gendering experiences of sport is also prominent in the work of Michael Messner (1992). He interviewed, among others, former professional American football players and his discussion concerning the injuries and health of athletes concentrated on contact sports. Messner suggests that the structure of masculine identity results in men becoming alienated from their feelings and, thus, prone to view their bodies instrumentally. These 'internal' factors, in conjunction with 'external' pressures from coaches, team-mates, fans and others, influence athletes to 'give up their bodies' by playing while injured (1992: 72). All of these gender-oriented studies focus on the manner in which male athletes 'normalize' (Albert 1999; Curry 1993), rationalize and legitimize their behaviour. They seek, that is, to comprehend the strategies developed by athletes in their attempts, in both the short and the long term (Young *et al.* 1994), to restore what constitute, for them, compromised and diminished notions of self.

In concluding the first section of this chapter, two very general limitations stand out. On the one hand, the focus of much of the earlier literature centred on men and tended to marginalize the pain and injury experiences of women athletes. On the other hand, few of the studies took serious account of sport physicians, physiotherapists and other sports medicine specialists who remained relatively peripheral in comparison to the central interdependent relationships between athletes and their coaches. In the next part of this chapter I focus on a number of studies of these two areas which have developed since the mid-1990s.

The experience of women athletes

Women athletes' experiences of pain and injury have received comparatively little attention from sociologists. Nixon's study of Division One NCAA athletes indicates that there are few noteworthy gender differences with regard to 'expressed pain thresholds' (1996a). Nixon argues that male and female athletes display similar dispositions to take risks and to play when suffering from pain and injury, and both male and female coaches exhibit a similar 'ambivalence' (Nixon 1994a) in their views of athletes taking these risks. Of greater relevance for the purposes of this chapter, however, are the findings of Young and White in 1995, and Theberge in 1997.

Young and White, in extending their earlier research on male athletes, examined the experiences of pain and injury among a sample of elite women athletes who had incurred a variety of injuries. In their view, female athletes were as willing as men to expose themselves to physical risk. Young and White suggest that, like the men in their earlier study, the women they interviewed appeared to 'normalize' the presence of pain in their lives in order 'to show courage and character; to consolidate membership and kudos in the group to avoid being benched; and to help make sense of compromised health in a lifestyle that demands and reveres fitness' (p. 53). They argued that, like male athletes, female athletes develop narratives about their experiences in which they deny, develop disrespect for, or show indignation towards, painful injuries. Young and White (1995) argue that there are some striking similarities in the attitudes of male and female athletes in relation to physical danger, aggression and injury.

The research undertaken by Theberge, which emphasizes the social construction of gender identities, concurs largely with the findings of Young and White. Theberge (1997: 83) suggests that the increasing evidence which indicates that 'women athletes readily accept violence inflicted on their bodies in competitive sport suggests an incorporation of, rather than resistance to, the dominant model of men's sport'. One of the objects of the work of Theberge is to examine the potential for political transformation embodied in women's ice hockey through an analysis of the construction and practice of sport. She argues, however, that 'while women's [ice] hockey provides participants with pleasure and a sense of personal empowerment, it does so in a context that reproduces the problems of institutionalized [male dominant] sport' (p. 85). This point requires further consideration.

In their earlier research, Young *et al.* (1994) focus on the role that physicality plays in the construction of dominant notions of masculinity. They draw on the work of sociologists such as Bob Connell (1992) and Michael Messner (1990) who similarly argue that by identifying their bodies as weapons to cause harm and be harmed, men have championed the physical basis of gender difference. The historical association of sport and masculinity has been most powerfully celebrated in sports that involve dramatic displays of physical force and courage. That said, however, throughout the twentieth century, sport came increasingly to be a public site for women to challenge 'commonsense' notions that privilege masculinity over an idealized femininity based on physical passivity (Young and White 1995). In other words, women's increasing involvement in contact sports such as rugby and football poses a particularly significant opposition to the association between athletic competition and masculine identity and has the potential to enable women to resist traditional ideologies of gender. Active involvement, therefore, may lead to feelings of empowerment for women athletes who display skill and force. Yet, the challenge to masculine hegemony posed by female athletic involvement is diminished to some extent for, as Theberge (1997: 84) argues, 'the transformative possibilities of women's sport are seriously compromised by the uncritical adoption of a "sports ethic" that celebrates toughness in the face of physical violence'. So, while women are participating more and more in what were traditionally male-exclusive sports, much of this involvement, rather than contributing to a deliberate reconstruction in the meanings of sport, appears to be consolidating the very traditional and masculinist sports structures that are full of violent, excessive and health-compromising qualities and attitudes (Young and White 1995). What stands out with respect to this body of literature, however, is the need for further theory-guided research to be undertaken.

The research of Young and White (1995) and Theberge (1997) adds significantly to the stock of knowledge related to the sporting (as well as injury) experiences of female athletes. It seems clear that more studies are required for, as Pike and Maguire (2003: 246) aptly point out, many women athletes 'tread on traditionally male territory . . . and so must do more complex work in managing their gender identity'. Female athletes, they argue, 'should not be reduced to the terms of taking on masculine norms' (p. 243). Understanding these processes more adequately would seem to be profitable and relevant sociological research.

The social arrangements of medical care

The sociologists discussed in this chapter so far all raise questions about the lived contradictions, for athletes, between the supposed healthfulness of competitive sport and the real experiences of pain and injury in sport (Safai 2003). However, most of these academics have paid only marginal attention to sports medicine clinicians who, as Safai (2003) argues, are at the front line of the sport/injury/pain complex. Stephen Walk in 1997, and Ivan Waddington, Martin Roderick and G. Parker in 1999, were among the first sociologists to address the relationships between athletes who risk pain and injury in order to participate and sports clinicians with whom participants must negotiate treatment and health care.

Using the work of Nixon as a backdrop to his qualitative study, Walk (1997) examined the beliefs and work orientations of those studying to become athletic trainers, who form part of the medical and support staff for athletes. Walk's work questions the notion developed by Nixon (1992) of a 'conspiratorial' alliance among members of sportsnets who perpetuate the acceptance by athletes of a culture of risk. What is interesting about Walk's study is that he examines sportsnet members other than athletes and coaches, focusing on young athletic trainers who are in the process of becoming embedded among the social relations of the health care of athletes, even though they are not yet qualified or fully accepted with respect to, for example, decision-making about fitness levels. By focusing on this interesting passage of time for aspiring sports clinicians, Walk highlights well the contradictory behaviours and discourses to which such inexperienced network members are exposed, a good illustration of which concerns the ways in which particular athletes feign injury in order, among other pressures, to relieve themselves of burdensome role expectations. In summarizing his data, Walk indicates that student athletic trainers had conflicting allegiances to student athletes and to staff trainers, held competing beliefs about athletic pain and injury, and struggled with athletes who did not properly use health care services and advice.

Safai (2003) argues that Walk's interviewees exhibited, on the one hand, concern for the health and welfare of the student athlete and, on the other, support for the reproduction of injury-legitimating norms, patterns of behaviour which indicate a rather more complex picture than the one initially painted by Nixon. In this connection, therefore, Walk (1997: 50) concludes that Nixon's model of 'an insulated, culturally homogenous, and "conspiratorial" sportsnet is both intuitively suspect and without empirical support'.

Of particular interest in Walk's study are the speculative points he raises with respect to chronic injuries and women athletes. Identifying the need for further research in this area, Walk argues that women athletes may be harmed disproportionately in the light of the fact that it is more socially permissible for them to display the emotions associated with pain. Their reports of pain may be undermined therefore by the tendency for medical staff to 'normalize' and generally underestimate or ignore their reporting of pain, in particular if these athletes continue to participate. Walk argues that further study of the ways in which the injuries of women athletes are managed is required in order to highlight assumptions about women athletes including, for example, the tendency for their injuries to be viewed as less serious versions of those of men simply because they are less likely to be the result of violence. Walk hypothesizes that the injuries and pain of women athletes may be just as severe but less socially visible (Duquin 1991) than those of men.

Waddington and Roderick (Roderick *et al.* 2000; Waddington *et al.* 1999; Waddington *et al.* 2001; Waddington and Roderick 2002) have also focused attention on sports medicine clinicians in their study of the management of injuries in professional football clubs in England. Some key aspects of this research, particularly those relating to ethical dilemmas in the roles of club doctors and physiotherapists, and to quality of care issues, are addressed by Waddington in Chapter 11 of this volume.

The tensions among network members highlighted in the work of Walk, and of Waddington and Roderick, are drawn out particularly well in the research undertaken by Parissa Safai (2003), who examines the negotiation of treatment between sport medicine clinicians and student-athletes (and sometimes the coaches) at a large Canadian university. While Safai acknowledges that her work does not extend beyond intercollegiate sport – a common characteristic of related North American literature – she does try to develop a more adequate way in which to 'conceptualize the pain/injury negotiation complex' (p. 142). Safai attempts to address the inadequacies of the notion of a 'conspiratorial' sportsnet (Nixon 1992) and extend the idea of the 'culture of risk' beyond simple over-conformity to a sport ethic (Hughes and Coakley 1991). This she does by examining the negotiation of treatment with respect to three-way inter- play between 'the culture of risk', 'the culture of precaution' and the promotion of the concept of 'sensible risks'.

The backdrop to her study, and one which is central for her analysis, is the idea that the network members under scrutiny were committed to the *desire to heal*; in the work of Waddington and Roderick by contrast, many of the clini- cians were committed to managing the level of pain and discomfort experienced by professional footballers and getting players 'fit' to return to play as quickly as possible. For Safai, the 'culture of precaution' resists, or at least tempers, the pro- motion and tolerance of injury as a normalized dimension of high-level sport. During negotiations, therefore, perceived risks are weighed against the perceived benefits of continuing to play while injured. Such deliberations, however, are predicated on the 'free and honest' exchange of information such that a realistic decision may be arrived at: a decision that is based primarily on long-term health and well-being and not on the immediate capacity for the student- athlete to compete. In addition to this idea of a 'culture of precaution', which interacts with the more commonly scrutinized 'culture of risk', is the promotion of what Safai refers to as 'sensible risk-taking'. This notion refers to the facilita- tion of re-entry into competition, physically, psychologically and emotionally, and involves the student-athlete and the clinician in a process of setting goals for recovery and testing out the 'injury' as well as the athlete's mental state of mind prior to competing, a process that is integral for an athlete who may have been marginalized socially by his or her inability to participate and main- tain a positive sense of self. The concept of 'sensible risk-taking' applies much more to the negotiations which take place during the latter stages of rehabilitation, it seems, rather than those that occur prior to, or accompany, the treatment of injury, such as those that may relate, for example, to the timing of surgery (Waddington *et al.* 1999: 30). Nevertheless, Safai adds significantly to the body of literature that examines the social relations of injury and introduces concepts that may in time direct sociologists to alternative issues focused around negotiations concerning the treatment and rehabilitation of injury and pain.

Before concluding this section, which has focused on the social arrangements of medical care, mention should be made of two additional studies that have contributed to the understanding of pain and injury in sport. Working within a model that sets out to explain the wider networks of relationships among high-level sportsmen, including sports physicians, Malcolm and Sheard, and Howe have studied the management of injury as a dimension of the process of the professionalization of rugby union in England and in Wales respectively.

Using an anthropological approach, Howe (2001) spent two years as general assistant for the Welsh professional rugby club, Pontypridd, and his research data shed light on the social relations of managing pain and injury in a club in which the process of professionalization extended increasingly to medical staff and methods of treatment. Howe describes the ways in which the process of change from amateurism to professionalism impacted on the playing and non-playing staff at the club. Of all the changes described by Howe, among the most interesting sociologically are those associated with the structuring of the passage of time. Howe argues that shifts in treatment patterns – such that the recovery of players is hastened so they can return to 'fitness' as quickly as possible – can be related directly to the economic value of players. He suggests that, for club officials, the players' pain is no longer a 'prime concern', for the attention of club directors, in the professional era, is now focused on 'getting more value for money in relation to player contracts' (p. 298), value that can be realized only if the player is active at the point of production for the duration of his tenure.

Howe employs the work of Bourdieu, particularly his concept of *habitus*, to examine his research findings. It is Howe's contention that Pontypridd rugby club has a specific habitus that was transformed by the way in which pain and injury are treated in the club environment. Howe suggests that specific embodied practices come in time to be imprinted on to players, physiotherapists, doctors and coaches in relation to the management of pain and injury and that distinctive patterns of social conduct are internalized [as second nature] by all members of the rugby club.

In contrast to the work of Howe, Malcolm and Sheard (2002) use a figurational sociological framework to interpret their data on the social relations of managing injury in professional rugby union in England. In an interesting departure from other research in this area, in particular the research undertaken by Howe, Malcolm and Sheard discuss what they consider to be the relatively equal power-relations between rugby club members that influence the long-term outlooks of players, coaches and club medical staff with respect to considerations of health. The orientations to work hinted at, they suggest, are associated with, first, the relatively middle-class status of rugby club members and, second, the fact that many people perceive rugby to be a public school sport. The central finding of Malcolm and Sheard (2002: 154), and one they suggest is consistent with Eliasian ideas of civilizing processes (Elias 2000), is that the professionalization of rugby seems to have entailed, on the one hand, an increasing acceptance of playing while in pain, but on the other, a decreasing tolerance towards playing while injured, with its associated risk of longer-term physical damage.

Both studies are interesting as they focus on a sport – rugby union – currently undergoing dynamic social change, particularly with respect to the organization of the health care of players. It seems clear that research focusing on the association between the professionalization of rugby union and the management of injuries offers the potential for sociologists to obtain time-series data such that, for example, longer-term processes may be analysed and connected with changes to the social habitus of players and other club members.

Risk

In much of the literature referred to so far the focus has been on high-level sport undertaken mostly by men. In addition, it has been taken for granted by most contributors to this area of interest that the concept of risk is clear and understood. In mainstream sociological studies, however, this term is widely discussed and applied.[1] Sociologists such as Anthony Giddens (1991), for instance, consider the cultivation of risk by individuals as personal experimentation, such that particular extreme sports may be viewed as actively testing the limits of the psycho-social security blanket which, he claims, normally surrounds us (Lupton 1999). Arguably, however, a central influence in terms of the links between risk-taking and sport has been the work of Stephen Lyng, who employs the term 'edgework' to apply to participants' experiences in dangerous activities that are voluntarily undertaken as part of leisure (Lupton 1999).[2] Lyng (1990: 859) argues that 'edgework' is underpinned by the skilled performance of the risky activity, which involves 'the ability to maintain control over a situation that verges on complete chaos' and that requires, in short, 'mental toughness'. Lyng suggests that this view is especially important among participants in more athletic activities. In this regard, encounters with danger undertaken voluntarily, often in extreme sports such as skydiving, hang-gliding and downhill skiing, link risk and pleasure (Lupton 1999), thereby normalizing risk for people who participate in activities for the purpose of seeking excitement and the production of a sense of self-actualization.

In relation to the analysis of risk in sports, Edward Albert has examined the sub-culture of recreational cycling, which he characterizes as a form of 'edgework'. Rather than examining phenomenologically the experiences of, and meanings imbued in, pain, Albert focuses on physical risks, thereby centralizing 'risk' as an orientating concept. Specifically, Albert (1999) examines the normalization of risk in cycling, looking specifically at whether narratives about injury can be seen as a form of 'membership talk' (p. 159). Thus, rather than examining the strategies developed by athletes for coping with pain, Albert addresses the ways in which cyclists construct normative practices which give order and place to risk and danger in their sport. In other words, he explains how falls, crashes and pile-ups come to be considered taken-for-granted features of participation.

Building on work undertaken by, for example, Hunt (1995), who discussed risk normalization among deep sea divers, Albert adopts a social constructionist framework examining the sets of norms and practices that construct risk-taking behaviour as 'normal, salient and often valued' (p. 159), such that danger in serious recreational cycling might be understood as constitutive of participation in the first instance rather than a peripheral element of sport. By placing the concept of risk at the centre of his analysis, Albert departs from other sociologists in this field who have tended to conceptualize risk only as it relates to people's experiences of pain and injury. The distinctiveness of his approach lies in the fact that Albert seeks to understand voluntary risk-taking as a dimension of *the lived experiences* of people engaged in sporting endeavours. As noted above, his focus stems in part from a relatively recent, yet rapidly growing area of interest in which the notion of risk has gained importance and is treated as a key concept.

Conclusion

In the world of sport, injury and the threat of injury are routine. Sport, as a profession or even as 'serious leisure' (Stebbins 1992), is not just something that you do – it is something that you are and, thus, being an athlete is an embodiment of identity (Turner and Wainwright 2003). Injuries to athletes may lead to a situation in which their sense of self-identity may be diminished (Charmaz 2003). The body of an athlete, therefore, may be considered as the *location* where injuries, and the baggage that tends to accompany injuries, receive their social manifestation.

In this chapter I have presented and considered some of the main perspectives and central problems addressed by sociologists who have examined the 'culture of risk' (Nixon 1992) in high-level and professional sport. Research in this area is relatively new. I have drawn attention, therefore, to some areas of interest that are currently under-researched and under-theorized. Most prominent in this respect is the relative lack of attention which has been paid to the experiences of female athletes, a situation which has only recently started to be addressed (see the contribution of Charlesworth and Young in this volume). Notwithstanding its newness, the sociological study of the pain and injury experiences of athletes has made a significant impact on the academic study of sport, and I believe that the chapters in this volume, and future research which addresses the shortcomings identified, will in time come to have important implications for health care policies constructed by sports organizations for all athletes, and not solely those who compete at elite levels.

Notes

1 Much of this literature analyses the ways in which people in Western societies give meaning to and deal with the globalization of risks. For some time, academics have examined economic risks, particularly with respect to investment and other business-related activities, but the sociological study of risk emanates in part from the writings of German sociologist, Ulrich Beck. Beck (1992) argues that in modern social life, debates and conflicts over risk are coming to dominate public, political and private arenas; there exists greater awareness of risks and people are forced to deal with risks on an everyday basis. Individuals in contemporary Western societies, he argues, are living in a transitional period in which industrial society is becoming a self-endangering civilization, or 'risk society'. Our heightened sense of risk therefore stems to some degree from the most pressing threats to modern social life, such as nuclear war, global warming and large-scale pollution. Much of the early literature in this field seeks to establish the relationship of risk to the structures and processes of late modernity and how risk is understood in different social-cultural contexts.

2 Lyng combines Marxist and Meadian perspectives to explore voluntary risk-taking among skydivers. Lyng suggests that the conflict and alienation produced in industrialist capitalist societies have profound implications for individual experience. People are constrained from fully realizing 'their species being' through material production and are separated from the general community. This results in a dearth of opportunities for spontaneous, creative, self-realizing action. 'Edgework', a form of play that involves risk, skill and planning, compensates for this lack and serves to facilitate self-actualization and an illusory sense of control.

Bibliography

Albert, E. (1999) 'Dealing with danger: The normalization of risk in cycling', *International Review for the Sociology of Sport*, 34: 157–71.

Beck, U. (1992) *Risk Society: Towards a New Modernity*, trans. M. Ritter, London: Sage.

Bellaby, P. (1990) 'What is genuine sickness? The relation between work-discipline and the sick role in a pottery factory', *Sociology of Health and Illness*, 12: 46–68.

Bendelow, G. (2000) *Pain and Gender*, London: Prentice Hall.

Charmaz, K. (2003) 'Experiencing chronic illness' in G. L. Albrecht, R. FitzPatrick and S. C. Scrimshaw (eds) *Handbook of Social Studies in Health and Medicine*, London: Sage: 277–92.

Connell, R. (1992) 'A very straight gay: Masculinity, homosexual experience and the dynamics of gender', *American Sociological Review*, 57: 735–51.

Conrad, P. (1987) 'The experience of illness: Recent and new directions' in J. Roth and P. Conrad (eds) *The Experience and Management of Chronic Illness: Research in the Sociology of Health Care*, 6, Greenwich: JAI Press: 1–31.

Curry, R. and Strauss, T. (1994) 'A little pain never hurt anyone: A photo-essay on the normalisation of sport injuries', *Sociology of Sport Journal*, 11:195–208.

Curry, T. J. (1991) 'A little pain never hurt anyone: "Positive deviance" and the meaning of sport injury', paper presented at the North American Society for the Sociology of Sport annual meeting, Milwaukee, WI, November 1991.

Curry, T. J. (1993) 'A little pain never hurt anyone: Athletic career socialization and the normalization of sports injury', *Symbolic Interactionism*, 16: 273–90.

Davies, H. ([1972], 1996) *The Glory Game*, Edinburgh: Mainstream Publishing.

Drawer, S. (2000) 'Risk evaluation in professional football', unpublished Ph.D. thesis, University of Loughborough, UK.

Duquin, M.E. (1991) 'Choosing pain: The meaning, myth and reality of self-inflicted pain in sport', paper presented at the North American Society for the Sociology of Sport annual meeting, Milwaukee, WI, November 1991.

Elias, N. (2000) *The Civilizing Process*, Oxford: Blackwell Publishers.

Freidson, E. (1970) *Profession of Medicine: A Study of the Sociology of Applied Knowledge*, New York: Dodd Mead.

Giddens, A. (1991) *Modernity and Self-Identity: Self and Society in the Late Modern Age*, Cambridge: Polity Press.

Goffman, E. (1961) *Encounters: Two Studies in the Sociology of Interaction*, Indianapolis: Bobbs-Merrill.

Guttmann, A. (1988) *A Whole New Ball Game: An Interpretation of American Sports*, Chapel Hill: University of North Carolina Press.

Hargreaves, J. (1994) *Sporting Females: Critical Issues in the History and Sociology of Women's Sports*, London: Routledge.

Howe, P. D. (2001) 'An ethnography of pain and injury in professional rugby union: From embryo to infant at Pontypridd RFC', *International Review for the Sociology of Sport*, 35: 289–303.

Howe, P. D. (2004) *Sport, Professionalism and Pain*. London: Routledge.

Hughes, R. and Coakley, J. (1991) 'Positive deviance among athletes: The implications of overconformity to the sports ethic', *Sociology of Sport Journal*, 8: 307–25.

Hunt, J. C. (1995) 'Divers' accounts of normal risk', *Symbolic Interaction*, 18: 439–62.

Kotarba, J. A. (1983) *Chronic Pain: Its Social Dimensions*. London: Sage.

Leder, D. (1990) *The Absent Body*, London: University of Chicago Press.

Lupton, D. (1999) *Risk*, London: Routledge.

Lyng, S. (1990) 'Edgework: A social psychological analysis of voluntary risk taking', *American Journal of Sociology*, 95: 851–86.

Malcolm, D. and Sheard, K. (2002) ' "Pain in the assets": The effects of commercialization and professionalization on the management of injury in English rugby union', *Sociology of Sport Journal*, 19: 149–69.

Messner, M. (1990) 'When bodies are weapons: Masculinity and violence in sport', *International Review for the Sociology of Sport*, 25: 203–18.

Messner, M. (1992) *Power at Play: Sports and the Problem of Masculinity*, Boston: Beacon Press.

Monaghan, L. (2001) *Bodybuilding, Drugs and Risk*, London: Routledge.

Morris, D. (1991) *The Culture of Pain*, Berkeley: University of California Press.

Nichols, T. (1997) *The Sociology of Industrial Injury*, London: Mansell Publishing.

Nixon, H. (1992) 'A social network analysis of influences on athletes to play with pain and injury', *Journal of Sport and Social Issues*, 16: 127–35.

Nixon, H. (1993a) 'Accepting the risks of pain and injury in sports: Mediated cultural influences on playing hurt', *Sociology of Sport Journal*, 10: 183–96.

Nixon, H. (1993b) 'Social network analysis of sport: Emphasising structure in sport sociology', *Sociology of Sport Journal*, 10: 315–21.

Nixon, H. (1994a) 'Coaches' views of risk, pain and injury in sport, with special reference to gender differences', *Sociology of Sport Journal*, 11: 79–87.

Nixon, H. L. (1994b) 'Social pressure, social support, and help seeking for pain and injuries in college sports networks', *Journal of Sport and Social Issues*, 18: 340–55.

Nixon, H. (1996a) 'The relationship of friendship networks, sport experiences and gender to expressed pain thresholds', *Sociology of Sport Journal*, 13: 78–86.

Nixon, H. L. (1996b) 'Explaining pain and injury attitudes and experiences in sport in terms of gender, race, and sports status factors', *Journal of Sport and Social Issues*, 21: 33–44.

Parker, A. (1996) 'Chasing the big-time: Football apprenticeship in the 1990s', unpublished Ph.D. thesis, University of Warwick, UK.

Pike, E. C. J. and Maguire, J. A. (2003) 'Injury in women's sport: Classifying key elements of "risk encounters"', *Sociology of Sport Journal*, 20: 232–51.

Roderick, M. J. (1998) 'The sociology of risk, pain and injury: A comment on the work of Howard L. Nixon II', *Sociology of Sport Journal*, 11: 175–94.

Roderick, M., Waddington, I. and Parker, G. (2000) 'Playing hurt: Managing injuries in English professional football', *International Review for the Sociology of Sport*, 35: 165–80.

Roth, J. A. (1962) 'The treatment of tuberculosis as a bargaining process' in A. M. Rose (ed.) *Human Behaviour and Social Processes: An Interactionist Approach*, Henley: Routledge: 575–88.

Roth, J. A. (1963) *Timetables: Structuring the Passage of Time in Hospital Treatment and Other Careers*, Indianapolis: Bobbs-Merrill Co.

Sabo, D. F. and Panepinto, J. (1990) 'Football ritual and the social reproduction of masculinity' in M. A. Messner and D. F. Sabo (eds) *Sport, Men and the Gender Order: Critical Feminist Perspectives*, Champaign, IL: Human Kinetics: 115–26.

Safai, P. (2003) 'Healing the body in the "culture of risk": Examining the negotiation of treatment between sport medicine clinicians and injured athletes in Canadian intercollegiate sport', *Sociology of Sport Journal*, 20: 127–46.

Sparkes, A. C. and Smith, B. (2002) 'Sport, spinal cord injury, embodied masculinities, and the dilemmas of narrative identity', *Men and Masculinities*, 4: 258–85.

Sports Council (1991) *Injuries in Sport and Exercise*, London: The Sports Council.

Stebbins, R. A. (1992) 'Serious leisure: A conceptual statement', *Pacific Sociological Review*, 25: 251–72.

Theberge, N. (1997) ' "It's part of the game": Physicality and the production of gender in women's hockey', *Gender and Society*, 11: 69–87.

Tombs, S. (1990) 'Industrial injuries in British manufacturing industry', *The Sociological Review*, 38: 324–43.

Turner, B. S. and Wainwright, S. P. (2003) 'Corps de ballet: the case of the injured ballet dancer', *Sociology of Health and Illness*, 25, 4: 269–88.

Waddington, I. (2000) *Sport, Health and Drugs: A Critical Sociological Perspective*, London: Routledge.

Waddington, I., Roderick, M. and Parker, G. (1999) *Managing Injuries in Professional Football: The Roles of the Club Doctor and Physiotherapist*, Leicester: University of Leicester.

Waddington I., Roderick, M. and Naik, R. (2001) 'Methods of appointment and qualifications of club doctors and physiotherapists in English professional football: Some problems and issues', *British Journal of Sports Medicine*, 35: 48–53.

Waddington, I. and Roderick, M. (2002) 'The management of medical confidentiality in English professional football clubs: some ethical problems and issues', *British Journal of Sports Medicine*, 36: 118–23.

Walk, S. R. (1997) 'Peers in pain: The experiences of student athletic trainers', *Sociology of Sport Journal*, 14: 22–56.

Williams, S. J. and Bendelow, G. (1998) *The Lived Body: Sociological Themes, Embodied Issues*, London: Routledge.

Young, K. (1991) 'Violence in the workplace of professional sport from victimological and cultural studies perspectives', *International Review for the Sociology of Sport*, 26: 3–14.

Young, K. (1993) 'Violence, risk and liability in male sports culture', *Sociology of Sport Journal*, 10: 373–96.

Young, K., White, P. and McTeer, W. (1994) 'Body talk: Male athletes reflect on sport, injury and pain', *Sociology of Sport Journal*, 11: 175–94.

Young, K. and White, P. (1995) 'Sport, physical danger and injury: The experiences of elite women athletes', *Journal of Sport and Social Issues*, 19: 45–61.

2 Sport and the psychology of pain

Kirsten Kaya Roessler

Pain research in general covers a wide field and has been the subject of historical, philosophical and cultural approaches (Bendelow and Williams 1995; Honkasalo 1998; Morris 1991; Rey 1998; Scarry 1985; Zborowski 1960). The medical, the psychological and the psychosomatic discourses on pain research are well developed and different methods of pain management have been identified (Baseler *et al.* 1996; James and Large 1992; McDougall 1989; Melzack 1978; Uexküll 1997; Zens and Jurna 1993).

This chapter focuses specifically on the psychological connections between sport and pain. The first part examines some theoretical approaches to the psychology of pain. The second part reports the results of a study of sport, pain and injury (Roessler 2002, 2004). The final part argues for the development of a more existentially orientated sports psychology.

Introduction

Sophie is 17 and has been playing tennis as a performance sport for ten years. She trains five to six times a week. When she began playing again after a six-month break following an injury, she had problems concentrating. She sees this as a personal psychological problem and is looking for help from any 'tricks' sport psychology might offer. In conversation, however, a very different story emerges. She had suffered from an unclearly diagnosed shoulder injury and had only recently been declared healthy. As she returned to her sports club she found her place in the first team occupied by another player, her team-mates ignored her, and she had lost her spare-time job in the club's kiosk. Her coach was not offering any special consultation and she felt a lack of support. Moreover, she still has problems with chronic pain in her shoulder.

Sophie is injured and really wants to start playing again. We can, of course, offer her classical sport psychology solutions, such as mentally focusing on her goal and working with stress management. We can show her how to improve her concentration on her second serve. But that does not really grasp the full range of the problems as we encounter them in this case. Following her chronic injury, Sophie is having problems with her identity, and communication between her and her coach and team-mates is not functioning well. For almost ten years she had structured her whole life around tennis. Like many athletes who are confronted with an unexpected injury, she suddenly finds herself in the middle of a crisis. What is her identity in relation to her sport after a six-month break? Has her education become just as important as her sport? Does she have the desire to fight and win back her place in the first team, or are other things becoming more important? Sophie's case shows how a deeper, more complicated situation can be hidden directly behind a simply posed sport psychology question.

Sophie's pain is more than a result of a physical process. It is the expression of the loss of personal equilibrium and an indication of the communication difficulties with her coach and team-mates. Her problems require a further look at the psychology of pain.

A psychology of pain: feeling, emotion, experience

Pain has been defined as follows: 'Pain is an unpleasant sensory and emotional experience associated with actual or potential tissue damage, or described in terms of such damage' (International Association for the Study of Pain 1979). This current definition is focused – like sport medicine – on damage. But it does draw attention to the emotional experience of pain. In the field of psychoanalysis, Sigmund Freud transferred the mechanical theory from the body to the psyche. If the body can be injured and experience pain, then so too can the psyche. Both can be treated according to the principle *cessante causa cessat effectus*: if the cause disappears, the symptoms disappear too. Freud treated pain as an objective phenomenon for which a cause could be found. He distinguished between somatic and visceral pain, and also connected pain and narcissism with one another (Freud [1926] 1971: 305), suggesting that somatic pain can lead to a narcissistic preoccupation with the painful part of the body. All energy – libido – is concentrated on the pain and, in this process, the ego loses energy. To express it another way, pain – seen psychoanalytically – empties the ego: 'With physical pain, a preoccupation with the painful point of the body occurs that is narcissistic in nature, increases more and more, and, so to say, has an emptying effect on the ego. . . .' (Freud 1971: 307f). These psychological distinctions have significance for sports and exercise because a major part of pain in sports cannot be understood on the basis of a mechanical model of pain alone. Athletes can suffer many things. They can feel alone and isolated on a team. They may feel that they have disappointed the expectations of team-mates. They can also experience extremely intense emotional 'highs' and, of course, emotional 'lows' between high points.

Pain cannot be understood simply in mechanical terms. It is more than a neuron-impulse set off by tissue damage. Pain in sports is also connected with willpower and with passion. Pain becomes a dimension of the psyche, a subjective feeling. In sport, this subjective side of pain may even become an aspect of hero worship in those who overcome pain and continue to compete.

Voluntarism

Ferdinand Sauerbruch, a German surgeon, criticized Freud's suggestion that pain leads to an emptying of the ego. He argued that 'in the declarations of Freudian psychoanalysis that we have before us, human practice remains on a level of unconscious staleness that contradicts all experience' (Sauerbruch and Wenke 1936: 85). He argued that the individual could mobilize her/his inner strength in order to cope with pain. Through the technique of distancing the rational ego from its sensations and from the circumstances under which it suffers (Sauerbruch and Wenke 1936: 92) a person could reduce pain. According to Sauerbruch, with the help of 'willpower' the individual is capable of changing the intensity of the pain and, in this way, is better able to bear it: 'illness is a misfortune for the body, but not for the will, if it does not want it to be (Sauerbruch and Wenke 1936: 93). Sauerbruch's emphasis on will and strength (and his critique of psychoanalysis) has to be understood in the political context, German fascism, which had the educational goal of being as strong as possible. But the attempt to fight pain and illness by the force of will has parallels with an understanding of pain in sports. The history of sports offers many examples of this way of thinking. Athletes who, despite pain and injury, are able to conquer themselves and 'overcome' the pain become heroes.

In the 1996 Olympics, the American gymnast Kerri Strug became a media star because, despite an ankle injury, she took a running approach into a jump over the horse, which brought the American team the gold medal. Kerri Strug's jump was not only a question of will, but also of concentration. The work of Ronald Melzack helps us to understand how people can be diverted from pain in such situations.

A holistic understanding of pain

In 1965 the Canadian psychologist Ronald Melzack (1973, 1996) revised the pain paradigm that had been shaped by Cartesian thought, in terms of which it was normal to separate the body from the psyche and, in that way, physical pain from psychic pain. In this traditional approach, pain is either a sign of tissue damage or, as in Freud's thinking, an injury of the psyche. Pain has the important function of warning the body and protecting the body and the psyche. But pain can also be interpreted differently.

The holistic understanding of pain received its theoretical basis in the early 1960s in the form of the Gate Control Theory. Melzack postulated that pain was not a simple mechanical process between a stimulus and a response, but was much more complex. Otherwise it would not be possible to explain phenomena like reactions which anaesthetize existing tissue damage – as in the example of the American gymnast Kerri Strug – or in the opposite circumstance, where pain is present without a somatic basis. In this regard, many people seek treatment within our health care systems without ever receiving a satisfactory explanation for their suffering. Doctors may be unable to identify the cause of the pain, but the patient does experience pain.

Pain can be described in many different ways: as a sensory quality (sharp, burning, pulsating), as an affective quality (merciless, punishing) or as a relative quality (uncomfortable, unbearable). What is important is that these qualities are subjective. The experience of pain depends on individual factors. Melzack (1973) discovered a 'gate' in the spinal cord, which controls and regulates whether pain impulses are sent on to a higher cerebral level or not. In this way, the intensity of the pain impulse becomes dependent on subjective factors such as awareness, fear or concentration. There is no such thing as objective pain; instead, the experience of pain is dependent on subjective factors. That is why, for example, in the highly emotional atmosphere of competition or sexual activity a person can go beyond the normal limits of pain and only later – occasionally painfully – become aware of it.

The Gate Control Theory has become a dominant paradigm in pain research, even though in the last decade theories that attempt to base pain sensitivity and pain memory in genetic factors (the so-called neuromatrix theories) have gained in importance. With the Gate Control Theory it became possible to explain many phenomena that cannot be understood within the Cartesian paradigm. These include phantom pain after amputations, the different experiences with birth pains, cultural differences in the experience of pain and also the experience of pain in sports, for example the different experience of pain in competition as compared with the training situation.

To conceive of pain as something 'whole' also requires an input from psychic forms of pain. *Necessary pain* is a concept which has developed out of psychologically based grief counseling. When someone close to us dies, we can go through a number of feelings: denial, anger, despair, fear and grief (Kübler-Ross 1969). To integrate the suffering and pain, and to accept our own grief, helps us to progress beyond the loss. To admit the pain, and to 'let it in', both protects and helps.

Sport and pain: Coping with sport injuries

Modern performance sports demand time and resources. This can lead to major psychic and social burdens. Recent sport research describes this milieu in terms of stress, social pressure and 'burnout' (Pensgaard and Ursin 1998; Raedeke 1997; Nixon and Howard 1994).

Since the subjects of pain and injury also play a central role in recent sport psychology literature (Brewer 2001; Gould *et al.* 1998; Taylor and Taylor 1998; Udry 1997; Williams 2001; Williams and Roepke 1993), a deeper analysis of the psychological aspects of sport injuries is essential. Who is injured, and when, and how a rehabilitation process will proceed, are not simply matters of coincidence. One model that has proved itself over the years is the Stress and Athletic Injury Model, developed by Williams and Anderson (1998). Recent research based on this model has been applied in many different ways with different populations (for example Johnson 1997; Kleinert 2000).

The research based on the model of Williams and Anderson has mainly concentrated on coping with pain and pain prevention following a sport-medical approach. It is also interesting to analyse how sport *expresses* pain, for sport is – besides masochism – one of the few fields where pain is expressed or accepted voluntarily.

Roessler (2002, 2004) sought to discover how high-performance athletes cope with and express their pain and injuries. The study used the experiences and data from 30 elite athletes (age 21–41 years, from fencing, football and judo) and 50 sports students (age 22–33 years). This research project, on 'Sport and Pain', was carried out in 1999–2001 and supported financially by the Danish Elite Sport Institution.

Results of the survey questionnaire

Which coping strategies do athletes use and how do they express the problems that arise in connection with sport injuries? Under 'coping strategies', all resources that a person employs in order to overcome a critical or problematic situation were included. This includes individual psychological attempts at solution as well as the use of friends or family.

The 30 performance athletes were first asked to fill out a validated questionnaire on the subject of coping strategies. The *Coping Strategies Inventory* (Keefe and Rosenstil 1983) examines different coping strategies. The results indicated that 'ignoring the pain' was the most commonly used coping strategy. The athletes' first reaction to the fact that something is hurting them is to try to ignore it. Another strategy is to be active and to look for diversion.

Interpretation

While noting that the small size of the sample means that the results are limited in terms of their generalizability, we see that, in the sports examined, the central coping mechanisms are to ignore the pain and to practise 'self-suggestion'. The attempt to ignore the pain and the use of 'self-suggestion' are associated with the fact that sport injuries and pain are generally not of a life-threatening nature. In similar studies on pain symptoms in clinical medical areas (Elsass 1994), thoughts of catastrophe and a need for interpretation predominate. In the case of sudden or chronic pain, the individual feels especially threatened, particularly when she or he cannot explain it.

By contrast, the strong inclination of athletes – who can also feel threatened by unfamiliar pain – to ignore it can be explained by the fact that they recognize a reason for the pain and can give it an intellectual explanation. When athletes consciously push pain aside in order to concentrate on training or competing in their sport, they make a choice that is connected with their ability to classify and rank the pain and thereby to control it. An unidentified chronic pain in the stomach, or in the head, sets off a fear reaction in athletes, as in other people, that health and control may be lost. When, by contrast, a person knows where the pain is coming from and when it is likely to go away, then she or he can decide to ignore it. In interviews, many of the athletes confided that it became possible to ignore their pain at that point where the physical therapist or doctor confirmed that they would incur no damage if, despite the pain, they continued to practise their sport. It is only when they learn that further strain would be damaging for their body that their exercise is impeded. 'When I notice that something hurts, I look for a physical therapist right away in order to get a professional opinion' (Julia, football player, 30 years). The athletes are insecure as long as they cannot classify and rank the pain but, where the pain is a familiar one resulting from physical injury, they handle it as a matter of will.

Evaluation and discussion

The study with performance athletes was first oriented towards the subject of coping with pain. In addition to the coping strategies outlined above, two additional factors were examined, namely the role of the coach and the role of Team Denmark, the Danish organization for the promotion of performance sports. Especially in team sports the athletes indicated that, in relation to coping with injuries, they are dependent on the care and interest of their coach. In connection with injuries, but also in relation to ending their careers, the support of Team Denmark was also reported as being important. The athletes clearly indicated that, when it comes to managing pain and injuries, they find it more difficult to cope without support from their coaches. This need for care occasionally ends up in contradiction to the performance interests of the coach, for the primary interest of the coach is often to return the injured athlete to training and competition as quickly as possible.

Breaking off contact – communication problems with the coaches

The way the athletes, their injuries and their coaches stand in relationship with one another reminds us of the Hippocratic unit of doctor, illness and patient: 'Our craft encompasses three: the illness, the one who is ill and the doctor' (Corpus hippokraticum, quoted in Uexküll 1997: 14). That is why sports injuries cannot be treated as the problem of an isolated individual, for at this level the injury always involves contact and communication between coaches and athletes. Injury to an athlete seriously disrupts a key element of the contract between athlete and coach, for the ability of both to perform is disrupted. The coach cannot give any training directives and the athlete can no longer train, or can do so only in a limited way. At the same time, however, they are dependent on each other. That leads to disappointments, frustration or indifference. Many athletes report that they were disappointed when, after an injury, they heard nothing more from their coach. In that situation they suddenly felt like a 'thing' and not like a worthwhile human being. The period following an injury is sometimes described as a 'radical descent':

> It wasn't enough that my body was so restless because it couldn't train like it wanted. They also shut me out of the team when I asked if I could continue to practise along with the others until the injury was completely healed. That was a real blow.
>
> (Lars, gymnast, 37 years)

Some athletes also expressed a wish for more support from their coaches or their sport institutions following the end of their career. One five-time world champion expressed her disappointment as follows: 'I haven't heard a single word since I stopped. In football they're beginning to reflect on the problem because so many athletes become addicted to drugs or alcohol after their career' (Maria, fencer, 38 years). Many athletes expect a more explicit acceptance and recognition of their suffering from their coach. Athletes suffer when they are injured, and they want their coach to empathize with them. It is here that communication can break down because the coaches often hold themselves at an emotional distance. 'I don't concentrate much on an injured athlete. The game must go on', said a football trainer. While pain is in other contexts often the occasion for showing increased concern – for example, when a child falls down or when an illness is diagnosed – here it becomes the occasion for backing out of a communication-based situation. The athlete can no longer participate in normal communication, and the coach withdraws because his duties lie in a different area. For many athletes, and especially for female athletes, this feels like rejection. The role of the 'other' – and particularly the coach – is central in the treatment and understanding of pain.

The interpretation of pain

Pain as individual trauma

> The psychological pain came later when it became clear that my ligament was torn. The injury required a major operation, and I had to break off my stay at the sport boarding school. As that became clear to me, I was paralysed. I had to bid my friends a premature good-bye, and that was connected with the uncertainty as to whether or not I'd ever be able to play my sport again.
>
> (Pia, gymnast, 22 years)

Pia's ligament is torn, she is in pain and her future is suddenly insecure. The worst thing, however, is that now she must say good-bye to the school and her friends. For others, the trauma can be connected with an unexpected rupture in preparations for competition and, in a worst-case scenario, with the sudden end of a sporting career. Young athletes in particular may build their whole lives around a sport. A sudden injury can quickly lead to a crisis that sometimes requires professional help. When a 24-year-old who is completely committed to her/his sport can no longer compete because of a serious injury, then that person's self-identity may be shattered. That is difficult to overcome.

The experience of pain as trauma or crisis is not limited to physical injuries. It can hurt to lose, not to be selected, or to doubt one's own performance abilities. Pain may be an expression of the disruption of contact, for example when a person no longer feels he or she belongs to the team. The pain of a sport injury signals that the body has become a different one and, in the worst case, that it has become one's own enemy. Athletes report that it is as though the body betrays a person, but people who are suddenly taken ill can also feel this way. Pain can also be an expression of the reality that the significant 'other' is not responding to the desire for contact, that the coach is ignoring the athlete. Many performance athletes describe the role of the coach as central to overcoming their own pain. Experiences with the health system can also be a cause of crisis: 'I experienced the greatest pain of my life when an orthopedist told me that I should change . . . to flower arranging or ballet. I was 17 then' (Jonas, football player, 28 years). As individual trauma, pain appears on three communication levels. The first involves the subject her/himself with her/his wishes and expectations. The second relates to the roles that others play within sport. And the third level is connected with the reaction and roles of those within the health care system.

Pain as an expression of self-realization: the 'good' pain

Although pain is often experienced as trauma, it can also be experienced as an opportunity, for example when pain is interpreted as a means of self-enhancement or self-development. Here we can see a parallel with the ideas of Sauerbruch: the will is an important instrument in overcoming the pain. Sanne, a 25-year-old runner said: 'Another form of pain is the "pain of endurance", pain as experienced in marathon racing or in a ski expedition. This pain is chosen and therefore positive. I can often enjoy it because it conveys an indescribable, intoxicating contentment.' Sanne describes the 'high' experienced by endurance athletes. The limits of the body are explored out of a simple desire to do so and, out of curiosity, the question of how far a person may extend her or his own limits, how far a person can grow beyond their 'normal' self, is explored. Pain appears to serve as an indicator that the limit has been reached and 'self-enhancement' has begun.

Christianity has endowed pain with the religious vision of asceticism. In the identification with the suffering of Christ, but also in the overcoming of physical pain, is the promise of a higher vision that opens up one's self. Although it is hard to find religious motivations among contemporary sports students, many would readily describe a kind of vision in which the overcoming and mastery of pain is present – a vision that reminds us of pain in the tradition of Christian asceticism.

The athletes interviewed often described the painful search for physical limits as a search for identity. That could explain the increase in participation in extreme sports and sports with high-risk factors. For whom or what are they searching in this confrontation with their own limits? Sports students reported again and again that it has to do with 'overcoming one's self' in a clearly marked area, to experience the 'good' pain, to test the limits. As Pernille, a 25-year-old runner put it:

> Pain does not have to be negative. Pain makes you conscious of your body and shows you your body's limits. Suddenly something happens and I go over a threshold and have the feeling that I'm 'resting' in pain. When I reach this stage I can get the feeling that I'm invincible.

According to athletes, the pain of a challenge is the 'good' pain that is inherent in the personified self. The acceptance of a challenge occurs consciously – one is not surprised by it but, rather, one seeks out the challenge.

Sports allow total commitment to a particular action, to a motion, that shuts everything else out. 'I throw myself at the ball'; 'I rest in pain'; 'I overcome my limits'; the statements themselves substantiate the notion that sports students connect personal meaning with the endurance of pain, that pain helps to move them along in a search for personal realization: 'The experience of pain can be marvellous when it has to do with hard training in which I'm challenging my body, my muscles' (Janne, football player, 25 years).

Sports can be intoxicating and can evoke pleasure even when it hurts. It is not a *product* (performance), but rather the *activity* itself (the search for limits) that is central.

Pain as an accepted by-product: no pain, no gain

Another form of pain is not as something that one values, but as something that simply comes with the package. It is a reluctantly accepted by-product. As Mette, a 24-year-old footballer put it:

> 'It hurts before it helps' is a phrase that runs through my head when I start training for a new season. It is only after the pain has been survived that there's time and place for everything else that sports really mean to me, and what really motivates me: namely, joy, exuberance, victory and, certainly not lastly, development. For me sports become bigger, merrier and more meaningful after I've lived through a pain phase.

Mette's motivation for playing sports is not to seek pain, but rather to look for joy and exuberance. At the same time, pain is an inseparable part of it, and is accepted more or less as an expression of physical development.

To play sports, to exercise and to train, to move the body, can hurt, but the pain is a means for improving performance. Training gives one the experience of how far one can go. It is a good experience for the athlete when, after a hard training session, everything hurts, because this is what is required to improve one's performance. In a tough handball or football game a player may collide with an opponent. That hurts, but it is accepted as a part of the game:

> In the heat of battle, the ball is in focus and I'm not aware of physical 'bangs'. I throw myself around . . . All this gives me the feeling of being tough and unbreakable, and of being physically as well as psychically strong.
>
> (Lene, football player, 25 years)

Most of those who actively practise sports express this distinction between 'good' and 'bad' pain. The pain of an injury is unpleasant and bad. But the pain that is connected with hard training or with competition is good. Sometimes athletes may reflect on it with a shrug of the shoulders – as when a sprinter talks about the awful conditioning runs in the forest, for example. They are not pleasant, but there is nothing you can do about it: 'I'm O.K. with the pain that follows a hard period of training. This pain gives me a satisfying feeling that I've done something healthy or wise' (Steffen, judo, 26 years). Pain is part of sport – on that athletes are in agreement. And pain is acceptable, as long as it does not have anything to do with injury.

Pain as an expression of a relationship

On a commonsense basis, one might assume that, when one is in pain, one is first and foremost concerned with one's self. However, this idea is not supported by the research reported here. While the occurrence of pain often expresses an individual's relationship with her/his own body, additionally – at least in sports – it is an occasion for posing ethical questions, for aesthetic dimensions and for social-political confrontations. In this sense, pain not only belongs to the individual and her/his body, but also expresses other relationships – with the fans, and with the wider society.

Pain and aesthetics

> When you dance, you have a love for dancing and you're strong. A dancer begins when they're six to eight years old, and that means that they've danced their whole life and they've learned to live with the pain. As a child it does not hurt so much, and at that point the ballet is more fun than anything. The pain first comes later . . . Out of the pain emerges the beauty.
>
> (Rose Gad, dancer with the Royal Danish Ballet, quoted in Gad 2000)

According to Melzack, the concentration of the dancer is not focused on pain, but on the dance. That is why the spectator is not aware of the physical pain behind the dance. Dance and ballet are forms of movement where people are constantly operating on the edge of their pain tolerance level in order to express beauty or powerful emotions. One does not see pain; unspoken, it lies hidden in the biography of the individual dancer – behind the movements. Pain is a powerful expression of emotion and aesthetics in dance and gymnastics, an emotional condition that is beautiful. 'This form of art production is not free', said the ballet queen Rose Gad.

To observe pain in sportspeople or other performers has an effect on others – on spectators or team-mates. The dancer who has stylized or almost sublimated the pain enchants her audience and unites it in breathless admiration. The footballer who lies motionless on the ground after an injury, the ski racer who is hurled off the trail on a downhill run, the boxer who sinks to the canvas as he is knocked out – they grip the others and move them to cry out. The cry that goes through the crowd contains compassion as well as a sense of yearning participation. In every case pain brings contact. The spectators feel connected.

Pain as an expression of contact with others

> I'm a football player. I love the physical contact, the small conflicts with opponents. I like it best when after a game or practice I can really notice that I used my body. It does not matter if it is the tiredness in my legs or the bruises that the opponents left behind on my thighs.
>
> (Janni, football player, 24 years)

Pain in the case of an acute sports injury was also described as an expression of a relationship. In this situation it is related to the disruption of a 'normal' connection with the body. Suddenly one's own knee in pain has become separate from oneself, 'an other'.

In my interviews, there were clear differences between the sexes with regard to the inflicting of injury. Women consistently said it was a bad experience for them when they injure others. In fencing, where 'hitting' the other is the focus of the sport, it is readily observable that men approach hitting, as well as being hit, with less fear, while women often feel the need to excuse themselves when they believe they have injured someone.

It is also significant that some forms of behaviour – particularly behaviour involving violence – that are normally forbidden in other areas of social life are possible in sports: violent body contact, hitting and kicking. With their possibilities for inflicting and receiving pain, sports represent an alternative to most other forms of everyday social life in the relatively highly pacified societies of the West. This idea was clearly expressed by Mads, a 25-year-old judo player:

> In sports, pain is a natural substance on equal footing with other border experiences like joy or euphoria. This declares sports to be a free zone – a necessary emotional air hole. This is not possible in society to the same degree.

Pain in sport can be understood on different levels. The individual experience of pain, and pain as a mediator of relationships with others and the health care system are key points of orientation that can help structure the phenomenon of pain in sport. Pain can be an individual physical trauma, where a beginning and an end can be located. But it is also an expression of the story that athletes tell about their relationship to their bodies, to their sport and to the health system.

Pain can also serve as a means for discovery and enhancement of the self. Finally, it is – in many different ways – an expression of wider relationships: relationships with culture, with a personal biography and with the history of society.

Perspectives for sport psychology

The analysis in this chapter points to a number of key issues for sports psychologists to understand. These include:

1   Pain as an aspect of a communication (problem).
2   Health as an expression of a relationship, not a form of capital.
3   The existential and cultural dimensions of injury and pain-related crisis.

Why does Sophie – the tennis player whose case was cited at the beginning of this chapter – struggle with her shoulder for almost a year without being able to find out what is wrong? Why does she not get healthy again? Sophie does not get healthy again because health is not simply a form of *capital* from which one can live. On the basis of the interviews with the athletes, we are able to understand health in a different way, namely, as an aspect of communication and as an expression of a relationship. The communication in connection with an injury happens between four partners: the subject and her/his relationship with her/his own body, the health care system and the surrounding culture. Sophie often spoke to her shoulder as if it were another person: 'Stop bothering me', or 'you have to keep up the fight', she would say. Pain is a condition in which the body is observed and 'heard' as if 'another' is speaking. Sophie believes that her pain is her personal affair, a private conflict between her body and her will. But other communication partners are also part of the game and share the responsibility for her health. These include the doctors and physical therapists who are unable satisfactorily to diagnose her problem; her club, her coach and her team-mates, who are not effectively supporting her; and finally there is a common way (in western societies) of interpreting pain as a private thing instead of seeing it as a general problem.

If sport psychologists want to be a necessary complement to sports medicine, then they must turn to the communication processes connected with pain and open up for analysis the existential and cultural dimensions of injury-related crisis. In connection with their pain, many athletes expressed their dependence on the form of communication with coaches and doctors. In contrast to those who do not practise sports, athletes are used to controlling their bodies to a very high degree. An injury makes them vulnerable and brings them into an unfamiliar dependence on other people. For most athletes, that is very difficult to endure.

Sport psychology must become a health psychology that treats people in motion and integrates the subject into the health sciences once again. Illness and injury should not only be treated, but rather must be seen as involving communication with those providing the treatment and with the people who are involved in the health care system. A sport injury says something about the communication between those practising the sport, coaches, the health care system and treatment providers – and something about the athlete her- or himself.

On the basis of the importance that communication has for health, one can pose critical questions to sport psychologists whose first approach involves techniques centred on the individual. It is certainly legitimate to apply these techniques. Sophie, however, would not have progressed very far with them because too many other problems stood in the way.

At the start of an injury or pain stands the personal story of the athlete. One athlete may see an injury as a legitimate break, but for another athlete it may be a serious existential threat. Without an understanding of crises and without an interest in past history, chronic injuries in particular cannot be understood. Chronic pain lies in a no-man's land between sport medicine and psychology, especially when an exact cause for the pain cannot be found. If one works with injured athletes, then it is important to overcome the gap between somatic and psychic suffering, the gap between sport medicine and sport psychology.

In the face of pain, a person can react in different ways. She or he can turn to treatment or can search for other information and diagnostic possibilities. Here medical, psychological and other alternative treatment possibilities are offered. The door is opening towards the understanding of the expressive dimensions of pain. Pain is more than something that must be removed. Pain can express cultural phenomena or neurotic disturbances. Pain in sports can be understood and managed as individual trauma, as self-enhancement, as a by-product and as the disturbance of a relationship. But above all, pain tells a story about the lives of people. That story deserves our attention.

Bibliography

Baseler, H.-D. *et al.* (1996) *Psychologische Schmerztherapie*, Berlin, Heidelberg and New York: Springer.

Bendelow, G. and Williams, S. (1995) 'Pain and the Mind–Body Dualism: A Sociological Approach', *Body & Society* 1, 2: 83–103.

Brewer, B. W. (2001) 'Psychology of Sport Injury Rehabilitation' in R. B. Singer, H. A. Hausenblas and C. Janelle (eds) *Handbook of Sport Psychology*, New York: Wiley: 787–809.

Dörner, K. and Plog, U. (1986) *Irren ist menschlich. Lehrbuch der Psychiatrie/Psychotherapie*, Bonn: Psychiatrie Verlag.

Elsass, P. (1994) *Sundhedspsykologi. Et nyt fag mellem humaniora og naturvidenskab*, København: Gyldendal.

Freud, S. (1971) *Hysterie und Angst*, Frankfurt a.M.: Fischer.

Gad, R. (2000) Interview med Rose Gad. *Ud og Se*, Maj: 20–30.

Gould, D. *et al.* (1998) 'Coping with Season-Ending Injuries', *The Sport Psychologist*, 11: 379–99.

Heil, J. (1993) *Psychology of Sport Injuries*, Champaign, IL: Human Kinetics.

Honkasalo, M.-L. (1998) 'Space and Embodied Experience: Rethinking the Body in Pain', *Body & Society*, 4, 2: 35–57.

International Association for the Study of Pain, 'Pain Terms: A List with Definitions and Notes on Usage', *Pain*, 6, 1979: 240.

James, F. R. and Large, R. G. (1992) 'Chronic Pain, Relationships and Illness Self-Construct', *Pain*, 50: 263–71.

Johnson, U. (1997) 'A Three-year Follow Up of Long-term Injured Competetive Athletes: Influence of Psychological Risk Factors on Rehabilitation', *Journal of Sport Rehabilitation*, 6: 256–71.

Keefe, F. J. and Rosenstil, A. (1983) 'Coping Strategies Questionnaire', *Pain*, 17: 33–44.

Kleinert, J. (2000) 'Dimensionen adaptiver Schmerzbewältigung im Sport', *Psychologie und Sport*, 7, 1: 1–12.

Kübler-Ross, E. (1969) *On Death and Dying*, New York: Macmillan.

Kugelmann, R. (1997) 'The Psychology and Management of Pain: Gate Control as Theory and Symbol', *Theory and Psychology*, 7, 1: 43–65.

McDougall, J. (1989) *Theatres of the Body: A Psychoanalytic Approach to Psychosomatic Illness*, London: Free Association Books.

Melzack, R. (1973) *The Puzzle of Pain*, New York: Basic Books.

Melzack, R. and Wall, P. D. (1996) *The Challenge of Pain*, London: Penguin Books.

Morris, D. B. (1991) *The Culture of Pain*, Berkeley: University of California Press.

Nixon, H. L. II (1994) 'Social Pressure, Social Support, and Help Seeking for Pain and Injuries in College Sport Networks', *Journal of Sport & Social Issues*, 18, 4: 340–55.

Ogilvie, B. and Tutko, P. (1966) *Problem Athletes and How to Handle Them*, London: Pelham Books.

Pensgaard, A. M. and Ursin, H. (1998) 'Stress, Control, and Coping in Elite Athletes', *Scandinavian Journal of Medicine & Science in Sports*, 8: 183–9.

Raedeke, T. D. (1997) 'Is Athlete Burnout More Than Just Stress? A Sport Commitment Perspective', *Journal of Sport & Exercise Psychology*, 19: 396–417.

Rey, R. (1998) *The History of Pain*, Cambridge, MA: Harvard University Press.

Roessler, K. K. (2002) *Når idræt gør ondt . . . – skader, smerter, stress*, Aarhus: Klim.

Roessler, K. K. (2004) *Sport und Schmerz: Ein sportpsychologischer Ansatz zur Schmerzforschung*, Immenhausen: Prolog.

Sauerbruch, F. and Wenke, H. (1936) *Wesen und Bedeutung des Schmerzes*, Berlin: Junker und Dünnhaupt.

Scarry, E. (1985) *The Body in Pain: The Making and Unmaking of the World*, New York: Oxford University Press.

Schmid, W. (1999) *Philosophie der Lebenskunst: Eine Grundlegung*, Frankfurt a.M.: Suhrkamp.

Taylor, J. and Taylor, S. (1998) 'Pain Education and Management in the Rehabilitation from Sports Injury', *The Sport Psychologist*, 12: 68–88.

Udry, E. (1997) 'Coping and Social Support among Injured Athletes Following Surgery', *Journal of Sport & Exercise Psychology*, 19: 71–90.

von Uexküll, T. (1997) *Psychosomatische Medizin*, Munich, Vienna and Baltimore: Urban & Schwarzenberg.

Williams, J. M. (2001) 'Psychology of Injury Risk and Prevention', in R. B. Singer, H. A. Hausenblas and C. Janelle (eds) *Handbook of Sport Psychology*, New York: Wiley: 766–86.

Williams, J. M. and Anderson, M. B. (1998) 'Psychosocial Antecedents of Sport Injury: Review and Critique of the Stress and Injury Model', *Journal of Applied Sport Psychology*, 10: 5–25.

Williams, J. and Roepke, N. (1993) 'Psychology of Injury and Injury Rehabilitation', in R. N. Singer et al.: *Handbook of Research on Sport Psychology*, New York: 815–39.

Wundt, W. (1913) *Grundriss der Psychologie*, Leipzig: Alfred Körner.

Zborowski, M. (1960) *People in Pain*, San Francisco: Jossey-Bass.

Zens, M. and Jurna, I. (1993) *Lehrbuch der Schmerztherapie*, Stuttgart: Wissenschaftliche Verlagsgesellschaft.

3 Three approaches to the study of pain in sport

Sigmund Loland

The aim of this chapter is to sketch and critically discuss, with the help of practical examples, three ideal-typical approaches to the study of pain in sport. I have chosen to focus on pain, rather than injuries and illness, because pain is a borderline case between what can be physically located and medically diagnosed and what is seen to belong to the subjective, experiential sphere that must be explored by other means. Studying pain involves challenges to the traditional understandings of athletes and their bodies and, more generally, to traditional understandings of the physical and the natural, of body and mind, and of nature and culture.

In the first section, I will discuss the classical, medical approach, in which the aim is to describe accurately and to explain causally pain as a physical phenomenon. The second section deals with a radically different approach in which pain is conceived of primarily as a product or a construction of the social and cultural context in which we find ourselves. The third perspective is inspired by phenomenology and departs from the immediate and subjective experiential qualities of pain: from pain as *qualia*. In the conclusion, I will reflect upon some possible implications of these approaches for future research into pain in sport.

The classical approach: Pain as nature

In a tight duel over the ball, soccer player X is 'stamped' on the knee by another player and falls down. The knee hurts, and X stays down and is in pain. X is carried off the pitch where she is met by the team medical doctor Y. Y follows a standard procedure. The primary aim is to locate and explain the pain. Are there visible marks on the knee? Does palpation hurt, and if so where and how? What kind of movement produces pain? Y has to make a preliminary diagnosis. Should the knee be cooled down for X to continue or should X be taken off the pitch to receive further treatment? If the latter is the outcome, a more extensive examination is undertaken to determine a more precise diagnosis and to decide which therapeutic measures are required to heal the injury as quickly as possible.

In their understanding and management of pain and injury, most athletes and doctors think and act within what can be called a traditional or classical approach. In simple terms, its premises can be described as follows. The body is understood as a physical object existing within a deterministic, natural world. In principle, any bodily phenomena can be described accurately and explained causally. Moreover, given knowledge of initial conditions, bodily processes can be predicted and controlled in therapeutic contexts. The paradigm scientific disciplines of the classical approach are anatomy, physiology, bio-mechanics and traditional medicine.

The premises of the classical approach are built more or less directly on what is referred to as a Cartesian, dualistic worldview (Stricker 1970). To the seventeenth-century French philosopher René Descartes, the world could be separated into two substances, *res extensa* or the extended substance, and *res cogitans*, the thinking substance. The extended substance refers to physical objects and natural phenomena that follow the deterministic laws of nature. Thinking substance is without extension. Here are found consciousness, spirit, mind, rationality and freedom. The two substances are considered qualitatively different and totally independent of each other. Whereas the mind belongs to thinking substance, the body as extended substance is to be understood as deterministic nature. Hence, a human being is considered a radically divided being. Descartes presents a clear-cut dualistic philosophical anthropology.

The dualistic worldview has been of fundamental importance in the development of science in the West (Wright 1971). In an ideal-typical sense, the natural sciences, from physics to biology, imply the exploration of extended substance, or deterministic nature. We talk here of nomothetic sciences which aim for accurate descriptions and causal explanations and predictions in terms of universal laws covering all physical phenomena and biological processes. This approach, it should be noted, has been immensely successful. In the context of pain, it should suffice to point to the role of classical medicine and pharmaceutical research in the development of general pain reduction and management, and to the many medical techniques and therapeutic measures in dealing with pain in sport.

However, the classical approach has also been subject to severe criticism. There seem to be key issues in human experience that this approach simply cannot adequately explain. One such issue is the common experience of close interaction, indeed of unity, of body and mind. Performances involving human movement provide paradigmatic cases. As argued by, among others, Dreyfus and Dreyfus (1986), in skilled performances in various fields, for instance by expert pilots, athletes, or surgeons, there seems to be a transcendence of the body–mind distinction and an experience of a total, unified commitment to the task. Cartesian, dualistic anthropology cannot conceptualize this. Descartes saw the challenge of the mind–body problem, in particular when it came to the reception of sensations from the body, and to intentional movement (Stricker 1970). However, through the *ad hoc* hypothesis of *glandula pinealis*, the pineal gland, through which a non-specified interaction between body and mind was supposed to take place, the dualistic view was upheld.

Although Descartes' *ad hoc* assumption is commonly rejected, the classical approach still builds on the philosophical premises of Cartesian dualism. This can be exemplified by current standard descriptions and explanations of pain. Pain is considered part of physical reality and must be treated accordingly. The International Association for the Study of Pain defines pain as 'an unpleasant sensory and emotional experience associated with actual or potential tissue damage, or described in terms of such damage'.[1]

More specifically, pain is understood functionally as a process which, via sensory experiences, informs the higher centres of the organism (i.e. the brain) of threats and dangers which have physical causes (injury and illness). In the case of soccer player X, for instance, a physiological-medical explanation would include descriptions of how signals from pain receptors, which are defined as the distal parts of the nerve system located in the knee, are sent to the spinal cord and then up to the higher centres of the brain. These centres send signals back down on a different nerve path via the mid-brain and the medulla. When they reach the spinal cord, where the pain message is being relayed, processes are activated to counter and reduce pain, for instance in terms of the production of endorphins.

The standard critique of the classical view and its dualistic underpinnings is that it is reductionist. It reduces a complex phenomenon such as pain in simplistic ways. Imagine that X's knee pain has no obvious physical explanation. There are no marks on the knee and no abnormalities when it comes to knee function. Medical doctor Y finds no physical evidence to suggest pain and injury. Still, X reports pain. Does X's pain not exist? Is it not real? And how can X and Y deal with the situation? Another problem is that pain patterns seem to vary from one individual to another. Identical medical diagnoses can be associated with different pain patterns as experienced by different people. For instance, X' s knee problem might be diagnosed in exactly the same way as player Z's, but player Z reports little or no pain. How can we account for such individual differences in the experience of pain?

In cases such as these, representatives of the classical approach appear to have two strategies. One strategy is to see X's report of pain as real and to assume that the missing diagnosis is due to a lack of knowledge and scanning technology. If a cause is found, treatment will start accordingly. If no cause is found, strategy two comes into play. The problem is redefined. In the classical approach, dualistic anthropology sets the explanatory scheme. Experiences of pain belong to non-extended substance, to *res cogitans*, that is, to the mind. In this view, pain without physical causes is a psychological problem infused with subjectivity and non-controllable factors and should be treated with different means. One possibility is psychological therapy. Another possibility is neglect and rejection. Either way, in a performance-oriented sport environment, athletes with no clear physical basis for their pain are likely to find that others are reluctant to accept that they have 'real' pain. Athletes with 'mental' or 'imagined' pain are often considered to lack the required attitudes and mental toughness to succeed

in sport. I will return to a more detailed discussion of the socio-cultural interpretation of pain below.

Critics argue that examples such as these illustrate the reductionist character
of the classical approach and the need for challenging its basic presuppositions.
An increasing amount of experiential and scientific evidence indicates that
pain, injury and illness are best understood as the complex products of interaction between bodily and mental processes (Melzack and Wall 1982). Moreover, the reductionist metaphysics of the classical approach, and in particular
the view of the body as an object and as part of deterministic nature, is considered to have ethically problematic consequences. For instance, in the hard
drive towards performance enhancement, the body is easily treated as an
object and, in particular, as a means open to extreme manipulative techniques
(Hoberman 1992). One expression of this attitude, critics may claim, is the
medically based use of bio-medical performance-enhancing means such as doping.

This does not mean that the classical approach ought to be rejected. As noted
earlier, this approach has provided the ground for impressive and important
medical and bio-technological developments with great potential for improving
the quality of human life in general, and the quality of sport and sport medicine
in particular. However, problems arise if the dualist view is seen, not as a working hypothesis in science and clinical practice, but as a total view designed to
explain human embodiment in all its aspects. The phenomenon of pain is particularly well suited to demonstrate the inadequacy of the classical approach
in this respect.

Interestingly, the very idea of humans as dualistic beings opens up the possibility of alternative conceptualizations of the problem. The Cartesian insistence
on the mind as a non-extended, non-deterministic substance has influenced the
development of theories of the mind and conscious experience which are built
on understandings and methodologies radically different from those found in
the classical approach. One such alternative is what can be called the contextualist approach.

The contextualist approach: Pain as culture

A contextualist approach to pain includes several explanatory schemes. On the
practical level, the contextualist has no problems with classical explanations.
On the contrary, if the causes of pain can be accounted for and therapeutic
regimes designed, this is considered important and valuable. However, contextualists would criticize the view of the classical approach as a complete and
objective understanding of pain. Like any conceptualization of the world, the
classical approach is a product of particular historical, cultural and social contexts. In simple terms, the development of classical medicine can be situated
within the frameworks of Cartesian dualism, the Enlightenment beliefs in
science and rationality, and the modern belief in progress and technology and
technological innovation. These frameworks are still strong and dominant. For
instance, Rheinberger (1995) sees in the current 'molecularization' of medicine

and the development of genetic technologies the full realization of the Cartesian idea of the body as an engineered machine.

Furthermore, contextualists hold that the classical understanding of the body and of injury and pain is only one among many which are possible, and that its hegemonic status has to be understood in terms of its coherence with basic ideas and norms of the socio-cultural context within which it has developed. One of the primary aims of the contextualist is to demonstrate how such contexts shape and reshape our understanding of what injury and pain are all about.

The contextualist approach is based largely on scholarly disciplines such as history, sociology and anthropology and, at first sight, appears to have no immediate and obvious practical application. However, on second thoughts, contextualist knowledge can be of significant relevance to the practitioner. Let us return to the case of soccer player X. After the hard tackle, X's experience of pain will vary according to her individual situation, the norms and values of X's team and the more extensive socio-cultural normative schemes of which X is a part. Being a young and successful player leading her team towards victory, X's knee pain might be repressed by strong enthusiasm and motivation. X wants to get up and continue playing. However, if X is a player with career problems and has performed unsuccessfully on a losing team, her knee pain might be experienced as more intensive and worse. In that case, X may stay down and be carried off the pitch. If the culture of the club and the sport is such that pain is supposed to be neglected and repressed, X may be reluctant to complain about it. If there is acceptance of reports of pain, and if the medical support system takes it seriously, X will communicate openly about her experience of pain. Obviously, to Y as a practising doctor, knowledge of socio-psychological and socio-cultural context will be crucial to treat X in an appropriate way, and to reflect critically upon the premises upon which the treatment of X is based.

A contextualist approach is built on different philosophical premises from the classical approach. The philosopher Georg Henrik von Wright (1971) draws a basic distinction between two ideals of Western science: the ideals of explanation and of understanding. Explanation belongs to what he calls Galilean science (after Galileo Galilei, the founding father of modern scientific methodology). It can also be called Cartesian science. The methodological and epistemological ideals are those of the classical approach described above. The alternative Aristotelian tradition is built on a teleological, holistic understanding of the phenomenon under study. It was revitalized in the eighteenth and nineteenth centuries with the reconstruction of the human sciences (*Geisteswissenschaften*) and the development of modern hermeneutics. In this view, quantitative descriptions and causal explanations are considered inadequate for a proper understanding of human action and the socio-cultural world. There is also a need for qualitative insights into the diversity and complexity of human intentions and experience, and into how socio-cultural norms and values shape and reshape such intentions and experiences.

Within the social sciences, the contextual approach has been further developed from classic hermeneutics towards social constructivist theories that can be found in, among others, the works of Norbert Elias, Michel Foucault and Pierre Bourdieu. A new sociology of the body has emerged, seeking an understanding of the body as a social construction (Featherstone *et al.* 1991; Shilling 1993; Turner 1984). The body is seen as a social symbol and a means in, or actually as the very site of, the construction of identity.

This has implications for the understanding of medicine, and of pain and injury. For instance, the sociologist Zola (1972) writes of the medicalization of society in which discourses of illness and health play an increasingly important part in people's lives. According to Zola, medicine in the West has become a means of social control. More specifically, contextualist-inspired analyses of pain see the phenomenon as culture and not as nature (Kotarba 1983). Pain is inscribed with meaning (or meaninglessness) based on the socio-cultural context in which it is situated. Contextualist studies of pain and injury in sport can be found in the anthropology and sociology of sport, among others in works of Howe (2004), Nixon (1996), Roderick *et al.* (2000), Waddington (2000), White *et al.* (1995) and Young *et al.* (1994). Typically, certain kinds of pain without injury, such as the pain of hard training and competition, are taken as signs of development and athletic growth. The well-known slogan, 'no pain, no gain', illustrates the point. The acceptance and endurance of pain are necessary to succeed. The body is seen more or less as a productive tool. There is almost a masochistic perspective in some sport cultures, such as the Welsh rugby sub-culture studied by Howe (2004). Pain is not an obstacle to, but a means towards, liberation and salvation.

In addition to describing these 'pain discourses' (as some sociologists would term it) the contextualist weighs them against each other and attempts to distinguish hegemonic discourses from the more marginal ones. In general, in performance sport coping with pain is seen as a test of the spirit of an athlete. Pain has to be fought and conquered. Strong athletes are expected to work hard on their recovery and return to competition as soon as possible. Injury and pain should be turned into success stories of human growth. In sport, the hegemonic pain discourse as portrayed by contextualists is heavily influenced by masculine values such as individualism, toughness and competitiveness, and by the classical medical approach (White *et al.* 1995). To complain of pain without detectable physical causes is considered a sign of weakness and problematic attitudes. Contextualists also describe marginal pain discourses, for instance feminist discourses concerning the experiences of female athletes that to a larger extent emphasize empathy, mutual understanding and solidarity with those in pain.[2]

There are many advantages of the contextualist approach. It makes explicit the many discourses of pain in sport and how they are intertwined or stand in contradiction to each other. A contextualist approach is also reflective; it opens up possibilities for alternative understandings and stimulates critical thought. Moreover, contextualists take seriously the ambiguity, subjectivity and particularity of pain. Within the constructivist approach, pain exists as long as there are reports of, or human expressions of, pain, independent of physical signs and causes. There are no absolute normative evaluations and hierarchies of pain here. The criterion of the seriousness of pain is the felt seriousness among those concerned. This is a deeply humanistic aspect embedded in the approach.

However, this approach is not without criticism. The humanism described above is a double-edged sword. One problem is that the approach offers empathy and understanding, but few possibilities for critical and systematic articulation of normative standpoints in the many moral dilemmas in the field. In some sport cultures, extreme and problematic pain regimes are pre-eminent. For instance, the so-called hegemonic masculinity discourse may have repressive and destructive implications that damage athletes for life. Some contextualists may seek to resolve the problem with forms of practical activism that are kept separate from their academic work. With the intention of developing an open and tolerant articulation of all 'voices' of pain in sport, other contextualists may end up in moral relativist positions within which even activism becomes difficult. Paradoxically, the admirable quest for understanding and tolerance may undermine moral engagement in practice.

A final criticism is that, just as in the case of the classical approach, if contextualism is taken as a worldview and given ontological status, strange implications arise. In the study of pain, contextualists might underestimate the value of the classical approach in terms of the role of physical realities and causes of pain and the value of classically based therapeutic regimes. In extreme versions, pain might be understood in purely social and cultural terms, with no reference to bio-medical aspects at all. In a sense, then, contextualism might be seen to represent a kind of reversed dualism. The distinction between body and mind, or nature and culture, is upheld but now with an emphasis on *res cogitans*, or the mind and culture.

There is, however, a third approach that attempts to overcome the dualisms of the classical and the contextual approaches. This is the phenomenological approach.

The phenomenological approach: Pain as subjective experience

The phenomenological approach has its roots in a reaction against what was considered a distanced and scientistic approach towards human experience, especially as found in the psychology of the late nineteenth and twentieth centuries. The aim of the founding father of philosophical phenomenology, Edmund Husserl, was an analysis of human intention 'in itself'. Husserlian phenomenology is concerned with the basic features of human intentionality. The main influence from phenomenology on psychology and social science is the idea of human beings as intentional beings constructing meaning through an active interaction with, and interpretation of, the environment (Bell 1991). As is evident from the earlier discussion of the constructivist approach, phenomenologically oriented psychologists and sociologists are also concerned with the analysis of this interaction. However, there is another line of development that follows a stricter philosophical path, and it is towards this approach that I now turn.

The phenomenological approach builds on a particular conception of the body and pain in sport. In the discussion of the classical approach, I referred to its inability to conceptualize adequately the relationship between body and mind. In this respect, the phenomenological approach seems to have more to offer. During a game, soccer player X can be totally absorbed by play and transcend distinctions between body and mind, and between self and the social and physical environment. The focus is on the ball and on the movements of team-mates and competitors. The game is experienced as a continuously changing totality (Hughson and Inglis 2002). X 'lives' totally within the game. Phenomenologists and psychologists label experiences such as these as 'peak experiences' (Maslow), 'deep play' (Czikscentmihalyi), 'being in the zone' (Standish), or in Gallwey's well-known phrase from tennis, as playing 'the inner game'. X is best understood as a unified soccer-playing intentionality and plays with a spontaneous and unreflective experience of the body. In the words of Marcel (1979), X 'is' her body.

This state of affairs is, however, regularly disrupted. In our example above, X is tackled brutally by an opponent and falls down with instant pain in the knee. X moves dramatically from being absorbed by the game towards focusing on a body part that hurts and that is outside her control. The hurting knee makes its appearance and breaks up the unified, experiential flow of the game. The focus of attention is turned towards the knee as an object, and to the pain resulting from the tackle.

Disruptions such as these affect all players and the game as a whole. The referee blows the whistle for a free kick, there is a sudden halt to the game. Some players move towards X to check out the possible injury. Some talk together about tactical moves. Some are aware of the gaze of the public and the cameras and think of their appearance. Some bend over with their hands on their knees and rest. After a while, the game restarts, player focus shifts, and players re-enter the play zone.

Phenomenologists are interested in exploring such shifts of intentionality and attention and examine how they are experienced and given meaning. The aim is to reveal the presuppositions of our experiences of the world. The point of departure is the classic phenomenological reduction, the Husserlian 'to the things themselves'. In line with the work of Merleau-Ponty (1962), most phenomenological analyses of sport build on an understanding of the body as intentional consciousness through which we establish meaning in a dialectic relationship with the world. Sudden pain, as in the case of X above, can be understood as breaks in this continuous meaning construction, or as a communication gap between intentionality and the environment. The description of X's play and pain demonstrates that we are both body objects and body subjects, and that we shift constantly between deep, unified experiences of the world, and distance and objectification. Phenomenological analyses of sport are analyses of 'the lived body', or the body in 'the life world' (*Lebenswelt*).

There are a number of arguments in favour of a phenomenological approach to human experiences such as pain. The perspective attempts to bridge the dualist gap. It gives an account of how the human mode of existence is in a constant flux and is in close, meaning-producing interaction with the environment. As with the contextualist approach, there is a deep humanism embedded in the project, in the sense of taking individual experiences seriously. From the phenomenological point of view, medicine is 'a *human* science that has, at its centre, the suffering embodied human being who seeks help and the professional who responds (is responsive) to the call for assistance' (Toombs 2001: 19). Methodologically, a phenomenological investigation of pain can build on $n = 1$. There is no aim here of describing objectively and explaining pain experiences causally; nor is there any necessary focus on how pain is understood by the majority of a certain social group or culture. Phenomenologists study the richness and diversity of subjective experiences of pain and, in this way, the existential role of pain in human lives (Morris 1991).

How is it possible to proceed from this sketchy phenomenological description of X's experiences above to a more systematic, phenomenological analysis of pain? A first step could be a tentative categorization of the experiential diversity and qualities of athletic pain (pain as *qualia*). Distinctions can be made between sudden and emerging pain, between sharp and well-defined pain and general muscle pain after a hard training session, between neurological pain in the joints and pain as the result of external impact, *et cetera*. A second step is to understand pain within the framework of individual athletes' life world. A basic phenomenological idea is to see pain as an expression of a communication gap, that is, as a gap in X's interaction with and interpretation of the world.

A third step can be a move to a more general analytic level. Kleinman (1988) describes intensive and chronic pain as a gradual loss of the self. To the phenomenologist, the classical, medical analysis of X's injury is of value as *one element* in the interpretation of X's understanding of the situation. In the situation on the pitch, and in the therapeutic measures afterwards, the close follow-up in terms of closing the communication gap and reconstruction meaning would be of crucial importance. Here, as in Jeff Fry's chapter in this volume, phenomenological categorizations and narratives of individual experiences of pain can be reflected upon, and the nature of pain as an existential theme can be described and discussed.

However, the phenomenological approach is not without its critics. From the perspective of the classical approach, phenomenology may appear as speculative and with only a loose relationship to conventional research standards and methodology. Critics could also point to the diversity of phenomenological understandings of the same phenomenon. For instance, two analyses of an athlete in pain can result in two different descriptions and there seems to be no clear, critical criterion to evaluate the adequacy of the descriptions. It could be argued that phenomenology might be interesting and good reading but, just like the good novel, it is fiction and based more or less on the free and associative interpretations of the researcher.

Although they are significant, these criticisms can be countered. First, since the early 1900s, the phenomenological movement has included a strong methodological discourse and has been a key inspiration to the development of qualitative methodology in the social sciences. In this respect, the classically based, methodological critique perhaps misses the target. Second, in a phenomenological universe, objective criteria and the search for only one valid or true description and explanation of a phenomenon make little sense. One aim of phenomenology is to provide descriptions and understandings of human experience in all its diversity and complexity. As long as they meet the internal standards of good phenomenology, the existence of two different descriptions of the same phenomenon is not a problem but, rather, an asset.

Another criticism of the phenomenological approach focuses on what is seen as a lack of critical potential. From a contextualist point of view, phenomenologists analyse individuals' experiences in more or less introvert ways and underestimate the social realities and broader power relations that shape those experiences. What seems to be ignored or underplayed in the phenomenological perspective is the basic premise of human experience as a result of socialization and of the social environment in which individuals are born and raised. Phenomenological analyses of pain in sport, for instance, portray pain and suffering as potentially meaningful and significant elements in individual development, instead of focusing on the socio-cultural contexts that make the infliction of pain and suffering acceptable and even admirable. Hence the approach becomes a-contextual and idealistic and conceals the social realities of the sporting culture.

Combining approaches: Possibilities and limitations

I have given an ideal-typical overview of three approaches to the study of pain in sport, sketched their philosophical premises, and referred to some possible criticisms of each approach. The classical approach offers accurate descriptions and clear-cut causal explanations of pain and has significant practical implications. Within this approach, strong and efficient therapeutic regimes can be developed. However, the classical approach seems unable to account for the subjective experience of pain, and there are difficulties with the understanding and acceptance of pain which has no clear physical causes. The contextual approach provides explanations and understandings of how the experience of pain is interpreted and shaped within the social and cultural context in which people live. It offers a critical, reflective perspective but can be attacked for maintaining the dualist distinction between nature and culture, and for its lack of ability to handle the normative challenges linked to pain in sport. The phenomenological approach takes as its starting point individual athletes' immediate experience of pain and attempts to overcome dualistic accounts of the phenomenon. The aim is not to provide objective descriptions and explanations but, rather, to give inter-subjective accounts of pain as an existential theme. It can be criticized for being introvert, individualistic and idealistic and for ignoring or underplaying the social and cultural context of pain and injury.

It might be argued that, to some extent, these three approaches complement each other. The weaknesses of one approach, it might be suggested, seem to be covered by the strengths of another. Is it possible to combine the various approaches to get the best of several theoretical and methodological worlds? What are the possibilities and limitations here?

In real (research) life, the distinctions between these approaches are not as strict or clear as portrayed in my ideal-typical account. Most research projects combine approaches. In particular, as can be seen in sport sociological and anthropological literature, contextualist and phenomenological perspectives overlap, while relevant 'facts' from the classical approach serve as an informative background.[3] Much research in the area seems to represent an attempt at syntheses between approaches and appears to build on the ideal of thematic and inter-disciplinary sport research.

On the other hand, my ideal-typical sketch of perspectives above illustrates the need for caution when it comes to thematic inter-disciplinarity. The classical approach is built on radically different metaphysical, epistemological and methodological premises from the contextualist and phenomenological approaches. Whereas the classical approach understands pain in terms of objective, deterministic nature, the contextualist and phenomenologist approaches share the focus on pain as subjectively experienced and 'lived' within the socio-cultural contexts in which athletes find themselves. In a sense, this makes the classical approach and the contextualist and phenomenological approaches incommensurable (Boyd 1991). Key theoretical concepts of the classical approach cannot be translated in meaningful ways into contextual and phenomenological frameworks (semantic incommensurability), and *vice versa*. Semantic incommensurability implies methodological incommensurability (Boyd 1991). There seems to be no single method acceptable to all approaches to settle possible disagreements or disputes between them. The choice of one conceptual framework excludes incommensurable alternatives by necessity.

Hence, the quest for inter-disciplinarity needs modification. If incommensurable theories and methods are incorporated into all-embracing conceptual schemes, there is a risk of ending up with systems of knowledge that are either theoretically inconsistent or articulated in such a general way that they lack epistemological value. The idea of the body as a physiological cause–effect mechanism is radically different from the idea of the body as subjectively 'lived' and socio-culturally constructed.

This does not necessarily represent a limitation in pain research. On the contrary, an alternative viewpoint is to see the very existence of a variety of incommensurable approaches to pain as being of epistemological value. For instance, the three approaches described above seem to lead to broad and complementary knowledge of the phenomenon. Pluralism, and not inter-disciplinarity, seems to advance insights in the phenomenon both in depth and width and ought perhaps to be the ideal strategy in thematic research fields such as sport science.

However, the pluralist ideal needs modification. First, a plurality of approaches is not an unconditional good. To reach systematic and critical knowledge, the internal quality standards of each approach have to be reviewed and controlled. The ideal here is *critical* pluralism. Furthermore, in general it has to be said that connections between approaches and syntheses of previously separated bodies of knowledge enhance insights and knowledge of a phenomenon. In this sense, inter-disciplinarity is good. The condition for a meaningful integration, however, is commensurability and/or the acceptance of one dominant conceptual framework within which other approaches are subordinated. For instance, an epidemiological study that builds on a classic conceptualization of pain can use both contextualist inspired surveys and phenomenologically inspired qualitative interviews, but as sub-elements within the classical approach. And, *mutatis mutandis*, a contextualist or phenomenological approach could build on the shared ideas of persons as intentional meaning-constructing beings and use data gathered using the classical approach as components and illustrations of contextualist and phenomenological points.

A sound research strategy here, then, as in other fields of thematic sport research, seems to be critical pluralism combined with conditional inter-disciplinarity (Loland 1992).

Concluding comment

A final comment concerns the current status of the various approaches in the study of pain and injury in sport. Traditionally, this has been the domain of the classical bio-medical approach. This approach still seems to have hegemonic status. However, new research, overviewed in volumes such as this one, indicates an increasing interest in pain and injury from psychological, sociological, anthropological and philosophical points of view. The hegemonic, classical approach is challenged. If this volume can serve as a contribution in this respect, one of its most important goals has been reached. Critical pluralism and conditional inter-disciplinarity, I believe, are signs of a research field that is flourishing.

Notes

1 International Association for the Study of Pain, 'Pain terms'.
2 For an overview of research on pain and injury in women's sport, see the chapter by Charlesworth and Young in this book.
3 For an overview, see Roderick's chapter in this book.

Bibliography

Bell, D. (1991) *Husserl*, London: Routledge

Boyd, R. (1991) 'Confirmation, Semantics, and the Implication of Scientific Theories' in R. Boyd, P. Casper and J. D. Trout (eds) *The Philosophy of Science*, Cambridge, MA: Bradford.

Dreyfus, H. B. and Dreyfus, S. E. (1986) *Mind over Machine: The Power of Human Intuition and Expertise in the Age of the Computer*, Oxford: Basil Blackwell.

Featherstone, M., Hepworth, M. and Turner, B. S. (1991) *The Body: Social Process and Cultural Theory*, London: Sage.

Gallwey, T. (1974) *Inner Game of Tennis*, New York: Random House.

Guttmann, A. (1978) *From Ritual to Record: The Nature of Modern Sport*, New York: Columbia University Press.

Hoberman, J. (1992) *Mortal Engines: The Science of Performance and the Dehumanization of Sports*, New York: Free Press.

Howe, P. D. (1997) 'Professionalism, Commercialism, and the Rugby Club: From Embryo to Infant at Pontypridd RFC' in T. L. C. Chandler and J. Nauright (eds) *The Rugby World: Race, Gender, Commerce and Rugby Union*, London: Cass.

Howe, P. D. (2004) *Sport, Professionalism and Pain*, London: Routledge.

Hughson, J. and Inglis, D. (2002) 'Inside the Beautiful Game: Towards a Merleau-Pontian Phenomenology of Soccer Play', *Journal of the Philosophy of Sport*, XXIX: 1–15.

International Association for the Study of Pain, 'Pain terms: a list with definitions and notes on usage', *Pain*, 6, 1979: 240.

Kleinman, A. (1988) *The Illness Narratives: Suffering, Healing and the Human Condition*, New York: Basic Books.

Kotarba, J. A. (1983) *Chronic Pain: Its Social Dimensions*, London: Sage.

Loland, S. (1992) 'The Mechanics and Meaning of Alpine Skiing: Methodological and Epistemological Notes on the Study of Sport Technique', *Journal of the Philosophy of Sport*, XIX: 55–77.

Marcel, G. (1979) 'I am my Body' in E. W. Gerber and W. J. Morgan (eds) *Sport and the Body – A Philosophical Symposium*, Philadelphia: Lea and Febiger.

Melzack, R. and Wall, P. (1982) *The Challenge of Pain*, New York: Penguin.

Merleau-Ponty, M. (1962) *Phenomenology of Perception*, London: Routledge and Kegan Paul.

Morris, D. (1991) *The Culture of Pain*, Berkeley: University of California Press.

Nixon, H. (1996) 'The relationship of friendship, networks, sport experiences, and gender to express pain thresholds', *Sociology of Sport Journal*, 13: 78–86.

Rheinberger, H-J. (1995) 'Beyond Nature and Culture: A Note on Medicine in the Age of Molecular Biology' in M. Heyd and H. Rheinberger (eds) *Medicine as a Cultural System, Science in Context* 8, 1 (spring): 249–63.

Roderick, M., Waddington, I. and Parker, G. (2000) 'Playing Hurt: Managing Injuries in English Professional Football', *International Review for the Sociology of Sport*, 35, 2: 165–80.

Shilling, C. (1993) *The Body and Social Theory*, London: Sage.

Stricker, S. F. (1970) *The Philosophy of the Body: Rejections of Cartesian Dualism*, New York: Quadrangle.

Toombs, S. K. (2001) 'Introduction: Phenomenology and Medicine' in S. K. Toombs (ed.) *Handbook of Phenomenology and Medicine*, Dordrecht, Netherlands: Kluwer: 1–25.

Turner, B. S. (1984) *The Body and Society*, 2nd edn, London: Sage.

Waddington, I. (2000) *Sport, Health and Drugs*, London: Routledge.

White, P. G., Young, K. and McTeer, W. G. (1995) 'Sport, Masculinity and the Injured Body' in D. Sabo and F. Gordon (eds) *Men's Health and Illness: Gender, Power and the Body*, London: Sage.

von Wright, G. H. (1971) *Explanation and Understanding*, Ithaca, NY: Cornell University Press.

Young, K., White, P. and McTeer, W. (1994) 'Body Talk: Male Athletes Reflect on Sport, Injury and Pain', *Sociology of Sport Journal*, 11: 175–94.

Zola, I. K. (1972) 'Medicine as an Institution of Social Control', *Sociological Review*, 20, 4: 487–504.

Section II

Pain, injury and performance

4 The place of pain in running

John Bale

Where is the place of pain in sports? Most studies of pain focus on the discomfort that is induced by injuries of various kinds. The object of such work is, it seems, to relieve or eliminate pain. Studies into injury-induced pain are mainly scientific in nature and focus on facts rather than feelings. They employ the techniques of medical and statistical science and are undertaken by medical and social scientists. However, there are other contexts in which pain in sports is worthy of study. There is the pain experienced by athletes that is unrelated to injury. Such pain may be the result of fatigue or exhaustion during a competition; it may also be pain that is imposed by the coach or trainer; and there is also the emotional pain of failure or retirement. Another context for pain in sport is that experienced by spectators, mainly through the sense of sight. Spectators consume pain in a different way from performers and little has been done in the sports literature that addresses spectators' attitudes and feelings when watching athletes in pain. Additionally, I adopt here a somewhat 'non-scientific' approach, drawing more on the humanities than on the social and physical sciences.

In this chapter I make some tentative observations on pain in relation to 'non-injured' athletes and to spectators. For convenience (and personal interest) I concentrate on some aspects of pain experienced by top-class runners – almost entirely middle-distance runners – and those who watch them perform. Though I take running as an example, much of what I have to say may be applicable to other sports. However, it is worth noting that sports-workers from sports other than running may report pain in different terms and with different emphases. In order to illuminate the forms and meaning of pain in the context of running I utilize, on the one hand, the inspirational work of humanistic geographer Yi-Fu Tuan (see Bale 2004) and, on the other, biographical sources that, I think, describe the place of pain in running in a more sensitive way than scientists are able to do.

Running as pain

Elaine Scarry has noted that there 'are very great impediments to expressing another's sentient distress' (Scarry 1985: 6). After all, those in physical pain are unlikely to be in a position to record how they feel at the time. While scientific studies have been used to measure pain, it is arguable that literature – that is, novels and biographies (including autobiographies) – provides fertile sources for addressing pain from a humanistic perspective (Morris 1991). In autobiographical writing, runners record feelings of pain. Attempting to describe the pain while training for the 1,500 metres, the former French record-holder Michel Jazy noted that pain 'starts to hurt deep in your throat. The blood rushes up. You feel sick, your stomach muscles knot up and your legs feel like lead' (quoted in Brohm 1974: 24). Even in her first year at university, following years of running in high school, Leslie Heywood (a rare example of a professor of English literature writing about sports) sometimes felt that she had:

> Already given too much, all my blood and my driving, pounding heart and guts, I cannot possibly keep doing it, giving it more again and again . . . Since I don't know what else to do, I just keep giving more but I am so tired.
> (Heywood 1998: 186)

At the age of 19, her joints thought they were 50 (Heywood 1998: 141). From a neo-Marxist perspective, this might be taken as an illustration of the 'reactionary ideological functions of sport' (Brohm 1974: 26).

Pain is frequently thought to be an essential ingredient of a serious runner's career. It has been suggested that 'the essence of sport is the feeling of muscular pain and exhaustion' (Heikkala 1993: 81). In long-distance running athletes 'choose to torture themselves – to entertain other people and to make a living' (Phillips 2001: 31). Pain is greatly encouraged in running. Pain is thought to benefit runners despite the fact that it is often read as a warning signal. 'No pain, no gain', goes the well-known locker-room saying, an exhortation to train and race hard. The Hungarian coach Mihaly Igloi urged his charges to 'Go on, kill yourself' (quoted in Vinnai 1973: 101). The Austrian track and field coach Franz Stampfl exhorted his pupils to run harder with the words 'Don't worry, it's only pain' (quoted in Smith 2001). In his study of top-class sprinters the sports anthropologist Robert Sands (1995) further reveals the centrality of pain in training. He describes it as the deposit, the investment, through which speed is extracted. Pain is a form of bodily or physical capital, a bearer of symbolic value (Shilling 2003: 111).

Coaching pain

Pain is not something that merely happens to an athlete. As Juha Heikkala notes, 'man is not born a morally responsible agent, he becomes one in the "civilization process"; the athlete is not born with the desire to sweat and feel muscular pain, he will mould himself to possess this desire'(1993: 79). And the title of David Morris's (1991) book *The Culture of Pain* explicates that pain is part of culture – it is 'cultivated'. But these days pain is not so much cultivated and nurtured by the individual. As part of what Heinilä (1971) termed the 'totalisation process', the place of the coach and the trainer – indeed, the 'sports system' – is today of paramount importance in the production of pain. It is many years since elite runners were held personally responsible for the pain that they endured during training and racing. It is parents, coaches or trainers who do such moulding and are central in encouraging the runner to consume pain. At the same time the trainer seeks to cancel pain, to teach stratagems for neutralizing it and to apply 'painkillers' to eliminate it.

Such learning, of course, may give pleasure to the teacher (coach) even if the athlete endures pain in the process. If cruelty is the deliberate infliction of pain (Tuan 1999a: 109), can coaches and trainers be called cruel? They certainly – and surely deliberately – inflict pain, but perhaps in an unthinking way, disconnecting their instructions at the training ground from the possible serious injuries and pain that may be the result. If one believes the cliché that one can be cruel to be kind, there may also be a case for taking seriously Tuan's question: 'How, after all, is human life possible unless we are able to inflict pain unthinkingly?' (Tuan 1999a: 110). The coach certainly induces pain beyond the physical varieties involved in training and racing. Emotional and mental pain also may leave their mark from the coach for whom dominance is more important than affection.

In his book, *Dominance and Affection: The Making of Pets*, Tuan (1984) invites a comparison between the athlete and the pet. A characteristic of a pet is ownership. Often the trainer–pet relationship is one of affection but even so, at the same time it is necessarily one of dominance. The pet has to be trained. But to be over-dominant is to be cruel. Tuan defines a pet as a 'diminished being'. The degree of dominance assumed by coaches can vary but they 'often view their athletes as possessions' (Burke 2001: 229). As Tuan comments, 'Play is such a sunny word that we forget its darker side. It is bad to be "used", but it can be worse to be "played with"' (Tuan 1999b: 102). The result of a taught willingness to endure and suffer pain could be read as a form of diminished humanity – someone who has suffered through little choice of his or her own. Indeed, as Michael Burke (2001) has pointed out, the coach–athlete relationship is encapsulated by the words, 'obeying until it hurts'.

Pain as pleasure

Can the pain endured by athletes be a perverse source of pleasure? Although the fatigue that an athlete experiences in the course of enhancing performance has been described as 'positive pain' (Howe 2004: 85), such pain is hardly enjoyable. But Jack Lovelock, in James McNeish's 'biographical novel' of that name, is said to have recalled: 'I suddenly realized what running had given me, an enjoyment of heightened tension. I actually enjoyed the agony' (McNeish 1994: 340–1). Perhaps he had learned this from the German world record holder, Otto Peltzer, who was said to possess 'a fanatical quality'. He was seemingly able to 'submit himself to the worst kind of body-abuse' and 'to run at varying speeds to the point of exhaustion, and then to answer a summons and run three hundred yards more' (McNeish 1994: 69). Australian coach Percy Cerutty (1964) urged his charges to 'love suffering' (quoted in Elliott 1961: 39). This can be read as similar to the pain felt in asceticism. His most famous pupil, Herb Elliott (the former Australian Olympic champion and world record holder for the mile and 1,500 metres) likened pain caused through training to a religious experience, perhaps that of an ascetic. He observed that the 'purifying quality of the pain that has to be suffered is like that of a confession' (Phillips and Hicks 2000: 219). Gordon Pirie went somewhat further, stating that 'an athlete who isn't enjoying himself even in moments of the most agonizing effort at the point of exhaustion, might as well give up' (Pirie 1961: 27). The egotistical athlete, seeking to be out of the ordinary, may seek pain 'to lift himself above the plane of everyday life' (Morris 1991: 262).

To enjoy oneself at the point of exhaustion in running may be related to the fact that the runner has achieved a target, for example, achieving a record number of repetitions during a session of interval running, or setting a world record. Exhaustion may be the result of having run a personal best time. In such a case, it may be the personal best, not the exhaustion felt in obtaining it, which provides the enjoyment. Agony showed on the face of Roger Bannister, the first man to have recorded under four minutes for the mile, as he crossed the line in his world record breaking run. He writes that he:

> Collapsed almost unconscious [but] it was *only then* that real pain overtook me. I felt like an exploded flashlight with no will to live; I just went on existing in the most passive physical state without being quite unconscious. Blood surged from my muscles and seemed to fell me. It was as if my limbs were caught in an ever-tightening vice.
>
> (Bannister 1955: 165, emphasis added)

Yet within a few minutes Bannister was on his feet scampering 'around the track in a burst of spontaneous joy'. For Bannister, then, pain is separated from the pleasure. The pain is the result of exhausting running; the pleasure comes from breaking the record. The pain that seems to be experienced is not described as pleasurable. However, the pain Bannister recalls having felt as a schoolboy rower seems different. He remembers 'the intense pleasure of utter exhaustion from rowing' (Bannister 1955: 165). In this case it was the pain (i.e. the exhaustion) that seems to have provided the pleasure.

The notion of pain being pleasurable takes us into the realms of masochism, the tendency to take pleasure (including sexual pleasure) from one's own pain and suffering. Sado-masochism is the enjoyment of suffering and inflicting pain at the same time. Yi-Fu Tuan writes: 'Dominating and being dominated is, to say the least, morally ambiguous, but what if it were being done playfully, with affection for the thing [or person] dominated and with the dominated thing itself participating more or less willingly?' (Tuan 1999a: 113). Surely this is the situation in which athletes find themselves. Surely also, it appears to be the condition of sado-masochism. These are subjects that seem to be linked to running but about which we have little information. The former British 400 metres runner Adrian Metcalfe described the experience of racing over that distance as 'the virtual masochism of pleasure through prolonged pain' (quoted in Magnusson 1981: 45). The maverick Australian coach Percy Cerutty argued that 'the more it hurts, the harder we try to run' and, in a more explicitly masochistic tone, observed that 'it is not normal to dislike pain, since all true men realize that nothing worthwhile was ever accomplished without it' (Cerutty 1964: 81, 159). Was Cerutty here thinking about the pain of Jesus on the cross, the pain that made him human? Cerutty elevated the endurance of pain to goodness. He stated that 'you only ever grow as a human being if you're outside the comfort zone' (quoted in Smith 2001). Cerutty taught his pupils to believe that 'pushing yourself . . . beyond what you thought were the borders of endurance is of great moral benefit' (quoted in Phillips and Hicks 2000: 219).

Describing the running of a marathon as masochistic is common enough in popular writing but such language tends to be used frivolously and the actual pleasure (sexual or not) that might be derived from painful running is hardly ever mentioned. Allen Guttmann claims that there exists, at the start of a race, 'that strangely masochistic sexualized sensation of mingled pain and pleasure known to every serious athlete' (Guttmann 1996: 108), though I cannot say that, during many years of running and racing, I have ever experienced any such sexualized sensation myself. We seem to know little about pain being enjoyed in sport and it borders on the perverse. Yet it is hard to deny the possibility that pleasure during pain is experienced by at least some runners while running (see Vinnai 1973). At the very least, racing can be seen as a kind of deferred gratification in which runners may absorb a lengthy period of pain before the joy of the final result.

A context in which athletes might enjoy pain is when they know that they are inflicting it on an opponent. The double meaning of 'beating' an adversary implies a mildly sadistic side to running. Some runners, who like to run from the front, seek to 'burn off' their opponents, to 'run them into the ground', to 'make it hurt'. Their fast pace serves to inflict pain not only on themselves but, more importantly if they are to succeed, more pain on those who try to keep up with them. They are even encouraged by some coaches to hate their fellow runners.

During training painful fatigue may be satisfying because it signifies improving strength. In a race, however, there is more at stake for the athlete: 'In a close race, runners experiencing painful fatigue will probably react with distress because the pain means they are running out of steam' (Lazarus 2000: 54). But pain may also be ameliorated by the body's natural opiates (endorphins) that make running a pleasure rather than a pain. Such natural opiates allow runners to continue running with minor or even major injuries. This suggests that natural opiates, by encouraging the body to run while injured, contribute to the body colluding in its own oppression. Opiates may also contribute to running addiction, which may be read as a condition to improve fitness but, at the same time, a means of self-destruction – a machine out of control.

The use of the machine metaphor and its application to the human body has been common since the end of the nineteenth century among novelists, physiologists and biologists whose ambitions seem to have been to understand how far the body could be transformed into a machine (Hoberman 1992; Rabinbach 1990; Seltzer 1992). The idea of the athletic machine, or the 'human motor', reflected the nineteenth-century desire to see the end of exhaustion, pain, fatigue and neurasthenia that were associated with industrial work (Rabinbach 1990). The rationale of such thinking is that machines do not feel pain. John Hoberman paints a dismal scenario of the cyborg future. If the ability to catch athletes taking dope becomes increasingly successful, the outcome may well be that even more severe training will be necessary. Should that be the case, Hoberman notes that:

> Harder training will mean more pain, and the athlete will require a trainer of some kind to help him or her inflict and endure this suffering. One extreme development . . . would be 'torture contracts' between athletes and their handlers that would attempt to establish the trainer/torturer's legal immunity from prosecution. In this scenario, the athletes of the future . . . would literally require protection from their 'trainers'.
>
> (Hoberman 1992: 282–4)

It would be the retention of pain that would define their humanity.

Emotional pain

In addition to physical pain, running may be associated with emotional pain and distress. Although this has been seen as an inappropriate dichotomy, I use it here for organizational purposes. Such distress may be related to pride. During the women's 3,000 metres final at the 1984 Los Angeles Olympics, the American favourite, Mary Slaney, was accidentally knocked over by the South African-British runner, Zola Budd. The collision affected the performance of both athletes, but Slaney left the track, distressed and in tears. For someone who undoubtedly attached great importance to winning the race, it was more than physical pain that she endured as she fell and withdrew to the infield. Her pride was more than simply dinted. Athletes who fail to win races are often reduced to tears, perhaps from pain, perhaps from chagrin.

How does it feel when a runner no longer feels like participating? Consider Jim Denison, writing about the experiences of an American college miler who had ambitions to compete in the Olympics:

> That whole season I had been running right around four minutes – 4:04 in Philadelphia, 4:05 in Durham, 4:02 in Indianapolis. And in practice the week before I'd run 4:03 all by myself. But for some reason I had started feeling like I was just going through the motions. As if I really didn't care anymore how fast I ran or whether I won or lost, which just made no sense at

all. I mean, considering the years of training I'd put in, you'd figure I would've been raring to get out there and get it done. It didn't add up that I was willing to chuck all of that hard work away. As if suddenly running had become something I did for somebody else – a job, a requirement, a responsibility – when it always used to be so fun: heading out to the track each day, spending time with my friends, pushing myself, feeling so strong.

(Denison 1999: 66)

The loss of any fun, its replacement by work and cooption and 'going through the motions', seemed to be crucial.

Some 18-year-old runners look into the mirror and see that they are starting to look old (Heywood 1998: 143). Here is the start of the emotional pain for athletes whose promising careers are terminated by illness or injury. Emotional pain may be greater and may stay with them for many years. Jim Denison recalls how the route to athletic ruin began:

I should have listened when the pain started. But it was hardly anything at first. Just an occasional ache, nothing I couldn't tolerate. I kept training on it every day, most days twice. [I]t was my senior year and I had big plans. When it started to get bad I swore to myself every night before going to sleep that if it still hurt in the morning I'd take the day off. Rest it. Give it a chance to heal. But I never did.

(Denison 1999: 33–4)

Physical pain caused emotional pain. Watching from the sidelines would not do. He was a runner, not a spectator. He continued running, each morning breaking his promise to stop. He was addicted, despite the pain. In August 1984, instead of meeting his friends for a twenty-first birthday celebration in an Irish pub, he was at home with his parents. Neither knew much about running. They had no idea what a 'good runner' was, and the only runner with whose name they were familiar was Roger Bannister. They watched the 1984 Olympics on television. He wrote:

[W]hile I was at home with my parents watching the Olympic Games on television a queer feeling in my gut told me it was too late, that I was in serious trouble. And somehow I knew it to be true. So like a man who senses his lover drifting away, who realises that he's about to get dumped, I began to prepare for the worst.

(Denison 1999: 36)

In the case of Leslie Heywood, her doctor told her that she had a female athlete triad: eating disorders, exercise compulsion, leading to amenorrhea, loss of bone. Unless she stopped running her immune system would eventually start attacking her vital organs, her heart and her liver. She would have to do something other than running (Heywood 1998: 186–9).

Ethnographic studies of former runners reveal the emotional pain they experience following retirement. Michael Messner (1992) has recorded how runners act differently to a 'mid-life crisis' when their speed diminishes and younger athletes surpass their achievements. One of his respondents noted that he had managed to transform himself from a 'racer' to a 'runner', shifting his focus from achievement to welfare. He learned how to take pressure off himself, he dared to be a 'normal person'.

> My wife had a T-shirt [made] for me. It says 'Dare to be average', and it gets funny reactions from people. I think it gets at that place where somehow we all think that we're going to end up on the cover of *Time*, or something, you know? Do you have that? That some day you're gonna be *great*, and everyone will know, everyone will recognize it. And I think I used that to somehow disengage from that, because that's part of the competitor, the racer, the vicious person. And it's a *disease*! It's *hard*! I'd rather be great now because I'm *good*.
>
> (Messner 1992: 147)

The emptiness in a life that has had to leave running behind can also be a relief (Heywood 1998: 188).

Spectators attend sports events for various reasons (Loland 2002). Many gain pleasure from a record result, a winning performance, a stirring victory, national success over a disliked nation, or for voyeuristic sexual pleasure. However, it is also possible that pleasure could be obtained from seeing athletes in pain and suffering. Imposing pain on others is less attractive to many spectators than the self-inflicted pain that, according to Phillips (2001: 38), is 'more entertaining, more a commodity', to which spectators are drawn. Like Houdini and his self-torture, the agony of the runner is not considered to be in any way offensive.

Adam Phillips (2001), in his remarkable book on the escapologist Harry Houdini, writes in terms that relate to the runner as well as the escapologist. The spectators watch a runner in pain; it is a safe risk as there is medical support available, if needed. Runners rarely die as a result of their exertions but do, nevertheless, experience a manifestly punishing ordeal that people have paid to see. The runner may not die but he might suffer and still be defeated. In its own small way, running perhaps becomes part of a market for torture.

How many of the spectators at track meets or marathon races display sadistic tendencies is simply unknown but it is surely plausible that at least some do. Many spectators hold weakness and failure in contempt, by extension enjoying seeing painful losers (Tännsjö 2000). To see one's favourite runner exhausted at the finish is heroic; to see one from a stigmatized nation in a similar state may be enjoyable in a different way. W. R. Loader (1962) refers to the famous 5,000 metres race between Chris Chataway and Vladimir Kuts at the White City Stadium, London, in 1954. He observes that 'the physical agony both of the Russian trying to break away and the Briton refusing to let him, was *cruel*. It couldn't only be seen by the spectators. It could be *felt*' (Loader 1962: 154–5).

Kirsten Roessler has pointed out that spectators' enjoyment of watching a race can, on the other hand, be understood as an identification with the suffering person, a kind of catharsis, or as a 'voyeur' interested in other people's suffering (Roessler 2001).

Is there a point at which self-torture becomes heroic in the eye of the spectator? What are we to make of the courage of the long-distance runners who overcome the pain of fatigue and injury, perhaps endangering their health and even life in so doing? Perhaps spectators are happier to watch such *self-inflicted* pain, being more acceptable and more entertaining, but in some track races, when only two runners may be left to contest the result, it becomes almost a case of one person torturing another. Drawing again on the work of Adam Phillips, the modern runner, in his profession, exposes what spectators take pleasure in seeing being done to bodies – or what they want to see bodies doing to themselves (Phillips 2001: 88). With the commercialization of running, spectators see what economics can do to biology. Athletes show spectators new ways in which the body may be tested, endangered, exploited, or confined by time and space.

In some cases, the pain induced by long-distance running leads to considerable distress, collapse and hospitalization. Recall the collapse of Pietri Dorando in the 1908 Olympic marathon, and of Jim Peters, staggering into the stadium and collapsing, dehydrated, before the finish line in the 1954 Empire Games in Vancouver. In the latter case, perhaps the athlete had gone beyond pain; he came close to death. In more modern performances of this kind, athletes appear to torture themselves to make a living and to provide entertainment. In the cases noted above, however, their grotesque perseverance, pain and distress were admired. The pain endured by the two marathon runners was felt worth rewarding. In the case of Dorando (the 'moral winner' according to de Coubertin, quoted in Müller 2000: 417–18) he was awarded a special medal for his pain by the King of England and Peters was similarly rewarded by the Duke of Edinburgh.

Grace, poise and apparent effortlessness are central features of the aesthetically pleasing body in movement. However, grace and poise can be read as hiding pain. In recalling his visit to Wembley Stadium in 1948 to witness the London Olympics, Yi-Fu Tuan (1995) can still remember watching 'with bursting excitement' the women's 100 metres final:

> The athletes *looked* beautiful to me from a distance, but if I could see their faces I would no doubt see them twisted and ugly. But then the same could be said of ballet – how elegant the dancers look from a distance, how ugly from up close. And how close this elegance is to violence! At the end of a performance, the ballet slippers are stained by blood.
>
> (Tuan 1995)

The two-time winner of the Olympic 800 metres title, Douglas Lowe, observed that 'Whenever it is said of an athlete, "How easy it looks!" one can be sure that he possesses a good style' (Lowe 1935: 17), but in modern track running, there have never been any prizes awarded for style. What count are measured times. Aesthetics are secondary, almost incidental, to success and the quantified result. In running, beauty is often, literally, skin-deep and hides behind the trainer's dominance or the athlete's obsession. It is not always possible to mask pain. Emil Zátopek, regarded by many as the greatest middle- and long-distance runner of all time, was a highly effective athlete but his apparently ungainly style and tortured facial expressions belied his efficiency. The French writer Magnan said of Zátopek that he was a runner 'who paid dearly for his victory . . . a man whose face is in anguish when running and who struggles for breath' (quoted in Kožík 1954: 84). The same could be said about the British marathon runner Paula Radcliffe, who runs with an inelegant style that often displays agony but does nothing to detract from her popularity. Gunther Gebauer implies that spectators do enjoy witnessing pain. He observes that these days 'audiences want to see passion in all shapes and sizes' (Gebauer 1998: 85).

Conclusion

Most research from the multi-disciplinary field of sports studies that addresses the notion of pain has come from scientists – social, psychological or medical. Little work of a humanistic or literary nature has addressed the topic of pain in sport. This chapter has sought to identify certain dimensions of pain in the study of sport by drawing on biographical and philosophical studies. Taking running as an example, it seems that pain is an absolutely central feature of the achievement configuration of running. It can plausibly be added to Guttmann's (1978) 'characteristics' of modern sport. It is endured by athletes and admired by spectators. By drawing attention to pain in its broader context – by including the place of pain among non-injured athletes and spectators – suffering in sport may be read as being even more pervasive than first thought.

Bibliography

Bale, J. (2004) *Running Cultures: Racing in Time and Space*, London: Frank Cass.
Bannister, R. (1955) *First Four Minutes*, London: Putnam.
Brohm, J.-M. (1974) *Sport: A Prison of Measured Time*, London: Ink Links.
Burke, M. (2001) 'Obeying until it hurts: Coach–athlete relationships', *Journal of the Philosophy of Sport*, 28, 3: 227–40.
Cerutty, P. (1964) *Middle-distance Running*, London: Pelham.
Denison, J. (1994) 'An elephant's trunk', *Sport Literate*, 2, 3: 64–85.
Denison, J. (1999) 'Boxed in' in A. Sparkes and M. Silvenoinen (eds), *Talking Bodies: Men's Narratives of the Body and Sport*, SoPhi: Jyväskylä: 29–36.
Elliott, H. (1961) *The Golden Mile*, London: Cassell.
Gebauer, G. (1998) 'On the role of everyday physical-fitness sport in our time' in K. Volkwein (ed.) *Fitness as Cultural Phenomenon*, Münster: Waxman: 83–91.
Guttmann, A. (1978) *From Ritual to Record*, New York: Columbia University Press.
Guttmann, A. (1996) *The Erotic in Sports*, New York: Columbia University Press.

Heikkala, J. (1993) 'An introduction to a (non) fascist sporting life', in L. Laine (ed.), *On the Fringes of Sport*, Sankt Augustin: Academia: 77–9.

Heinilä, K. (1971) 'Notes on inter-group conflicts on international sport', in E. Dunning (ed.), *The Sociology of Sport*, London: Frank Cass: 343–51.

Heywood, L. (1998) *Pretty Good for a Girl*, New York: The Free Press.

Hoberman, J. (1992) *Mortal Engines: The Science of Performance and the Dehumanization of Sports*, New York: Free Press.

Howe, D. P. (2004) *Sport, Professionalism and Pain: Ethnographies of Injury and Risk*, London: Routledge.

Kožík, F. (1954) *Zátopek, the Marathon Victor*, Prague: Artia.

Lazarus, R. (2000) 'Cognitive-Motivational-Relational theory of emotion', in Y. Hanin (ed.), *Emotions in Sport*, Champaign, IL: Human Kinetics: 39–64.

Loader, W. R. (1962) *Testament of a Runner*, London: Sportsman's Book Club.

Loland, S. (2002) *Fair Play in Sport: A Moral Norm System*, London: Routledge.

Lowe, D. G. A. (1935) *Track and Field Athletics*, London: Pitman.

McNeish, J. (1994 [1986]) *Lovelock*, Auckland: Godwit.

Magnusson, S. (1981) *The Flying Scotsman*, London: Quartet Books.

Messner, M. (1992) *Power at Play: Sports and the Problem of Masculinity*, Boston: Beacon Press.

Morris, D. (1991) *The Culture of Pain*, Berkeley: University of California Press.

Müller, N. (ed.) (2000) *Olympism: Pierre de Coubertin 1963–1937: Selected Writings*, Lausanne: International Olympic Committee.

Phillips, A. (2001) *Houdini's Box: On the Arts of Escape*, London: Faber and Faber.

Phillips, M. and Hicks, F. (2000) 'Conflict, tensions and complexities: Athletic training in Australia in the 1950s', *International Journal of the History of Sport*, 17, 7/8: 206–24.

Pirie, G. (1961) *Running Wild*, London: W. H. Allen.

Rabinbach, A. (1990) *The Human Motor*, Berkeley: University of California Press.

Roessler, K. (2001) 'Pain'. E-mail communication.

Sands, R. (1995) *Instant Acceleration: Living in the Fast Lane*, Lanham, MD: University Press of America.

Scarry, E. (1985) *The Body in Pain: The Making and Unmaking of the World*, New York: Oxford University Press.

Seltzer, M. (1992) *Bodies and Machines*, New York: Routledge.

Shilling, C. (2003) *The Body and Social Theory*, 2nd edn, London: Sage.

Smith, A. (2001) *The Sports Factor*, 12/01. Online. Available HTTP: <http://www.abc.net.au/rn/talks/8.30/sportsf/stories/s226388.htm> (Accessed 5 February 2001).

Tännsjö, T. (2000) 'Is it fascistoid to admire sports heroes?' in T. Tännsjö and C. Tamburrini (eds) *Values in Sport*, London: Routledge: 9–23.

Tuan, Y.-F. (1984) *Dominance and Affection: The Making of Pets*, New Haven: Yale University Press.

Tuan, Y.-F. (1995) 'Pain'. Postal communication.

Tuan, Y.-F. (1999a) 'Geography and evil: A sketch' in J. Proctor and D. Smith (eds) *Geography and Ethics: Journeys in a Moral Terrain*, London: Routledge: 106–19.

Tuan, Y.-F. (1999b) *Who am I? An Autobiography of Emotion, Mind and Spirit*, Madison: University of Wisconsin Press.

Vinnai, G. (1973) *Football Mania*, London: Ocean Books.

5 Pains and strains on the ice

Some thoughts on the physical and mental struggles of polar adventurers

Matti Goksøyr

Exploring and adventuring in polar areas have been human interests for centuries. For different reasons people have taken on immense and risky physical challenges in some of the most hostile natural environments of the world. Historically the feats of these adventurers can be compared with other sport-like physical achievements in extreme environments, such as mountaineering or deep-sea diving. On occasions these adventurous achievements may have a clear sporting link, as in the case of the Norwegian polar explorer, skier and gentleman, Fridtjof Nansen (1861–1930) who achieved fame as a skier through his polar explorations. More recent polar adventurers have also often had a direct link to sports, as the main objective has sometimes been to record physical achievements and performances, even to race and set records, in an extreme and uncontrollable environment.

Walking on thick ice

Does this practice provide or provoke any special kind of pain that is different from the pain of 'normal sports'? As with all voluntary physical activity, pain is more or less self-inflicted. But are the questions relating to pain that occurs in extreme environments different from the more 'ordinary' questions of pain? Here I shall try to discuss these and other questions and ask whether they can add something to the general discussion about 'pain and sport'. As a basis for my debate I will use some of the generous amounts of autobiographical materials offered by the adventurers themselves.

I will present historical examples from a wide time period, from the late nineteenth century up to today. The cases mentioned will have a Norwegian bias, although international and, particularly, English references will be included (Drivenes and Jølle 2004). My sources are literary, and these exist in abundance as most adventurers considered their achievements worthy of a book. I have also interviewed some of the more recent participants in what must now be regarded as a cultural practice, as many of the earlier political, scientific and, to a certain extent, economic motivations for these adventures have disappeared.

In order to answer questions about 'polar pain', we must look at what these people actually do. What are the special challenges these adventurers have to cope with, challenges which separate them from other sportspeople? To answer briefly: they try to cover long distances on foot, usually with skis, on the most deserted fringes of the earth, the polar areas, or other ice-covered geographical areas of a certain size (such as Greenland). Traditionally they have been aiming to do this before anybody else, to claim a 'first'. After these feats were accomplished, the interest did not disappear; instead adventurers sought to reproduce these achievements in other places or, in recent decades and after all distances had been covered, new and special, mostly more difficult and demanding, ways of covering distances were invented. These new and difficult ways could usually be defined by the absence of something, most often company, equipment or 'support'. For so-called unsupported travel, new rules have developed. In these 'classes' competitions exist, mostly based on being the 'first' or fastest to achieve a particular target. Polar explorers are, then, still involved in the process of coping with enduring pain for perhaps longer than most other 'sportspeople'.

What is the typical pain experienced by people who, for whatever reason, set out to do these things? Most of those involved in these activities will say: drudgery, toil and exhaustion. Existing polar literature tales are a strange mix of enormous physical efforts which nevertheless seem to get done in a rather elegant or unstrained manner. The endeavours bring with them physical difficulties and pain which are there all the time, as a caption in the narrative of polar adventuring. Swollen and painful skin, backache and frostbite are prevailing themes in the polar literature. Of course, one might say that such physical pains are also typical of many other sports. If we consider frostbite as a temperature-related pain, it might be argued that similar problems, such as heat-stroke or dehydration, also occur in other sports. Is, then, the typical polar pain just 'more of the same'? Or can we detect more specific features of pain? To understand this more adequately, we need to study how the acknowledged polar pain interacts with the physical hard work.

In his latest book on the eternal and lost hero Robert Falcon Scott, the British adventurer Sir Ranulph Fiennes summarizes his own polar experience in three words: 'deprivation, stress and physical pain' (Fiennes 2003). One could argue that these are also conditions that are found in – some would say they are inherent parts of – high-level sports. However, what are also found in the polar tales are more original, distinguishing forms of pain such as freezing and hunger, and the mental pains related to the void of place and space: loneliness and fear.

These four conditions – freezing, hunger, loneliness and fear – are usually regarded as controllable in 'normal' modern, sportive settings. We can adjust how much or how little clothing we wear, how much nutrition we prefer to eat and drink, and choose what kind of social setting we wish to be a part of before or during a performance. We also perform in an environment where we can usually call for help and do not have to look out for lethal obstacles like polar bears or crevasses. In many respects freezing, hunger, loneliness (as physical isolation) and fear/anxiety (in the form of everyday physical threats) are former challenges which modern, civilized people have minimized or put an end to some time ago – provided you come from the affluent part of the world, which most modern explorers do. These torments are, however, introduced again through the invented tradition of polar adventuring. And the pains they pro-duce are as self-inflicted as other sportive pains. The similarities to the process of sportization, in the way Norbert Elias portrays it, in which modern, civilized people introduce extra strains, challenges and norms to make traditional efforts become more sport-like, is apparent (Elias and Dunning 1986).

Mental strength a long way from home

Temperatures of minus 50 degrees Celsius and below, combined with strong winds, make human existence very difficult. Food is also extremely scarce in polar areas; there is nothing to gather and little to hunt. That is why no one lives there, as was pointed out by the rather reluctant Inuit Ekaksat Amagoalik, who assisted in Ragnar Thorseth's North Pole expedition in 1982 (Thorseth 1982). However, it can be said that for the 'modern era' of polar adventuring, the most physiological of the specific polar pains – the freezing and the hunger – can be controlled. Technological developments have made comfort-able clothing and sufficient nourishment possible, provided there is sufficient economic sponsorship, which is a necessary precondition for taking part at all.

In other words, what we are left with as the distinctive forms of polar pain are not the typical physiological ones – the hurting knees, legs, backs or whatever, even if they certainly exist. Hence, the psychological pains, loneliness and fear, and perhaps also a psychological strain, the need for patience because of the long time periods involved, seem to be the most distinctive challenges and obstacles to polar adventuring.

It is on these matters, loneliness, fear and patience that I wish to focus, though they must always be seen against the background of immense physical endeavours. However, technological development has also changed these more subtle aspects of polar explorations. While it is today still perfectly possible to be alone in the polar areas, the modern polar adventurer is not as alone as his or her colleagues were a century ago. Modern adventurers are usually compelled by legislation to bring satellite navigation and communication equipment which makes contact with the rest of the world possible. This contact option will also influence the fear factor involved. Although much reduced, the fear factor certainly still exists. A lone polar skier's success or failure is, in the last analysis, dependent on his or her daily ability to cope with routine or extra-ordinary challenges in an extreme environment. Related to this is patience. While in the pioneering era explorers and adventurers aiming for the Poles and similar areas had to expect and adjust to the thought of being away for a year or two, the test of patience for modern adventurers has been reduced. It is now a question of months of absence, rather than years. How have these various 'pains' been described and narrated in polar literature?

Two obvious epochs of polar adventuring can be distinguished. The first was the age of the pioneers from the 1880s to 1911/12, culminating in the Scott–Amundsen race to the South Pole. After the conquest of the Poles, modern technology, especially aircraft, reduced the human physical effort in the expeditions. However from the 1960s, and especially from the 1980s, a new interest in expeditions with human effort as the decisive force once again emerged. In this modern era, adventurers sought to reintroduce what they saw as the 'spirit' of the pioneers, most notably by travelling 'unsupported', meaning without any help or assistance from outside, and by travelling without the help of dogs and motorized vehicles. The precise meaning of the term 'unsupported' was much debated, but at its heart was a reinstatement of human physical effort, and thereby also a willingness to forsake some (but not all!) technological gains and to accept increased pain as part of polar expeditions. Unsupported travel in this sense takes the activity closer to sport, and is supposed to involve an acceptance of more of the 'original' pain. What was this original, 'pioneering' pain in the polar regions?

Pain in the pioneering era

The classic challenges and races to both Poles were settled in this period. Robert Peary claimed the North Pole in 1909, though his claim was not undisputed.[1] Roald Amundsen was acknowledged as the first to the South Pole in 1911, beating Robert F. Scott in what turned out to be a race. Norwegians and Britons were among the nationalities heavily involved, supposedly applying different techniques for mastering hostile nature (Kirwan 1962). They also seemed to approach the subject of pain in different ways.

Fridtjof Nansen was a brave explorer, and also a gentleman and scientist – a practical person, who responded to polar risks with firmness and determination. His motto for his first major expedition, the crossing of Greenland on skis in 1888, was: 'The West Coast or death'. No return was possible, because there was nothing to return to on Greenland's east coast from where they started, in contrast to the west coast which housed permanent settlements. Hence, an element of anxiety accompanied Nansen's group of six as they struggled over the Greenland inland ice. Nansen's account of the tour does not hide the dangers involved. In his story his men seem to be aware of and conscious of the fact that what they are doing is dangerous. However, they seem to cope with this in a rational, almost scientific way. The only ones who deviated from this 'civilized' view on life and its dangers were the two Lapps (Sami) whom Nansen had brought from the north of Norway because they were expected to be familiar with the challenges the expedition were to meet. In a way which must be called patronizing, Nansen refers to how these two proclaimed and believed that their last hours had come when the expedition, in its early phase, was stranded on an ice-floe heading for the open sea (Nansen 1890). Their attitude towards fear very much contrasts with the rather laconic way Nansen reports from his next major expedition, on skis towards the North Pole in 1895: '5 August: Two good things happened. The first was that Johansen was not eaten by a polar bear. The other that we could see open water.' (Nansen 1994: 108). Nansen and his companion Hjalmar Johansen were attacked by a polar bear, one of the most lethal animals one can encounter in the northern hemisphere. The bear was holding Johansen in a firm grip ready to finish him off, when he appealed to Nansen who was trying to load his gun: 'You'd better hurry now Mr. Nansen, if it is not going to be too late.'(Nansen 1994: 109). (Johansen used the formal Norwegian form of 'you', even though they had slept in the same sleeping bag for four months!). The two remaining dogs of this expedition distracted the bear enough for Nansen to kill the bear. The two men had until then fought off serious starvation threats by managing to find an occasional seagull or a seal to shoot and eat just in time. This could not help their dogs to escape starvation. As usual on these pioneering trips, none of the dogs who set out reached the goal. Nansen reports the killing of dogs in a resigned but rational way. The remaining dogs needed the meat, but the slaughtering was nevertheless done with unease. The last dogs were always the ones with which they had developed a relationship. Therefore he and Johansen used two bullets on them (and not a knife), and each shot the dog of the other.

Fridtjof Nansen had his own way of portraying polar pain, especially during optimistic periods. From the same journey he says, after having made good progress through the massive and almost impenetratable ice masses: 'the only thing that is unpleasant now is the cold. Our clothes change into ice body armour during the day and wet wraps during the night' (Nansen 1994: 25–7). The only way to melt the ice-armoured clothing was to put them on their chests and legs at night. This was less pleasant with a night temperature of minus 42.7 degrees. After a couple of hours in the shared sleeping bag, their bodies started to return to normal temperature, but as Nansen says 'very warm it cannot have been, as I had frozen the feeling out of all my fingertips as I awoke one night' (Nansen 1994: 25–7). Although writing his diary in an optimistic voice, Nansen admits other torments as well: he did not like to slaughter dogs in such cold weather, but worse still was the weariness; 'sometimes', he says: 'we could be so sleepy and exhausted that the eyelids slipped down and we fell asleep as we were walking. Once my head fell forwards and I awoke from diving forwards on my skis' (Nansen 1994: 49).

'How can people wish so much suffering on themselves?'

The initial polar explorations no doubt involved serious amounts of pain. And Nansen, the gentleman skier, admits pain; there is no doubt that the natural environment was very hostile. They froze and they struggled. One of the members of Nansen's Greenland expedition, Kristian K. Ravna, raised the fundamental question: 'How can people wish so much suffering on themselves that they do this?' (Sale 2002: 82). Sometimes the adventures ended up with the most serious pain of all: death. People died in accidents or from injuries, froze to death, or died of malnutrition leading to illness or direct starvation sometimes leading to cannibalism.[2] Even more encountered so-called 'near death' experiences. A thin line, such as the edge of a crevasse, was often the only thing separating life and death. I do not intend here to enter a philosophical debate on what death is, if it really can be called pain, interesting though this might be (Elias 1985). Even though death in many settings can be regarded as a reward, as a transition from suffering and unease to stillness, tranquillity and peace, in this case, among the polar explorers, death rarely was intentional. Even if it could mean an end to suffering, it was almost always a result of (too much) suffering. The risk of dying was always present, and had to be countered by careful preparation.

Though not calculated, the idea of a 'heroic death' could, and did, come up. The English polar adventurer Wally Herbert claims that the English 'love for their heroes to die' (Kagge 1994: 70). Among the pioneers there seems to have been a clear acknowledgement that what they set out to do was dangerous, and involved a fair chance of losing their lives. Their rather unstrained descriptions of the dangers they encountered, and the feelings that ran through their heads, must be read from the perspective of such a determined and settled state of mind.

However, the mental pain in the form of fear and anxiety must also have been there, no matter how the pioneers themselves tried to disguise it with what Francis Spufford has called 'their appalling understatement' (Spufford 1996). The story of Robert Falcon Scott and his men is of course *the* story of polar pain: having used more energy than they really possessed, they struggled underequipped to the South Pole in January 1912 only to find that Roald Amundsen had been there one month before them. The pain of defeat was neatly described in Scott's diary: 'The Pole, yes, but under very different circumstances from those expected [. . .] none of us having slept much after the shock of our discovery [. . .] Great God! This is an awful place and terrible enough for us to have laboured to it without reward of priority' (Sale 2002: 192).

Next day he noted 'Now for the run home and a desperate struggle. I wonder if we can do it.' (Sale 2002: 192) They did not. As the unavoidable end became clearer, Scott continued to write his diary. The title of Francis Spufford's book about Scott and the English polar tradition, *I may be some time*, is a direct quotation from one of Scott's men, Edward Oates, who had been educated at Eton, in the English public school tradition. As Oates left the tent where Scott and the others were sitting, enfeebled from illness and lack of food, he spoke his last words. To use an understatement like 'I may be some time' in such a situation, as he struggled – with his frostbitten and damaged feet he could barely walk – into a blizzard to disappear, is one way to cope with pain and to face a certain death. It was also a way for Scott to write himself and his men into a heroic death.

Even if he, like a true 'gentleman amateur', with a lack of preparation and competence (Spufford 1996: 5), led his men to nothing but pain and suffering, it was Scott's words which survived. Fridtjof Nansen expressed great admiration for Scott's writing abilities under the circumstances: 'The ice-cold eye of certain death has captured him, and he calmly leads his pencil . . .' (Bomann-Larsen 1995: 550). He may have led his men into certain death, but he brought the

living word out of the ice desert. Nansen's praise of Scott's 'manliness' was interpreted as a clear downgrading of the man who defeated Scott, Nansen's fellow-
citizen and compatriot Roald Amundsen.

However, the lack of effort in the final days of Scott and his men could also be
interpreted in a sportive way. If Scott's expedition had won the race to the Pole,
they might, perhaps, have gained the momentum and spirit that characterizes a
sportsman who is injured in the process of, for example, scoring a goal; the feeling of elation in success makes it possible to stand on your feet a moment longer
than if you had failed to score, to take one more step. Scott failed to score, and
his expedition ended not very far from a depot which would have re-supplied
them with food.

Exposed to nature and time

The polar experience could be called sublime. The raw, deserted and pure
characterizes the place. It is difficult to withdraw from races going on here.
The determination and firmness of purpose which characterized most of the
adventurers could not prevent them from feeling the force and the pressure of
the void, of hostile nature – no matter how romantic or idyllic what modern
polar tourists, with their back-up systems, have described as 'the polar light'.
The names the pioneers gave to the places through which they struggled are
revealing. These names can be divided into three types: places named after
sponsors or other dignitaries to whom it was considered appropriate to give
such an honour; places named after geographical formations where the names
'naturally' suggest themselves; and places named after the feelings the places
invoked. This last category is the most interesting one in the context of this
chapter; the feelings that Shackleton and Amundsen believed these places
evoked clearly were not joyful ones. Names such as 'The Devil's Ballroom',
'The Gate of Hell', and 'Old Nick's Glacier' point to places which the pioneers
had to cross, traverses that involved both physical and mental pain and which
were clearly not associated with pleasurable feelings. The polar places demanded
respect, and sometimes fear. The first Norwegian to reach the North Pole, as
late as 1982, said that many of his memories of the place were like a nightmare.
The thundering sounds of ice-floes battering against each other, colliding, were
not music to the ears of people trying to sleep in a tent on an ice-floe.

Another ingredient of the Arctic was the wildlife – interesting from a distance, but more disturbing at close range. The threat of polar bears was a permanent worry which produced fear among North Pole adventurers. Related to this
was the awareness that to reach the North Pole, it was necessary to travel on
frozen salt water, which could easily break up. Ice on firm land, such as Greenland or the Antarctic, presented its own version of this threat (of falling down);
crevasses, sometimes covered with a thin layer of snow, so deep and narrow that
they were impossible to escape from if somebody had the bad luck to fall into
them. Frightening, scary, ghastly and sickening were among the words used

both by pioneers and by modern adventurers to describe encounters with such unsafe and perilous natural conditions.

The long time period necessary for polar expeditions put an extra mental strain, both on the traditional explorer and also on the modern, solo un-supported traveller. The expedition and the absence last much longer than any sporting event. The ability to cope with day after day of more and more of the same, ice of various kinds, was and is a mental test. Fridtjof Nansen reported depression and desolation as he and his partner struggled without making any real progress in the 1890s. The patience required is perhaps the hardest test for modern adventurers as they strive, well-equipped and almost safe, but never-theless doomed to a long period of time isolated on the cold ice. Imagine then, how the pioneers must have felt as they launched expeditions that meant an absence not of weeks or months, but of years. In this respect, Amundsen's South Pole expedition was a rather short trip, taking only two years (Kvam 2004). The capacity men had for struggling, surviving and tolerating the absolute or relative loneliness and each other's closed company, in a cold and hostile climate, eating a very limited and often reduced diet, coping with a special and demanding form of personal hygiene, coupled with the knowledge that this stay in a foreign place, far away from home, would take its time, was decisive. Mental strains like loneliness and fear were coupled with demands for patience and mental strength. The feeling of mastering and coping with all this was after all a reward. Physical strains like toil and drudgery, freezing and under-eating could then be coupled with experiences of freedom, and of being privileged.

The efforts required during polar adventuring in the pioneering age were extreme. It was painful and exhausting. Unlike other sporting performances, there were rarely any possibilities for changing one's mind, of withdrawing, or pulling out of the race; it was 'the West Coast or death'. To accomplish such extreme goals, 'no prisoners could be taken', no sick or injured dogs could be cared for, no excessive empathy could be shown. Only what could contribute to the reaching of the goal could be brought along. It was necessary to become hard. 'Forward we *had to* go – for this purpose all other things had to give way. It is sad that such an adventure systematically kills all your good feelings and just leaves the cold-hearted egoist back' (Nansen 1994: 29). These feelings are perhaps not different from what the ordinary egocentric sportsperson goes through. However, performing on the deserted ice makes it a more pressing and demanding reality.

The modern era

Can this pioneering way of experiencing pain really be reconstituted in modern times? The idea of 'unsupported travel', meaning explicitly self-supplied and self-carried, was and is a special way of compensating for the 'advantages' of modernization, such as lighter and better equipment, by a deliberate attempt to return to earlier, more painful and difficult ways. As Elias and Dunning

(1986) have noted, clearly defined rules and means for their enforcement are central features of modern sports and, like other sports, unsupported polar travel is defined by rules limiting some of the more efficient means to reach the desired goal. Motorized vehicles are as forbidden here as in normal cross-country skiing. But like other modern sports, within these limitations there is room for development and improvement. In relation to the special sport of polar racing, the quest has always been for lighter and, at the same time, more robust equipment. This technical side of the performance also has a cultural side. The emphasis on the need to be well and rationally equipped was part of a claimed Norwegian self-image and tradition. It has also been given explanatory power when dealing with the relative success of Norwegian adventurers from Amundsen to Erling Kagge and Børge Ousland. Serious dedication to the planning and choice of equipment was thought to be the 'Norwegian way' (Goksøyr 2004). By such attention to the detail of planning and equipment, one could reduce the uncertainty of the enterprise.

Good equipment, then, meant that more emphasis could be put on the more 'normal' sportive pains: the physical struggles of the body and the need to stay sharp and focused, to keep up the pace. It is interesting though, that this human side of the polar challenge is also often described in technical terms. The body may be seen as the performing sporting 'machine' which could break if not taken care of. Preparation and training, as well as carefully planned diets, were ways to minimize the physical pains of the machine that was going to take you to the Poles. Many modern descriptions are written from this perspective. The main problem of modern travel seems to be not freezing and hunger, as in the pioneering days, but how technically to provide an input of energy to prevent the inevitable weight loss which comes from struggles like these over long time periods. To store extra kilos of fat in the body before the expedition and to try to keep as many as possible of them is indeed a special relationship between sport and weight. Fantasies about food, and about favourite recipes, seem to be in many an adventurer's dreams.

The physical challenges of unsupported polar travel are immense. The skiing and sledge tracks to the Poles are also tracks of pain. Børge Ousland's training procedures before big events were similar to the training regimen of other sports demanding stamina and strength. Severe back pain is common among modern polar adventurers. Because of improved equipment, frostbite can now be regarded as an accident. But accidents do still occur, as the very experienced Englishman Sir Ranulph Fiennes admitted on what seems to have been his last major polar expedition. In 2000 he had to amputate lower portions of all the fingers on his left hand and undergo extensive medical treatment in hospital, after being exposed to an unfortunate combination of extreme cold and water (Richards 2001).

One of the modern polar adventurers who took the suffering part seriously was Asle T. Johansen, who crossed Greenland on skis in 1988. That year marked the hundredth anniversary of Nansen's first crossing of Greenland, and Johansen's idea was to make his trip an exact copy of Nansen's, just a hundred years later. The idea was, of course, hard to realise even though a great deal of effort was put into making the equipment – skis, sledges, clothing and food – a true replica of Nansen's. Johansen's idea however, was also to make the physical performance a copy of Nansen's. This is where we approach the pain concept. A physician by education, Johansen held that the human organism had remained basically the same during the hundred years that had passed since 1888. He therefore set out to do medical testing during the expedition, which he believed could give a valid picture of general pain during polar expeditions. What he perhaps missed out was the subjectivity of pain, and also the historicity of pain; Nansen's clothing seemed to be colder 100 years later.

On modern expeditions, freezing seems to be more a question of balance between intensity of physical effort and layers of clothing, where the idea is to avoid sweating. Areas like the face are still vulnerable though. 'The only place where we did not lose weight was in the face' (due to swollen cheeks and noses), Erling Kagge reported from the North Pole (1990: 118).

Unsupported by back-up

The expeditions of the 1990s illustrated this modern relationship between the will to sacrifice comfort and the will to reach ambitious goals. In 1992 three young men, Per Einar Bakke, Willy Gautvik and Arild Vegrim, tried to cross the North Pole on skis from Siberia to Canada, unsupported – a test no one until then had attempted. They each hauled a heavy loaded sleigh. With such a distance to cover they had to start in early spring when daylight was short and, in the beginning, almost absent. From the beginning they met difficult conditions with heavy winds and ice ridges together with lots of open channels in the ice. To cross such channels they had to use the sleighs as vessels for paddling. During these attempts to cross the channels they had to fight against heavy winds that blew their vessels further back than they managed to paddle forwards, and frozen ice that was too thick to paddle and too thin to walk. It meant lots of toil, but positive, physical toil. In their own words: 'Ice barriers, three bears, everything ok' (Polarboken 1991–92: 70) After a month of hard work Vegrim hurt his back. Trying to ignore the injury did him no good, and – as modern expeditions are in a position to do – they had to call for help. A Russian helicopter picked him up, while the two remaining men continued their struggle towards the North Pole. After 'several encounters with polar bears, harsh cold (minus 50 degrees Celsius and below) and amounts of drudgery, they reached the North Pole 12 May [1992].' (Polarboken 1991–92: 70). Here they would be rejoined by their old mate Vegrim, parachute diving from a Russian supply aircraft. Having recovered from his back injury, he very much wished to carry on with the original plan of going all the way to Canada. However, conditions and luck were not on their side. They had to throw in the towel after 18 more days. In this modern sport, that meant that they had to pick up their satellite telephone and call for the rescue plane (Polarboken 1991–92: 70).

As we have seen, the challenges are not only physical. The mental pressures are still there, even if in a slightly changed and reduced form. For the non-solo expeditions, special mental capacities seem to be required by expedition leaders. Bjørn Staib, who attempted a North Pole crossing in 1964, sought people who were willing and able to struggle and fight and at the same time keep their good humour. He also required a willingness to obey orders from the team leader (Staib 1965). Asle T. Johansen defined his model participant as a 'social horse', a not unreasonable description as they had to pull heavy sledges as well as sleep with three other people in the same sleeping bag (Johansen 1988).

The solitude of the modern unsupported polar adventurer is well described by Børge Ousland. He had to overcome fear, isolation and depression in order to reach his goal, and this meant three months of solitude around the North Pole in 2002. He had to 'peel away all layers of civilisation' as he 'was pushed to the limit'. His way of doing this was to try to resemble 'an animal of the environment' and be 'part of the ice' (National Geographic online 2003). This is the idealized version of how to cope with polar strains. And Ousland was of course dependent on the quality of the equipment he brought along, in order to be able to function as he wished.

Modern polar adventures are still risky, especially for the lone traveller who has nobody to assist him or her if an accident should happen, even though a survival dry suit is of immense help. However, the amount of danger involved is not comparable to that experienced during the age of the pioneers. The existence of satellite phones and Twin Otters (planes) reduces the experienced and imagined danger, both for performers and spectators.

Gender and culture

Traditional polar adventurers were, almost exclusively, men. Men are also in a clear majority among modern polar explorers. However, enough female polar trekkers have emerged in the modern period to raise issues concerning gender differences regarding lived and imagined pain. One difference which is rather clear from the modern polar tales is that male adventurers emphasize their physical struggles, their hazards and their pain more openly than their female colleagues. The will to be a heroic male adventurer who overcomes immense and gruelling physical struggles, fighting his way through precisely described pain – neither too much nor too little – and other obstacles, still seems to be a vital ingredient in men's polar narratives. This aspect of the tale does not seem to be as prominent among female adventurers. In their tales, the physical pain seems to be downgraded, leaving more room for contemplation and feel-good components (Arnesen 1995; Sørensen 1991; Kristensen 1987).

These are preliminary impressions, mainly based upon Norwegian polar litera-ture, and the data need to be studied further before any serious conclusion can be drawn. However, perhaps women do not have to buy into the conception of polar adventures as masculine and exhibitionistic tests of strength? Certainly the Norwegian discourse on polar trekking invites the conclusion that solid preparation and planning can enable both men and women to master a polar adventure. A question of cultures could also be raised here: is the gender difference always the primary one? Could it be that English women along with their male counterparts, differ, for example, from their Norwegian colleagues of either sex, in relation to issues such as heroism and the pain involved in reaching heroic status? Websites and media coverage of English–American female expeditions seem to contain more discussion about frostbites and other injuries than similar Norwegian narrative sources (Oliver 2002). It could be that this simply reflects the publishers' views about what sells a polar book. However, the male tale of 'deprivation, stress and physical pain' (Fiennes 2003) seems to be replicated in some ways.

Concluding comments

Polar tales, though elegant, are not about the marginalization of pain. On the contrary, pains hold a central place in polar narratives. Sometimes one can be led to believe that pain is indeed the purpose of the whole thing. Without pain there would not be much to write about. However, in modern polar tales, agonies, torments and pain are described in a clearly utilitarian way. The toil gives the reward, the pain gives the pleasure. The greater the struggle, the greater the reward. Unlike in the pioneering days when people risked their lives for king and country – and other more trivial motives – modern adventurers insist that their reward is a personal reward, one which comes from succeeding in one's own endeavours by breaking mental boundaries. In this way self-inflicted pain can be legitimized even now.

Notes

1 Frederic Cook had made a claim for the North Pole in 1908. Peary's claim was the most generally accepted at that time. Later research has put some question marks around both these achievements (Sale 2002: 126). E. A. Drivenes and H. D. Jølle (eds) (2004).
2 Sale 2002: 88–9, tells the story of the two Danes Ejnar Mikkelsen and Iver Iversen who miraculously survived a two-year ordeal in the north of Greenland. At one point 'Iversen was so desperate for food that he asked Mikkelsen to carry their rifle as he feared he might shoot and eat him'. They also discussed whether one could eat the other if one died from more 'natural' causes. Earlier search teams for the missing, and lost, Franklin expedition (1845–) had reported findings of skeletons with their hands removed, corresponding to the belief that hands are what make a person human (Sale 2002: 89).

Bibliography

Arnesen, L. (1995) *Snille piker går ikke til Sydpolen*. Oslo: Damm.
Bomann-Larsen, T. (1995) *Roald Amundsen. En biografi*, Oslo: Cappelen.
Drivenes, E. A. and Jølle, H. D. (eds) (2004) *Norsk Polarhistorie*, 1, Oslo: Gyldendal.
Elias, N. (1985), *The Loneliness of the Dying*, Oxford: Blackwell.

Elias, N. and Dunning, E. (1986) *Quest for Excitement: Sport and Leisure in the Civilizing Process*, Oxford: Blackwell.

Fiennes, R. (2003) *Captain Scott*, London: Hodder and Stoughton.

Goksøyr, M. (2004) 'Kappløp i gamle spor' in E. A. Drivenes and H. D. Jølle (eds) *Norsk Polarhistorie*, 1, Oslo: Gyldendal

Johansen, A. T. (1988) *På ski over Grønland. 100 år etter Nansens ekspedisjon i 1888 – i 1988*, Oslo: Metope.

Kagge, E. (1990) *Nordpolen. Det siste kappløpet*, Oslo: Cappelen.

Kagge, E. (1994) *På eventyr*, Oslo: Damm.

Kirwan, L. P. (1962) *A History of Polar Exploration*, Harmondsworth: Penguin Books.

Kristensen, M. (1987) *Mot 90° syd*. Oslo: Grøndahl

Kvam, R. *Aftenposten*, 1 October 2004.

Nansen, F. (1988) *På Ski over Grønland*, Oslo: Aventura.

Nansen, F. (1994) *På Ski over Polhavet*, Oslo: Aschehoug.

National Geographic (2003) Online. Available HTTP: <http://www.nationalgeographic.com/speakers> (Accessed 22 December 2004).

Oliver, M. (2002) 'Frostbite forces polar woman to abandon trek' *The Guardian*. Online. Available HTTP: <http://www.guardian.co.uk/northpole/story/0,11743,707728,00.html> (Accessed 30 April 2002).

Ousland, B. (1994) *Alone to the North Pole*, Oslo: Cappelen.

Polarboken 1991–92, 70, Oslo: Polarklubben.

Richards, L. (2001) 'The January Interview', *January Magazine*. Online. Available HTTP: <http://www.januarymagazine.com/profiles/rfiennes.html> (Accessed 15 October 2002).

Sale, R. (2002) *Polar Reaches. The History of Arctic and Antarctic Exploration*, Seattle: The Mountaineers Books.

Spufford, F. (1996) *I May Be Some Time. Ice and the English Imagination*, London: Faber and Faber.

Staib, B. (1965) *On Skis toward the North Pole*, New York.

Sørensen, M. (1991) *Jentenes tur! Nuliaq-ekspedisjonen over Grønland 1990*, Oslo: Cappelen.

Thorseth, R. (1982) *Ferden mot Nordpolen*, Oslo: Hjemmets bokforlag.

6 Injured female athletes

Experiential accounts from England and Canada

Hannah Charlesworth and Kevin Young

Introduction: Studying women and sports injury

While sociological attention has, to date, been primarily directed towards male athletes and their experiences of risk, pain and injury in sport, the counterpart experiences of female athletes have been relatively under-researched. The bulk of the sociological literature has, for example, been concerned with male sports environments, the impact that dominant notions of masculinity have on legitimate uses of the male body, and the ways in which 'social forces work upon male athletes in such a way that they become willing to subject their bodies to injury' (Young *et al.* 1994: 179). Clearly, these are important areas of study. However, it is equally clear that sociological research on sports-related pain and injury has been unquestionably male-orientated. Simply put, more research on how women experience sports injury is needed.

In this context, this chapter considers the previously neglected pain and injury experiences of female athletes. Attention is drawn to recent work carried out with female athletes on both sides of the Atlantic, which suggests that women are often as willing as their male counterparts to take risks with their bodies and to 'hide', 'deny', 'disrespect' and 'depersonalize' (Young and White 1995) injury and pain on a routine basis. More specifically, as part of broader and ongoing work, cross-cultural comparisons of the experiences of female athletes in England and Canada are offered. Our discussion is based on interview and survey data gathered from a sample of women athletes involved in a range of campus sports at an English university and earlier samples of female university athletes in Western Canada.

The central aim of the chapter is to begin to understand the similarities and differences between the ways in which male and female athletes understand, respond to, and manage sports-related injury and pain. The evidence that exists so far suggests that both male and female experiences are strongly shaped by certain risk-promoting elements in mainstream sport culture, about which much is already known (Coakley and Donnelly 2004; White and Young 1999). A deeply embedded 'culture of risk' (Nixon 1992, 1993a and 1993b, 1996; Young *et al.* 1994; Young 2004a) is internalized by athletes who, regardless of their gender, learn to tolerate injury and normalize pain. However, trans-Atlantic data considered in this chapter also indicate that there are a number of apparent differences between men's and women's experiences of pain and injury, which are likewise representative of the social production of health, illness and injury along gender-based lines. In this respect, attention is paid to gendered nuances of injury and pain in sport, the impact of injury on notions of feminine identity and the role of gender in sports rehabilitation and medical treatment. Using the experiential accounts of English and Canadian female athletes as evidence, the possibility that sports-related pain and injury encounters may be outcomes of *both* sport and gender socialization processes is considered.

Methodological approach and rationale

This chapter grows out of ongoing research into the relationship between sport, gender and health conducted in Canada (Young 1993; Young *et al.* 1994; Young and White 1995; Young 1997) and from research undertaken for a doctoral thesis concerned with the sports-related pain and injury experiences of female university athletes in England (Charlesworth 2004). In both cases, over 60 women participants at the university level or above were closely studied. A range of research techniques – including surveys, semi-structured interviews and observation – was used to explore how these female athletes felt while they were injured, and how they understood and negotiated sports-related pain. Respondents were involved in a variety of team and individual sports, including rugby, soccer, basketball, tennis, downhill skiing, body building, swimming, volleyball, field hockey, triathlon, canoeing, shoe jumping, lacrosse, and track and field events. The decision to examine these particular sports was not arbitrary; they were chosen initially as they embody a number of sport 'types' and because, consequently, their characteristics (that is, their structures, their athletic requirements, and the reasons why they appeal to certain athletes) differ in a number of key respects. More specifically, the selected sports represent team (soccer, rugby, field hockey, volleyball, lacrosse) and individual sports (track and field, tennis, triathlon, swimming, show jumping, canoeing), contact (soccer, rugby) and non-contact sports (tennis, field hockey, volleyball), sports which have been traditionally male-defined and male-dominated (soccer, rugby), as well as a number of sports that have been 'marginal' to the mainstream of dominant sport structures (triathlon, show jumping, canoeing).

It was anticipated that experiences of pain and injury within these heterogeneous sports might vary. For instance, due to the repetitive nature of their sport, tennis players and track and field athletes often encounter a range of over-use injuries which may result in forms of chronic pain (Harries *et al.* 1998). Due to the non-contact nature of their sport, they are, however, less likely than, for instance, rugby players to sustain serious or catastrophic injuries (Adams *et al.* 1987). In contact sports such as rugby, collisions with other participants are the most common cause of injury (Sports Council 1991) and can lead to a number of serious injuries including spine trauma 'severe enough to cause either death or complete quadriplegia' (Harries *et al.* 1998: 878). In rugby, injuries may be accidental (such as those resulting from a collapsed scrum, for example) but, whether accidental or not, they are often related to aggressive collisions and dangerous play.

Methodologically speaking, it was felt that casting the net widely would be helpful when attempting to understand the pain and injury experiences of female athletes in general, and would help to provide a sense of how diverse and varied their experiences can be. As one of us had written some years previously, 'early evidence suggests that [there is] no homogeneous experience or set of values on the part of women athletes, no fixed or monolithic "femininity", and that variation and contradiction are common' (Young 1997: 298). Women's experiences of sports involvement are not only often very different from those of their male counterparts, but are also likely to be unique in their own right, differing from one female to another, both between and among sports. But more information is needed to verify this assumption. As Halbert (1997) argues, while women are now more seriously involved both in traditionally male-defined and male-associated sports, and in sports that have been considered more appropriate for female involvement, very little is known about women's experiences of pain and injury. Moreover, the sociological evidence that does exist (Friis-Thing 2004; Halbert 1997; Pike 2000, 2004; Theberge 1997; Young and White 1995; Young 1997) suggests that there is a greater need than ever to understand the gendered experiences of female athletes in a range of sports since, as athletic opportunities for female athletes expand, they appear as willing as male athletes to place their bodies at risk in a variety of sports contexts.

The women involved in the research were aged between 19 and 31 years, had participated at the university level of sport or higher, and had all experienced at least one major injury. Many of the respondents had encountered multiple injuries, had been hospitalized, and/or had undergone corrective surgery. All members of both samples were white, and could broadly be classified as middle class.

Injury, gender and dominant sports culture

Charlesworth's (2004) research carried out with English female university athletes confirms earlier findings by Young and White (1995), in their work on pain and injury in Canada, that there are a number of important similarities between how men and women experience injury and pain in sport. Examining the data we gathered from female athletes alongside the existing sociological literature on male sports environments suggests that many women are as likely as men to take risks with their bodies when they are involved in a range of sports at a range of levels.

Interviews with Canadian and British women indicated that their attitudes to pain and injury are as likely to be shaped by a culture of risk that pervades mainstream sport environments and the associated ideological structures that support them, as are the sports-related pain and injury experiences of male athletes. As Nixon (2004) argues, while there may be some minor differences in the nature, extent and degree of this 'culture of risk' in female sports environments, there is nevertheless a broad acceptance among female participants of a set of beliefs that normalize, rationalize and indeed champion the risks of playing with damaged bodies. Perhaps most significantly, the data gathered in Canada and England support the notion that, regardless of gender, athletes may adopt a range of by-now familiar techniques for neutralizing pain and 'managing' injury. As Young *et al.* (1994) and Young and White (1995) have shown, both male and female athletes may hide, deny and disrespect pain, as well as depersonalize its 'physical manifestations'.

Hidden pain

Sociologists of sport have indicated that, within the context of male sports environments and especially at elite levels of play, injury and pain are usually viewed unfavourably by coaches, trainers and athletic peers alike. For these reasons, and as Young *et al.* (1994) have argued, many men involved in sport may find that hiding pain is an important and widely understood subcultural tactic. Concealing injury, however, is equally likely to be a strategy for female athletes who may also 'decide to hide [their] suffering from others when the costs of disclosure appear too high' (Kotarba 2004). Indeed, pain was 'ignored', 'avoided', 'blocked out' and 'forgotten about' both by Canadian and by British female athletes involved in our respective studies. For example, Jane, an English javelin thrower, spoke of masking pain as a routine characteristic of her daily involvement in sport, as a strategy for coping with physical hurt:

> I think you just get used to it [pain] because when you train you usually hurt anyway. I guess you just consider it as normal pain really. Pain is something you just deal with. It's something you go through and you just try to ignore it.

In a similar way, Carol explained that she felt that achieving distinction as a swimmer necessitated shielding and disguising pain from her coach:

> I would sometimes perceive that I wasn't made to feel as much a part of the session [by my coach] when I was injured. You'd expect that, though, because he'd be concentrating on those who weren't injured. Sometimes he wouldn't ask me how I was until the end of the session and I'd be in pain, so sometimes I felt a bit cut off. Often I'd keep quiet about injuries though. If I had a competition coming up, I'd not tell him if I was hurting because I wouldn't want him to reduce my training load.

In these ways, Carol's experiences were not dissimilar to those of Canadian basketball player Laura, whose words indicate that suppressing pain can become a subcultural 'imperative' (Young *et al.* 1994: 182) for many female athletes. Here, Laura describes her responses to a dislocated kneecap:

> The first thing I remember is being very scared after hearing the 'pop' and the feeling of no control as I hit the ground. I knew immediately it was my knee, but tried to deny it. I hunched over my leg grabbing my shin and waiting for the referee, which seemed like 10 minutes. I kept telling myself that it was only some pulled muscles, and even when my leg went into contractions, I refused to believe it was bad. I didn't give in and actually waited out the entire game. It was the first step on the way to admitting defeat and acknowledging my injury.

In brief, interviews with these English and Canadian women indicated that female athletes involved in a number of different sports mask injuries and hide pain from potentially judgemental significant others whose reactions they clearly often feared. For a number of female athletes, and like their male counterparts, coping with pain thus entails 'suppressing its physical and mental prescriptions on the body' (Young *et al.* 1994: 183) on a regular basis.

Disrespected pain

Research carried out by Young *et al.* (1994) with male athletes in Canada indicated that men often cope with pain by adopting an attitude of indignation or resentment towards their injured body parts. While the ability to show irreverence towards injuries was, on the whole, less extreme among the women we spoke to, it was nevertheless still apparent. For example, Dalaura, a Canadian athlete, described how she learned to cope with severe lower leg and ankle pain from a very young age:

> Even at school years ago . . . I never skated or played basketball without constant pain. However, this just made me push harder to beat it. I was often sore and stiff. The pain, while playing, was often enough to make me cry once I got home (but never at the rink!). I dealt with it through the use of painkillers and denial.

Such an attitude of indignation towards injury and pain was not unusual in the Canadian data but was also reflected in the accounts of a number of female athletes in England. For instance, Vicki 'blocked out the pain', Lisa was 'annoyed and irritated' by it, and Gemma was 'resentful and bitter' about her injuries and wounded body parts.

Dealing with pain in this way was, then, a strategy employed by both sets of women. Along with other female university athletes in the UK, Gillian (gymnastics) dismissed pain as something to be 'managed with the help of a few painkillers and an ice pack'. Troublingly, Gillian underscored this point in connection with the pressures she felt during competition and tournaments, when coaches' expectations – and the pressures on athletes – were especially high:

> Sometimes at competitions you might take some painkillers which the physio gives you. I don't do it too often, and not usually when I am training because it's usually just numbing the pain. Sometimes in competitions, though, you might not be able to get through without some help. If you have a goal of a competition or a championship, then that can often blind you to the fact that you could be damaging your health.

While over-the-counter painkillers and a certain cynicism towards injury were enough to enable Gillian to compete regardless of pain, they were not sufficient for a number of more seriously injured athletes to whom we spoke. Kelly, a rugby player, required 'regular pain-killing injections' when suffering with ankle ligament damage, while Emily (soccer) had needed morphine and other drugs to cope with the pain resulting from a torn anterior cruciate ligament. Similarly, and on the advice of an impatient coach, Sandra (track and field) explained how she had taken weekly cortisone injections in order to reduce the inflammation caused by a back injury. She explained:

> I think I knew that it wasn't really doing me any good, but I also knew that if I wanted to compete then I had to somehow numb the pain. My coach said that the best way for me to do that was to have cortisone injections. Once they wore off, though, I'd be in as much pain, if not more, than before, so I stopped having them in the end. They managed to stop the pain and helped me to cope for a while, but it wasn't making the injury any better.

Such descriptions of the 'disrespected pain' of Gillian, Kelly, Emily and Sandra were far from unusual; indeed, most of our respondents had similar strategies and accounts to report.

That the women involved in our research dealt with pain in similar ways to many male athletes indicates that learning to hide intense physical (and, relatedly, emotional) pain may be a result not only of socialization into the rules and norms of 'masculinist sport' (Young et al. 1994: 185), but also of socialization into a harsh and often dehumanizing culture of sport more generally. Moreover, these women's accounts remind us that when athletes are seriously committed to sport, they may be willing to take excessive risks with their bodies by taking pain-killing injections and drugs and using other compensatory strategies that are not necessarily in their long-term health interests – once again, regardless of gender.

Unwelcomed pain

Data gathered on both sides of the Atlantic indicate that injuries are often poorly received in both male and female competitive sports environments. We found that with female athletes, outward expressions of pain were simply not appreciated by coaches and peer groups, and in some cases were not even tolerated. In this respect, we found that coaches and team-mates, while described by our respondents as important potential sources of social/emotional support for injured athletes, often viewed injury as a 'nuisance', a 'hassle', or an 'inconvenience'. Prior work (Curry and Strauss 1994; Nixon 1992, 1993a, 1993b, 1996; Young 1993) has indicated that the pain and injury experiences of athletes may be best understood within the context of a network of social relationships which may 'contribute to the willingness of athletes to play hurt and knowingly or unknowingly to risk greater pain, injuries, and possible long-term disability' (Nixon 1996: 34). Our data from English and Canadian female participants similarly suggest that pressure from administrators and significant others, in particular coaches and team-mates, may impact on athletes' decisions to play while in pain or to return to play prematurely from injury, and thus risk even further discomfort and disability. The data suggest that coaches are particularly influential in this respect and they were, in some cases, described by respondents as unambiguously unsupportive of, even hostile to, their injured athletes and their pain and rehabilitation needs.

As Nixon argues, coaches are 'central figures in the sub-cultures and social networks of athletes, and as central figures they may influence athletes' choices about taking risks with their bodies' (Nixon 1994: 80). Elizabeth's experience of injury within track and field provided a classic example of pressure being placed upon athletes by coaches. Coaches may, perhaps inadvertently at times and as a result of their own occupational/sub-cultural pressures, rank performance and success above the well-being of the athlete. Elizabeth explained that while suffering from a partial rupture of her Achilles tendon, 'One coach tried to persuade me to race despite the doctors advising me not to . . . he wanted me to have a steroid injection which masks the pain and then to run regardless of the injury'. That coaches may wield organizational power over athletes to persuade them to return to action too early is neither responsible nor, in the long term, athlete-friendly.

Similarly, a coach who was outspokenly unsympathetic towards injured players in his squad made it difficult for Lucy (tennis) to voice concerns about her recurring injuries. Lucy's experiences appear to be consistent with the findings of Young *et al.* (1994) and with the claim of Roderick *et al.* (2000), based on their all-male samples, that athletes will often hide emotional responses because 'those who are not prepared to play through pain and injury are likely to be stigmatized as not having the right attitude' (Roderick *et al.* 2000: 169). In Lucy's words:

I just told my coach of a sore shoulder and he doesn't really understand players saying they are injured. He presumes it is an excuse or being 'soft', so I don't make a fuss about it . . . He never believes you are injured, so you feel pressured to play and keep quiet.

Not unlike Lucy, Catherine (volleyball) described how her coach was abrupt and unsympathetic towards her when she was in pain, and had made it clear that he was unwilling to 'waste' valuable training time discussing her injuries:

Our coach doesn't take much interest in injuries . . . he just wants us back training. I saw the physio before a training session and was told I could do some light training that night. I told my coach and he replied 'you're damn right you're training'. This pressurized me into taking part in every drill and I was in a lot of pain during the session as a result.

As with the evidence from male sports environments, Catherine's account indicated that coaches can make athletes' lives so difficult that some would rather train in pain than 'be injured' and on the sidelines and thus vulnerable to the critical eyes and sharp tongues of impatient coaching staff. She noted, for example, that despite being injured, her coach made her attend and watch every training session. In her words: 'This was ok at first but, as we train twice a day, I became frustrated that I couldn't be involved and my attitude toward my injury became negative. I was tempted, therefore, to come back earlier than I knew I should.' On this dimension, Canadian findings were extremely similar. For example, basketball player Robin described her coach's reaction after she had decided to withdraw from her sport as a result of cyclical and very painful knee injuries. Here, once again, pressure to return to competition too soon was also experienced as early as high school:

My parents wanted me to quit. They didn't agree with my basketball coaches who pushed training beyond what was physically reasonable for that age group and development. My swim coach was concerned and barred me from the pool. But my basketball coach in Grade 10 had me pulled into the Principal's office for refusing to go to practice, even though I told him I'd quit because I was going for surgery.

Although most of these English and Canadian women described their team-mates as being supportive of and sympathetic towards them *as people* while they were injured, on a number of occasions their responses indicated that, along with coaches and trainers, athletic peers may also react in ways which influence an athlete's experience of pain and injury and her decision on when to return to play. Debbie, a high-level British water polo player, for example, considered that she had perhaps returned from shoulder damage too quickly as a result of the negative reaction of some of her team-mates to the injury. In her words:

I felt some pressure from my team-mates when I was injured . . . mainly to perform as well as usual and not to let the injury stop me from playing or affect me . . . some people actually accused me of faking the injury.

Similarly, Tamsin, an English Universities soccer player, described the pressure placed on her both by her coaches and by her team-mates to continue to play despite suffering with very sore and inflamed ankle ligament damage:

I was just told to strap it up and carry on, and for the BUSA [British Universities Sports Association] Final, I was told to strap it up really tightly and go to the hospital after. The second time I did it, I refused to play, but that wasn't a very popular decision . . . My team-mates did pressure me. I didn't mind the first time, but the second time I wanted to rest it properly, but I was made to feel bad as we had a couple of FA Cup games that I missed.

Canadian athlete Donna also explained how she minimized her injury after facing similar pressures from the players around her, and became willing to return to play before healing properly:

The other players at the club pretty much ignored [my] injury and downplayed its seriousness. It wasn't cool to admit your body wasn't finely tuned and healthy, so I downplayed it.

In brief, it is evident from the data that a network of significant others in female sport may act in ways which influence women to tolerate injuries, ignore pain and return to action prematurely. In their cases, our respondents often accepted the risks associated with participating in their sport because their 'sports nets' (or the networks of social relationships to which they belonged – Nixon 1992) constructed such experiences as 'natural' or 'worthwhile'. In a Goffmanian (1968) sense, these women had learned to manage their bodies in a certain way – by hiding pain, tolerating injury and returning to play sooner than one should – because they realized that an 'inappropriate' presentation of self might have led to their athletic identity being 'spoiled' by the reaction of others; a clear effect of being labelled, for example, 'weak', 'unreliable', or 'uncommitted' as several of our athletes were by their coaches and peers. Our data also indicated, however, that these athletes were very rarely, if ever, *forced* into playing while hurt or returning to their sport too quickly after injury. Rather, they were more likely to be subtly persuaded into hiding pain and concealing injuries by significant others and audiences perceived to be critical and unforgiving (Young *et al.* 1994) as well as by a pervasive 'sport ethic' (Coakley and Donnelly, 2004) within most mainstream athletic subcultures which tends to equate practices such as playing through pain and taking risks with qualities like commitment, reliability and character.

Depersonalized pain

Because injuries may be so poorly received, or *perceived* as being so poorly received within the sub-culture of competitive sport, athletes are often inclined to deal with them in an intensely private manner (Young and White 1995). In this respect, our research showed that both male and female athletes use techniques of depersonalization in order to make sense of pain in their lives. As with the male athletes involved in the study by Young *et al.* (1994), Canadian and British women objectified their injured body parts and tended to interpret injury as a form of self-weakness and bodily betrayal. In this respect, Heidi, a Welsh International netball player, noted how she felt 'cheated' by her anterior cruciate ligament injury, and described how her desire to stay involved in her sport meant ignoring the pain her injury caused on a routine basis:

> At one point, I went on court with my ankle so heavily taped up, and some of my friends who had shin splints would have both legs taped up the whole time. I'd just think, well I suppose this is letting me play. Everybody had ankle supports through their laces and it was just accepted. It was nothing unusual at all for people to be taped up.

Rather than being solely a characteristic of male athletes, it was not uncommon for the female athletes in our samples to speak in 'impersonal and techno-rational' ways (Young *et al.* 1994: 186) about their injuries being 'iced', 'strapped', 'mended', 'worked on', 'fixed' and the like. The general consensus appeared to be that acknowledging responsibility for injuries was also to acknowledge personal weakness and dubious moral fibre.

In sum, it is apparent that athletes may adopt a number of coping strategies or techniques in order to deal with injuries when they belong to sports sub-cultures in which they learn, regardless of gender, that *feeling like and being perceived as* a serious and committed athlete entails taking risks and accepting pain. Data gathered in the UK confirm Young and White's (1995) earlier Canadian claims that these strategies are adopted by both male *and* female athletes who have learned that revered qualities such as courage, character and grit can be demonstrated through pain suppression and that maintaining core membership in their group or team means being willing to compromise health.

The gendering of pain and injury through sport

The parallels that we imply between how male and female athletes respond to and manage injury and pain indicate that sports-related pain and injury experiences are, at least to some extent, a result of socialization into the culture of sport itself. The complex of relationships and expectations forged within sport figurations encourages athletes to internalize the belief that normalizing pain and rationalizing injury are appropriate, even laudable, orientations, regardless of gender. The important differences identified within the research carried out

with female athletes in both Canada and the UK and prior sociological investigations into the sports-related pain and injury experiences of male athletes suggest, however, that orientations towards injury and pain are also partly a result
of gender socialization processes. Considerable sociological work (Anderson
and Blue 1991; Frank 1991; Goldsmit 1994; Graham 1984) has illustrated that
health and illness are rarely experienced in *exactly* the same ways by men and
women. Instead, health and illness experiences may reflect traditional gender
roles and are a product of inequality in ideological, political, economic and
cultural power in social settings, whether vocational or avocational. Having
indicated that some female athletes take risks with their bodies in similar ways
to male athletes, the next section underscores how sports-related pain and
injury, as with experiences of health and illness more generally, are also likely
to be shaped to some extent by *gendered* expectations and experiences.

While a great deal of sociological attention has been given to the ways in
which dominant notions of masculinity can shape the male athlete's experience
of sports-related pain and injury, interviews with female athletes indicated that
ideological assumptions about appropriate uses of the female body may also
strongly impact on how women understand and manage injury and pain.
Compared with data from studies with injured men, there were some noticeable
differences in female player responses to injury and pain, to the impact that
injury had on the female athlete's body, and with regard to the material
resources available to the female athletes involved in our research when they
were injured and in need of medical care. The following discussion provides
illustrations of these 'gendered' dimensions to injury and pain in sport.

Pain stories and the gender order

Our data suggest that, unlike most male athletes who – existing research shows –
nearly always deal with their pain and injury experiences privately, female
athletes are more likely to discuss injury openly with team-mates, peers and significant others and that this may assume the status of a critical coping strategy.
For example, like a number of other female athletes involved in the research,
discus thrower Jodie found sharing 'pain stories' with team-mates and other
athletes to be both therapeutic and practical:

> I think if you can share what's happening to you and what's happened to
> [team-mates] in the past it can help. If they've had a similar injury, for
> example, you can talk about how long it took them to recover and what
> sorts of things they did to help the injury. So, I think it definitely helps to
> talk to people. My boyfriend is a javelin thrower and has been injured in
> the past, and I think he finds it helpful that he's got someone close to
> him that understands.

Instead of isolating themselves when in pain, which Young *et al.* (1994)
certainly found with most of their male respondents, Belinda, a track and field

athlete, explained that the women in her training group 'talked through' their injuries in small groups, or even collectively as a team (though rarely in the presence of coaches):

> In general [pain] would be the content of every conversation walking back after a session. We talk about how sick we feel or how much something is hurting. It would be a really common thing for us to be in pain, nothing unusual really, so talking about it usually helps.

We found such injury-sharing among female team-mates to be a common pattern in both sets of samples. The fact that the female athletes involved in our research appeared more willing than their male counterparts to share and communicate sports-related pain and injury experiences is perhaps best understood in relation to historical notions surrounding acceptable 'masculine' and 'feminine' conduct, and to traditional norms with regard to gender-appropriate emotionality. The silencing of male athletes' voices in relation to sports-related pain and injury experiences discussed by Young (1993), Young *et al.* (1994) and others can be at least partly attributed to the fact that illness has traditionally been associated with perceptions of flaws in the power of the body and conceived, therefore, as a compromiser of masculine status. Women, on the other hand, are likely to report ill-health more frequently than men and share sports-related injury and pain experiences because they feel that it is more culturally acceptable for them to show affect, and express emotion publicly. Of course, this links with known disparities in the gender composition of workers in the health care industry and similarly gendered patterns of illness-sharing which have also been identified by sociologists of health and illness (cf. Lupton 1995).

As the data from our samples show, there are undoubtedly some striking similarities, yet also a number of important variations, in the ways in which male and female athletes understand, respond to and manage injury and pain. Since men and women have traditionally understood health and illness in rather different ways, it is not surprising that within the context of sport they also communicate these experiences in different ways that serve, ultimately, to reproduce patterns of 'gender logic' (Coakley and Donnelly 2004) as well as 'gender order' structures (Messner and Sabo 1990) more broadly.

Injury and feminine selves

Speaking to women about their experiences of pain and injury indicated that female athletes continue to face a number of practical and ideological barriers to their involvement in sport. On an ideological note, socially constructed stereotypes about appropriate uses of the female body had made a clear impact on the lives of our respondents in both England and Canada. For example, these women talked of the conflict they experienced as a result of the *perceived* inconsistencies between being an athlete and being a woman. While meeting social and cultural norms surrounding appropriate uses of the female body often requires women to be passive, dependent and subservient, the traits required to achieve success in sport (for example, confidence, power, physical and mental fortitude) are often quite different, especially in competition at high levels. For example, as discus thrower Jodie noted:

> As a high school student everybody knew I was a thrower because I was quite good. The lads at school used to tease me, though. It was like, 'Oh look it's Jodie, the big butch thrower'. Friends would tell me not to listen, but inside it makes you feel like you are a bit different to everyone else. Also, when we had school photos in our little netball skirts, I'd be the one with the big thighs. At one point, it really got to me and I felt as though I wasn't feminine and wasn't 'girly'. My event definitely meant that I needed to be more powerful and more toned than other girls and, for a while, that did bother me.

It became apparent with the British and Canadian data that when women's bodies become *athletic* bodies they are often constructed by non-players (who may include significant others such as boyfriends, parents or siblings) as 'deviant' and their behaviour stigmatized as 'unfeminine' or suspicious in some sense (Young and White 1995). Such stigmatization can often lead women to question their involvement in sport, or sometimes to withdraw from participation completely. As Harris (1980) has noted, crisis can ensue for the female athlete when she 'perceives a disparity between how she sees herself and how society expects her to be'. For some women, the experience of often striking physical markers of sports-related injury only served to compound this sense of uncertainty.

Already very painful injury experiences were made even more disruptive for athletes such as Liz (rugby) who identified injury as having a negative impact on how she felt about being an 'attractive' or 'sexy' woman:

> I have to say that when I kept getting black eyes all the time it did bother me. It isn't very feminine and I did feel less attractive. Also, because of my knee injuries, I had scars all down my legs. I didn't wear skirts for a while because they looked a mess, really not very attractive at all.

Similarly, Estelle (rugby) worried that her injuries made her feel and appear less feminine, and even made her question her place in the public sphere:

> When I broke my cheekbone, I wouldn't go out for ages, I just didn't want people to see me, it didn't look very nice at all. I have thought about how I'd feel if it happened again, it was really painful and it made me feel crap about how I looked. I'm still playing, though, so I guess that says something.

It has been shown that injury can be particularly problematic for male athletes when it brings about changes in their bodies, including diminished strength, decreased fitness and reduced body tone (Young et al. 1994). As our data indicate, injury poses similar problems for female athletes, although perhaps in different ways. While some of the women involved in the research viewed injury as a sign of being a dedicated athlete, many of the women in Canada and England also clearly expressed the view that injury impacted negatively on their sense of femininity and even sexuality, especially when it involved facial wounds such as 'black eyes', cuts, bruises and stitches – that is to say, visible signs that one had rejected stereotypical notions of 'frail' femininity and was willing to place oneself at physical risk.

In brief, many of the women in our samples acknowledged that these sorts of facial/body injuries are considered to be threatening to notions of femininity and a marker of gender-ambiguous behaviour. Similarly, physical scarring from sport may be deconstructed by audiences, in the words of our respondents, as 'unattractive', 'unfeminine' and 'unsexy', and thus unsettling to the sexual identities of their bearers. For the most part, these sorts of deconstructions of the meanings of such injury markers have not been uncovered in research on male athletes who, indeed, may apply precisely opposite meanings to them to gain kudos and even honour in their respective sports environments (cf. Young 1993; Young et al. 1994). Crucially, however, it is important to recognize that our samples are limited in size and representativeness. As such, it is entirely possible that other female athletes from other samples, but perhaps the same sports, may express views on injury and wounds that are far more closely aligned with the kudos and badge-of-honour 'models' of injury reported by many male athletes to date.

Injury rehabilitation and gendered opportunity structures

While ideological notions about acceptable uses of the female body had an impact on the way in which our respondents understood and responded to injury and pain, their experiences of sports-related pain and injury were also clearly shaped by a number of practical constraints that cannot be divorced from questions of gender equality. The gendered nature of the infrastructure of sport injury was, for example, perhaps best illustrated by the medical treatment our respondents received for their sports-related injuries. Although treatment processes, as Roderick (2004) argues, are also often inadequate for male athletes, conversations with these women indicated that with regard to availability, expense and quality of treatment, sports medicine and rehabilitation facilities and services are often far worse for female players.

Accounts of treatment for pain and injury incidents/experiences among this group of women were replete with words and phrases such as 'double standards', 'misdiagnosis', 'expense', 'dissatisfaction' and 'mistrust'. Medical advice and financial support for physiotherapy and rehabilitation appeared to be routinely worse for female athletes throughout a range of sport types and across the continuum of ability levels. Liz, for example, described the gender-based inequalities between the men's and women's rugby teams at her university in the following way:

> The men's rugby team have a triage session on a Monday night with the physio who takes a look at any injuries and says what might be wrong. If you are really badly injured then you are allowed to go along, but only if you are a first team player [on the women's team]. There's no real support system surrounding the girl's team, we aren't that lucky.

In a similar way to Liz, Emily (soccer) noted how belonging to a 'low status' team on campus had a clear impact on the quality of support available to injured female athletes:

> We aren't counted as one of the top teams, we aren't male rugby players, so we're not a major priority. There is a physio on campus but we don't get that free like some of the men's teams do. I don't actually go to see the campus physio, I sort my own out, it's very expensive but there isn't really any other option.

Regardless of the sport played, the majority of female athletes involved in the present research found that the medical treatment they received for their injuries was often inadequate, and sometimes completely lacking. Astonishingly, given their level of competition, these women were very rarely, if ever, provided with specialist sports rehabilitation. Instead, treatment processes were very much self-initiated and self-funded. In this way, already painful injury experiences were accompanied by feelings of vulnerability, anxiety and uncertainty that Roderick (2004) argues are key features of modern-day medical diagnoses and treatment processes in elite sport. Research in Canada and England indicates that there are important differences in the structures of medical treatment options available to male and female athletes. These differences were clearly recognized by our respondents. Similarly disturbing disparities have been reported by female handball players in Denmark (Friis-Thing 2004).

Undoubtedly, further comparative analysis of treatment for injury among male and female athletes is necessary in order to make any concrete assertions about the gendered nature of such processes. However, on the whole, our data indicated that there are likely to be some very important similarities, but also a number of significant differences, between how men and women experience health, and between the ways in which they are treated for ill-health, including injuries that result from athletic participation.

Gender counts: Avoiding singular explanations for sports injury

English and Canadian female athletes participating at the university level and beyond are willing to take risks with their bodies in the pursuit of athletic commitment, character and identity. Talking to these women indicated that, in order to understand more adequately the sports-related pain and injury experiences of female athletes, the roles of both sport socialization *and* gender socialization must be taken into account. Parallels between the ways in which male and female athletes understand, respond to and manage their bodies when they are injured and in pain provide evidence of the influence of a sport culture within which athletes learn that they must 'have the right attitude' if they wish to remain part of a competitive sport setting. This attitude requires normalizing risk, living with pain and tolerating and rationalizing injury. However, some important differences, identified in this chapter, suggest that orientations towards, and sense-making strategies about, injury and pain are also partly a result of gender socialization. Data gathered from female athletes in both Canada and England illustrate that health and illness experiences may be deeply gendered and shaped by broader hegemonic power relations which include gender stereotypes and ideologies. These processes impact upon sport injuries in a series of ways, as we found with respect to notions of precisely how men and women athletes feel that they should or should not 'accept', 'display' and understand injury.

Sociological research on pain and injury in sport is clearly still in its infancy (Young 2004b). While the earliest phases of this work have focused almost entirely upon relationships between the social construction of masculine identities and male experiences, our work shows how dominant ideologies about acceptable uses of the female body can also impact on how girls and women experience sports-related pain and injury. Women's orientations towards sport, injury and pain can, without a doubt, be moulded by potentially discriminatory reactions of social observers towards female athleticism, which might include the notion that physically blemished (that is, injured, disfigured or hurt) female bodies equate with spoiled identities.

Our research suggests that there is no compelling singular or uniform explanation with regard to the sports-related pain and injury experiences of women *or* men. Rather, these experiences are marked by ambiguity, complexity and contradiction and are a product of an interweaving of both gender and sport socialization processes. Certainly, more research on female athletes is necessary before we can claim with confidence to understand the place of pain and injury in women's lives. Where the present chapter is concerned, due to the size and nature of our English and Canadian samples, claims as to the generalizability or representativeness of our findings need to be made cautiously, and early data gathered from female athletes need to be bolstered by further inquiries with girls and women in a range of sport contexts. For instance, while we found a number of common strategies that women adopted to interpret the meanings of pain, more work on possible variance in these sense-making techniques is needed, especially with and between the many and varied sports that women play. Similarly, more developed investigation into the apparent contradictions of pain and injury experiences for female athletes (such as the willingness to both 'hide' and 'share' pain stories) would be helpful. Nor was it our intention to suggest that coaches are unilaterally hostile to sport injury. Though our respondents had critical evidence to report in this respect, such a position hardly seems fair or realistic, and other studies may find coaches to be far more sympathetic to and tolerant of their 'damaged' athletes. These sorts of limitations notwithstanding, we hope that the data presented here on the experiential accounts of Canadian and English female athletes make a modest contribution to the sociological literature on injury and pain in sport, on which future researchers may be able to build.

Bibliography

Adams, S., Marlene, A. and Bayless, M. A. (eds) (1987) *Catastrophic Injuries in Sport*, Indianapolis: Benchmark Press.

Anderson, J. M. and Blue, C. (1991) 'Women's Perspectives on Chronic Illness', *Social Science and Medicine*, 33, 2: 101–13.

Charlesworth, H. (2004) 'Sports-Related Injury, Risk and Pain: The Experiences of English Female University Athletes', unpublished doctoral dissertation, Loughborough University, UK.

Coakley, J. and Donnelly, P. (2004) *Sports in Society: Issues and Controversies*, Toronto: McGraw-Hill Ryerson.

Curry, R. and Strauss, T. (1994) 'A Little Pain Never Hurt Anyone: A Photo-essay on the Normalisation of Sport Injuries', *Sociology of Sport Journal*, 11, 2: 195–208.

Frank, A. W. (1991) 'For a Sociology of the Body: An Analytical Review' in M. Featherstone and B. Turner (eds) *The Body: Social Process and Cultural Theory*, London: Sage: 36–102.

Friis-Thing, L. (2004) 'Scars on the Body: The Risk Management and Self-Care of Injured Female Handball Players in Denmark' in K. Young (ed.), *Sporting Bodies, Damaged Selves: Sociological Studies of Sports-related Injury*, Oxford: Elsevier Press: 195–210.

Goffman, E. (1968) *Stigma: Notes on the Management of Spoiled Identity*, Harmondsworth: Penguin.

Goldsmit, E. M. (1994). 'All in Her Mind! Stereotypic Views and the Psychologisation of Women's Illness' in S. Wilkinson and C. Kitzinger (eds) *Women and Health: Feminist Perspectives*, London: Taylor & Francis: 7–13.

Graham, H. (1984) *Women, Health and the Family*, Brighton: Harvester Press.

Halbert, C. (1997) 'Tough Enough and Woman Enough: Stereotypes, Discrimination and Impression Management among Women Professional Boxers', *Journal of Sport and Social Issues*, 21, 1: 7–37.

Harries, M., Williams, C., Stanish, W. D. and Micheli, L. J. (eds) (1998) *Oxford Textbook of Sports Medicine*, Oxford: Oxford University Press.

Harris, D. V. (1980) 'Femininity and Athleticism: Conflict or Consonance' in D. F. Sabo and R. Runfola (eds) *Jock: Sports and Male Identity*, Englewood Cliffs, NJ: Prentice Hall: 222–39.

Kotarba, J.A. (2004) 'Professional Athletes' Injuries: From Existential to Organizational Analyses' in K. Young (ed.), *Sporting Bodies, Damaged Selves: Sociological Studies of Sports-related Injury*, Oxford: Elsevier Press: 99–116.

Lupton, D. (1995) *The Imperative of Health: Public Health and the Regulated Body*. London: Sage.

Messner, M. and Sabo, D. (1990) *Sport, Men and the Gender Order: Critical Feminist Perspectives*, Urbana-Champaign, IL: Human Kinetics.

Nixon, H. (1992) 'A Social Network Analysis of Influences on Athletes to Play with Pain and Injury', *Journal of Sport and Social Issues*, 16, 2: 127–35.

Nixon, H. (1993a) 'Accepting the Risks of Pain and Injury in Sports: Mediated Cultural Influences on Playing Hurt', *Sociology of Sport Journal*, 10, 2: 183–96.

Nixon, H. (1993b) 'Social Network Analysis of Sport: Emphasising Structure in Sport Sociology', *Sociology of Sport Journal*, 10, 3: 315–21.

Nixon, H. (1994) 'Coaches' Views of Risk, Pain and Injury in Sport, with Special Reference to Gender Differences', *Sociology of Sport Journal*, 11, 2: 79–87.

Nixon, H. (1996) 'The Relationship of Friendship Networks, Sport Experiences and Gender to Expressed Pain Thresholds', *Sociology of Sport Journal*, 13, 1: 78–86.

Nixon, H. (2004) 'Cultural, Structural and Status Dimensions of Pain and Injury Experiences in Sport' in K. Young (ed.) *Sporting Bodies, Damaged Selves: Sociological Studies of Sports-related Injury*, Oxford: Elsevier Press: 81–98.

Pike, E. C. J. (2000) 'Illness, Injury and Sporting Identity: A Case Study of Women's Rowing', unpublished doctoral thesis, Loughborough University, UK.

Pike, E. C. J. (2004) 'Risk, Pain and Injury: "A Natural Thing in Rowing"?' in K. Young (ed.), *Sporting Bodies, Damaged Selves: Sociological Studies of Sports-related Injury*, Oxford: Elsevier Press: 151–62.

Roderick, M. (2004) 'English Professional Soccer Players and the Uncertainties of Injury' in K. Young (ed.), *Sporting Bodies, Damaged Selves: Sociological Studies of Sports-related Injury*, Oxford: Elsevier Press: 137–50.

Roderick, M., Waddington, I., and Parker, G. (2000) 'Playing Hurt: Managing Injuries in Professional Football', *International Review for the Sociology of Sport*, 35, 2: 165–80.

Sports Council (1991) *Injuries in Sport and Exercise*, London: The Sports Council.

Theberge, N. (1997) '"Its Part of the Game": Physicality and the Production of Gender in Women's Hockey', *Gender and Society*, 11, 1: 69–87.

White, P. and Young, K. (1999) *Sport and Gender in Canada*, Don Mills, ON: Oxford University Press.

Young, K. (1993) 'Violence, Risk and Liability in Male Sports Culture', *Sociology of Sport Journal*, 10, 4: 373–96.

Young, K. (1997) 'Women, Sport and Physicality: Preliminary Findings from a Canadian Study', *International Review for the Sociology of Sport*, 32, 3: 297–305.

Young, K. (ed.) (2004a) *Sporting Bodies, Damaged Selves: Sociological Studies of Sports-related Injury*, Oxford: Elsevier Press.

Young, K. (2004b) 'Sports-related pain and injury: Sociological notes' in K. Young (ed.) *Sporting Bodies, Damaged Selves: Sociological Studies of Sports-related Injury*, Oxford: Elsevier Press: 1–28.

Young, K. and White, P. (1995) 'Sport, Physical Danger and Injury: The Experiences of Elite Women Athletes', *Journal of Sport and Social Issues*, 19 (1): 45–61.

Young, K., White, P. and McTeer, W. (1994) 'Body Talk: Male Athletes Reflect on Sport, Injury and Pain', *Sociology of Sport Journal*, 11, 2: 175–94.

Section III

The deliberate infliction of pain and injury

7 Sport and the systematic infliction of pain

A case study of state-sponsored mandatory doping in East Germany

Giselher Spitzer

Since the fall of the Communist regime in the German Democratic Republic (GDR), a great deal of material has become available which sheds light on the practice of systematic state-sponsored doping in that country. The analysis of archival material and interviews with former athletes has revealed the centrality of doping in sport and the harmful medical side effects of doping (Spitzer 1994a, 1994b, 1994c, 2001c). These data reveal that up to 10,000 male and female athletes were doped, often without their knowledge or consent, while 2 million doses of anabolic steroids were used annually in the preparation of Olympic sports in the GDR.

The use of performance-enhancing drugs not only improved strength and endurance but also had another important effect: it reduced recovery time and thereby made it possible for athletes to train harder, and for longer, than at any time before. The upper limit of time spent on training was increased from about 1,500 to 1,800 hours a year, making it possible for athletes to train for five 45-minute sessions every day, including weekends and holidays.

The Communist Party – or The Socialist Union Party, or SED, to give it its proper name – and the organs of state security integrated doping into the training plans of athletes while techniques of doping were developed in applied sport science. (For an analysis of GDR science as a system and its links with doping and the secret service in East Germany, see Spitzer 1997.) The goal of sport for all was officially declared to be government policy (Spitzer *et al.* 1998), but this policy was in effect underdeveloped while the government devoted huge resources to the use of drugs in developing elite-level sport for political purposes.

Elite sport and doping in the GDR: Some organizational aspects of the background

The main elements of the GDR doping system can be described as follows. From the early 1950s a structure of politically dominated professional sport developed. Within this structure, in return for their unquestioning commitment to the sporting goals of the regime, athletes were offered lifelong employment. This was the nature of the 'social contract' into which athletes were expected to enter. After the 1970s, a system was developed which ensured a flow of athletic 'new blood', through the selection of the top 3 per cent of young athletes. From an analysis of the entire East German youth population, approximately 60,000 children were selected for *enforced* – not voluntary – entry into the 1,800 'training centres'. From those who were admitted to these training centres, almost 10,000 athletes were selected for promotion to the second level. From this selection system, some 2,000 top athletes emerged as, in effect, full-time professional sportspeople, many of whom were to suffer bodily damage as a result of doping.

In reality elite athletes in the GDR were exceptionally well-paid civil servants, soldiers, policemen or officers of the secret state security with a guaranteed career but also, as the other part of the 'social contract', with the obligation not to convey to others information about their day-to-day lives as athletes, including the systematic doping of athletes. Sport was organized on military lines: athletes were expected to follow 'orders' from all those above them in the hierarchy. Athletes were forbidden to have any contact with any persons or organizations not affiliated with the government and, as such, were subject to very rigorous social control. The integration of sport within the political and security system can be illustrated by the fact that the Secret Service, the 'Stasi', needed volunteers or 'unofficial supporters' of the state security system and between 11 and 15 per cent of those involved in sport (coaches, athletes and so on) acted as state security volunteers, with the Socialist Unity Party being the dominant influence in the organization of sport.

There was a massive investment in elite-level sport. More than 4,700 professional trainers were employed in high-level sport, and nearly 1,000 medical doctors and 5,000 administrators were employed in sport – and all this in a country with a total population of just 17 million. All these people were legally employed within sport; in addition, almost 1,500 individuals were active in research or the illegal application of doping substances and techniques (for research on the Stasi volunteers and blood doping, see Spitzer 2002a, 2002b).

This massive investment was made in sport because the Communist Party aimed to beat the West in all things, including sport. The leaders of the GDR set a target of achieving the number three ranking in world sport for East Germany, while the secret internal plans for 1984 and 1988 (now available to scholars, following the collapse of the East German regime) indicate that they later came to see the number one ranking in the world as a realistic target.

Special aspects of GDR doping as a system

The organization of doping in the GDR was highly systematic – about 10,000 athletes were victims of what may be described as *industrial doping*. There were some aspects of the doping system in East Germany which made it quite different from the use of particular performance-enhancing drugs by athletes in most other societies (Spitzer, 2001b, 2001c). In particular: as a rule athletes were exposed to mandatory (or compulsory) doping without their active cooperation; only a few athletes knew about the practice of doping. In addition, *every* selected athlete was doped – it was impossible to refuse.

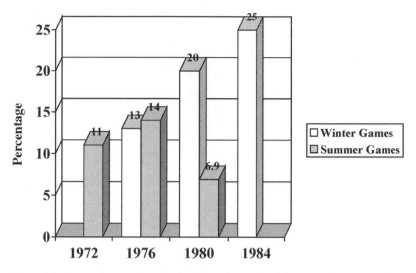

Figure 7.1 Active Stasi-volunteers in Olympic teams of the GDR (in per cent) at Winter Games and Summer Games

Source: Spitzer 2004c

Compulsory (or mandatory) doping was financed by the state, without *de facto* legal restrictions. The sport associations' central doping guidelines even regulated the dosage for every athlete. The supply of drugs was guaranteed by the state-run Secret Service and the military as well as the Communist Party. Doping was a highly secret, closed system of abuse of children, young people and adults, who were not provided with any real information about what was happening to them (Spitzer 2004a: 416). The President of the East German Sports Federation (DTSB), Manfred Ewald, supervised the work of Dr Manfred Hoeppner of the Sports Medical Service (SMD) and Professor Dr Alfons Lehnert of the secret Research Institute of Leipzig (FKS). These people were responsible for determining the doping guidelines for a four-year period and approving the application of doping policy for the various Sports Federations in the East German Sports Federation on an annual basis for all sports clubs. The acquisition and financing of doping substances took place through the State Secretary's office, the state-run Sports Medical Service and the Elite Sport Commission of the GDR (*Leistungssportkommission der DDR*, LSK). Those responsible for organizing sport in the Army (*Armeesportvereinigung Vorwaerts*, ASV) and the Security Services (*Sportvereinigung Dynamo*, SVD) were able, through their own pharmacy distribution, to obtain additional doping substances without approval from the Federation (DTSB) or the Sports Medical Service.

Dr Hoeppner of the Sports Medical Service and his co-workers in Berlin directed couriers to transport doping substances and the list of athletes to whom the drugs were to be administered, with applicable dosages, to the sports federations. Occasionally the appropriate federation medical doctor (*Verband-sarzt*) collected the doping substances personally, to distribute them according to the central directive. As a general rule athletes were required to take the 'supporting substances', as the drugs were called, in the presence of the trainer. Injections were administered by the federation's divisional doctor. Athletes received no explanation regarding the purpose, risks or side effects of the drugs used. Occasionally, if this was unavoidable, athletes were told either the truth or a partial truth, though when this happened, they were required to sign a 'confidentiality' paper.

Drugs were frequently administered to young people, even children; in gymnastics, weight lifting and swimming, drug use often began in childhood, from 10 years up. The result was, in many cases, long-term drug abuse. An assumption of this system was that athletic achievement was of higher value than the athletes' actual or future state of health. Inevitably this policy involved the systematic infliction of long-term suffering and pain on athletes. After the end of an athlete's career the health data in relation to that athlete were falsified – the victims were given no information about damage to their health and future health risks. In some cases those responsible for the doping programme were not able to provide reliable data, for some applications involved experimental substances the side effects, particularly long-term side effects, of which were often not known.

There were, however, some exceptions to this pattern of doping. In football, within the national leagues, doping was forbidden, because of the need to guarantee equality of chances *within* the GDR league. However, national football teams were required to use drugs in order to compete successfully against other nations (Spitzer 2004b). It is not surprising that knowledge about doping in soccer at the national team level filtered down to the club level, where doping was organized and financed, not as part of the state system, but by the club itself. However once again, the victims – the players – were often given no information about the drugs being administered to them, or the possible side effects.

Side effects of doping within the GDR system

An official doping manual indicates that many side effects of doping were well known, but kept secret. Generally doping had, particularly on women, negative side effects on health status (Manual of FKS 1982 in Spitzer 2004c). Although the harmful side effects were known, this did not lead to the cessation of doping. Typical side effects noted in the Manual from 1982 include the following: for men, inhibition of production of sperm as well as *gynaecomastia* (enlargement of the male breast to female profile; for that reason the anti-cancer medicine Tamoxifen was also administered to male athletes) and, for women, 'cycle-anomalies and virilisation when high dosages were used for long periods; these effects are partly irreversible'. These are taken from the written text in the original source (Spitzer, in preparation). Similar data are presented in the official study of the effects of anabolic steroid use on athletes in the long jump and high jump (data provided by W. W. Franke, Heidelberg). Side effects were recorded on the skin, and on organs such as the liver (higher serum-transaminase or cholestase) and the heart, as well as problems such as high blood pressure, and fluid retention in body cells and connective tissue. There is also evidence of psychological damage. Specific side effects on female athletes include the growth of facial and bodily hair, abasement of the sexual hormones and increasing virilization, reduction of the breasts and lowering of the voice. Problems with menstruation and hypertrophy of the clitoris may be followed by polycystic ovary-syndrome. Side effects among male athletes include testicle atrophy, enlargement of the prostate and *gynaecomastia*. There is also evidence that some of these dangerous side effects were passed on to the next generation, for children born to athletes who used drugs appear to have higher risks of developing skin allergies and asthma.

The above list of side effects was associated with anabolic steroid use. However, other, experimental drugs were also used, the side effects of which were not known. Athletes did discuss secretly among themselves some of the side effects which they experienced and, in particular, the possible effects on any children they might have. Psychological and behavioural disturbances were also noted by the victims: an increase of aggression, libido change, strong mood alterations (for example, mood swings between euphoria and depression) and mental disorder. The enlargement of the male breast caused mental problems for men and, for women, virilization and hirsutism (growth of beard and hair on the body) caused many more problems. Pain, injury and fear about what was happening to their bodies were a part of the sporting life of high-level athletes, as a consequence of the enforced use of performance-enhancing drugs.

Pain in GDR sports: Case studies

In this section we will have a glimpse into what was a *terra incognita*, because drug-related pain was not a topic for official investigation in high-level sports in East Germany. In the following case studies, I want to address two key questions:

1 Was there an intention to (ab-)use pain (e.g. to structure and direct training) or was the existence of pain and injury something which was an undesirable, though not a planned, result of participation in sport?
2 What was the function of pain in East German elite sport, within and beyond the use of doping?

The case studies that follow are based on interview data; the interview data from athletes were then checked against information provided by other athletes and also against other data sources such as photographic evidence and medical data.

Case study 1: Pain as a means of producing absolute discipline

The athlete in this case is a female shot-putter, with a weight of about 95 kg and height of 1.72 metres. The treatment of this athlete was described by another athlete who was present and who described what happened.

> It must have been the spring of 1975, when a sportswoman in our *Trainingsgruppe* (a small group of cadre athletes, competing against each other in the GDR Elite Sport System) did not unconditionally follow our trainer's instructions during the training session. Because of that, our trainer made her do additional training immediately after the regular training session. She had to run another 4000 metres. The reason was, in the coach's words, that she obviously still had some 'reserves' left. She needed even more endurance training, said the coach. Remember: the training partner weighed 95 kg weight and was only 172 cm tall!
>
> For shot putters of both sexes there is hardly any harder training than endurance running, because of the high body-weight of the athletes. After this sportswoman had run 2800 metres, she vomited . . . she also interrupted the run against the coach's orders, lay down by the outside of the lane, vomited again and wept, because she was in so much pain from the running and also because she was very ashamed and upset that she vomited in front of the members of the camp. Maybe 100 of the 300 world class athletes of the club were on the ground at that moment.
>
> She wanted to leave the stadium because of the pain and to go into the washroom, to wash herself. However the coach prohibited that, saying that she would have to run three more laps on the track. After that she might take a break. Because of fear of further penalties in the form of being made to do more sprints in future training sessions, she ran with tears and pain the remaining required 1,200 metres.
>
> That day had consequences. We had trained on the same stadium, and had to look on that scene. So the consequence for us was that we were so frightened that we planned, because of that horror, to obey our trainer in future even more unconditionally. The reason for that was to avoid penalties. It was because of fear of the penalties by our coach.

In the above example, the sportswoman describing the situation did not demonstrate her opposition to what the coach was doing and thereby risk losing her job as a well-paid athlete. Solidarity between athletes was rarely seen: year-long selection and socialization into the professional East German sports system made the option of opposition to the infliction of pain in training impossible. The shot putter in the above incident was also a victim of doping and still has the side effects today; the virilizing side effects of anabolic steroids finally become so obvious that eventually she was no longer allowed to take part in public sport-events.

Case study 2: Ignoring athletes' pain

Coaches and doctors may ignore the athletes' pain as a way of imposing discipline, but this may also have results that are the opposite of those intended, as the following case study shows:

> In January of 1976 we visited the winter-training camp, in which we had to practise first downhill-ski. So we had only downhill boots, and when we had to do cross-country ski training after that with these hard boots, we all got problems.
>
> The reason for downhill skiing was that the coaches wanted us as athletes to fight against the fear of mountains to develop a better morale, and of course we had to do endurance training in winter also. After a few days almost all of us were bleeding . . . from different parts of the feet.
>
> The chief coach had planned for the next day as part of the training programme a journey to Oberwiesenthal, a big winter-ski resort [in Thuringia]. We started with luge-training, but we had to sleigh with the hard ski-boots which had hurt before. The pain in our feet caused by the ski-boots was hard to bear. So we asked our trainer if, instead of the luge-training, endurance-training using running-shoes would be accepted, because we would have less pain. We wanted to avoid the hard and heavy ski boots. The coach did not accept this change of his training programme – the aching feet of our shot put group were no problem for him.
>
> The next morning the bus for the journey . . . arrived. Our coach gave an order that we should practise the luge-training as ordered, but in running-shoes. The dangers associated with training for the luge with only light running-shoes on the ice were ignored. However because of the threat of penalties, none of us dared to remind him of the high risk of injury of wearing sport shoes in the downhill luge.
>
> On that day we were all afraid of driving downhill in these dangerous shoes, but our chief trainer demanded to start the race. If we did not do as instructed, it would be a case of 'non-obedience' [like acting against military orders: G. Spitzer]. The consequence would be to get pushed out of the sport club and the school as well as the international college. We would have to pack our things and go home.
>
> But none of us wanted to risk the end of our career. Some of us had been Champions at the last East German Junior competitions, the *Spartakiade* [in 1975; G. Sp.]. So we got on the sleigh, another sportswoman seated in front.
>
> Our chief trainer took a rope and tied his sleigh behind ours. The hill was very uneven, so we hit the ground. Because the two sleighs were connected by the rope, the chief trainer's sleigh went over my right ankle.
>
> At once I had a very strong pain, the ankle swelled up very quickly and turned blue. There were only a few metres to go to the ground station of the hill, which had a rescue-station. However the head coach answered my question, as to whether I should visit a doctor, by saying 'Don't be so

snivelling – everything is O.K. with you'. Although my foot was very painful and continued to swell, I had to walk two more hours with the other members of the group.

Back in our hotel, our female club-doctor saw me, not a doctor from the public medical service of the city. She declared that it was only a little sprain which needed no special treatment. The pain became more and more unbearable, so throughout the night the other sportswomen tried to help me with compresses.

My condition worsened during the night, and the doctor allowed me to have an x-ray in the local hospital. It showed a bone had splintered in the ankle, as well as a torn ligament. They advised me to have an operation immediately in the hospital there. The operation in the local hospital was not accepted by our coach and the sports doctor. They wanted the operation to be done in Berlin-Pankow by Professor Kurt Franke. So I had to wait a whole week to be treated at Berlin.

Three operations and 20 months later my sporting career ended, because the doctor could give me no hope that the broken ankle would ever work properly again or be pain-free. He was right, I regret. It was the end of my dream.

The central character in this case study was an elite female athlete who was also the person who observed and described the events in the first case study above. This former high-performance sportswoman now says: 'Nobody should forget that pain, especially in sport, is an alarm-signal of the body, which should not be ignored.' She had herself been given anabolic steroids as a young girl, without her knowledge, by the coach, who was also a woman but one with little concern for the health of her athlete. Pain was a normal part of the working day in training. The accident and the associated pain were alarm-signals which were disregarded by those in charge of the East German system.

Case study 3: Pain and enforced competition

The next case is based on a letter from a leading gymnast seeking help. It was sent to the Socialist Unity Party in the 1980s, and personally directed to the person with responsibility for Sport in the Central Committee, Egon Krenz. The author was an elite female gymnast; her request for help was ignored. Her letter says nothing about doping, because the use of performance-enhancing drugs in female gymnastics was not revealed until the collapse of the GDR. In her letter to one of the most powerful leaders of the GDR, this young woman sets out her pain and suffering within sport. The letter writer was a leading gymnast for 12 years. She was many times GDR Champion and won medals at the Olympics and European Championships. She wrote in a very open manner to the leading Communist Secretary for Sports (the letter is in *Die Bundesbeauftragte für die Unterlagen des Staatssicherheitsdienstes der ehemaligen Deutschen Demokratischen Republik*):

I have devoted my . . . life entirely to the sport; I . . . left my parental home eight years ago. All I have done I have done with pleasure, and always with a firm will, to represent our state as a worthy athlete . . . I had to stop competing for almost one and a half years because of an injury to my back. During that time I lay in a plaster-bed [bed with gypsum for injured back]. Then, however, unfortunately an old injury to both ankles stopped me from taking part at the World Championships again. Since then I have done gymnastics constantly with a lot of pain, both my feet had to be strapped constantly, but I fulfilled my job as a successful participant at the Olympic Games.

The wear and attrition to the tissue in my feet necessitated operations on [my feet]. My personal experiences about the *Antrainieren* [the quick return to training in high-level sports after a break caused by an injury; G. Spitzer] reminded me that . . . after these surgical operations . . . it is not possible for me to take part in the World Championships. The continuous backaches have accompanied the problems with the legs and made it impossible to train effectively to come back to medal ranking. A third problem is that the breaks in training have led to weight problems . . .

(Following this she wrote about problems with weight and weight control and associated problems. She discusses the role of her parents who were excluded from the training process in order to stop their influence, and shows how the coaches and the club cheated – they promised that she could end her career with honour after the next international championship or Olympics, but then did not allow her to retire.)

Therefore I want to leave elite sports now, with honour, because I did everything and had great results. I personally have wept enough tears through all that pain in all the years . . . Writing this letter is based on the fact that you met us, the Olympic Winners, at Berlin after the Games and you spoke cordial words to me.

This young woman asked for help. However, she was not allowed to end her career for health reasons. After 12 years of training with increasing and extreme pain, she expressed a desire to retire with honour, but those who controlled the sport system ignored her pain and denied her request. It is important to add that retiring from sport without the permission of those who ran the sport system would have caused major difficulties for the athlete: she would have had no access to a specialist medical service, no sports or training possibilities, no fees or money, no chance to sit exams at high school and no possibility of studying in the GDR. So she asked for permission from the Party in a final attempt to end the pain without losing her existence as a normal citizen. In reply, the letter from Egon Krenz did not answer her question. It simply said that she is a fine athlete and that Krenz hopes she will have good results (a copy of this letter is in the possession of the author). The athlete received no help from anybody in sport. On the contrary, she was given instructions to train for the next competitions: the World Championship and after that the Olympics in 1992. In that desperate situation, it was the opening of the Berlin Wall in November 1989 and the collapse of the GDR regime that saved her. This third sportswoman in our case studies fought against what might be called the functionalization of her body and the enforced acceptance of pain in high-level gymnastics. The data in this case study were confirmed because in 2002 the original sports medicine files became available. In addition, secret medical files indicate that she had been given anabolic steroids, beginning in childhood, and without her knowledge. Training when in pain was accepted by coaches and doctors as well as by the politicians at every level. Pain was seen as a condition for success at the international level. The destruction of the bones and connecting tissues as a result of continuing to train and compete when in pain, as well as the destruction of internal organs by steroids, were recognized as major health problems, but these were kept secret as a means of reaching the goal of international sporting success.

Case study 4: Pain, drop out and defection from East Germany

The captain of the East German gymnastics team in the years between the Mexico and Munich Olympics was told by his coaches to take steroids, though he was not given information about their side effects. He was simply told they would help in training. However, major health problems followed. His muscles developed and he became more powerful, but the steroids reduced his ability to concentrate and, as a consequence, he frequently failed in training to catch the horizontal bar or the parallel bars. As a result, he often fell and was injured and required surgery. (We now know that lapses in concentration may be one of the side effects of anabolic steroids.)

To improve his concentration, the gymnast was given another medication, to be taken shortly before training. This improved his concentration and coordination on the bars, but led to aching in the muscles and joints, tiredness and severe headaches. (It now appears that the gymnast was given Oxytocin, which improves concentration, but is associated with exhaustion and fatigue as side effects.)

The gymnast also required surgery to his foot, legs and shoulders, but the surgery was cancelled in order not to jeopardize his participation in the next world championships. The gymnast was also a member of the army-sport *Vorwaerts* and therefore had the legal status of a soldier. On one occasion, he stopped practising because he was in pain and was afraid of falling, and left the hall. This was interpreted as the refusal of a serving soldier to obey orders.

Manfred Ewald, the President of the gymnastic and sport federation of East Germany and a Central Committee member of the Socialist Unity Party (SED), immediately visited the gymnast. Ewald demanded that the gymnast and national team captain should act 'like a real man and a tough soldier'. The gymnast was suspected of malingering and of refusing to train because of minor aches. The

President promised that, if the national team captain would resume training and take part in the coming world championships, then he would afterwards be allowed to retire with honour and would be provided with health care. The 'breach of discipline' would also be forgotten. But if he refused, he would leave sports without *Abtrainierung*. This is the term used to refer to the process of 'detraining', that is the process designed to allow athletes to make a controlled transition from the life of an elite athlete to that of a 'normal' citizen, and would usually involve medical supervision to manage the health risks associated with any long-term sports injuries they had suffered and, of course, the management of the process of coming off drugs and managing the side effects of drugs. This is a highly complex process lasting one or two years, and to end one's career without guided 'detraining' would have meant continued pain and threats to one's health. As a consequence, athletes would not wish to retire without 'detraining'.

For these reasons, the gymnast in this case study returned to training and competition in the short term, but secretly he decided to defect from East Germany and used the occasion of the next world championships to escape from the country. As a result, the East German state and its sport system lost one of its best competitors because he was no longer prepared to suffer the pains associated with enforced training and competition. (This case study is based on five interviews with the former gymnast at Leverkusen, 1998–2000, and on Stasi files which recorded his escape. Defection from East Germany was, of course, a crime and those who were caught trying to defect were liable to imprisonment, so the gymnast was running a considerable risk in defecting.)

These case studies reveal what might be described as the 'dark side' of East German elite sport. The inhumane aspects of the system can be seen clearly. But let us return to a question raised earlier: What was the function of pain in the East German elite sport system, within and beyond doping?

The abuse of pain as a means of maintaining discipline [*Disziplinierungsmittel*]

East German elite sport was based on a military-like structure. Approximately 20 per cent of all elite athletes were actually in the army, or were soldiers of the ministry for state security, or police officers. The other 80 per cent belonged to 'civil' sport clubs, but even here the system was not based on free choice, but on the military concept of 'delegation', which involved assigning soldiers to another service or command; in sport it involved assigning people to a new employment as, in effect, professional athletes. Elite sports people were required to support the regime and, in return, were provided with relatively high incomes and other privileges such as foreign travel and cars.

Under the cloak of coaching, pain was inflicted as a punishment for disobeying instructions and as a means of instilling and maintaining discipline; the similarities to military culture were clear. In the everyday life of sport clubs, the athletes themselves became brutalized and, on occasions, even used aggression, including collective beatings, against other, 'dissident', athletes. Such situations indicate the effectiveness of this system of instilling obedience and discipline in athletes.

Hart sein: Being tough and ignoring pain

Interviews and contemporary written sources show that being 'hard' or 'tough' with athletes was seen as a precondition of high performance. Being 'soft', in contrast, was seen as feebleness. Athletes were required to be hard with their own bodies, disregarding their pain in order to fulfil the extreme coaching plans. However, if coaches ignored the pain of the athletes, this could lead to athletes dropping out of sport. By ignoring pain, injury and illness, coaches could precipitate the end of an athlete's career, so this form of oppressive coaching could be counter-productive.

Drugs and pain as aspects of coaching

The use of anabolic steroids brought a new dimension to the relationship between athletes and coaches in the GDR. Coaches had to learn how their individual athletes reacted to the new doping substances and when and how the individual limits of performance by their athletes were to be reached. In this new process, pain was given a fascinating new function as an aspect of control within the training regime. The use of anabolic steroids dramatically increased the endurance and strength of athletes and reduced the recovery period after intense training. Many athletes were fascinated by these new possibilities of their bodies. But on the other hand there was also a multiplicity of negative changes which they experienced in their everyday lives: muscle cramps, difficulty in relaxing, strong mood changes, manic phases or difficulties in concentration. However, coaches and medical doctors were able to shelter behind the fact that information on these side effects of drugs was not made public and not revealed to the athletes. Thus the athletes did not know the real reasons for either their enhanced performance or the associated pain which they experienced. What they did know was that the more intensive training of which they were now capable was associated both with significantly improved performance and with an increase in pain which was part of their training: such was the life of the elite athlete.

There were two other influences on the coaches and medical doctors in elite sports. First, coaches transformed their own athletic biographical experiences, which for many consisted of the experience of pain as a permanent aspect of the status of the elite athlete, and developed this philosophy in an extreme way.

A second aspect concerned the role of the centralized sport system in setting targets for athletes. The training figures from the science centres indicated that a given level of performance should guarantee a specific haul of medals at championships (and also the income and continued appointment of the coach or doctor of the sport club). However, this centralized sport system in East

Germany had failed to take into account the individuality, the distinctive features, of each individual athlete.

We can find many sources indicating the presence of permanent conflict between central 'scientific' plans and the everyday practical work carried out by coaches with performers on the track. To coaches and doctors, watching the efforts and reactions of athletes in relation to pain was a better measure of athletes' performance than abstract computer-generated plans from East Berlin or Leipzig.

Moreover, the coaches had no trust in general plans because they knew their genesis. The highly complex, secret training plans came from the 'scientific centres' of the national federations and the even more highly secret plans from the doping researchers at Leipzig. But the plans were founded on incorrect premises. The perfect *Norm-Erfüllung* (fulfilling the central orders from Berlin for each individual athlete) was practically impossible. In gymnastics in the 1980s the real performances as compared to the plans were about 40 per cent lower, in soccer 30 per cent and in track and field about 20 per cent.

Because they lacked reliable data, trainers tended to use extreme measures of both training and drugs. This was a crucial element of the success of the East German sport system.

Pain and the role of 'detraining' in the social control of athletes

The continuous abuse of pain as a means of maintaining discipline in training was an aspect of the East German system. But what happened if an athlete was sufficiently mentally strong to resist such pressure? Here the ultimate threat was to terminate the athlete's career without 'detraining', the process designed to manage (relatively) safely the transition from a peak of physical strength and fitness, based on the use of drugs, to a more 'normal' life, and to manage any associated health problems. 'Detraining' was therefore very important for the health of the athletes leaving the cadres of the national teams. But such help was denied to those who were dismissed for political reasons or because they refused to obey instructions.

The consequences of withdrawal without 'detraining' were numerous and could result in continued pain and illness. The athlete would be denied the use of sport facilities after retirement. He or she might have to cope with heart and circulatory problems, associated with drug use, without specialist help from others. The withdrawal of the drugs might also be associated with pain as athletes became dependent on the drugs to help them manage the pain of training and competing.

This threat of withdrawing 'detraining' was frequently used to maintain discipline or to compel an athlete to continue competing when he or she wished to retire. In this situation, athletes were likely to choose the lesser evil of continuing the high-level training and competition as a form of self-protection. By making that decision, the athlete ensured that he or she would continue to have access to medical advice and any specialist care which was required, after retirement. The experiences of those who left without help became part of the culture in the sport clubs and therefore reinforced the process of producing discipline on the training grounds.

Ignoring pain as a means of pushing beyond the limits of endurance

Athletes were expected to ignore pain and risk. This was also true for new forms of training or coaching methods. 'Overloading' in training was practised with extremely high weights and to the complete exhaustion of the athletes. There were experiments with a heavy backpack containing a gas cylinder used in hypoxia training. Subterranean bunkers, where there was no daylight, were used in bonding sessions. These sessions produced fear in athletes.

In many sports the objective was to harden athletes against their own experiences of pain. At the army sport organization *Vorwaerts* ('Onwards') athletes were required to take part in repeated sprints wearing a gasmask, which restricted breathing, and amphetamines were administered to athletes in order to enable them to endure excessive training sessions. Athletes who took part in new forms of 'experimental training' did so formally as volunteers, but in reality athletes who had the legal status of soldiers were expected to take part in experiments with untested substances and/or techniques and unknown side effects. A refusal by the soldier-athlete could lead to exclusion from sport, with the consequences noted above.

Relationships within the sport system

What was the pattern of relationships within this system? It is important to understand the hierarchical patterns within the East German sports system, as well as the patterns of communication.

The athlete

His (or her) performance was the focus of the organization. The individual athlete had little power; his or her main source of personal support was the family, from which the athlete was physically removed while at the sport school.

The doctor

Medical doctors wielded considerable power over athletes. The doctor oversaw the administration of appropriate drugs and determined whether an athlete's aches were 'real' or 'imagined' and whether they were pains associated with peak performance or pains which would hinder peak performance.

Data gathered both from archives and interviews indicate that doctors within the sports system were expected to practise in a 'hard-line' manner. Doctors who were more oriented towards the welfare of athletes were removed from the system and relocated into the general medical service.

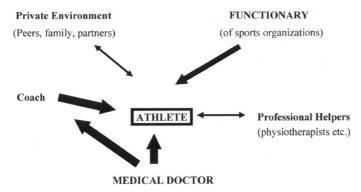

Figure 7.2 Relationships within GDR Sport Clubs: the dominance of the doctor and coach

Note:
↔ = two-channel communication: with equal rights of both parties; → = one-channel communication with direction of hierarchy against individual actors

Source: Following the interpretation (modified) of A. Delow, 'Leistungssport und Ideologie: die Vorbereitung der Olympischen Spiele in einem DDR-Sportclub', *Sozial- und Zeitgeschichte des Sports*, 11 (1997), 2: 62

Analysis of files and interview data covering the last 10 years of the East German system indicates that approximately 10 per cent of the doctors left the sports medical service annually, in most cases for ethical reasons and, in particular, because they did not accept mandatory doping and did not accept the principle of placing athletic performance above the welfare of athletes.

The coach

The trainer had even more power over the athletes than did the doctors. The trainer had daily contact with athletes and observed them closely, and also had absolute authority in the group of elite athletes. As was the case with doctors, trainers who were considered 'soft' were removed from the system.

If excessive dosages of drugs led to serious health dangers, the trainer still retained his or her position. Trainers responsible for giving excessive doses of drugs continued to be supported by the state security service. For example in Berlin, a female trainer (with the support of the doctor, who was also a woman) gave five times more steroids to female shot putters than were given to the men in the same event. The Stasi was aware of this practice but concealed the side effects and the criminal activity involved.

On a day-to-day basis, it was the trainer in the GDR system who was most closely connected with the athletes. On him or her the juniors, and even older athletes, projected their wishes and needs. So, trainers became in some cases substitute parents, or even sexual partners; in some cases (usually male) trainers became the sexual partners or spouses of athletes 20 or 25 years younger than themselves. In such cases, where close partnerships developed, athletes were to some extent protected within this relationship, but more usually athletes suffered at the hands of their coaches the typical mixture of gratification, doping and infliction of pain.

Summary

Sport in East Germany was a highly complex system. It treated both male and female athletes as objects. The pursuit of sporting performance was the objective of sport scientists, physicians and biologists, even if this meant breaching the law and the conventional understanding of medical ethics.

The masculinization of female athletes through the use of drugs was also an aspect of this system. (Berendonk and Franke have referred to this as 'androgenization' and the virilization of women; see Berendonk 1991). Because of these processes, several female athletes admitted having attempted suicide.

This system was also premised on the view that being 'hard' on athletes was a precondition for athletic success, while 'softness' was seen as weakness. This led to a dominance of a masculine pattern of thought and action which was reinforced through the biological effects of using anabolic androgenic steroids.

This system also reflected subjectively and objectively based theories of training. In relation to the latter, athletes who became coaches reproduced with their athletes the experiences they had to go through in their own careers. Objective reasons are to be found in the widespread misconception that only toughness and the overcoming of pain-barriers would lead to maximum performance in the Olympic arena. Pain was therefore to be understood as an indicator of the most effective training. The coach made the decision as to whether the athlete could take no more pain, or whether he or she was just pretending. In summary, one could say that in the East German system, pain was seen as an index of the effectiveness of training.

Seen from this perspective, the body of the athlete was a prison. The body was 'disciplined' as part of a victory-oriented but totalitarian athletic system; within this secret system of sport, there was little transparency and bureaucratic instructions were protected as state secrets.

The case studies in this chapter give a glimpse into pain in East German sport: as a means of producing absolute discipline. But this could also produce opposite, unwanted effects: drop out from sport or escape out of dictatorship. In East Germany, pain, injury and doping were central to the whole system. Causing pain was a method of coaching. Doping generated painful and dangerous side effects. These activities were organized by the state and covered by state security, and athletes were not given accurate information about the health risks to which they were exposed.

To return to the opening question: It is clear that there was an intention to (ab-)use pain to control training programmes. In this regard, pain has to be understood as a component of fundamental significance to the system.

Bibliography

Berendonk, B. (1991) *Dopingdokumente, Von der Forschung zum Betrug*, Berlin Heidelberg: Springer.

Berendonk, B. (1992) *Doping, Von der Forschung zum Betrug*, Reinbek.

Delow, A. (1997) Leistungssport und Ideologie – die Vorbereitung der Olympischen Spiele in einem DDR-Sportclub, *Sozial- und Zeitgeschichte des Sports* 11, 2: 26–56.

Digel, H. and Dickhuth, H.-H. (eds) (2002) *Doping im Sport. Ringvorlesung der Universität Tübingen*, Tübingen: Attempo: 166–91.

Franke, W. W. (1995) 'Funktion und Instrumentalisierung des Sports in der DDR: Pharmakologische Manipulationen (Doping) und die Rolle der Wissenschaft' in Enquete-Kommission (ed.) *Aufarbeitung von Geschichte und Folgen der SED-Diktatur in Deutschland*, Bd. III, 2, Baden-Baden: Nomos: 987–1089.

Hoberman, J. (1994) *Sterbliche Maschinen. Doping und die Unmenschlichkeit des Hochleistungssports*, Aachen, Meyer & Meyer Verlag (Original title *Mortal engines*).

Seppelt, H.-J. and Schück, H. (eds) (1999) *Anklage: Kinderdoping, Das Erbe des DDR-Sports*, Berlin: Transit.

Singler, A. and Treutlein, G. (2000) *Doping im Spitzensport, Sportwissenschaftliche Analysen zur nationalen und internationalen Leistungsentwicklung*, Aachen: Meyer & Meyer Verlag.

Singler, A. and Treutlein, G. (2001) *Doping – Analyse und Prävention*, Aachen: Meyer & Meyer Verlag.

Spitzer, G. (1994a) 'Aktuelle Konzepte zur Zeitgeschichte des Sports unter besonderer Berücksichtigung der aktuellen Diskussion im Bereich der Geschichtswissenschaft', *Sozial- und Zeitgeschichte des Sports*, 8, 3: 56–76.

Spitzer, G. (1994b) 'Eine überflüssige Generation im deutschen Sport? Spitzensportler und Leistungssport unter den Bedingungen der Nachkriegszeit' in G. Spitzer, G. Treutlein and J.M. Delaplace (eds), *Sport und Sportunterricht in Frankreich und Deutschland in zeitgeschichtlicher Perspektive*, Aachen: Meyer & Meyer Verlag: 163–83.

Spitzer, G. (1994c) 'Une génération superflue dans le sport allemand? Sportifs de pointe et sport de compétition dans les circonstances de l'après-guerre' in *Le Sport et L'Education Physique en France et en Allemagne*. Contribution à une approche socio-historique des relations entre les deux pays. Sous la direction de J. M. Delaplace, G. Treutlein et G. Spitzer, Montpellier: 188–212.

Spitzer, G. (1997) 'Die DDR-Leistungssportforschung der achtziger Jahre als Subsystem: Thesen zur interdisziplinären Systemkritik eines historischen Phänomens in differenzierungstheoretischer Perspektive' in N. Gissel, J. Ruehl and H. J. Teichler (eds) *Sport als Wissenschaft*, Hamburg: Czwalina: 151–86.

Spitzer, G. (1999) 'Spätschäden durch Doping bei Sportlern der ehemaligen DDR' in C. Müller-Platz (ed.) *Leistungsmanipulation: eine Gefahr für unsere Sportler. Wissenschaftliche Berichte und Materialien des Bundesinstituts für Sportwissenschaft, Bd. 12.* Cologne: Sport und Buch Strauss: 27–46.

Spitzer, G. (2001a) 'Auswirkungen von Doping bei Frauen. Ethische Grenzen und ihre Missachtung im DDR-Leistungssport', in G. Anders and E. Braun-Laufer (eds), *Grenzen für Mädchen und Frauen im Sport. Wissenschaftliche Berichte und Materialien des Bundesinstituts für Sportwissenschaft, Bd. 6*, Cologne: Sport und Buch Strauss: 83–100.

Spitzer, G. (2001b) 'Doping in the former GDR' in C. Peters, T. Schulz and H. Michna (eds) *Biomedical Side Effects of Doping, Project of the European Union, Bundesinstitut für Sportwissenschaft. Wissenschaftliche Berichte und Materialien, Bd. 13*, Cologne: Sport und Buch Strauss: 115–25.

Spitzer, G. (2001c) 'Doping with Children' in C. Peters, T. Schulz and H. Michna (eds) *Biomedical Side Effects of Doping, Project of the European Union, Bundesinstitut für Sportwissenschaft. Wissenschaftliche Berichte und Materialien*, Bd. 13, Cologne: Sport und Buch Strauss: 127–39.

Spitzer, G. (2001d) 'Remarks to the Hidden System of State-Organized Doping in the German Democratic Republic (G.D.R.)' in J. Buschmann and G. Pfister (eds) *Sport und sozialer Wandel: Proceedings of the ISHPES Congress 1998. Sports and Social Changes. International Society for the History of Physical Education and Sport: ISHPES Studies Vol. 8*, Sankt Augustin: Academia-Verlag: 161–70.

Spitzer, G. (2002a) 'Stasi-Agenten im Olympiatrainer. Der Münchner Terroranschlag von 1972 aus der Sicht des früheren DDR-Ministeriums für Staatssicherheit. Am 5. September jährt sich der Terroranschlag', *Neue Zürcher Zeitung*, 5 September.

Spitzer, G. (2002b) 'Blutdoping als Domäne im Wintersport. Eine Therapie, die in der DDR der Leistungsmanipulation seit 1972 gebräuchlich war', *Neue Zürcher Zeitung*, 16 March.

Spitzer, G. (2004a) 'Doping in der DDR. Ein historischer Überblick zu einer konspirativen Praxis. Genese – Verantwortung – Gefahren. Wissenschaftliche Berichte und Materialien des Bundesinstituts für Sportwissenschaft' (3rd edn), Bd. 3, Cologne: Sport und Buch Strauss.

Spitzer, G. (2004b) *Fussball und Triathlon. Sportentwicklungen in der DDR*, Aachen: Meyer & Meyer Verlag.

Spitzer, G. (2004c) '*Sicherungsvorgang Sport'. Das Ministerium für Staatssicherheit und der DDR-Spitzensport. Projektbericht für den Vorsitzenden des Sportausschusses des Deutschen Bundestages im Rahmen des Forschungsprojektes 'Die Kontrolle von Sport und Sportwissenschaft durch das Ministerium für Staatssicherheit'*, Schorndorf: Hofmann Verlag.

Spitzer, G. (ed.) (2005) *Doping in European Sports* (forthcoming).

Spitzer, G., Teichler, H. J. and Reinartz, K. (eds) (1998) *Schlüsseldokumente zum DDR-Sport, Ein sporthistorischer Überblick in Originalquellen*, Aachen: Meyer & Meyer Verlag.

8   Pain and injury in boxing
The medical profession divided

Ken Sheard

This chapter is underpinned by a number of major premises. The first is that boxing, because it involves people striking each other, is unavoidably physically painful. This pain is taken for granted by all those involved in it: the managers, promoters, trainers and, of course, the boxers themselves. Pain is such an obvious part of boxing that even the most personalized accounts seldom feel the need to draw further attention to it (see for example Wacquant 1995). In this chapter, the focus is not on the taken-for-granted pain of boxing but upon its associated injurious nature. More particularly, the focus is not merely on the nature of injury in boxing, but also on how that injury has been defined and managed over the past hundred years or so. The main source of data in this respect is the debate between medical practitioners which developed in the British medical journals between 1838 and the end of the twentieth century (Sheard 1992, 1998).

The second major premise is that the controversy about the injurious nature of boxing has never just been about the physical injury for which it may be responsible. It has also been about the morality of boxing, the possible social harm or good it may involve and the psychological harm or benefits with which it may be said to be associated.

Third, this chapter is premised on a central point of Elias's theory of civilizing processes, namely that one aspect of social development in the West has involved an increasing sensitivity to pain and to the infliction of pain and injury, and that what is defined as acceptable or unacceptable in both these respects – in sport and in society more generally – is both historically specific and highly variable (Elias 1994). I shall also argue – and related to the latter point – that boxing over the past 100 to 150 years has become less obviously physically damaging and, in many respects, safer for its participants. However, correlatively, as boxing's more obvious brutalities have become more controlled and subject to greater social constraints, the attention of its critics has become increasingly tightly focused upon the more subtle injuries it is claimed to cause and, in particular, upon less obvious forms of brain damage which advances in medical technology have made easier to detect.

In order to understand adequately the changing nature of the debate surrounding the injurious, 'uncivilized' character of boxing, one has to be aware of the changing figuration of social interdependencies within which all those concerned are involved. The main focus will be on the changing responses of members of the medical profession to the injuries, psychological as well as physical, believed to be incurred by boxing, but these responses cannot be fully understood without also taking account of changing power relations within the medical profession and other influential groups in the wider society.

The changing structure of the medical profession

These general propositions about power relations, the changing nature of the medical profession and concern with injury and its nature can be illustrated by a brief examination of the early development of medicine and the relationship between such developments and the lack of interest taken by doctors in the health of prize-fighters. The market for medical care in Britain for much of the period from the Middle Ages until the late nineteenth century was not only extremely small but also highly localized and dominated by the needs of high-status social groups (Waddington 1979, 1984, 1985). Medical knowledge was also relatively limited and readily understood by the clients who consequently, and because of their high status, were able to demand from their physicians the sort of treatment that they themselves thought appropriate (Jewson 1974: 369–85). Unsurprisingly, the medical problems of low-status pugilists were regarded as of little concern to the medical profession. If pugilists received medical attention after their bouts it was at the hands of local 'healers', or of their patron's physician, and involved the healing of cuts and bruises and the application of the rudimentary techniques of the day, including bleeding and the administration of opium. It is entirely possible that these techniques contributed to the health problems of the pugilists, rather than alleviating them (Sheard 1998: 75).

Even the developments in medical knowledge and techniques which occurred later in the nineteenth century, and the changes in the doctor/client relationship partly associated with the developing hospitals and growing market for medical services (Waddington 1984), did little to improve the type of medical treatment available to the low-status, working-class groups from among whom the bulk of prize-fighters were drawn. Given the scale of the epidemics which characterized the nineteenth century, and given the relative lack of knowledge about disease causation, it is again unsurprising that the cuts and bruises suffered by pugilists, the occasional death due to exhaustion or heart failure, and cases of deafness or blindness apparently resulting from the 'sport', should not have been regarded as of pressing concern to the medical profession. Prize-fighters' wounds were seen as self-inflicted and, if significant numbers of them appeared to end their days in asylums or as alcoholic wrecks, this was as likely to be attributed to their own bad habits as to any physical damage caused by their fighting. Moreover, prize-fighting was illegal and, like being present at duels, to be avoided by an increasingly status-conscious medical profession.

The significant point for present purposes is that the medical knowledge, medical techniques and medical ideologies which existed prior to, and during, the nineteenth century did not allow the accurate pin-pointing of the threats to a boxer's health in the way which became possible in the twentieth century (Sheard 1998: 75–6).

The medical journals and boxing

The medical journals, the *Lancet* and the *British Medical Journal* (*BMJ*), may be utilized to show how the debate about boxing, and the pain and injury it occasioned, developed and changed its form throughout the nineteenth and twentieth centuries. From the late eighteenth century, boxing was a subject of some controversy in the local and national press, but it was not until the end of the nineteenth century that the *Lancet* began to pay it any attention. It is significant that the first appearance of boxing as an 'issue' was not focused unambiguously on the medical dangers of the activity. The first mention in the *Lancet* in 1883 was concerned with the 'very discreditable proceedings' at a private club in Manchester where a prize fight took place for 'the delectation of the members'. The fact that one of the participants was hospitalized was mentioned almost as an afterthought (*Lancet*, 30 September 1883: 842). Almost four years were to pass before boxing received another mention. On this occasion, the *Lancet* commented upon a boxing 'accident' in Birmingham. Again, it is significant that the *Lancet* made no *medical* objection to boxing contests on this occasion but was censorious on moral and social grounds alone, suggesting that boxing contests were 'brutal and degrading' and that the law should be used to prohibit them 'in the interests of humanity and social order' (*Lancet*, 14 August 1897: 417).

It was not until the early twentieth century, when professional boxing had, to a certain extent, been controlled and legitimized by being taken under the wing of the National Sporting Club (NSC), that medical journals turned their critical gaze more fully and openly upon the sport. Ironically, the first letter on the subject in the *Lancet* after the turn of the century referred to three deaths which occurred under the jurisdiction of that same NSC (*Lancet*, 11 May 1901: 1366).

Although these cases were admitted to have involved 'inter-cranial haemorrhage' and 'laceration of the brain', there was reluctance among medical professionals to attribute this damage unambiguously to the boxing. One medical professional's explanation of one of these deaths is highly revealing:

> [Turner] was to be married . . . after the contest . . . and . . . supported a widowed mother. What could he have died from but nerve collapse due to over-excitement and anxiety? Yet public opinion put it down . . . to boxing pure and simple – killed by it.
>
> (*Lancet*, 11 May 1901: 1366)

This doctor elaborated upon this hypothesis – or rationalization – in a way curious to modern ears but one taken extremely seriously at the time. He said:

> Can it be that the very strict rule of 'silence during the boxing' at the National Sporting Club has the effect of making a contest a much more intense mental strain . . . conducing . . . towards nerve collapse and apoplexy? In all other clubs spectators are allowed to cheer . . . during the boxing, thereby letting off the steam of excitement for onlookers and competitors.
>
> (*Lancet*, 11 May 1901: 1366)

The medical argument here appears to be that controlling oneself in the way that was becoming increasingly the norm was a health hazard. This doctor was not alone, for Herbert Spencer (Spencer 1897) and others talked of the nervous strain of modern life, and death by apoplexy was frequently used to explain deaths in other sports such as rugby football.

For the first 40 years of the twentieth century the *Lancet* was rather quiet on boxing injuries despite the fact that in 1928 H. S. Martland had drawn attention to the possible link between boxing and brain damage (*Journal of the American Medical Association* 1928, 91: 1103–7). It was Martland who introduced the term 'punch drunk' to describe the tendency for some experienced boxers to become unsteady on their feet and to move and think more slowly. Although Martland described the clinical features of the syndrome he could only conjecture on the underlying cerebral damage. Neither Martland nor anyone else then had direct evidence of the nature of cerebral damage or even of its existence, and it was not until the 1950s that clinico-pathological case reports began to appear (British Medical Association 1984: 6).

In 1941 boxing did come under greater scrutiny in the medical journals. This was because of the publication of *The Medical Aspects of Boxing* by E. Jokl MD (Jokl 1941) who at the time was head of the Department of Physical Education, Witwatersrand Technical College, Johannesburg. Jokl, in a world-wide review of the literature, examined the claimed medical dangers of boxing. His book seems to have been relatively detached, for a *Lancet* review claimed that:

> The critical reader will not find it easy to form an opinion about the facts presented nor will he easily learn from the conclusion . . . what the author's attitude really is.
>
> (*Lancet*, 14 June 1941: 756)

Nevertheless, Jokl's book, and his letters to the *Lancet* from 1942 to 1959, did much to alter medical opinion in Britain regarding the hazards of boxing. However, the *Lancet*'s faintly dismissive reaction to it needs explanation, even allowing for the fact that it appeared in 1941, two years into Britain's participation in the Second World War when fighting qualities were presumably in demand. This reaction was probably connected with Jokl's 'multiple outsider' status (Elias and Scotson 1965), for he was a colonial, employed by a South African technical college, and head of a physical education department. It would appear that the British medical establishment was unwilling to accept the authority of a 'foreign' doctor, and especially that of one involved in what they regarded as the low-status occupation of physical education. Indeed, the British establishment refused for years to recognize the validity and applicability of the American data used by Jokl and others to support their case. They were, perhaps, wise not to do so for conditions in the US were, and still are, very different and the lack of effective controls over boxers and the sport generally in that society made comparisons between the two countries difficult (Sheard 1998: 81).

There was support for Jokl but the *Lancet* remained critical. It was said that his work was not systematic and that none of the cases of abdominal injury he reported, or the heart injuries, were due to boxing (*Lancet*, 14 June 1941: 759). The 36 cases of inter-cranial haemorrhage admittedly deserved more serious consideration but the *Lancet* added that given that 'this report covers the . . . world literature, and that fatal cases hardly ever escape public attention, this number is . . . not large, as sports accidents go' (*Lancet*, 14 June 1941: 759). The specific problem of 'punch drunkenness' – the term's first appearance in the *Lancet* – was said to be more complicated than Jokl allowed. The author of this review concluded that 'some like or dislike pugilism for moral and aesthetic reasons; these are not a medical concern' (*Lancet*, 14 June 1941: 759). However, ironically, it was these moral and aesthetic considerations that formed a major part of the debate in the years which followed the publication of Jokl's book. In fact until 1969, when the highly influential Report of the Royal College of Physicians on the *Medical Aspects of Boxing* (the Roberts Report) was published, every conceivable medical, social, moral, legal and aesthetic condemnation of – and support for – boxing was aired in the pages of the *Lancet* and other medical journals.

There were four major strands in the public and medical controversy over the desirability of boxing which developed in the medical journals. First, there were calls for increased medical intervention in the sport. Second, the morality of boxing was discussed, with much of the debate centring on the differences between amateur and professional boxing. Third, the ethical distinction between sports which involved deliberate intention to hurt, and sports where damage was accidental, was raised. Fourth, there was discussion of the parliamentary movement to have boxing banned.

Increasing medical intervention

Before 1950, and the annual general meeting in that year of the British Boxing Board of Control (BBBC), boxers had to be medically examined only *before* entering the ring. Following a decision at that meeting, all boxers were required to undergo a medical examination both before and after every contest. A doctor had to be within call to give immediate attention to any boxer meeting with an accident (Wilson 1952: 130–1). The debate in the *Lancet* which helped to lead to these changes was triggered by the possibility of a fight between the

British boxers Bruce Woodcock and Freddie Mills in 1946. In May 1945, a Dr E. Cunningham Dax had drawn attention to the fights which these boxers had recently had with American opponents. Mills, in his fight with the world title-holder, Gus Lesnevich, was said to have been 'out on his feet' in the second round but survived to be knocked out in the tenth. Woodcock was ahead in his fight against another American, Mauriello, when he was knocked out in the fifth round. After a clash of heads, Woodcock suffered memory loss for the remainder of the fight. The *Lancet* correspondent pointed out:

> With . . . injury produced by other means . . . both would have been rested in bed for ten days and forbidden to take any strenuous exercise for at least six weeks . . . however, Woodcock has been allowed to fly home 36 hours after the fight, and both are resuming training in a few days so that they may be pitted against one another on June 4th.
>
> (*Lancet*, 25 May 1946: 835)

Other doctors pointed out that the absence of legislation to enforce medical supervision meant that boxers were free to ignore medical advice, and argued that more stringent medical examination might be one way of ensuring that unfit men did not fight (*Lancet*, 25 May 1946: 835).

Such change was on the way. In 1950, the New York State Athletic Commission required all contestants to be medically examined just before a bout and, for championship matches, a further special examination five days before that was required. During bouts the attending doctor was empowered to enter the ring to evaluate injury. If a contestant was held to be in serious danger the referee should be advised to end the contest (*Lancet*, 25 May 1950: 1006–7). In 1951, the BBBC initiated the changes referred to earlier and, in 1953, its medical sub-committee laid down the conditions for compulsory examination. A professional boxer was to be examined after he had been knocked down and taken a count, or after a fight had been stopped for any reason and, if four consecutive fights were lost, a boxer and his manager had to be interviewed by the Board (*Lancet*, 7 February 1953: 282–3). The death of the French boxer Pratesi revived discussion over the adequacy of these precautions. The BBBC took the view that no other method had yet proved superior and although the *Lancet* examined the suggestion that periodic electro-encephalograph (EEG) examinations should be made, it concluded that they did not necessarily show up the type of brain damage experienced by boxers and that, without more evidence, the compulsory EEG examination of professional boxers in Britain was inappropriate (*Lancet*, 7 February 1953: 282–3).

An immoral practice?

The *Lancet*'s position on the morality of boxing was typical of its ambivalence towards the sport, which had earlier been evident in its lukewarm response to Jokl's book. One doctor attempted to pin down the editor by saying: 'Boxing is either a good sport or a bad one and I cannot make out . . . which category you favour' (*Lancet*, 27 September 1941: 382). The editor, Egbert Morland, felt obliged to answer this justifiable criticism not by concentrating on the *medical* issues, but by drawing a moral distinction between professional and amateur boxing. He wrote:

> Boxing may be a good sport but, like love, it acquires an evil smell when it becomes a business proposition. Amateur boxing has merit in harmonising courage and self-control. As a training in self-defence boxing is popular with the police and the military. But that has no comfort for the poor loons who get punch-drunk in the ring for other people's profit.
>
> (*Lancet*, 27 September 1941: 382)

On this occasion, perhaps understandably given the editor's interpretation of the uncertain nature of the medical evidence, this was all he was prepared to say (Sheard 1998: 81).

This distinction between amateur and professional boxing was to remain significant. Many doctors had themselves been amateur boxers when young and, in the 1940s, some claimed that punch-drunkenness, if it occurred, was not due to boxing but to lack of 'quality' in the human beings involved, possibly those suffering from diseases such as syphilis: 'Punch-drunkenness is a very rare condition, found in second-rate sparring partners. Some . . . have a history of syphilitic disease which accentuates the symptoms. I have never seen punch-drunkenness in first-class amateur or professional boxers' (*Lancet*, 25 October 1941: 500–1). By 1958, however, there were increasing numbers of medical practitioners who agreed with another writer in the *Lancet*, a Dr Edelson, that the effects of *professional* boxing were entirely harmful:

> We live in an age as brutal, violent, vicious and immoral as any of those in recorded history that preceded the Christian era . . . Boxing promoters, . . . journalists, and patrons of the prize ring, lacking the courage of those who provide the 'entertainment' but gloating nevertheless on knockouts, cut eyes and pouring blood, are the ferocious and brutalised descendants of those who, in gladiatorial times, without mercy turned down their thumbs to make a Roman holiday. It is as monstrous, wrong, and indefensible to cause gratuitous injury to the miraculous organs of the body as it would be to detonate an H-bomb without provocation, and it is as necessary for the Government of the country to enact legislation forbidding it as it was for the same authority to legislate against crime.
>
> (*Lancet*, 14 June 1958: 1280)

This correspondent went on to say that it was time for those: 'alarmed at the continued debasement of human life and values, to cry out upon a disgusting outrage against human dignity that has killed some and reduced many others to a state bordering upon idiocy' (*Lancet*, 14 June 1958: 1280). This impassioned condemnation of the 'evils' of boxing, with the stress placed upon the unhealthy implications for the spectator and its scarcely veiled accusations of sadism and moral decline, touched a responsive chord and was taken up by others who saw boxing as appealing to deeply rooted atavistic instincts which were not responsive to reasoned argument (*Lancet*, 23 January 1960: 209–10).

It is not surprising, then, that supporters of amateur boxing felt themselves threatened and attempted to dissociate themselves from the professional sport. The Amateur Boxing Association (ABA) constantly stressed the medical steps that had been taken to make amateur boxing safer, while also emphasizing its beneficial health and character-building effects. In 1952, for example, J. L. Blonstein, then Honorary Medical Officer of the London ABA, who eventually became President of the Medical Commission of the Amateur International Boxing Association, appealed for doctors to help out at contests in London and the suburbs, offering them the satisfaction 'of knowing that they (were) assisting to foster a high physical and moral standard in the health of the nation's youth' (*Lancet*, 6 September 1952: 487). In 1956, Blonstein and Dr J. Sharp-Grant repeated this contention that for boys' health the benefits of boxing were both psychological and physical:

> Psychologically boxing benefits inadequate, insecure or aggressive boys alike, affording both the opportunity to develop discipline and the art of self-defence. The physical training and road-work . . . the moderation needed in smoking and drinking, lead to physical fitness and good health.
> (*Lancet*, 13 October 1952: 791)

Other doctors were less convinced and one asked for evidence to support the claims made for the physical and moral benefits of boxing:

> Physically the muscular development produced by training will raise the performer's ability for muscular work, but much of this is temporary or even permanently offset by injuries. I do not know of any evidence that muscular development protects an individual against disease.
> (*Lancet*, 13 September 1952: 535)

Moreover, he continued:

> As regards moral betterment I feel Dr Blonstein has a much weaker case. The training of individuals to dominate . . . by physical force is surely a poor training in social adaptation and peace.
> The educational effect of watching such contests is . . . as high as that of reading the baser comics.
> (*Lancet*, 13 September 1952: 535)

There was to be no resolution of these issues and, like many such controversies concerning boxing, the same or similar points were to be raised, defended and attacked for years to come. However, the claim made in 1960 by the Director of Physical Education at Winchester College, that boxing had great educational benefits, was the last of this type to be made in the pages of the Lancet (*Lancet*, 23 January 1960: 209–10).

The ethical distinction

In May 1950, the *Lancet* introduced a crucial distinction between boxing and other sports which provided a major plank in the abolitionist argument and which was firmly based on an ethical, rather than a medical, premise:

> In most . . . sports the risk of sprains, fractures, or even visceral damage is accepted as inevitable; indeed the element of danger is . . . an attraction. But boxing is unique in that the chief aim of the contestant is to disable his opponent.
>
> (*Lancet*, 25 May 1950: 1006–7)

This criticism lay dormant for a while, only to re-emerge in 1959 when a Dr Waycott, Chief Medical Officer of Charterhouse School, drew attention to that aspect of the sport which was to continue to exercise its proponents and antagonists into the twenty-first century:

> In many games there is . . . risk of injury. Footballers and cricketers are occasionally killed. Players accept these risks . . . and the rules are partly designed to keep the chances of injury low. Injury, when it does occur, is accidental. It is otherwise with boxing. In this sport alone it is the single purpose of the boxer to defeat his opponent and the best way to do this is by knocking him out. The more we know about the structure and function of the brain the more we should understand the utter folly of allowing young people to sustain repeated head injuries.
>
> (*Lancet*, 17 May 1958: 1076)

This argument was repeated in the *Lancet* in 1960 (27 February: 492), 1962 (10 March: 1962), 1963 (16 November: 1062), 1970 (7 November: 986) and 1974 (23 November: 1270). It was an argument that was never directly denied in the pages of the *Lancet*, although in 1962 Blonstein, by this time Senior Honorary Medical Officer for the ABA, came very close to denying it in the pages of the *British Medical Journal*. In questioning a statement by Dr G. C. Sheriff that boxing alone involved *deliberate* attempts to produce a cerebral concussion and other bodily damage, he asked: 'has he not observed the kicking, kneeing, elbowing, gouging and other deliberate attempts to injure one's opponent at Rugby football, the ankle-tapping at soccer, and the "accidental injuries" sustained at judo and wrestling?' (*BMJ* 2 June 1962: 1556).

Blonstein's apparent attempt to cloud the ethical issue was challenged by the surgeon F. R. Brown, who suggested that this approach to the *relative* risks of death and injury in sports was both unrealistic and illogical:

> [I]n rugby – a game played by 30 players for 80 minutes – there is occasional rough play, but the essential difference between boxing and rugby is that in the former deliberate intention to damage the opponent is permitted by the rules. In all other sports intention to hurt or disable incurs a penalty.
>
> (*BMJ*, 11 August 1962: 1556)

Many of boxing's supporters refused to recognize this ethical distinction which is, perhaps, a rather nice one where the *health* of sportspeople is involved. As Muhammad Ali's former doctor, Ferdie Pacheco, pointed out in a 1985 television interview, a sport where there were only a few serious injuries *deliberately* inflicted was perhaps preferable to one in which there were many more *accidental* injuries. Pacheco appeared to be suggesting that it was irrational to attempt to ban on *health grounds* an activity which was less damaging than other similar activities simply because the intention was different. It seemed perfectly reasonable, then, using these and similar criteria, for the proponents of boxing to condemn its critics as 'hysterical':

> People have been struck on the head by cricket balls and died therefrom . . . no more cricket?
>
> Necks have been broken playing rugger . . . no more rugger? A tough doctor friend who won the inter-hospitals boxing at both middle and heavy weight in the same competition played rugger for his University and cricket and tennis for his county, and for many years rode to hounds . . . came to no harm till in his riper years he took to golf. Leaning over to scoop his ball out of a . . . bunker he slipped and fell, dislocating his shoulder. Clearly, then, no more golf.
>
> Meanwhile . . . let there be no more mountaineering, steeple chasing, or polar exploration: all too risky.
>
> Most of us . . . die in bed. Perhaps we should sit up all night. Really, Sir, do we want, or expect, to live for ever?
>
> (*Lancet* , 21 June 1958: 1339–40)

There was no organized medical opposition to boxing in the 1950s and 1960s and this elicited expressions of surprise from some correspondents of the *Lancet*. One pointed out that, from 'time immemorial', medical students had been taught to take the most *trivial* head-injury seriously. But, puzzled, he asked, 'have (their) teachers ever made any serious attempt to inform the public how much permanent damage to the brain can and does follow the minor injuries which are normal and inevitable in boxing?' (*Lancet*, 10 May 1958: 1018).

One outspoken critic, F. B. Byrom of the Maudsley Hospital, insisted that effective opposition required *united* action from the profession if the issue was to be kept alive and before the public. This job, he believed, was too big for individuals and he asked why no medical research council had become involved (*Lancet*, 7 June 1958: 1226). An answer came from B. G. Edelston of the Chest Clinic, Folkestone. In a bitter attack upon his own profession and upon boxing, Edelstone wrote:

> it would be as futile to marshal the facts about boxing and to keep them before the public as it has been on the subject of cigarette smoking, bronchitis, and bronchial carcinoma. . . . [M]ost of the . . . profession seem . . . indifferent to these evils and have given neither a lead nor an example to the laity; the majority of doctors smoke . . . and many attend boxing matches. Only lonely and individual voices . . . are heard crying in the wilderness of crass indifference.
>
> (*Lancet*, 14 June 1958: 1280)

The medical profession was not united in opposing smoking in the 1950s and early 1960s, and did not agree about the link between smoking and various illnesses and cancers. It took 10 to 15 years for such opposition to cohere. Similarly, during the 1950s and into the 1960s there was little hard research evidence on the possible short-term and long-term medical dangers of boxing, although 'common-sense' and the medical evidence which was available seemed to provide a strong *prima facie* case. However, many doctors had a vested interest in supporting boxing and remained unconvinced by the 'evidence' then available that boxing was a serious risk to health. It was not until the 1970s that such evidence was accepted as overwhelming and indisputable (Sheard 1998: 88).

The parliamentary campaign

The political struggle which developed in the 1950s and 1960s was led by Dr Edith Summerskill, who was both a medical doctor and a Member of Parliament. Her book, revealingly called *The Ignoble Art* (1956), not only presented the medical case against boxing, but stressed the psychological and moral harm suffered by audiences. In December 1960, Summerskill tried to introduce a Parliamentary Bill to prohibit professional boxing, a motion which was lost by 120 votes to 17 (*Lancet*, 31 December 1960). On 7 April 1962, she again asked the Government to prohibit prize-fights in Britain or, alternatively, to charge fight promoters with incitement to manslaughter in the event of a fatality. This request was also refused. Undeterred, on 14 April, Summerskill – who had by this time become Baroness Summerskill – introduced a Bill in the House of Lords to prohibit the authorization of boxing matches for profit (*Lancet*, 14 April 1962: 799).

This Bill was an event of immense significance for the struggle over boxing. It was Summerskill's intention, if the House gave the Bill a second reading, to ask that it be referred to a Select Committee so that a full investigation could be made into professional boxing, which she described as: 'This unsavoury traffic in young bodies' (*Lancet*, 19 May 1962: 1078). The Bill was again lost, although only by 29 votes to 22. Greatly encouraged, the anti-boxing lobby was able to set up a committee under the aegis of the Royal College of Physicians to examine the medical aspects of boxing. After its report, known as the Roberts Report, was published in 1969, it was much more difficult to deny the medical dangers of boxing.

The Roberts Report 1969: A case to answer

Roberts demonstrated conclusively that not only were there 200 severely punch-drunk ex-boxers in Britain and a further 400–500 with damage only likely to be recognizable on physical examination, but that the length of a boxer's career and the number of bouts fought were closely related to the severity of the ultimate neurological damage (Royal College of Physicians 1969).

The report recognized that better supervision, reduction in the number of bouts that a boxer was allowed to have each year and other safeguards introduced by the boxing authorities, had considerably reduced the frequency and severity of injuries, but that further studies, using information from both professional and amateur bodies, were essential if public confidence in the management of boxing was to be increased.

Inevitably, perhaps, the findings of the Roberts Report were not immediately embraced by the boxing establishment, or by those sections of the medical profession engaged in supervising the sport, as unequivocal evidence that the risk involved in boxing was unacceptable. It was argued that the picture presented was of the health dangers of an earlier, less controlled, period and that modern boxing had moved on (*Lancet*, 10 November 1973: 1065). Although the debate continued, one significant change was that after the publication of the Roberts Report, boxing was banned in state-funded educational establishments, a lead shortly to be followed in many of the public schools also.

The next, and probably the most significant, step in the medical campaign occurred in 1984 with the publication of the British Medical Association report on the medical dangers of boxing (BMA 1984). This report was less detailed than that of 1969, but was characterized by a significant change of emphasis. Attention was switched from the dramatic deaths of boxers in the ring to the insidious or chronic brain damage which was claimed to be a *normal* part of boxing, both professional and amateur. Furthermore, the report had been updated in two very significant respects. First, it made use of advanced scientific techniques for brain examination, particularly the CAT scan and, second, it focused attention on groups who had previously appeared to be at little, or even no, risk.

Previous testing of brain function had relied on clinical neurological examination, psychological tests and the EEG. The CAT scan, however, could reveal marked pathology of various kinds in the brain which all three of the other tests failed to indicate. Moreover, the new techniques revealed the extent of brain damage long before there was any outward or visible evidence of deterioration.

Of almost equal significance was the fact that the report stressed that amateur boxers were also exposed to the risk of long-term damage and that not only were 'serious' amateur boxers at risk, but also youngsters, police cadets, and boys' club members who had the occasional bout or sparring session in the gym (*Guardian* 9 March 1984). The ABA, which had over the years attempted to establish a moral and medical divide between itself and the professional sport, was alarmed to discover that it, too, was threatened by the 1984 report. Since then, all medical discussion of boxing has taken place within the framework which the report established; the medical dangers are now fully accepted and all concern is with minimizing those dangers (Sheard 1998: 98).

The stance taken by the medical profession over injuries in sport is obviously important in arousing public interest and concern but, equally obviously, such medical campaigns occur within broader social contexts. This particular campaign developed within a society in which people were becoming increasingly sensitive to risk. However, attempts to minimize risk can have potentially serious, and often hidden, consequences and repercussions.

Developments in the use of boxing gloves provide a good example of this process. It is popularly believed that one of the great leaps forward in the acceptability of boxing was the increase in the use of gloves, which followed the drawing up of the Marquess of Queensberry's rules in 1865. It is ironic, then, that the introduction of the Queensberry Rules and of boxing gloves – which cut down on the outward signs of injury, the blood and gore – not only increased the popularity of boxing at a time when it was under sustained attack, but also increased the likelihood of more serious, if less noticeable harm, most notably in the form of brain damage (Sheard 2004, 1997). Before the Queensberry rules were drawn up, punches were straight and cutting, not slogs to the side or back of the head, and a fighter would think twice before throwing a punch unnecessarily because of the risk of hurting his hands. There was also no point in knocking someone out temporarily because, in the absence of a count, the seconds could drag their man to the 'scratch' ready to fight again (Sheard 2004, 1997; Queensberry 1942).

In modern times bare-knuckle fighting is condemned as barbaric and uncivilized. However, it is now generally recognized that the purpose of boxing gloves is not to protect the opponent's head but the hands of the puncher. They also add weight to a boxer's blows. Gloves increase the rotational forces which cause the brain to swirl within the skull, catching on the uneven surfaces and causing bleeding (Sheard 1997, 2004).

The use of headguards, which appear protective and unambiguously safer, may be subject to similar reservations. The 1984 BMA report into the dangers of boxing, while admitting that headguards could protect against minor cuts and eye injuries, was at pains to point out that they were of little use in preventing brain damage (1984: 26), which tends to occur when the jelly-like substance of the brain is shaken around inside the skull. In fact headguards, by making the head heavier, are also more likely to cause the swirling movement which is likely to contribute to long-term damage to the brain. Furthermore, many boxers and managers believe that headguards, because they obscure vision and encourage carelessness, make boxing *more* dangerous, not less so (Sheard 2004: 28; 1997: 52).

At first sight, it would also appear self-evident that moves over the years to place restrictions on the length of contests and the length of rounds have increased the safety of boxing or, at the very least, helped to change the balance in contests between skill and strength in favour of the former. Most professional championship contests in Britain now follow the lead given by the European Boxing Union and are fought over 12 rounds. In America until relatively recently the stipulated 'distance' was 15 rounds. And before this – in both the US and Britain – the usual distance was 20 rounds of three minutes each. By contrast, prior to the 1860s, a round ended with a fall, and fights would be fought to a finish or until one of the fighters could not continue for any reason. In Britain, the largest number of rounds to be fought under this system was the 276 fought between Jack Jones and Patsy Tunney, in Cheshire in 1825 (Golesworthy 1983: 136; Sheard 2004: 17–18, 1997: 36). However, while the round-reduction which occurred over the nineteenth century would clearly appear to be in the interests of the boxers and their safety, more recent innovations in this area are not as clear-cut. For example, it is often suggested that the number of rounds in professional boxing contests was reduced as a safety measure. However, Cashmore has suggested that this was not the reason behind the change. In discussing what he sees as the effect of *television* on sports, Cashmore (1990: 146–7) points out that:

> There was little conclusive evidence that the serious injuries associated with boxing were incurred in the final three rounds, but in the mid-1980s, the World Boxing Council, World Boxing Association, and International Boxing Federation all changed their rules. Fifteen three-minute rounds, as well as fourteen one-minute intervals, preamble and post-fight interviews amounted to an awkward seventy to seventy-five minutes. Twelve rounds yielded forty-seven minutes, as well as, say, thirteen for padding, which fitted perfectly into a one-hour time slot.

Cashmore thus argues that this change was primarily designed to fit in with commercial interests and considerations, particularly the interests of television companies and producers.

The introduction of weight divisions into boxing has also been viewed as part of an on-going civilizing process (Sheard 1997). In the early days of the prize-ring there were no weight divisions and men fought each other irrespective of poundage. It was not until the 1880s, and the widespread adoption of the Queensberry Rules of 1865, that a real effort was made to standardize weight divisions, both in Britain and the United States. This innovation, of course, allowed boxing skill to have a greater impact upon the outcome of a contest than extra poundage or extra reach and helped to eliminate dangerous mis-matches (Sheard 2004: 17; 1997: 36).

However, in the modern situation things are not as straightforward. The number of weight divisions has enlarged considerably with the lead coming from the United States. In the early 1960s, when the television boom in boxing began, the power of the gambling interests in Las Vegas meant that the big fights were increasingly attracted away from New York and the power of the New York Boxing Commission was undermined, creating a vacuum in the governance of boxing. This was soon filled by the major promoters – each of whom usually worked exclusively with a particular television company – who recognized a need for more championships to keep their paymasters happy. With only one, or occasionally two, world champions in each of the existing eight categories – fly, bantam, feather, light, welter, middle, light-heavy and heavy – there were not enough championships to go around (Mullan 1998: 33). The perceived solution took two forms: first, the creation of 'world governing bodies' (there are now at least eight) and, second, the expansion of the number of weight classes from the classic eight to the present 17.

Although there was some justification on safety grounds for expanding the categories – the gaps between the original eight were recognized as being too wide and, it was believed, often resulted in dangerous mismatches – many of the new divisions in the lighter weight categories reflected commercial pressures from the expanding Oriental market, where fighters weighing more than 10 stone were rare (Mullan 1998).

Although at least part of the motivation to introduce weight categories, and to refine those categories, may be attributed to a desire to increase safety and avoid mismatches, it is important to recognize that these changes were also to have unintended consequences which, in some respects, actually made boxing more dangerous. In this regard boxers, in their efforts to 'make the weight', have been constrained to take diuretics and resort to other dubious practices in order to lose weight rapidly before a fight. One consequence of rapid fluid loss of this kind has been dehydration, and this may be associated with shrink-age of the brain within the skull, allowing it to swirl damagingly against the sharp edges of the cranium, possibly leading to the internal bleeding partly responsible for several recent tragedies in the ring.

Conclusion

In the sociological literature the medical profession is often presented as one of the most powerful of occupational groups (see for example Johnson 1972). How-ever, the anti-boxing campaign provides a good example of how difficult it can be, even for such a supposedly powerful social group, to manipulate 'public opinion', or to create the unity necessary for a concerted campaign against entrenched interests. Over the years the medical profession has not presented a united front in its campaigns. Historically, as the struggles in the medical journals clearly show, the profession has been characterized by internal divisions

and intra-professional rivalries. Indeed, the unity necessary to organize successful campaigns is forthcoming probably only when members feel that the
interests of the whole profession are threatened, which was not the case with
boxing. In non-crisis situations, in any organization, it is often small, pioneering
groups who initiate action. This was certainly the case with the pressure, prior
to 1984, emanating from sections of the medical profession that 'something
should be done' about boxing. The decision taken at the BMA conference in
1982 to campaign for the abolition of boxing was made by a very small section
of the profession (Whiteson 1985). In 1980 there were over 54,000 doctors in
Britain, not all of whom were members of the BMA. Only 600 registered for
the 1982 conference, and only 254 were present during the debate on boxing.
Of these, 114 voted in favour of the motion to abolish boxing and 110 against
(Whiteson 1985).

Moreover, one should not assume that campaigns organized around the
health implications of particular sports stand or fall according to the internal
medical logic of the supposed threat to health. As the case of boxing illustrates,
in such ideological struggles medical evidence and debate constitute only part of
the debate, and moral issues are either implicitly or explicitly incorporated into
the argument. The development in medicine of neuropathology and diagnostic
brain techniques may have allowed the brain damage which can be caused by
boxing to be painstakingly detailed, but this medical evidence is seldom left to
stand on its own. In more recent years, perhaps influenced by the more general
medicalization of society (Waitzkin and Waterman 1974; Zola 1972) and sport
(Waddington 1996) and increasing health-consciousness, the specifically medical case against boxing is given greater prominence. Nevertheless, moral issues
are still smuggled into such discussions, and are still given significant, if more
subtle, emphasis (Sheard 1998).

Bibliography

British Medical Association (1984) 'Boxing', *British Medical Association*, London.
Cashmore, E. (1990) *Making Sense of Sport*, London: Routledge.
Elias, N. (1994) *The Civilizing Process: The History of Manners and State-Formation
  Civilization* (single integrated edition), Oxford: Blackwell.
Elias, N. and Scotson, J. L. (1965) *The Established and the Outsiders: A Sociological
  Enquiry into Community Problems*, London: Frank Cass.
Golesworthy, M. (1983) *Encyclopedia of Boxing*, London: Robert Hale.
Guardian (9 March 1984), London.
Jewson, N. (1974) 'Medical Knowledge and the Patronage System in Eighteenth
  Century England', *Sociology*, 8: 369–85.
Johnson, T. J. (1972) *Professions and Power*, London: Macmillan.
Jokl, E. (1941) *The Medical Aspects of Boxing*, Pretoria: Van Schaik Publishers.
Journal of the American Medical Association, Stanford University, CA.
Lancet, London.
Mullan, H. (1998) *Boxing: Inside the Game*, Cambridge: Icon Books.
Queensberry, Tenth Marquis of (1942) *The Sporting Queensberry's*, London.

Royal College of Physicians (1969) *Report on the Medical Aspects of Boxing* (The Roberts Report), London.

Sheard, K. G. (1992) 'Boxing in the Civilizing Process', unpublished doctoral dissertation, Anglia Polytechnic.

Sheard, K. G. (1997) 'Aspects of Boxing in the Western "Civilizing Process"', *International Review for the Sociology of Sport*, 32, 1: 31–57.

Sheard, K. G. (1998) '"Brutal and Degrading": The Medical Profession and Boxing, 1838–1984', *The International Journal of the History of Sport*, 15, 3: 74–102.

Sheard, K. G. (2004) 'Boxing in the Western Civilizing Process' in E. Dunning, D. Malcolm and I. Waddington (eds) *Sport Histories: Figurational Studies of the Development of Modern Sports*, London: Routledge: 15–30.

Spencer, H. (1897) *The Principles of Sociology*, 1876–96, 3 vols., New York: Appleton & Co.

Summerskill, E. (1956), *The Ignoble Art*, London: Heinemann.

Wacquant, L. J. D. (1995) 'Through the Fighter's Eyes: Boxing as a Moral and Sensual World' in C. C. Robert (ed.), *Boxing and Medicine*, Champaign, IL: Human Kinetics.

Waddington, I. (1979) 'Competition and Monopoly in a Profession: The Campaign for Medical Registration in Britain', *Amsterdams Sociologisch Tijdschrift*, 6: 288–321.

Waddington, I. (1984) *The Medical Profession in the Industrial Revolution*, Dublin: Gill and Macmillan.

Waddington, I. (1985) 'Medicine, the Market and Professional Autonomy; Some Aspects of the Professionalization of Medicine', in W. Conza and J. Kocka (eds) *Bildungsburgertum im 19 Jahrhundert*, Stuttgart: Klett-Cotta: 388–416.

Waddington, I. (1996) 'The Development of Sports Medicine', *Sociology of Sport Journal*, 13, 2: 176–96.

Waitzkin, H. and Waterman, B. (1974) *The Exploitation of Illness in Capitalist Society*, Indianapolis: Bobbs-Merrill.

Whiteson, A. (1985) 'Open Letter to the British Medical Association', in B. Hugman (ed.) *British Boxing Yearbook*, Feltham: Newnes Books.

Wilson, P. (1952) *How to Watch Boxing*, London: Sporting Handbooks Ltd.

Zola, I. K. (1972) 'Medicine as an Institution of Social Control', *Sociological Review*, 20: 487–504.

9 The intentional infliction of pain in sport

Ethical perspectives

Jim Parry

Introduction

This chapter explores a variety of ethical issues concerning the intentional infliction of pain in sport, both in the actual playing of the game and in the overall care of the athlete. It will make special reference to the cases of boxing and systemic doping, already the subjects of chapters by Ken Sheard and Giselher Spitzer.

It begins with conceptual preliminaries, since some attention should be given to the common focus of enquiry of chapter authors. We should ask, 'The intentional infliction of . . . what?', so this section considers a range of pain-related concepts, followed by a range of violence-related concepts.

Next we focus on 'intra-contest violence' – the intentional infliction of pain or injury by one athlete on another within the contest itself – taking as examples football, rugby and boxing; and then on 'pre-contest violence' – examining the morality of the systems that surround and support the athlete in preparation for the contest, with special reference to the practice of systemic doping.

Finally, we look at the self-infliction of pain and the responsibility of the athletes themselves for the pain they undergo, asking whether sport is sado-masochistic.

Pain-related concepts

Sport brings pain

Consider someone on the street breaking into a run – for example, so as to be on time for an appointment. He would not run himself too hard. He would slow down or even rest awhile to recover his breath, so as indeed to arrive earlier, but without undue or unseemly distress. If the effort were so great as to begin to hurt in some way, this would normally be taken as a sign to give less effort, or even to desist. He would certainly never consider running himself to exhaustion unless motivated by some very important aim.

Or consider the person running through meadows for the sheer frolicking joy of it – gambolling like a new-born lamb. Since motivated by pleasure or delight, it would seem counterproductive to put himself through the pain or suffering of excess effort, or to risk harm or injury in the process.

Sport begins where such everyday attitudes end. For the person running for sport will indeed extend him/herself and may even run to exhaustion – all in the service of no aim other than the aim internal to the sport of winning the competition. One will accept discomfort, hurt and even quite severe pain. One will undergo training, hard and possibly even painful in itself, in order to accustom oneself to the pains of competition, the better to be able to cope with or ignore them – and one may even welcome them as signs of improving powers or of resilience. In certain sports one will freely risk harm, damage and the possibility of permanent impairment, in others the peculiar sufferings of endurance, or anguish of failure or defeat.

If we add to this picture certain external aims and motivations, such as fortune and fame, we can easily see how sport may become an arena of suffering and injury.

In the foregoing paragraphs I have employed a wide range of pain-related concepts, which are often confused, or used interchangeably. It may be useful to review and refine our usages here, since my title invites the question: 'The intentional infliction of . . . what?', and the responses to that question might suggest some important distinctions for the ways in which we express our concerns.

This section, then, considers the use of a range of pain-related concepts, with a view to arriving at a view as to what kinds of pain it might be useful to distinguish.

Pain

Pain refers to a variety of sensations, for example: a sensation felt when hurt (bodily or emotionally), a sensation accompanying physical injury, a distressing sensation (as of soreness, not injury), a chronic ache (sometimes the result of disease), the suffering and anguish of endurance, and extreme discomfort (accompanying extreme exertion, etc.).

Hurt and harm

The difference between hurt and harm is that, while hurt has to do with causing pain or anxiety, harm is centrally to do with causing bodily injury or damage. In sport, then, it may be part of the game to cause hurt, whereas intentional harm may be outlawed.

Discomfort and distress

Distress means experiencing stress, strain, pain or anguish, or the exhaustion of extreme stress, strain, pain or anguish, whereas discomfort means feeling uncomfortable or experiencing mild distress. The pain of exertion, for example, brings hurt, discomfort or distress, rather than harm or injury.

Anguish

Anguish is primarily an emotional pain (and there may be similar others in sporting experience). As Matti Goksøyr shows (in Chapter 5 of this book), the arctic explorer Scott's pains included those bodily pains characteristic of the peculiar sufferings of endurance, but for him there was also the acute disappointment of having been beaten to the North Pole, evoking the emotional pain of anguish. Maybe to a different degree, or in a different way, such pain may also be felt by any athletic competitor who fails – *just* fails? – to win.

Suffering

Suffering may be seen as the bearing or undergoing of (experiencing or being subjected to) any of the above – pain, hurt, harm, discomfort, distress, injury, impairment or anguish. Suffering also has some overtone of chronicity, so it is unsurprising to find that it frequently forms part of the pain-descriptions of those in long-distance and endurance sports, or of those experiencing long-term injuries.

Pain and injury

To 'be injured' is ambiguous. It might mean either to *incur* (to suffer) an injury or to *have* an injury (to be in an injured state – to be 'carrying' an injury). This distinction helps us to see how the connection sometimes held to obtain between pain and injury (see Howe, in Chapter 13 of this book) does not necessarily hold.

In the first case (to *incur* an injury), pain may or may not be an accompaniment. Often, of course – even usually – injuries cause pain. But I may become injured without present pain. For example, I might be anaesthetized – possibly by some analgesic agent, or by extremely cold conditions, or because of the physiology of traumatic impairment.

In the second case (to *have* an injury), similarly, pain may or may not be an accompaniment. I may of course be in agony for weeks while my broken leg heals. But I may be carrying a hamstring tear without present pain, even though it prevents me from competing in my sport.

The question might be asked: If there is no present pain, then how do I know that I am injured? The suggestion here is that the pain is what makes me notice my injury, and that, without pain, no injury is noticeable. The former is of course often true, but the latter is not necessarily so: I may know that I am injured because of immediate and apparent impairment, or lack of function – with or without pain. Alternatively, I may entertain a legitimate suspicion of likelihood of breakdown under activity – I feel that I dare not maintain or prolong my effort, perhaps because I feel a certain tension or tightness in the muscle. I feel that, if I persist, then I *will* feel pain, or do myself a further injury.

In both cases, attention to the idea of 'being injured' has led us to deny the necessary relation between injury and pain.

Kinds of pain

In the sports setting, then, it might be useful to distinguish a number of different kinds of pain (see also Roessler, in Chapter 2 of this book): pain of hurt (not necessarily harm, or at least not lasting harm), pain of harm (or damage, or injury), pain of exertion (including discomfort and distress), pain of suffering (and endurance), and pain of anguish (including fear of annihilation).

All of these may be either positive or negative, they may all be expressive (of relationship, of self-realization, etc.), and they may all be accepted by-products of sporting participation.

Intentional infliction of pain (intra-contest)

Extra-contest violence (for example, spectator violence, or post-match fights between players) is violence which occurs 'on the occasion of the contest' but not 'as part of the contest'. This section focuses on intra-contest violence – the intentional infliction of harm, pain or injury by one athlete on another within the contest itself.

Elsewhere (Parry 1998) I have sought to distinguish assertion, aggression and violence. Let us begin with these basic concepts, and see if some informed conceptual stipulation might be useful.

Assertion and aggression

Some see the biological organism as active, positive, and see 'aggression' as a basic biological drive, or a pre-condition of existence, or human flourishing, or excellence. However, I prefer to call this capacity 'assertiveness' or 'self-assertion', because there is no suggestion here of a necessary forcefulness. Rather, there is the sense of affirming or insisting upon one's rights; protecting or vindicating oneself; maintaining or defending a cause.

Aggression, however, *is* forceful. Some see a possibility of defensive as well as offensive aggression, but both are served by force. Aggression is *vigorous* (trying to gain advantage by sheer force), *offensive* (in the sport context: battling for the ball) and *proactive* (striking first).

Such features may all be morally exceptionable or unexceptionable, according to context, in everyday life, but all are usually permitted according to the rules of team sports.

Violence

Just as it is possible to be assertive without being aggressive, it is quite possible to be aggressive without being violent. A player can be both forceful and vigorous without seeking to hurt or harm anyone. And we should distinguish between 'hurt' and 'harm'. 'Hurt' here means *'give pain to'*, *'knock, strike, give a blow to'* and 'harm' means *'injure, damage'*.

Violence, then, is centrally to do with intentional harm or injury to others, as well as attempts to harm, recklessness as to harm, and negligence. Since such injury is very often seen as illegitimate, legitimacy has often been seen as an important ethical issue in sport. Accordingly, violence in a sport might be seen as (i) harm or injury to others (or attempted harm) or (ii) something which is against the rules.

But there is a difficulty here. If the above account were to hold for 'combat sports', this would require the counter-intuitive notion that very hard punches aimed at knocking someone out do not constitute 'violence' so long as they are delivered legally. In this case, we might delete the criterion: 'which is against the rules'. Let us simply insist that violence is centrally to do with intentional harm or injury to others, as well as attempts to harm, recklessness as to harm, and negligence. It also suggests that we need one more category: illegitimate violence. For, sometimes, violence may be justifiable (in war, or revolution; or in boxing, where 'violence' within bounds is legitimate). Illegitimate violence must be characterized as the attempt to harm by the use of illegitimate force (e.g., in boxing, the rabbit punch).

There are further interesting problems arising from injuries which are caused instrumentally, but not through full-blown intention. Reckless challenges are those whose intent may be to gain advantage, but whose means are taken in the knowledge of risk or foresight of probable injury. Negligent challenges are those undertaken without appropriate due care for others. We need to rely not just on the concept of intention, but also on such wider concepts of culpability and responsibility. We should ask questions not just about intention, but also about the acts and omissions for which we should be held responsible, and for which we are culpable. A reckless or careless (negligent) driver may have no intent to injure someone, but is held to be to some degree culpable nevertheless. The same should apply in sport – a reckless or negligent challenge may maim as well as an intentionally injurious one.

Violent acts and acts of violence

Not all acts of violence are violent acts, and not all violent acts are acts of violence (see Harris 1982: Ch. 1). Almost any human act may be performed in a more or less violent manner – vigorously, forcefully, strongly, energetically, vehemently, furiously, etc. However, an act of violence is identified not by the manner of its execution, but by the human consequences flowing from it, such as harm, injury, distress, suffering, and so on.

We should also posit a parallel distinction between aggressive acts and acts of aggression. Aggressive acts are those acts marked by vigour, offensiveness and proactivity. Acts of aggression, however, are attacks or assaults on others – and these may be performed vigorously or not.

Examples

Let us look at a few practical applications of the above thoughts, and see how they fare when tested against examples.

Football

At every instant in the game of football, possession of the ball is being contested. Assertion is necessary at all times, and aggression is permitted in pursuit of legitimate ends. Games such as soccer are essentially exercises in controlled aggression. However, violent and dangerous play is strictly against the rules, so the case against acts of violence is simply that they are illegitimate.

Rugby

Here is a game which many see as violent, for part of the game seems to be to overcome others simply by violent force. One way of expressing this thought is to argue that, although rugby might be a violent sport, it is not a sport of violence. People may get hurt in the course of the game due to the extreme nature of honourable physical combat, but the aim of the game (and the way to win it) is to score points, not to hurt people.

Having said that, I am of course referring to what official sets of rules appear to say, as distinct from what 'custom and practice' appears to be. Among players, for example, there may exist a 'code of silence' which prohibits the reporting of acts of violence witnessed. If this is true, then hard questions must be asked about the moral basis of custom and practice. If the rules prohibit acts of violence, then any such collusion risks bringing the game into disrepute, to the disadvantage of all. If the rules actually *don't*, then perhaps they will require revision.

The special case of boxing

Nigel Benn ('The Dark Destroyer') beat Gerard McClellan by a tenth-round knock-out on 26 February 1995. McClellan was counted out while not unconscious, but down on one knee, obviously distressed and blinking heavily. As soon as he reached his corner it became clear that something was badly wrong, and he was rushed to hospital, where he had a blood clot removed from his brain shortly after arrival. His condition was critical.

British Boxing Board of Control (BBBC) officials were very quick on the night to explain the detailed precautions taken, including the presence of four doctors, one an anaesthetist (although the very necessity for such precautions is itself evidence of foreknowledge of risk to life). On BBC1 News the next night (1995a) a promoter, Frank Warren, and a BBBC official mounted a spirited defence of the sport, in the following terms (supplemented by later discussion on BBC1 Sportsnight, 1995b).

Boxing is a skilled sport, whose aim is to score points, etc.
This is true, but boxing also not only permits, but rewards ultimately the causing of grievous or actual bodily harm. If it were possible with one blow to decapitate one's opponent (let us call this move the 'knock-off'), this would not be against the rules or the spirit of the rules. A knock-out is a final knock-down. The knock-off would simply be a more final and spectacular way of ending the fight than a simple knock-out.

If the knock-off were possible, why should it not be permitted? You must say either that it is permissible, which dramatically exposes the sport's rationale, I think; or that it is impermissible for some reason – which reason would, I think, also provide a criterion for banning head punching at all.

Boxing should be treated the same as any other risk sport. Many other sports are as dangerous as boxing, and people die every year in many different sports.
The actual facts of the matter are in some dispute. Sports medics argue over the precise nature, degree, effects and probabilities of injury. The statistics given on the Sportsnight programme were that over the previous nine years in Britain there were 94 deaths in horse riding, four in cricket, and only two in boxing. Leave aside for the moment the fact that these are not properly weighted statistics (ignoring as they do participation rates, time spent during periods of activity, etc.), for they are simply irrelevant to the point. The argument is not about the facts of injury levels – but it is a moral argument about the aim of the activity. John might hurt someone in cricket, but he won't get runs or wickets for that. In boxing, he might *win* just by doing that. Indeed, hurting or harming someone so badly that he cannot continue the contest is a *sufficient* condition of victory – and surely this feature of the sport exposes its false appeal to the skill argument, as in the previous example. It is not as if there *is* no skill in boxing; but rather that a boxer might rationally aim at inflicting a simple debilitating injury as a *means* of winning.

Surely other sports take care not only to provide for casualties, but also to *avoid* those casualties as far as possible. So why not take the head out of the target area in boxing?

Answer: you can't have boxing without the head as a target. That's like having rugby without scrums; or the steeplechase without jumps.
Well, these are interestingly different cases: it is quite possible to envisage rugby without scrums, just as we can envisage rugby without line-outs. A steeplechase, however, is *defined* in terms of jumps. It means 'formerly, a race having a church steeple in view as goal, in which all intervening obstacles had to be cleared'

(SOED 1972). So: you could have rugby without scrums; but you could not have a steeplechase without jumps.

Now, what shall we say about boxing? That boxing without the head as target is a logical nonsense? Or that we could easily envisage a simple rule change that would preserve all that is good about the skill, fitness, endurance, etc. of boxing *except* for that proportion of those things relating to the intentional permanent damage of another human being? I vote for the latter. *If* boxing is about skill, endurance, etc., then it can survive such a rule change. But if it is really about the thrill and chill of the ultimate snuff sport, then shouldn't we do away with it, and with the promoters who profit from it?

One thought: most boxers are (in legal terms) reckless, and this is especially true of one who calls himself 'The Dark Destroyer'. One account of recklessness describes it as 'conscious risk-taking'. A professional boxer knows from the outset that it is entirely possible that he will 'destroy' his opponent; and perhaps he even hopes that he will. That is to say: it is almost certain that Benn fully appreciated the risk that he might kill his next opponent, and yet he went willingly and enthusiastically into battle after careful and serious preparation. This is not true of sportspeople in any other sport.

This means that there is a clear moral argument against professional boxing – the simple moral imperative against an activity of which not only the outcome but also the object is too often the injury, incapacitation or even death of a human being.

And yet I also acknowledge the particular virtues of boxing, which seem to differ only in degree from the virtues of many other sports: the courage involved in putting oneself on the line (think of individual compared with team sports); in putting one's entire *self* on the line (think of boxing *as opposed to* other individual sports); the facing of pain, injury, danger and risk; the absolute reliance on one's personal resources; the discipline involved in attaining and maintaining extremely high levels of fitness and endurance, and so on.

Conclusion

The intra-sport intentional infliction of pain in sport has many facets. Tactical hurt infliction is permissible in many sports. Its aim is to debilitate, or degrade the performance of the opposition, within the rules. Tactical harm infliction, however, will disqualify in most sports, whose rules prohibit 'personal' fouls. The very toleration of a sport such as boxing, which is at least reckless as to harm, and permits intentional infliction of injury, calls into question our moral sensitivities.

Intentional infliction of pain (pre-contest)

The previous section distinguished intra-contest from extra-contest pain infliction. This section examines the idea of pre-contest pain infliction, and in particular the systems that surround and support the athlete in preparation for the contest (even if this is just a trainer, or coach).

In Chapter 7 of this book Giselher Spitzer documents the systematic, state-sponsored doping system in the GDR, and the suffering which this inflicted on athletes who continue to suffer the side-effects of what was often 'compulsory' doping. Of course, our knee-jerk reaction is to see such practices as wrong, but this section seeks to provide some explication of just *why* it might be wrong.

The strategy here is to suggest a set of broadly acceptable considerations of principle, and then apply them to sport-related cases and examples of pre-contest pain infliction, with special reference to Spitzer's chapter. The idea is both to interrogate the particular cases and examples and also to test the principles for their adequacy and illuminative power.

Principles of biomedical ethics

In a standard medical ethics textbook Beauchamp and Childress (2001) offer a number of 'fundamental principles' as an integrated framework through which diverse moral problems may be handled. They see the cases they offer not only as illustrations, but also as explications and tests of the principles, since hard cases can sometimes lead to a rethinking or modification of principles.

They see ethics as the systematic examination of the moral life, designed to illuminate what we ought to do by asking us to consider and reconsider our ordinary actions, judgements and justifications. Although we rarely find knock-down arguments in debates about applied ethics, such debates are nonetheless subject to rational analysis. However – to paraphrase Aristotle – we can only expect such precision and degree of certainty as is appropriate to the subject matter. Sometimes the answers cannot be as tidy as we might wish, but the application of principles is one way of trying to be systematically rational about moral issues.

Another way of trying to be rational about moral issues is to apply the language of rights, but there is much controversy over the meaning, scope and possession of rights. Some see rights as *prima facie* claims – as making strong moral demands that nevertheless are defeasible, and may justifiably be over-ridden by a stronger claim, or by other considerations. Rights are also sometimes unjustifiably overridden – they may be violated or infringed. Others, however, have criticized the language of 'rights', because rights are often presented without justification as a set of claims or demands.

Yet another systematic approach recognizes that it is also possible to express our concerns through the language of welfare, and the duties and responsibilities we owe to others. Beauchamp and Childress believe that rights (and the correlative obligations and duties that they sometimes beget) are anyway to be analysed in terms of more basic principles and rules, and so we must turn to a consideration of those principles.

The principle of autonomy

Morality requires autonomous (self-governing) persons, who determine a course of action in accordance with a plan chosen by themselves – who think about and choose plans and are capable of acting on them. The principle of autonomy requires us to respect people's rights to self-governance – that is, to act without constraint by others. We should do this in order to recognize and respect an individual's personhood – for no other reason than that he or she is another person, having the same right to self-governance as myself.

A counter-example is the World Anti-Doping Agency legislation, where governments and the IOC intervene in order to secure their own ends against the autonomous choices of athletes who wish to take dope of various kinds. But here justifying reasons are part of the process of authoritative command. This is what distinguishes such legislation from simple *Parentalism*, which is the over-riding of someone's autonomy (and also their non-autonomous decisions) for beneficent reasons.

The principle of informed consent

The principle of informed consent exists to protect persons from (risk of) harm, and to protect their autonomy. The main elements of informed consent relate to information and consent. Information should first be disclosed, according to standards set by a professional community (where medical care standards operate), or by a legal rule set according to a 'reasonable person' standard (where patient rights operate). Second, information should be comprehensible and care should be taken to ensure that it is comprehended. Consent should be voluntary, and a presupposition of consent is competence to consent (for example, minors may be deemed non-competent).

The principle of non-maleficence

The Hippocratic oath expresses the principles of beneficence and non-maleficence: 'I will use treatment to help the sick according to my ability and judgement, but I will never use it to injure or wrong them.'

Let us begin with the principle of non-maleficence, which expresses the duty of '*primum non nocere*' – first do no harm. This is a strong duty – the duty not to injure is distinct from and more stringent than the duty to take steps to benefit. It is a duty as to actual harm, but also as to risks. It therefore imposes a duty of due care – to be thoughtful and to act carefully. In this context we must consider intention, recklessness, negligence, and legal and professional standards.

We should also mention here the *Principle of double effect*, where there are both good and bad consequences of an action. In order to be non-maleficent the action must be good, and the agent must intend only the good effect – the bad effect is foreseen, but not intended. In addition, the bad effect must not be a means to the good, and there must be a proportionality in the balance of good and bad effects.

So, in the sporting situation in general, and bearing in mind the provisions of autonomy and informed consent, we should take care not to harm athletes by avoiding undue physiological stress or damage, overtraining as a risk to health, well-being and the development of sporting potential, harmful nutritional regimes, food supplements and drug misuse, psychological pressure, stress and burn-out, over-specialization in sport to the detriment of other aspects of life, over-specialization in one sport and unreasonable lifestyle requirements (such as the denial of childhood – the 'Michael Jackson syndrome').

The principle of beneficence

The principle of beneficence should be seen as a duty to others, not as a virtue. (Benevolence is a virtue of persons, whereas beneficence is a quality of action.) It tells us not only 'do no harm', but also 'contribute to welfare', for example, by the prevention of harm, the removal of harmful conditions and the provision of benefits.

So, in the sporting situation in general, we should seek to contribute to the athlete's physical well-being, satisfaction and self-esteem in participation and achievement, confidence in facing challenge and in risk-taking, peer acceptance and peer relationships, and personal identity and role definition.

There can be no sharp distinction between the two principles of non-maleficence and benevolence. For example, risk/benefit analysis requires a balance of possible harms and benefits – a version of the principle of utility. And there is a genuine difficulty in ascertaining just what is the positive duty of beneficence (as opposed to supererogatory action). However, a failure to benefit others while in a position to do so violates social or professional duty, and this is one way of promoting preventive medicine, active public health interventions, etc.

Application to the case of systematic doping

Now we shall try to apply some of this to the particular case of the systemic doping regime operative in the former GDR, as described by Giselher Spitzer in Chapter 7.

The principle of informed consent

One of the chief criticisms of the regime lies in breaches of the principle of informed consent – failure to inform athletes of what was being done to them, failure to take steps to secure their understanding of what was being done to them, and failure to secure their consent. For this principle imposes duties and standards in respect of various elements.

DISCLOSURE OF INFORMATION

In this case, procedures were sometimes carried out without the knowledge of the athletes.

COMPREHENSION OF INFORMATION

Mere disclosure of information is insufficient, since this may not secure the comprehension of the athlete as to what procedures will actually take place, why they are being conducted, what are the possible effects and side effects, etc. In this case, too, athletes seem to have been used as guinea-pigs, i.e. used as experimental subjects in order to gain further comprehension for researchers. But, if the researchers do not yet have comprehension in the required sense, how could their subjects be in a position to comprehend?

VOLUNTARY CONSENT

This is possibly the most important element of informed consent. Subjects must give their fully informed and voluntary consent. In this case, athletes were exposed to compulsory doping, sometimes without their knowledge, which is a clear and obvious breach of the principle.

COMPETENCE TO CONSENT

A further important element is competence. For informed consent, researchers must be assured that subjects are competent. In this case, juniors (i.e. legal minors) were doped in gymnastics, weight-lifting, swimming, and other sports, without adequate ethical and legal safeguards having been obtained.

The principle of autonomy

As we have seen above, the principle of informed consent exists to protect persons from harm, and to protect their autonomy. Parentalism is intrusion into the sphere of autonomous choices and decisions of the subject. Justified parentalism may be seen as intrusion for the supposed best interests of the subject. In this case, there was intrusion, and it was not necessarily in the interests of the subject. To be sure, some of them might thereby have benefited, for example by achieving athletic success, but the systemic nature of the intrusion suggests that it was motivated by a concern for the best interests of the system, not of the individual. System success depends on the success of *some* individual – but not necessarily *this* one.

This kind of concern may be broadened by asking whether there is a potential conflict of interest for all sports medics. Do doctors belong to (or anyway do they share the aims of) the organization that employs them and gives them benefits of identification, collaboration, etc.? To whom are their loyalties – to club or to player – and is there a tension or conflict here? Do the medics facilitate autonomous decision-making by the athletes? Should they?

Such questions suggest why, from the point of view of athlete autonomy, a fully professionalized (and to that extent stronger and more independent) medical service for athletes is an urgent priority. Here the ethical and economic arguments often coincide. Isn't it simply prudent to do the ethically correct thing? Why exploit the talents of a £30 million asset in a way that fails to maximize the benefits those talents bring? One per cent of the player value of one of the top football teams would buy the best specialist sports medicine facility in England. One per cent of all transfer fees to be paid to the Professional Footballers' Association (PFA) for just this purpose would produce an even better and independent facility. We could ask, for example, why this is not top of the agenda for the PFA, since football is one of the few sports that could afford it.

The principle of non-maleficence

Primum non nocere – first, do no harm. Remember: this is a duty as to actual harm, but also as to risks. Can the GDR system pass this test of principle? No, for the procedures described by Spitzer carry with them great actual harms and risks of harm. Particularly damning is the allegation that, post-career, health data were falsified, and victims were given no information about damage and future risk. In this way, many preventable harms have not been averted.

We should ask about the medics involved – how did they, as medics, justify such practices to themselves, when they were clearly against the first principle of medical ethics since medicine was invented? What could have been their self-understandings?

It seems that many left for ethical reasons, even in the difficult conditions of dictatorship, when refusal to comply carried with it potentially very severe penalties. Of those who stayed, we might hypothesize that their rationale could have been one of the following: *identification* (belonging to – sharing the aims of – the system), *self-interest* (benefit from association with the authority; economic and social disbenefits of non-compliance) and *fear* (what will happen to me, my career, my family if I do not collaborate?).

The principle of double effect

But the principle of double effect might be invoked: we foresaw some of the possible harms, especially of experimentation, but the expected harms were relatively minor compared with the glory achieved for the motherland by these soldier-athletes. No one wants to lose soldiers in a war. But we foresee the possibility that they might die in combat – justifiably sacrificed in the defence of the motherland. So what price a few athletes?

The principle of beneficence

As we have seen, it is difficult to draw the line between non-maleficence and benevolence. But let us take Dominic Malcolm's evidence about the practices of professional rugby clubs (Chapter 10 of this book), and ask whether they are in a position to contribute to the welfare of their players, for example by the prevention of harm, removal of harmful conditions and the provision of benefits.

It seems to me beyond dispute that clubs pay inadequate attention to issues of corporate liability, managerial responsibility, duty of care, negligence and provision of developmental opportunities for their players. Clubs should, under the principle of beneficence, seriously consider some of the simple possibilities open to them to provide a harm-reduction and player-development environment. As we have already seen above, there is both an ethical and an economic justification for such a general policy.

Self-infliction of pain

This section focuses on the responsibility of the athletes themselves for the pain they undergo.

Acceptance of risk: consent and 'volenti non fit injuria'

In the ordinary course of the normal game, any participant might expect to face certain hazards and risks as 'all part of the game'. The operative legal principle here is 'volenti non fit injuria' (no injury is done to a willing person). So long as a participant is fully informed of the inherent risks of playing that sport, and voluntarily incurs the risk of harm, then he/she cannot complain of any injury that befalls him/her. To that extent, all participants consent to accept a range of pains that might be expected by an aware and reasonable person, and are therefore partly responsible for their own pains.

Acceptance of injury: Stingers and burners

Over the course of an average career, an athlete must accept the experience of the pain of injury, either as something inflicted on him/her by another, or as simply an occurrence. One example of such routinely experienced pain is the stinger.

> The stinger syndrome, or 'burner', represents one of the most common injuries seen in tackle football. It is thought to be caused by trauma to the brachial plexus and/or nerve roots. The injury most typically is characterized by muscle weakness involving the biceps, deltoid, and spinatus muscles. Because the pain, paresthesias, and weakness typically last only a few seconds or minutes, these injuries often go unreported to medical staff.
> (Shannon and Klimkiewicz 2002)

The most famous British sufferer of the stinger is rugby World Cup hero Johnny Wilkinson, who had a series of neck injuries. 'Another year, another injury . . . The bigger picture for me is that I won't let the injuries change the way I play my game' he says (Wilkinson 2004). He just takes a week or two off to recover.

> I've actually been dealing with [this type of neck injury] for six or seven years now, maybe more. The hit – or the sensation – is known as a 'stinger'; it comes when you take a hit on your shoulder, neck or head which sends a nerve pain down your arm, it makes your arm very hot and heavy and difficult to move. Stingers don't tend to last that long – you get pins and needles down your arm as the heaviness goes away. Sometimes it's ten seconds . . . sometimes maybe a minute . . . I've suffered stingers all my career . . . I had six stingers in one game.
>
> (Wilkinson 2004)

Wilkinson uses a range of terms in this article to refer to his experiences: pain, discomfort, distress and weak[ness]. When asked about the long-term effects, he says, 'I want to make sure it does not end my career early and . . . that I'll be in decent shape when my career's over'.

A month later, Steve Bale reflects on Wilkinson's recent injury trail – the World Cup Final injury in November 2003, then the disappointing breakdown in the 'come-back' match for Newcastle – and reports that he would not be fit for the Six Nations opener against Italy in February 2004. The title question of Bale's article: 'So just what is wrong with Johnny Wilkinson?' goes un-answered – instead we hear that he has undergone tests, and that an operation is unlikely. England head coach Clive Woodward says: 'At this stage I don't believe it needs more than rest and gym work' (Bale 2004).

But it did in fact require an operation, with many months on the sidelines, and a further injury shortly after returning to competition resulted in an oppor-tunity for Charlie Hodgson to stake his claim to Wilkinson's England place with a man-of-the-match performance in the 25–14 win over South Africa in November 2004.

This example illustrates the way in which pain experience and pain acceptance are part of athletes' engagement in sport. It also demonstrates the importance of injury avoidance and injury management, and the motivation for athletes to recover quickly and return to competition as early as possible.

Acceptance of training pain

'Sport brings pain.' The examples at the beginning of this chapter show how engagement in sport at any level requires us to exceed 'normal' levels of pain expectation and pain acceptance, and to adjust our attitudes accordingly. There follow three examples of pain acceptance from elite sport.

Sebastian Coe's father and coach, Peter, uses the term 'bodywashing' to bring out just how mentally tough an elite athlete must be, and how he must be able to accept pain levels beyond the experience of most of us:

> In the same way that you can brainwash somebody, you must bodywash an athlete so that even when the body is screaming out to stop, the messages to the brain are not so severe.
>
> (Quoted in Hughes 1987)

In the same article Steve Ovett likens pain to 'an old friend' to capture the attitude of someone who knows what it is to push themselves towards greater effort and achievement, and who goes beyond acceptance, even as far as welcoming the pain as a motivator, or as an indicator or marker of achievement:

> When you are training intensely, maybe three times a day through physical pain, you are constantly tired. You go through a retarded physical and mental condition where physical pain becomes like an old friend. When it starts to hurt you know you are doing what you should do.
>
> (Quoted in Hughes 1987)

These examples reveal the athlete as not necessarily the simple recipient of pain, but also as interacting with pain experiences in ways that are fundamental to sports engagement. One step further than this is the as-yet-undeveloped (but entrancing) idea suggested by Sigmund Loland (Chapter 3 of this book) of the empowered athlete who is the cultural operator and system manipulator – the Pain Artist, who conspicuously carries responsibility for his own pain and suffering, and their management.

Acceptance of pain culture

There is a genuine issue as to the extent to which the cultures that we inhabit control us, as opposed to our choosing them (or using them) as modes of expression for our selves. For each of us, doubtless, there is an element of both. We would not stay long in a habitus that we found uncomfortable or lacking in opportunities for self-expression, unless heavily constrained – and sport is (mainly) for volunteers. However, once on the inside, the powerful forces of practice culture and the expectations of significant others act so as to influence our choices and decisions.

Thus, Malcolm and Waddington (Chapters 10 and 11 of this book) refer to Nixon's idea of the 'conspiratorial alliance' that rationalizes risk and normalizes pain and injury, and the 'sportsnet' that entraps athletes into a culture of risk, insulating them and inhibiting them from seeking care.

Charlesworth and Young (Chapter 6 of this book) suggest that women are as affected as men by the dominant sports culture. They are as willing as men to

take risks with their bodies, and adopt the usual strategies of concealing, denying and normalizing pain and injury. They, too, make sense of compromised
health in terms of team membership and identity, avoiding being benched,
risk acceptance and others' evaluations of their courage and character.

These examples show the power of pain cultures to affect our behaviour. But,
despite the power over us of its very existence, we must all take responsibility for
the formation, preservation and development of the practice culture of our
sport. We all contribute to our sport's culture and ethos, which acts as a backdrop and a constraint for ourselves and for other athletes.

This applies, too, to its media representations. In *Nike Culture*, Goldman and
Papson (1998) provide a number of excellent examples of carefully constructed
and presented images and epithets from Nike advertisements, relating to receiving and inflicting pain:

> 'If you don't lose consciousness at the end, you could have run faster.'
> 'Some people quit when they reach their threshold of pain, some don't.'
> 'There are two sides to a sprinter. The side that wants to crush his oppo-
> nents and leave them blue and lifeless by the side of the track, (pause) and
> the other, darker, side.'
> 'There's a time and place for mercy. And it isn't here and it isn't now.'

One of Nike's adverts uses the theme of 'sport as war' and Iggy Pop's song
'Search and Destroy', featuring close-ups of falling hurdlers, blood-spattered
boxers and vomiting runners.[1]

We all need to ask to what extent we rejoice in these images, collude in these
representations, and bear contributory liability in their effects.

'No pain, no gain!': A note on sport and sado-masochism

The Marquis de Sade was famous for his crimes, which were characterized by
sexual perversion marked by a love of cruelty and a delight in or indifference
to another's pain and injury. Leopold von Sacher-Masoch was famous for his
descriptions of its partner perversion, that of finding pleasure in receiving
abuse and cruelty from another. In popular usage, however, the terms sadism
and masochism have lost their necessary implication with sexual activity, and
the notion of masochism has been extended to include finding pleasure in (or
at least a marked toleration of) one's self-imposed pain.

Applied to our present topic, we can see how sport might be seen as a rich
field for studies of sado-masochism. We have seen how athletes may accept
and even welcome pain. We observe the power and dependency of certain
coaching relationships, involving abuse and domination of athletes over training and lifestyle, and the use of pain and excessive exercise as punishments.
We observe the incidence of actual pain to athletes, and managers who do
not care – who become (and maybe need to become) hardened in order to
make the right decisions and to be effective.

So: is sport sado-masochistic? One answer is no, because sport is not a sexual perversion – but this is possibly too easy a route, which does not recognize the extended popular usage. Another answer is no, because in sport we are not taking pleasure in the pain itself, or in cruelty for its own sake. The pain is instrumental: no pain, no gain. It is pain and cruelty (if and when that exists) in the interest of winning, or of a better performance. It is acceptance (maybe even welcoming) of pain as an indicator or motivator of one's body doing well, and performing at its best.

That is to say: if coaches take satisfaction and delight simply in the discomfort, hurt, pain or suffering of their athletes, there is something amiss. They are sadistic perverts, because they take intrinsic pleasure in others' suffering. But if they are willing to inflict pains in the interest of getting results, the issues are different. Rights and wrongs now depend on levels of consent, pain, necessity and reward. A tough coach need not be oppressive, and the pains imposed by even the most oppressive coach need not be sadistic pains – but just because they are not sadistic does not mean that they are not wrong.

Where athletes are masochists, there seems to be little harm done, so long as no-one else is harmed. If athletes see pain as an inevitable or enjoyable part of (or accompaniment to) their greatest pleasure, they help us to see that simple pleasure is not all there is to life.

Note

1 I am grateful to Chris Kennet for the reference to *Nike Culture*.

Bibliography

Bale, S. (2004) 'So just what is wrong with Johnny Wilkinson?', *Daily Express*, 5 February 80.

BBC (1995a) *News*, 27 February, 9.00 pm.

BBC (1995b) *Sportsnight*, 1 March, 10.20 pm.

Beauchamp, T. L. and Childress, J. F. (2001) *Principles of Biomedical Ethics*, 5th edn, Oxford: Oxford University Press.

Goldman, R. and Papson, S. (1998) *Nike Culture*, London: Sage.

Harris, J. (1982) *Violence and Responsibility*, London: Routledge.

Hughes, R. (1987) 'The high, reckless price of being a superstar', *Sunday Times*, 7 June: 18.

McNamee, M. and Parry, J. (eds) (1998) *Ethics and Sport*, London: Routledge.

Parry, J. (1998) 'Violence and aggression in contemporary sport' in M. McNamee and J. Parry (eds) *Ethics and Sport*, London: Routledge: 205–24.

Shannon, B. and Klimkiewicz, J. J. (2002) 'Cervical burners in the athlete', *Journal of Clinical Sports Medicine*, 21, 1: 29–35.

SOED (1972) *Shorter Oxford English Dictionary*, 3rd edn, Oxford: Clarendon Press.

Wilkinson, J. (2004) 'New addition to hit list will not take sting out of my tail', *The Times*, 1 January: 36.

Section IV

The management of pain and injury

10 Sports medicine: A very peculiar practice?

Doctors and physiotherapists in elite English rugby union[1]

Dominic Malcolm

In their review of literature relating to the role of the club or team doctor, Waddington *et al.* (2001: 48) conclude that the vast majority of published work is prescriptive, describing not how doctors actually behave but how, in an ideal world, they ought to behave. They note that little of this literature is empirically grounded, and that the portion that is tends to be based on individual experience. Literature relating specifically to rugby union follows this general pattern. Davies (1990; see also Macleod 1989) provides a clear example of the empirically limited nature of existing work, drawing almost solely on his own experience in discussing the role of the team doctor in international rugby.[2] Kennedy provides an illustration of the prescriptive nature of the literature on the role of the rugby club doctor, listing the qualities that a doctor providing services in the rugby context 'ideally should have' (1990: 315). These are: knowledge of traumatology and the kinesiology of rugby, experience of rehabilitation and orthopaedics, good referral contacts and the ability to liaise effectively with physiotherapists. 'Most importantly', Kennedy notes, 'the doctor should have an affinity for the game and the people in it' (1990: 315). Limited though the literature relating to club doctors in sport is, literature relating to the role and working practice of physiotherapists is almost non-existent (Rennison 1999).

Prior to the research by Waddington *et al.* (2001) on English professional football, there had been no systematic investigation of the qualifications, experience and methods of appointment of doctors and physiotherapists practising in sport. The research of these authors demonstrated that the recruitment of football club doctors and physiotherapists constituted 'a catalogue of poor employment practice' (2001: 51) and that the limited qualifications and experience of medical personnel working in football clubs were also 'matters of concern'. The research attracted considerable press attention and was the subject of much debate on the letters pages of the journal in which it was published, the *British Journal of Sports Medicine* (Boyce 2001; Hay 2001; MacKay 2001). Contributors noted that the situation in football may have parallels in other sports, and a central objective of this chapter is to expand this emerging knowledge base by investigating similar themes with respect to club doctors and physiotherapists in English elite rugby union. Mention should be made of the groundbreaking

North American research of Safai (2003) and Walk (1997), but this chapter attempts to expand our knowledge in this hitherto neglected area.

The first part of this chapter outlines the level and range of qualifications and occupational experience typically held by doctors and physiotherapists at elite rugby clubs, the normal routes of recruitment and appointment, the ways in which the respective roles tend to be rewarded, and what motivates doctors and physiotherapists to fulfil the roles that they do. Within this context, I look at how the decline of amateurism in the sport has affected the employment practices to which rugby union medical personnel are subject. In the second part of the chapter I examine some of the consequences of these patterns of employ-ment (for example, in terms of practitioner autonomy and status within clubs) and the extent to which they contribute to what others have argued is the peculiar nature of sports medicine (Waddington 2000; Walk 1997).

Methods

Data were derived from a series of semi-structured, largely qualitative interviews with nine doctors (five with Premiership clubs, two with First Division clubs, one with a Third Division side and one with Premiership club experience, but who worked mainly with a representative side) and ten physiotherapists (three with Premiership clubs, three with First Division clubs, two with Second Division clubs and two with Third Division clubs). A total of 23 coaches and players were also interviewed as part of a broader research project, though their responses are not reported here.

In addition to the interviews, two postal questionnaire surveys were adminis-tered. These provided more quantitative data, and also a more secure basis for generalizing the findings from this study. A questionnaire survey was distributed to club doctors associated with the top 68 rugby union clubs in England; 34 questionnaires (50 per cent) were returned. Clubs in the three national divisions were disproportionately represented, with responses received from five of the 12 Premiership clubs (41.7 per cent), 12 of the 14 First Division clubs (85.7 per cent), nine of the 14 Second Division clubs (64.3 per cent), and just seven of the 28 clubs in Division Three North and South (25 per cent). The bias in the sample may reflect the administrative limitations of smaller clubs, although as some of our interviewees indicated, it may also be a consequence of the absence of an official or recognized club doctor at lower league clubs. A second questionnaire survey, sent to 'Head' or 'First XV' physiotherapists, obtained a response rate of 39.7 per cent. Once again, respondents were heavily skewed towards the top leagues, with responses obtained from physiotherapists at 10 Premiership clubs (83.3 per cent), four clubs from Division One (28.6 per cent), five clubs from Division Two (35.8 per cent), and eight from clubs in Division Three North and South (28.6 per cent).

Clubs in these divisions were selected partly because they represent the elite of the game in England, but also because it was felt that these would be the clubs which had experienced most acutely the relatively rapid professionalization and commercialization of rugby union since 1995. There is not the space here to describe fully the changes which have taken place in the game in the past 10 years, nor indeed the background to these changes and the networks of inter-dependence that have led to the 'rugby union figuration'[3] taking the shape that it does today (these changes are comprehensively covered in the work of Sheard 1997; Malcolm *et al.* 2000; White 2004). Briefly, however, the major changes include: the changing organizational structure of clubs, national governing bodies, leagues, etc.; the increasing monetization and growing seriousness (Dunning 1986) of the sport; and the growing media influence and spectacular-ization of the sport through the reform of its rules and styles of play. The effects of the commercialization of the sport on the number of injuries (Garraway *et al.* 2000; Malcolm *et al.* 2004) and the way in which injuries are 'managed' (Malcolm and Sheard 2002) have been discussed elsewhere.

Rugby club doctors: Qualifications, experience and methods of appointment

Waddington *et al.* (2001: 49) found that only about half a dozen of the leading football clubs employed full-time doctors, and no rugby club on which we have information did so. More closely resembling the situation in professional foot-ball, our research revealed that sports medicine specialists are poorly represented among rugby club doctors. Only two doctors – one interviewee and one ques-tionnaire respondent – described their primary employment as sports medicine. The majority of interviewees (78 per cent) and questionnaire respondents (67.6 per cent) were primarily employed in general practice. As one interviewee noted: 'the decisions as to whether people play are often made by either the GP (General Practitioner) who does not have sports knowledge or an orthopaedic surgeon who really knows how to operate but doesn't know about the rehab and things like that.' Without additional specialist training, GPs are unlikely to have the range of skills Kennedy identified as desirable for a club doctor, and the game's widespread reliance on GPs means that relatively few clubs have the expertise to cover all the medical areas identified by Kennedy as rele-vant in rugby union. Moreover, a number of questionnaire respondents came from medical sub-disciplines such as cosmetic surgery, radiology, urology and dentistry. Doctors working within such specialisms are even less likely to have the range of skills required in the rugby setting.

Few rugby club doctors had received appropriate specialist training. Just two (5.9 per cent) rugby club doctors who returned questionnaires cited an existing qualification in sport and exercise medicine, though three others (8.8 per cent) reported that they were currently undertaking such courses. Interviewees indi-cated that such courses, where taken, were normally funded by the doctor him/herself rather than by their clubs. There was, however, a relatively high degree of relevant occupational experience revealed by our questionnaire respondents. A total of 35.3 per cent of rugby club doctors had worked in other sports medicine contexts, either at other rugby clubs (11.8 per cent) or, more commonly, in other sports (23.5 per cent).

Given most doctors' lack of appropriate qualifications in sports medicine, it is perhaps not surprising that securing the position of rugby club doctor is rarely dependent on a candidate's qualifications or expertise. Rather, jobs were obtained largely on the basis of personal contacts. No rugby club doctor whom we interviewed or who responded to the questionnaire survey applied for the position as a result of it being advertised, either in the general or the medical press. Often the appointment of the club doctor developed from a personal contact with club coaches or committee members, or from their involvement with the club in another capacity (for example, as a coach, referee, parent of a player or simply a spectator). This may, on occasions, lead to a clash of interests and priorities. One physiotherapist whom we interviewed explained that the club doctor was also the club's official photographer and noted that, 'it doesn't help when he's on the touchline and you want someone stitched and he's more interested in taking photographs of the game'.

There was evidence that this casual kind of arrangement is becoming less common, though such changes may not be without conflict. One doctor explained that the club's new coach had approached him because, as he put it, they had heard 'on the grapevine' of his interest in sports medicine. However, this doctor experienced continual friction with the incumbent club doctor, and each left the club for a brief period. He illustrated one of the sources of the friction: 'I did find it difficult to believe that this guy was the doctor for seven years . . . he's never gone to any sports medicine training . . . all he cares about is rugby . . . and having that kudos of being the doctor and standing on the side watching the game'.

Given the informal way in which many club doctors were appointed, it is not surprising that only five (14.7 per cent) of those who returned questionnaires and, indeed, none of those doctors interviewed in the research, had been interviewed for the post of club doctor. Where interviews did take place, most commonly this involved a member of the administrative staff. Only two doctors on whom we have relevant information indicated that their interview was conducted by someone possessing a medical qualification (the club's physiotherapist and 'clinical director'). Many questionnaire respondents simply used the word 'informal' to describe the manner of their appointment. A Premiership club doctor, when asked if he had been interviewed, replied: 'No. Well they talked to me over a couple of pints of beer.' Indeed, only one doctor who responded to the questionnaire had a formal contract and, not surprisingly, he worked for a Premiership club with the formal contract having started shortly after the advent of professionalism in the English game.

There are signs, however, that medical appointment procedures are becoming more formalized in the professional era. Fifteen doctors in our questionnaire survey (44.1 per cent) had been involved in further medical appointments at the club, nine (26.5 per cent) in connection with the recruitment of other doctors and 12 (35.3 per cent) with the recruitment of physiotherapists. Four

(11.8 per cent) of the doctors in the questionnaire survey had sat on interview panels and two (5.9 per cent) had drawn up job descriptions. Others had been involved in the recommendation (26.5 per cent), and personal selection (17.6 per cent), of new recruits to the medical/health care staff.

Club doctors: Duties, routines, rewards and motivations

Often clubs can call upon a bank of doctors who rotate duties. Just 16 questionnaire respondents (47.1 per cent) worked alone. The mean number of doctors at a club was 2.03. Doctors also varied in terms of the frequency of their visits to the club and the number of hours worked. All the doctors who responded to the questionnaire attended first-team home matches and 64.7 per cent normally travelled to away matches. A small number (17.6 per cent) normally attended reserve or youth-team home matches.

Not surprisingly, Premiership sides have the most comprehensive cover. As one doctor with a Premiership side stated during an interview: 'Now that we're professional all the teams bring a doctor with them . . . It used to be the case that they didn't, five years ago . . . it's all changed.' Conversely, doctors with lower division teams explained the difficult position in which they sometimes found themselves: 'I've certainly been to away matches where there hasn't been a doctor, which is a little bit difficult when you actually have to treat one of the opposition's players.'

The number of hours worked per week by doctors responding to our questionnaire ranged from one to 18, with a mean of five and a mode of three. Though all the Premiership club doctors interviewed stated that, since professionalism, a Monday/Tuesday injury assessment clinic had been introduced at their club, most doctors (55.9 per cent of questionnaire respondents) had scheduled visits to the club only on match days. Of those who did routinely attend training sessions, most (60 per cent) visited the club just once a week. None of the clubs encompassed within the sample had a doctor in attendance at all, or even most, training sessions. More commonly, interviewees explained, the doctor's role was to use their referral contacts (as noted by Kennedy) to fast-track players through National Health Service (NHS) schedules. As a questionnaire respondent noted, 'we [the club doctors] provide an excellent service, with the club supported – probably unknowingly – by the NHS'.

Many rugby union doctors (28.4 per cent of questionnaire respondents) received no remuneration for their services. Most typically, other doctors received complimentary tickets/club membership (29.4 per cent), match day hospitality (23.5 per cent) or a match attendance fee (23.5 per cent), described by some doctors as 'modest'. Just three questionnaire respondents (8.8 per cent) received a salary. Questionnaire respondents described their role as a 'labour of love' and, somewhat resentfully, another crossed through all the categories of reward and wrote 'SOD ALL' in capital letters on the questionnaire. Yet most doctors, if not happy, are at least accepting of the lack of financial remuneration and some are even prepared to subsidize their clubs. One Premiership doctor explained that as companies had blacklisted his club for not paying its bills on time, he bore all strapping costs on his credit card.

Not surprisingly, only four doctors (11.8 per cent) cited payment as one of the main reasons why they acted as club doctor. Most commonly a doctor's motivation came from their 'support for the team' (82.4 per cent) or a 'general interest in sport' (67.6 per cent). Three (8.8 per cent) felt that the occupational experience was useful, with two (5.8 per cent) noting that their interest in sports medicine was a major motivational factor. More typically doctors stated that they enjoyed being 'part of the team', provided cover due to some personal tie (for example, because their son played for the club) or, as one doctor put it, because he wanted to 'give back to rugby something in return for years of great pleasure as a player'. Indeed, from the interviews conducted with physiotherapists it became particularly clear that some doctors were motivated by the social aspects of the role. One retired physiotherapist recalled travelling to an away match and having to assist the home team's doctor to stitch a player's wound because the doctor was too drunk to provide treatment! Another physiotherapist, recalling his experiences of the amateur game, noted:

> the club doctor was a social member that would turn up and frequent the bar. He would be available for stitching on a Saturday; they'd use a room out the back of the stand, complete with a bottle of scotch and an optic for members of the crowd to go down and get a quick shot during the game.

Rugby club physiotherapists: Qualifications, experience and methods of appointment

A total of 85.2 per cent of questionnaire respondents were chartered physiotherapists (this being the qualification required to work as a physiotherapist in the British National Health Service) as were all but one of our interviewees (who possessed a BSc in Sports Rehabilitation). It was notable that 13 (almost half of our questionnaire respondents) had a degree in physiotherapy and a further four (14.8 per cent) listed a relevant postgraduate qualification. In all, 63 per cent of questionnaire respondents had previous relevant occupational experience; 12 (44.4 per cent) had worked as physiotherapists at other rugby union clubs, and 11 (40.7 per cent) had practised in other professional sports. All but one interviewee had practised in other sports or at other rugby union clubs. In contrast to rugby union club doctors, physiotherapists tend to be well qualified and have prior experience of working in the sports setting.

Although rugby club physiotherapy posts are normally filled by appropriately qualified personnel, they are rarely advertised. Two questionnaire respondents (7.4 per cent) obtained their positions by replying to advertisements placed in medical journals/physiotherapy magazines, and one interviewee responded to an advertisement placed in a local newspaper. More commonly, positions were obtained through personal contact with other physiotherapists connected with the club (51.9 per cent), or through personal contacts with coaching or administrative staff at the club (48.1 per cent). Interviewees provided qualitative evidence to support this overall picture. A physiotherapist with a Second Division club recalled:

> I was working in the NHS in an outpatients physiotherapy department. One of the female members of staff was married to a doctor associated to the rugby club and they sent word through to our department that they were looking for a part time physio.

The recruitment of rugby club physiotherapists, like that of club doctors, is informal and, to a degree, reliant on an 'old boy'/'old girl' network, but for the majority it is at least a network based in the wider medical profession rather than the sport itself. Thus, in comparison with the recruitment of doctors, physiotherapists are likely to experience some 'vetting' by a medically qualified person, albeit only informally.

Thirteen (48.1 per cent) questionnaire respondents were interviewed for their positions, a finding which underscores the relative informality of the recruitment of physiotherapists. All 13 were interviewed by a member of the coaching staff. Four respondents had also been interviewed by a member of the administrative staff (14.8 per cent of all respondents), and five (18.5 per cent) had been interviewed by a member of the club's medical staff. Interviews, however, were often quite informal; one questionnaire respondent described his interview as 'a chat over the phone'.

As with rugby club doctors, it seems that medical staff are having an increasing input into recruitment processes. Sixteen (59.3 per cent) questionnaire respondents had been involved in the recruitment of additional physiotherapy staff at the club, nine (33.3 per cent) had been involved in the recruitment of doctors, and nine had been involved in the recruitment of other health care providers (e.g. masseurs). Most commonly this involvement entailed 'personally selecting' the appointee (cited by 40.7 per cent of respondents), though 10 (37 per cent) had drawn up job descriptions and eight (29.6 per cent) had sat on interview panels.

Twelve respondents (44.4 per cent) possessed formal contracts with their clubs, all of which post-dated the 'open' era of professionalism in rugby union. That the move towards the formalization of appointment procedures is relatively slow was highlighted by a questionnaire respondent with a Premiership club who wrote: 'Only just getting written contract and have been here for two years'.

Rugby club physiotherapists: Duties, routines, rewards and motivations

Where players are not full-time (i.e. in most clubs outside of the Premiership) there is too little contact time with players to justify employing a full-time physiotherapist. It is not surprising, therefore, that only 11 (40.7 per cent) questionnaire respondents identified the rugby club as their main source of employment. A further 48.1 per cent stated that they worked primarily in private practice (many interviewees, for instance were self-employed), and two others held positions in hospital practice.

Relatively few physiotherapists (22.2 per cent) worked alone at their clubs. Most commonly, clubs were serviced by two physiotherapists, though the mean number of physiotherapists at rugby clubs was 3.12. All respondents attended first-team home games and nearly all respondents (88.9 per cent) normally travelled to away fixtures. Over a quarter (25.7 per cent) also provided physiotherapy cover at reserve or youth-team matches. In contrast to rugby club doctors, almost all physiotherapists (92.6 per cent) attended the club on non-match days. Interviewees, however, explained that physiotherapists' regular attendance both at matches and at an increasing number of training sessions had developed post-professionalism.

Most commonly (40.7 per cent) physiotherapists attended the club twice per week though the mean was 3.44. Although 39.1 per cent of respondents worked 10 hours per week or fewer for the club, 30.4 per cent worked 40 or more hours, indicating that the availability of physiotherapy varies markedly from club to club, depending on whether players and physiotherapists are employed on a full-time or part-time basis. There is some evidence that this pattern of working hours leads to considerable variations in the quality of care that can be provided. Interviewees at the leading clubs expressed some satisfaction with the service they provided, but physiotherapists at lower league clubs felt that treatment was limited. A First Division physiotherapist explained:

> we can't control what a player does outside of Tuesday, Thursday and Saturday afternoon . . . it's just two hours a week and it's come in and wait to be treated, and it's a minimal kind of treatment and you've got to trust the players to do all their own work away from here.

He contrasted this with the treatment which patients in his private practice receive: 'at least half an hour with every patient . . . you can make sure that they are doing all their exercises correctly instead of just letting them go'.

All the physiotherapists who responded to our questionnaire were financially remunerated in some way. Ten (37 per cent) received a salary, and 14 (51.9 per cent) were paid an hourly fee. Others indicated that they received a fixed sum per match or were paid 'per treatment given to each player, at a reduced rate from my usual fee'. Questionnaire respondents also reported that they received expenses (29.6 per cent), hospitality (25.9 per cent) and complimentary tickets (22.2 per cent).

The vast majority of physiotherapists (81.5 per cent) stated that a significant motivation for their acting as rugby club physiotherapist was their 'general interest in sport'. In addition – and in contrast to rugby club doctors for whom tangible rewards were relatively unimportant – physiotherapists are often motivated by payment (48.1 per cent) and the ability to gain occupational experience (55.6 per cent). In contrast to some rugby club doctors who indicated that the work required of them at the club was relatively basic, practising in elite rugby union was described as 'a very exciting, challenging and progressive area of physiotherapy'. A Premiership doctor whom we interviewed put this in perspective:

> The physiotherapists . . . from what I've seen are absolutely stunning. They are very, very, very focussed and very well qualified. They are very sports specific. They don't want to deal with normal physio problems like back pain, swollen joints, old geriatrics . . . They want to deal with the sharp end.

Sports medicine: A very peculiar practice?

In summary, it can be noted that relatively few rugby club doctors have the range of skills and experience identified as desirable in an occupant of this position, that doctors are rarely appointed in line with conventional forms of employment practice, and that they generally receive little financial (though perhaps considerable 'social') reward for the service they provide. On the other hand, rugby club physiotherapists are often well qualified to practise in the sports club setting and, while the majority are again recruited informally (for example, few responded to job advertisements, few had been formally interviewed for the post), they are at least recruited by other medical personnel, and largely from conventional (that is, non-sport) health care backgrounds. What are the consequences of these patterns of employment for the practice of medical care in English elite rugby union clubs?

Waddington *et al.* (2001: 51) concluded their study of medical care in English professional football by stating that 'almost all aspects of the processes of appointing and remunerating club doctors and physiotherapists need careful re-examination'. The findings presented here suggest that in many rugby clubs, and despite the fact that rugby has a higher rate of injury than football (Garraway *et al.* 2000; Garraway and MacLeod 1995; Hume and Marshall 1994; Sports Council 1991) and therefore arguably has a particularly pressing need for skilled medical practitioners, the situation is, in some respects, worse. Although doctors in rugby union have marginally more experience of practising in sports contexts than do football club doctors, methods of appointment in rugby are even less rigorous than they are in football and formal contracts are very rare. The skills and commitment of rugby club doctors can, at best, be described as variable, and may expose some players, even at leading clubs, to what many might consider unacceptable levels of risk. The reverse is, however, the case in relation to physiotherapists, particularly when compared with their counterparts in football, for physiotherapists in elite rugby union are relatively well qualified and often possess relevant occupational experience. Physiotherapy appointments in football are often 'in the gift of the manager', but this situation appears relatively rare in rugby union. Many rugby club physiotherapists have good qualifications and, unlike many club physiotherapists in football, often also have experience of working in non-sport clinical settings, and indeed may even have their own private practice. Although we might say that rugby union club doctors carry many of the hallmarks of the amateur game, rugby club physiotherapists, and the ways in which they are recruited and employed, appear to have professionalized rather more rapidly.

Several writers have noted that one major respect in which sports medicine differs from other forms of medical practice is that the sports medicine practitioner – or more precisely, the sports medicine practitioner who is employed by a club – has dual, and potentially conflicting obligations, for club medical staff have to balance their responsibilities to the athletes whom they treat with their obligations to the club which employs or authorizes them to practise (Crane 1990; Waddington 2000). A similar reading of the characteristics specific to the sports medicine setting informed Walk's research into student athletic trainers (SATs) in an American university. Separating literature on pain and injury in sport into 'organizational' and gender studies analyses, he nevertheless concludes that the two approaches lead to a similar set of conclusions about the practice of sports medicine (1997: 27). For instance, Walk argues that the implication of Nixon's work on pain and injury (e.g. Nixon 1992), described in more detail in Roderick's chapter elsewhere in this volume, is that medicine is practised 'differently, more competently, and/or more ethically in non-sports contexts' (Walk 1997: 24). There is, therefore, some consensus that sports medicine is, in some respects, a 'peculiar' form of practice. In the remaining section of this chapter, I build on the empirical description of the working practice of medical staff in rugby clubs, and how these relationships contribute to, or represent an additional dimension of, this 'peculiarity' of sports medicine.

Through the interviews conducted with rugby club medical personnel it became apparent that there were considerable differences in the way in which doctors and physiotherapists as occupational groups perceived their obligations and autonomy. The majority of doctors, for instance, felt that any conflict of interests was minimal:

Interviewer: Who is your responsibility to as a doctor? Your employer? Or the patient?
Doctor: The patient definitely. Definitely first and foremost the patient. If you are being paid by the club, then obviously you have a certain duty to the club as well. But I think you always have to do that with the consent of the player.

Others recognized that although potentially there might be a clash of interests, this very rarely surfaced in their working lives. Asked about this, a Premiership doctor responded: 'I haven't, to be honest I haven't (experienced a clash of interests). I can't think of any one particular situation where I have been that perturbed.' Another, First Division, doctor argued, 'it's perhaps surprising how little real dilemmas arise. The interests of the players usually coincide with the interests of the club.' This opinion was reiterated by a Premiership doctor who said, 'I want them to play, I love the game, I love the club. I want them to be there, but not at all costs. If I'm saying they are not fit to play, that's for their own good, the club's good and everybody in it.' But it would also be true to say that most doctors recognized that the kind of treatment 'patients' in the sports setting received was, in some respects, different from that received by patients in their 'everyday' working lives. As a Premiership doctor noted:

> there are some things that happen in sports medicine now that other physicians will look at aghast. In actual fact I find . . . that sometimes when I am dealing with my players I allow them to do things which I normally wouldn't allow with Joe Public.

The following extract from an interview with a Premiership club doctor provides a similar picture.

Interviewer: But in general medical care, you err on the side of caution?
Doctor: Of course.
Interviewer: And it seems that from other doctors and physios that I have spoken to, and players as well, that in the rugby and sports context you don't always, the outcome is not always on the side of caution.
Doctor: You are probably right . . . again it is a professional thing, it's your professional integrity and yes you are attached to the club, and you want the best players to be playing. And wherever possible you will do that, but equally there is a line where you have got to be sure of yourself professionally. And you have to say, 'no I'm not happy'. And you have to be big enough and strong enough to do that, and if you are not you shouldn't be doing the job. You don't want to be bullied by the coaches. The managers and the union should be doing their job. You should walk out. And if that ever happens with my professional judgment, if it was challenged, then I would leave, that's what I'd do.

In summary, therefore, the doctors recognized that practising in the rugby club context was slightly different (for the majority) from their work in general practice, but none of them felt that the constraints within which they worked were particularly threatening to their professional integrity. Indeed, in such cases, the lack of payment which doctors typically receive may be 'enabling' in that the penalties attached to leaving their posts are reduced.

Physiotherapists, however, seemed to perceive these dilemmas and potential problems rather more acutely and this may be related to the remuneration and the other rewards (for example, occupational experience) they receive from performing the role. As one Premiership physiotherapist noted: 'I've got a very difficult role to play haven't I? I'm quite literally between the two. I'm not a player but I'm not anybody who has any say or view in selection.' A First Division physiotherapist explained that the more his role at the club expanded, the more difficult it became:

> Particularly now where you are employed, you are interested not just in a 'treating the injury' role, but you may be employed in ways that may be performance enhancing; you may be involved in the fitness training or in a small way in the coaching of the side, you may be involved in rehab which . . . includes a lot of coordination, quickness, speed, agility, type work . . . You may be very interested in the result, not that I've ever been on any performance related bonus but I know a lot of physios are. So on the one side you have all the performance of the players out there and you have the caring side of things and the players' long-term interests at heart. It is a difficult role to perform well. That isn't something that is written down and different people's positions lie in different places.

Thus, although almost all the interviewees suggested that practising sports medicine was in some ways peculiar, the ways in which individuals perceived this peculiarity varied. Physiotherapists' greater awareness or sensitivity towards these conflicts is probably related both to their more regular contact with players and also, to some degree, to the relatively more powerful position which doctors, as an occupational group, enjoy in terms of professional autonomy more generally. More particularly, it may well be the case that, because most doctors see their role as essentially voluntary and advisory, they may simply remove themselves from conflictual situations. On the other hand, the process of being financially rewarded by the club for their services may mean that physiotherapists encounter conflicts more acutely, for their greater degree of involvement with the club – and specifically their more regular contact with players and managers – may mean that these kinds of pressures are experienced more frequently.

An additional dimension of the peculiarity of sports medicine was pointed up by Walk (1997: 32) who observed that, 'Athletes frequently engaged in behaviours that demeaned the student trainers and resisted their wishes.' An analysis of the non-cooperation of athletes as patients would merit a paper in itself, but here it is pertinent to note that the research reported revealed a number of incidents where medical staff were demeaned by the behaviour of others within the rugby club setting. For instance, when I arrived at a Third Division club to interview a doctor on a training night, I found him sweeping out the changing rooms. Later the same doctor was systematically ignored by bar staff who, in the absence of anyone else to serve, busied themselves filling ice-buckets. Such an experience could be passed off as a one-off involving a not much liked or respected individual, had similar things not also happened elsewhere. While one Premiership club physiotherapist was being interviewed in a quiet corner of the clubhouse, a player shouted, 'why are you interviewing him? He's not important you know.' The physiotherapist, not surprisingly, looked somewhat discomfited at this remark. The level of respect afforded to some medical staff in some rugby club contexts again marks out sports medicine as being characterized by social rules quite different from those of other, 'normal', forms of medical practice, where great respect is usually accorded to medical practitioners.

Some interviewees brought up these status issues during the research. A Premiership doctor, for instance, argued that:

> It's always the same old story that you are never going to get the recognition that you deserve. You are almost certainly one of the most highly qualified people in attendance and you are treated as the butt of the jokes. You have got to be prepared to accept that.

Similarly a physiotherapist at a First Division club noted:

> I have been called Dr. Death, Healing Hans, and all manner of things! 'Oh, don't go and see Healing Hans, you won't be fit for two months!' You could take that personally or you could just let it run straight off your back.

This aspect of sports medicine can only be understood relationally. On the one hand, you have the confidence, arrogance perhaps, which characterizes elite sportspeople and comes to underpin their self-identity (see for instance the work of Adler and Adler 1985 in this respect). On the other hand, you have a group of medical staff who are prepared to forgo the respect which they can usually demand from patients because of the other benefits of the job, for example, the attraction of working with elite sportspeople. In what other setting, one might ask, would a doctor include in his/her duties, 'ground maintenance – painting, grass cutting, general labouring, etc.' as one Third Division questionnaire respondent told us?

Doctors also reported a number of clashes between themselves and physiotherapists. Such conflict, it may be suggested, is somewhat unusual in conventional medical settings, where the balance of power between doctor and physiotherapist tends to be more clearly defined. A First Division doctor, describing his appointment to the club, recalled:

> I had an interview with the physio you could say. The physio came and we had lunch and chatted through, and he told me what his thoughts were. And he was very clear. He was the physio. He was in charge of the medical set-up. And he would ask me if he wanted my advice. He said that the previous guy was always on the pitch and he said 'I don't need the other guy on the pitch'. I said 'Well that's fine, I'm cool with that'.

Another doctor described how a clash between one of the doctors and a physiotherapist at the club had led to the doctor's dismissal:

> This particular GP saw the physio as wanting to wield too much power. He thought the physio had an agenda whereby the doctor was dancing to

the tune of the physio, he was just rubber stamping his decisions and his management.

This is, of course, an inversion of the conventional division of labour in medical settings where the doctor's opinion (based on a longer programme of education and training leading to a more highly regarded qualification) would normally hold greater sway. However, the factors discussed in the first section of the chapter – recruitment, reward, contact hours, and so on – indicate that in the rugby club context it cannot be taken for granted that this conventional division of expertise exists.

During matches, again, we see an inversion of conventional medical practice. There can be few more familiar sights in professional sport than the physiotherapist running on to the pitch to treat a player. However, as a Premiership doctor noted: 'in theory I suppose the doctor should be the first person to get there to make the diagnosis . . . and assess the situation, and if it's not a fracture or a dislocation or something . . . let the physio deal with it.' But, this doctor continued, in the sports context this is rarely the case:

Interviewer: Does the physio usually go on first?
Doctor: Oh yes! Yes, yes, yes.

It is not unique that initial medical diagnoses are made by junior colleagues in the medical setting – for example in Accident and Emergency Wards nurses normally conduct the first assessment of a patient's needs – but this arrangement is based on considerations of cost rather than best practice, a point demonstrated by a doctor with a First Division club:

> I think problems did arise sometimes (from the dominance of the physiotherapist). Once or twice there were players, it's very easy in retrospect to say 'Oh I think I would have diagnosed that earlier' . . . (but) there were a few occasions I thought, 'well yes sometimes it would be better to have another view' . . . What annoyed me a bit was that (when injuries weren't) responding in the normal way, (players) weren't then referred to me for an opinion.

Some doctors indicated that they entered the field of play whenever they felt it necessary: 'I'm not the sort of doctor who sits in the stand. I'll sit at the side of the pitch. If I can see something that I am not happy about, I go straight on, I don't wait to be called, because the sooner I can get there the sooner I can assess . . . we all know it helps if you have got somebody else working with you.' Others stated more clearly that they left matters largely in the hands of the physiotherapist: 'They are literally and metaphorically "hands on". They see the players, they're the first port of call and they are dealing with the majority of problems.'

Conclusion

In conclusion, there appear to be at least four factors which ultimately determine the working relationship between the doctor and physiotherapist in a particular sports setting and which may, at times, lead to abnormal or 'peculiar' working practices. One, undoubtedly, is the type of injuries rugby players experience and the extent to which the majority of these can be, and indeed are, often best dealt with by a physiotherapist. Second, due to their respective 'contractual' duties, doctors are likely to have less, perhaps minimal, contact with the club and the doctor may regard him/herself as 'on call' rather than 'on duty' during the week and, in some cases, even on match days. Third, most doctors' own lack of appropriate skills and experience in sports medicine, relative to the often highly appropriate skills, qualifications and all-round professionalism of rugby club physiotherapists, means that doctors may often be less well equipped than physiotherapists to deal with many of the injuries which occur. Last, however, it seems that there is an unusual power balance in which the physiotherapist generally holds more influence over the players than does the doctor, and indeed may hold an abnormally high influence over the doctor him/herself. This is related not just to their relative skills and worth to the club, but also to commitment, the way in which they have been appointed, and the voluntary or paid nature of their positions.

The review of appointment procedures, and allied matters discussed above indicates that an additional aspect of the peculiarity of sports medicine, not found elsewhere in the medical world, is the informality of recruitment and employment procedures. Although some literature points towards the peculiarity of sports medicine in relation to the potential conflict of interests between the patient and the employer, it would be more adequate to see these two aspects as interdependent. That is to say, where jobs have been openly obtained in line with the normal equal opportunities principles, the appointees are likely to be accorded a certain amount of legitimacy and kudos. Where a post holder has been hand-selected, is not financially rewarded and is not particularly well qualified, their power relative to others in the rugby union figuration (for example, players, managers, and other medical staff) is likely to be low. The medical treatment that players receive can be adequately understood only if we locate the roles of club doctors and physiotherapists within this wider figuration of power relations in rugby.

Notes

1 I am particularly indebted to Ken Sheard who played an equal part in the data-gathering phase of this project and who has been highly influential in developing the ideas contained in this paper.

2 He highlights the need to gain players' confidence, his role in identifying emergent injuries in players (e.g. through a player favouring one leg) and, at a time when no tactical substitutions were allowed, the doctor's role in certifying that a player is unfit to continue playing (and thus be substituted). More specific to the international

context, Davies notes the significance of his role in providing vaccinations (for over-
seas tours), advising on drug testing, and information dissemination.
3 Elias described a figuration as 'a structure of mutually oriented and dependent people'
   (1978: 261). There is some debate over the use of this term (see Guilianotti 2004),
   but figurationalists claim that the concept of figuration represents a conceptual break-
   through in that it puts the problem of human interdependencies at the very heart of
   sociological theory, and serves as a simple conceptual tool to loosen this linguistic constraint to speak and to think as though the 'individual' and 'society' were separate and
   perhaps even opposing entities.

Bibliography

Adler, P. and Adler, P. (1985) 'From idealism to pragmatic detachment: The academic
   performance of college athletes', *Sociology of Education*, 58: 241–50.

Boyce S. (2001) 'The football club doctor system', *British Journal of Sports Medicine*, 35:
   281.

Crane, J. (1990) 'Association football: the team doctor' in S. D. W. Payne (ed.)
   Medicine, Sport and the Law, Oxford: Blackwell Scientific Publications: 331–37.

Davies, J. (1990) 'The team doctor in international rugby' in S. D. W. Payne (ed.)
   Medicine, Sport and the Law, Oxford: Blacwell Scientific Publications: 324–30.

Dunning, E. (1986) 'The dynamics of modern sport: notes on achievement-striving and
   the social significance of sport' in N. Elias and E. Dunning (eds) *Quest for Excitement:
   Sport and Leisure in the Civilizing Process*, Oxford: Basil Blackwell: 205–23.

Elias, N. (1978) *The Civilizing Process*, Volume 1: *The History of Manners*, Oxford: Basil
   Blackwell.

Garraway W. M. and Macleod D. A. D (1995) 'Epidemiology of rugby football injuries',
   The Lancet, 345: 1485–87.

Garraway, W. M., Lee, A. J., Hutton, S. J., Russell, E. B. A. W. and Macleod, D. A. D.
   (2000) 'Impact of professionalism on injuries in rugby union', *British Journal of Sports
   Medicine*, 34: 348–51.

Guilianotti, R. (2004) 'Civilizing games: Norbert Elias and the sociology of sport' in
   R. Giulianotti (ed.) *Sport and Modern Social Theorists*, Basingstoke: Palgrave Macmillan:
   145–60.

Hay, C. (2001) 'Club doctors and physiotherapists', *British Journal of Sports Medicine*, 35:
   207.

Hume, P. A. and Marshall, S. W. (1994) 'Sports injuries in New Zealand: Exploratory
   analyses', *New Zealand Journal of Sports Medicine*, 22: 18–22.

Kennedy, K. W. (1990) 'The team doctor in rugby union football' in S. D. W. Payne
   (ed.) *Medicine, Sport and the Law*, Oxford: Blackwell Scientific Publications: 315–23.

MacKay R, (2001) 'Club doctors and physiotherapists', *British Journal of Sports Medicine*,
   35: 207.

Macleod, D. (1989) 'Team doctor', *British Journal of Sports Medicine*, 23, 4: 211–12.

Malcolm, D. and Sheard, K. (2002) ' "Pain in the assets": The effects of commercialization and professionalization on the management of injury in English rugby union',
   Sociology of Sport Journal, 19, 2: 149–69.

Malcolm, D., Sheard, K. and White, A. (2000) 'The changing structure and culture of
   English rugby union football', *Culture, Sport, Society*, 3, 3: 63–87.

Malcolm, D., Sheard, K. and Smith, S. (2004) 'Protected research: Sports medicine and
   rugby injuries', *Culture, Sport, Society*, 7, 1: 97–110.

Nixon, H. L. II (1992) 'A social network analysis of influences on athletes to play with pain and injuries', *Journal of Sport and Social Issues*, 16: 127–35.

Rennison, M. (1999) 'Physiotherapy for the Scotland rugby team: An ever changing role', *Sports Care News*, 17: 10–11.

Safai, P. (2003) 'Healing the body in the "culture of risk": Examining the negotiation of treatment between sport medicine clinicians and injured athletes in Canadian intercollegiate sport', *Sociology of Sport Journal*, 20, 2: 127–46.

Sheard, K. (1997) '"Breakers ahead!" Professionalization and rugby union football: Lessons from rugby league', *International Journal of the History of Sport*, 14, 1: 116–37.

Sports Council (1991) *Injuries in Sport and Exercise*, London: The Sports Council.

Waddington, I. (2000) *Sport, Health and Drugs: A critical sociological perspective*, London: Routledge.

Waddington, I., Roderick, M. and Naik, R. (2001) 'Methods of appointment and qualifications of club doctors and physiotherapists in English professional football: Some problems and issues', *British Journal of Sports Medicine*, 35: 48–53.

Walk, S. R. (1997) 'Peers in pain: The experiences of student athletic trainers', *Sociology of Sport Journal*, 14, 1: 22–56.

White, A. (2004) 'Rugby union football in England: Civilizing processes and the de-institutionalization of amateurism' in E. Dunning, D. Malcolm and I. Waddington (eds) *Sport Histories: Figurational Studies in the Development of Modern Sports*, London: Routledge.

11 Ethical problems in the medical management of sports injuries

A case study of English professional football

Ivan Waddington

Writing from the perspective of a team doctor in water sports, Newton (1990: 309) has suggested that: 'Essentially the profile of the team doctor is that of the old-fashioned family doctor'. Although many sports physicians have a background in general practice (Waddington 2002), and although it is undoubtedly tempting to cite the example of the much-loved 'old-fashioned family doctor' as the model for the practice of sports medicine, this comparison is in some respects misleading. There are a number of important differences – and not simply in terms of the different kinds of medical problems with which they have to deal – between the role of the general practitioner and that of the sports physician. In particular, there are important differences in relation to the management of some potentially difficult ethical issues within the two contexts. The exploration of some of these ethical problems in the practice of sports medicine, by means of a case study of English professional football, is the central object of this chapter. In particular, the analysis will focus on three areas of the practice of sports medicine which raise medical ethical issues: (i) questions of informed consent; (ii) return to play decisions following injury and associated quality of care issues; and (iii) issues relating to medical confidentiality.

The relationship between doctor (or other health professional) and patient is normally underpinned by three fundamental assumptions: (i) the doctor's skill is used exclusively on behalf of the patient; (ii) the doctor is not acting as an agent on behalf of anybody else whose interests may conflict with those of the patient; (iii) the doctor may be trusted with private or intimate information which she/he will treat confidentially and not divulge to others.

However, these assumptions – which underpin the trust that is an essential part of relationships between doctors and patients in general practice – may not apply in the same way, or to the same degree, in the work situation of the club doctor or physiotherapist in professional sport. As the British Medical Association has recently noted in its handbook of ethics:

> Doctors who are employed by sports teams and by sports clubs may find themselves subject to the tension of conflicting loyalties. On the one hand they are agents of the team or club with the contractual obligations

of an employee, and, on the other, as doctors, they are advocates for the individual athletes or players who are their patients.

(BMA 2003: 595)

Clearly the club, which employs the doctor, has a legitimate interest in the management of players' injuries. But if the team doctor and physiotherapist are agents of the club, how can they simultaneously act as agents for, and on behalf of, the individual player-as-patient? How, in their day-to-day practice, do club doctors and physiotherapists resolve the potential conflicts of interest between their responsibility to their employer (the club) and their responsibility to the individual player-as-patient? What happens if the interests of the club and the player do not coincide, as inevitably will be the case from time to time?

Roy and Irvin (1983: 3) have noted that where members of the medical and related professions are employed by the team management, 'this may lead to an explicit expectation on the part of the management or coaching staff of loyalty to them' and they add that 'this arrangement may not always be in the best interests of the athlete'. For example there is in professional football, as we shall see, a strong and clear expectation that, wherever possible, players will continue to play through pain and injury and the club medical staff may be subject to strong pressure to agree – possibly against their better medical judgement – to players returning to play, perhaps with the help of painkilling injections, before they have fully recovered from injury. Should the doctor (or physiotherapist) concur, thereby possibly risking further and perhaps more serious injury to the player? Or should they insist that the player is rested, thereby possibly incurring the disapproval of the coach/manager? Are the long-term health risks of playing while injured explained to, and understood by, players? Or is relevant information withheld from, or simply not conveyed to, players? How do club doctors and physiotherapists balance the long-term health interests of the player with the short-term interests of the club/coach in fielding the strongest team?

A further problem relates to medical confidentiality. A club doctor at Arsenal (Crane 1990: 332) has written that the rules of confidentiality governing relationships between the club doctor and players are *not* those which apply in general practice, but rather those which apply to the relationship 'between an occupational physician and an employee of a company'. In this respect, he noted that the physician 'may be employed by the company primarily to serve its interest. *There may arise, therefore, a conflict of loyalties.*' Writing about the role of the team physician, Mellion and Walsh (1994) have similarly noted that confidentiality is 'often compromised' by the doctor's relationship to the club and that, in sports clubs, 'information is seldom held in the strict doctor–patient confidentiality'. A similar point has been made by Graf-Baumann (1997: 31). Writing as a member of the Sports Medical Committee of the Fédération International de Football Association (FIFA), he has noted that 'a particularly sensitive problem in football and in all prominent sports is that of confidentiality and professional secrecy in dealing with information on an athlete's physical and mental condition'. How, then, do club doctors and physiotherapists deal with delicate issues involving doctor–patient confidentiality? For example, how much information about the players' health is communicated to the team coach or manager? Is such information confined to the players' injury status, or does it include information which the manager might want, but which would normally be considered confidential to the doctor–patient relationship, such as information relating to a player's lifestyle? And what do club medical staff do if they discover that a player has a problem in relation to excessive alcohol consumption, or that a player is illegally using drugs? Are such problems handled within the confidentiality of the doctor–patient relationship, or do doctors feel constrained to inform the manager? And what happens if a player does not wish information to be passed on?

Research methods

The study reported here involved tape-recorded interviews of between 30 minutes and one hour with 49 respondents involved in managing injuries in professional football. Of these, 12 were club doctors and 10 were club physiotherapists; 19 current and eight former players were also interviewed about their experiences of injury and rehabilitation. Doctors in the Premier League were more amenable to being interviewed – a fact which probably reflected their generally greater involvement in their clubs. However, this did mean that the sample of doctors who were interviewed was biased towards club doctors in the Premiership; in this regard, the findings reported here tend to reflect practice in the largest and best resourced clubs, rather than in the smaller and poorer clubs. Of the 12 interviews, seven were with doctors at clubs in the Premier League (one of these had recently left the club to return full-time to general practice), two were with doctors at clubs in the First Division of the Nationwide League, two with doctors at Second Division clubs, and one interview was with a doctor in a Third Division club; one of the Premier club doctors had also previously worked in a Second Division club. Of the club physiotherapists, three worked in Premier League clubs, two in First Division clubs, two in Second Division clubs and two in Third Division clubs; in addition, one physiotherapist had formerly worked in two football clubs (one Third Division club, one Premier League club) but now worked as a club physiotherapist in another sport.

In addition to the interviews, a postal questionnaire was sent to 90 club doctors who were not interviewed; 58 questionnaires were returned, with the responses being evenly spread between Premier League clubs and clubs in the three divisions of the Nationwide League. This chapter draws only on the interview data; data from the questionnaires related mainly to the methods of appointment and experience of club doctors and physiotherapists and have been reported elsewhere (Waddington et al. 2001; Waddington 2002).

'Playing hurt' as an aspect of football culture

In order to understand some key aspects of sports medicine as it is practised within football clubs it is necessary to understand something about the culture of professional football and the associated constraints within which club doctors and physiotherapists work. In particular, it is important to note that playing when in pain, or when injured, is a central part of the culture of professional football.

One of the characteristics which managers look for in a player is that he should have what, in professional football, is regarded as a 'good attitude', and one way in which players can demonstrate to their manager that they have such an attitude is by being prepared to play when in pain or when injured. A good illustration of what, from a manager's point of view, constitutes a 'good attitude', was provided by the then Liverpool manager, Gerard Houlier, in an interview with the *Sunday Times* (6 December 1998). Houlier said that the kind of players a manager wants are those who 'will fight for you once they are on that grass'. He added: 'I'll name you one – Jamie Carragher. What a professional. He might have a niggly injury, but he'll always be out there giving you some of this' (Houlier smashed a fist into his other palm by way of emphasis).

Being prepared to play while injured is thus defined as a central characteristic of 'the good professional'; by the same token, those who are not prepared to play through pain and injury are likely to be stigmatized as not having the 'right attitude', as malingerers or, more bluntly, as 'poofters'. One of the players who was interviewed summed up what having a 'good attitude' entails in the following way:

> We had a player, I won't mention his name, but he has gone to [another club] now, and he had a fantastic attitude as in, he used to play constantly through injuries and they would get worse and worse. He'd be injured one week and . . . two weeks later he'd have the injury again. When you get a dead leg, you know, if you start running on it in the first twenty-four hours, you've got no chance, it can get worse . . . he'd play through to show the management that he had a fantastic attitude. But he was constantly injured. Constantly injured.

Asked how managers react to this kind of behaviour on the part of their players, he replied:

> They think it's fantastic. Brilliant. He's out there dying for the club. Dying for the club. Now, we have another player here who's from [another country] and his attitude is any little niggle, 'That's it, I'm not playing' . . . Everyone's attitude towards him is 'He's a poofter, he doesn't want to play, no heart.' You know, the manager says in front of the players, 'Look at him over there, he's pulled out of the game again. There is a big game coming

up . . . so he's pulled out.' It might be because he has genuinely got an injury. Only the player knows. But his title is that he's a f****** wuss, you know, he hasn't got the right attitude. But if you go out with an injury and you play for ninety minutes and it's doing you more harm than good, you know, you're Braveheart, you're brilliant.

A related aspect of football culture involves the idea that players who are unable to play as a result of injury and who can, therefore, make no direct contribution to the team on the field of play, may be seen as being of little use to the club, and may be stigmatized, ignored, or otherwise inconvenienced. The idea that the injured player is, at least for the duration of his injury, of little use to the club may be expressed in a variety of ways. The former Liverpool manager, Bill Shankley, regarded by many people as one of the greatest ever British managers, refused to speak directly to players who were unavailable for selection as a result of injury. Perhaps surprisingly, such attitudes are still commonly to be found among managers. One player told us that some managers 'have a theory that injured players aren't worth spit basically . . . You are no use to us if you are injured.' Another player described the attitude of one of his former managers towards injured players as follows: 'You're not meant to be injured. You should be playing. You get paid to play. He totally ignored you when you were in the treatment room. His attitude was: "You're no use to me anymore".' A similar point was made by one of the physiotherapists, who said that some managers took the view that, 'At the end of the day, you're a non-producer, as they say, if you're injured. You're not playing Saturday and you're no good to anyone. Some managers put it that way.'

From interviews with the players it is clear that the central value of continuing to play, whenever possible, through pain and injury is recognized and internalized by the players themselves; indeed, players learn from a relatively young age to 'normalize' pain and to accept playing while in pain and when injured as part and parcel of the life of a professional footballer. One player said that players 'are so desperately keen to get back that 90 per cent of them come back to play long before they have made a full recovery. I am no different . . . there is desperation to show that you are keen.' Another player described how he had changed his running style to compensate for a knee injury and, as a consequence, had suffered a number of other related injuries over a period of 18 months. He indicated that he had continually returned to play before he was fit to do so:

> We never gave it enough time [to recover]. We were always chasing our tail with every injury that I've ever had. You know, there's always been a cup semi-final, or there's been a quarter-final in the cup or there's another [international] game . . . you never give yourself time.

One indication of players' willingness to play while injured came in response to a question in which we asked them how many matches, in a full season, they played without any kind of pain or injury. Many players – and, in particular, senior players, who had often accumulated many injuries over the years – indicated that they played no more than five or six games in a season entirely free from injury and one senior player said: 'There's not one player goes out to play who's 100 per cent fit.'

'Playing hurt' and informed consent

As noted above, players accept playing while injured as a normal part of the life of a professional footballer, and they will try to play through injury for any one of a number of reasons. Foremost among these is the fear of losing their place in the team, which is a very real fear for all but a handful of very well-established players. Players will also try to continue playing if the team has a series of particularly important games coming up. In addition, most players have a strong self-image as professional footballers and a strong sense of professional pride; for many players, playing football is the only job they have ever done and the only job they know how to do, and many players described the frustration which they experience when they are unable to play.

Within this situation, doctors may be subject to pressure from players for the latter to return to play before they have fully recovered from injury. However this does not, in itself, present any special ethical problems. Numerous studies of doctor–patient relationships have indicated that a normal characteristic of such relationships is the bargaining between doctor and patient over such things as the nature of the treatment which is prescribed, and the time period during which the patient may be excused from work or other social responsibilities; in this respect, the pressure which players are able to exert on club doctors may differ in degree, but probably not in kind, from the pressures which patients more generally are able to exert in relation to their doctors, particularly in general (primary care) practice.[1] In this context we might note that, while players may return to play earlier than the doctor may feel is advisable, if the club doctor has provided the player with full information about any possible side effects of, for example, playing while receiving painkilling injections, as well as the possible long-term effects of playing while injured, then the doctor may legitimately feel that he/she has properly discharged his/her responsibilities to the player-as-patient.

Some players indicated that their decision to continue playing while injured had been taken under just such conditions. For example, the player described above, who had tried to compensate for his knee injury and who suffered several other related injuries as a consequence, said of his decision to continue playing following the initial knee injury and the associated surgery: 'It was a calculated risk . . . they [the doctors and physiotherapists] left it to me. I knew the implications. [I had] many, many, second opinions, third opinions . . . I was willing to take the risk.'

In the above situation, the player concerned appears to have been given the information required to make a relatively informed decision about whether or not to try to play while injured. *In some situations, however, relevant information about their medical condition may be not conveyed to players, or may even be deliberately withheld as a matter of club policy.* A particularly striking example of the latter was provided by a doctor who worked in a club which has only a small squad of players and in which, as a consequence, the pressures on players to continue playing, even when injured, are particularly acute. The following is part of the interview with that doctor:

Doctor:	I x-rayed somebody's tibia last season, as he had an injury there which could have been a stress fracture. I looked at the x-ray and saw an enormous smash on his ankle, a very old injury, but it was a very badly distorted, deranged ankle. He'd suffered a major fracture to his ankle, lower tibia at some stage, the whole thing had fallen half an inch. How can the guy play? So [the physiotherapist] said: 'Don't tell him. Don't tell the player that he's gone and broken his ankle otherwise he'll start being off'.
Interviewer:	The player didn't know he'd done it?
Doctor:	No, and I haven't told the player that the x-ray showed a hell of a fracture from some stage in the past. I said to him: 'Tell me, have you ever somehow damaged your ankle, have you been having any pains in the last few seasons at all, just out of interest?' So I haven't told him.
Interviewer:	But [the physiotherapist] didn't want you to tell the player – why?
Doctor:	Well, because he'll be off and will start asking what's wrong with it, and asking if he should retire now. And it decreases his value when you're sold. So it's a bit like a slave market.
Interviewer:	How did you feel about not giving the patient information about his own body?
Doctor:	I was asking my friends what I should do. What happens when that player actually finds out in 10 years time that that x-ray was taken by me 10 years before and I never told him, and he played on another 10 years, and has buggered his ankle so badly he can hardly stand on the bloody thing, with arthritis, which he will get?

The former Chelsea, Everton and Tranmere Rovers player, Pat Nevin (Nevin and Sik 1998: 83), has also suggested that managers may seek to withhold information from players about the extent of their injuries and may encourage their physiotherapists to do the same. This is, of course, not a problem which is specific to football; in the United States, there has been a good deal of litigation concerning informed consent in the field of sports medicine, with a central claim in many cases being that information was withheld – either negligently or intentionally – from athletes about the true nature of their conditions, thereby preventing the athlete from making a properly informed choice about his/her fitness to return to play (Herbert and Herbert 1991: 121). Such situations, like that cited above, clearly raise serious ethical issues in terms of the relationship between doctor/physiotherapist and the player-as-patient.

Return to play decisions: Quality of care issues

The need to get players playing again as quickly as possible after injury constitutes the essential backcloth to understanding the role of the club doctor and club physiotherapist in professional football and also has potentially important implications for the quality of care which players receive. One club physiotherapist characterized the culture of football, as it related to medical practice, in the following terms:

> Everything has to be done yesterday. The players have to be fit yesterday. If they miss a week, it's like a month to anyone else. The players will play when they're injured. You tend not to get the player injury-free. You . . . manage the level of injury irritation to play ninety minutes of football.

This physiotherapist, who also worked in a private sports medicine clinic in the evenings, described the key difference between his private practice and his practice in the football club as follows:

> In private practice, the client isn't desperate to be fit by Saturday. The client wants to be cured of the injury so it doesn't come back . . . In private practice, my *modus operandi* is to cure the injury. In professional football, my *modus operandi* is to get the player on the pitch as quickly as possible . . . you get people who are playing on injuries that need constant care. And you just end up performing maintenance on top of treatments in between games.

Being a physiotherapist in a football club was, he said, 'a different job' from being a physiotherapist in private practice or in the National Health Service. The different constraints under which he worked in private practice and in football meant that, in his view, he was able to provide better quality care to his private patients than to the players; asked about the quality of care he provided in the two contexts, he answered: 'Unequivocally, non-negotiable fact . . . my private clients will get better quality treatment than the players . . . Don't doubt this. Yes, a fact.'

The need, as this physiotherapist put it, to 'get players fit yesterday' is a strong and ever-present constraint within football and every club doctor and physiotherapist who was interviewed was, without exception, acutely aware of this constraint. Thus even where medical staff were working with coaches/managers who they felt respected their medical judgement and who did not place them under any direct pressure to return players to play prematurely – and, as we shall see, this was not always the case – they were nevertheless still very conscious of the need to get players off the injured list as quickly as possible. As one doctor put it:

> Obviously [the manager] wants players to play as soon as they can . . . It's a very, very grey area really whether a player is fit because we have to push things to the limit in respect that if an injury normally takes four weeks to get better, we want them back in three. But if they break down and are out for another four, then we're in trouble. So we've got to not push things too hard so they break down but, on the other hand, a week out of playing is a very expensive thing for the club . . . so we're always on a tight-rope really.

It was in the context of this need to get players fit – or, at least, able to play – as quickly as possible that another doctor talked of what he called the 'unfortunate' need to make medical compromises in his treatment of players:

> As you know, in this game, there's always compromise, unfortunately. If a player says, 'Well, I want to get on', we say to the manager: 'He's not quite ready, he could do with another week or two weeks' rest' and the manager is under pressure because he hasn't got a depth of staff to play or he's got other injuries and he needs this particular player, then sometimes we're overruled . . . I mean, in those situations it would be very nice for us to keep them out of playing but they're more or less three-quarters of the way there, maybe almost there and they're needed. Sometimes we get away with it and they play and they're alright, sometimes we don't and it puts them back again.

A good example of the kind of compromise referred to by this doctor was provided by the management of an injury to one player at this club. The player concerned, who was described by the doctor as 'a very important player for the club', had had a continuing problem with a groin injury for much of the season. Though he had been unable to do anything other than light training, he had continued to play while injured for several games but the injury limited his effectiveness as a player and eventually it was decided that he required surgery. The doctor explained that the operation:

> Should have put him out for something like six weeks . . . he recovered very quickly and after about four weeks he said he felt quite good. The manager was short of a striker and brought him in one to two weeks before we wanted to bring him in . . . the manager was aware that although he seemed alright, [he] still wasn't training with the team, or [was] training very lightly with the team. The player said: 'Yeah, I feel OK, it feels a lot better, I feel I can cope' . . . We said: Well, we'd like to give him another week to two weeks, but if the player is that keen . . . so he went and played and unfortunately within a week or two weeks it had broken down.

The player continued to play while injured, and was given a course of weekly steroid injections, with a local anaesthetic injection before matches. This again proved unsuccessful, however, and the player required a second operation. Asked whether he was happy for the player to continue playing while having the course of steroid injections and the local anaesthetic injections, the doctor replied:

> Not entirely happy, but one was hopeful that they would settle it down for him but knowing in the back of one's head that it probably wouldn't, and that what the player needed was a long rest. Asking for a long rest in football is asking a lot. But in all honesty . . . he needs a long rest. Now a long rest means, I don't know, maybe two or three months, by which time the season's over.

Thus even in those situations which would, at least within the context of football, probably be regarded as 'good practice' models – in the sense that doctors are working with managers whom they regard as 'reasonable', and where they do not feel under strong or direct pressure from managers – there is nevertheless a clearly felt need to make medical compromises which, ideally, they would prefer not to make. In other situations, however, managers may seek to have a much more direct involvement in the management of injuries and, in such situations, the clinical autonomy of doctors and physiotherapists may be much more directly threatened.

Return to play decisions: The limits of medical autonomy

We have seen that doctors may be subject to pressure from players to allow them to return to play before they have fully recovered from their injuries. However, club medical staff may also be subject to similar pressure from coaches/managers, and this raises much more serious ethical issues. In the first place, it may be more difficult for the doctor or physiotherapist to resist pressure from the manager, for the manager is normally the most powerful person in the club, at least as far as the playing side of the club is concerned. It is he who has the responsibility of selecting the team and, if he chooses, he can simply ignore the advice of the club medical staff concerning the fitness of players. If he does so, however, there may be adverse longer-term consequences for the health of the players though – and this is the second cause for concern – it is not the manager, but the players, who have to pay these health costs. Of course, in such situations the manager has to persuade the player to play but, as noted above, players are normally keen to play whenever possible and they may also be subject to a variety of pressures from the manager to continue playing through injury; younger players in particular, as well as less established players, may find it difficult to resist such pressures.

The precise nature of the relationship between club medical staff and the club manager varies considerably from one club to another, and it may also change radically within a club when there is a change of manager, as happens quite frequently. The 'best practice' model – 'best' in the sense that medical staff are allowed a substantial degree of clinical autonomy in their treatment of players – is one in which managers are only minimally involved in the direct management of injuries, and where they accept the medical judgement of doctors and physiotherapists concerning the fitness of players. An example of such a 'good practice' model was described by one doctor who said he was 'privileged' to work with his current manager: 'I've been very privileged to work with [the manager]. He does listen to what you say and he will actually support the decisions that you've made . . . He's always been very supportive.' Although several club doctors and physiotherapists reported similarly good relationships with their managers, others reported very different experiences.

One physiotherapist said that, at his present club, decisions about when injured players are fit to return to play are taken by the player, the doctor and himself. However he added that the situation varies from club to club: 'if you're working at another club, to my working knowledge, it's not worked like that. You have managers who interfere left, right and centre.' As an example, he cited the following case of an injury to the goalkeeper at a club where he formerly worked as the physiotherapist. The injury occurred in training on a Friday:

> He's done his lateral ligaments of his ankle, it's swollen, stiff, painful, he's strapped up, he's on crutches and sent home. And of course we've got no goalkeeper . . . the day before a game. So the manager's got till 5 o'clock to sign a goalkeeper to play the following day. Now, he's trying to make us bring the player back in to have a fitness test, which we were forced to do – I mean other than actually saying 'No, I am not doing it', and losing your job possibly. We said we'd bring him in but told him the bloke wasn't fit to play. 'But if you want him to kick a ball, you want him to jump up and do whatever the fitness test involves, we will do it.' So sheepishly I brought the player back in, strapped him up and told him that whatever I did just fall about in agony, basically, so the fitness test would end quickly. And so he did that . . . and the manager accepted that, but there could have been further damage caused to the player . . . I know for a fact, I've done it myself, that you've been involved in those situations, when you know he's not fit and you shouldn't be doing that but you've been told to do it by the manager.

Another physiotherapist described his difficulties in working with a manager who regularly sought to intervene in relation to injured players and to take key aspects of the management of injured players out of the hands of the physiotherapist. He described a series of disagreements which he had had with the manager about whether players were fit to play, and said that on occasions the manager himself did fitness tests on the players and passed them fit to play without reference to the physiotherapist. The physiotherapist said he had been 'very uneasy' about this and suggested that, in such situations, club medical staff have two options. The first of these was that 'if you bite your tongue, there will come a . . . time when that manager will then inevitably move on anyway. I reckon they probably have a three year life-span at a club.' Asked what happened if the club doctor or physiotherapist did not bite their tongue, he replied:

> Then he will either get rid of you or you will be forced to leave . . . What happened in my case . . . was the very day before pre-season training started. He just called me into the office and said 'I am not comfortable with the situation we have here. You want to be in charge of the treatment room, to treat the injured players your way, and I am not comfortable with that.' To which I said, 'What you are saying is that you want to be physiotherapist as well as manager . . . and I cannot work that way.' He said 'I think we are going to have to let you go . . . I don't want you to work here anymore' . . . I then said 'Have you spoken to the club's doctors about this?' Because I had a very good working relationship with the club's doctors. And he said, 'No. I am the manager of this football club and I make the decisions.' To which I said something in the terms of 'Well, f*** you', and I got up and walked out. I sued the club through the Chartered Society of Physiotherapists because obviously . . . it was unfair dismissal and I got compensation. They settled out of court. For a sum which . . . although it was quite nice, would be quite miniscule in the overall budget of the football club.

A not dissimilar situation was described by a club doctor who said that he was 'privileged' to work with his current manager but that he had had a difficult relationship with his previous manager, a relationship which the doctor described as 'tainted'. He explained:

> I think my experience with him was perhaps tainted by my own inexperience when I first joined the club . . . I'm older and wiser now . . . when you come into this sort of establishment it's very easy to be overpowered by the environment in which you're working and by the personalities and I found that very difficult . . . in that respect [the current manager] is a very different personality and I have a much closer working relationship with him than I ever did with [the previous manager].

Asked to explain in what respects his relationship with the previous manager was tainted, he said – with a very diplomatic choice of words – that 'perhaps he was a bit more forceful in his thoughts to injured players'. He went on to explain that when he became team doctor a few years previously, the club had not had a fully qualified (that is, chartered) physiotherapist on the staff and, as a consequence:

I was a single voice and if I disagreed with what was going on, then there were a lot more people around at that time to perhaps try to persuade me to change my mind . . . that the players were fit . . . All I could say in those situations [was that] players were not . . . fit and they [the managerial team] would then have to take the consequences of their playing. The majority of them [the players] would then break down and they would be out for a lot longer . . . And then the situation arose where I began to find it difficult to continue in my capacity here. My recommendations were not being considered.

It was at this time that the manager, who had not been successful in terms of results on the field, left the club; the doctor indicated that, had the manager not left the club then he, the doctor, might well have done so.

It is clear that an ever-present constraint on club doctors and physiotherapists is the perceived need to get players playing again as quickly as possible after injury and that all club medical staff are, without exception, aware of and feel the need to respond to this constraint. However, it is important to emphasize that the precise nature, as well as the strength, of this constraint varies considerably from one club to another. In some situations – for example, where managers take a relatively 'hands-off' approach towards the management of injuries – club doctors and physiotherapists may be allowed a significant degree of professional autonomy in their relationship with the player-as-patient. However, in other situations – and particularly where the manager insists on being involved in the management of injuries – their professional autonomy may be severely restricted and club doctors and physiotherapists may find themselves involved in situations in which players are regularly returned to play before they are medically fit to do so. Under these conditions, club doctors and physiotherapists are likely to react in one of two ways. They may simply adapt to and accept the situation, in which case the quality of care they are able to offer will be compromised to a greater or lesser degree. Alternatively, they may come to feel that their professional autonomy has been so circumscribed that they are unable to do their job in what they consider a properly professional manner. In the latter situation, doctors and physiotherapists are likely to find themselves in recurring conflict with the manager, a situation which may be ended only when one or other leaves the club.

Medical confidentiality

Another area which was probed in the interviews with club doctors and physiotherapists related to the way in which they dealt with information about a player which, in other medical contexts, would normally be treated confidentially. Do the normal rules governing confidentiality within the doctor–patient relationship apply within the football club?

The most general finding – and one which should be considered a matter of concern – is that there is among club doctors and physiotherapists no commonly

held code of ethics governing such matters, and there are considerable variations in terms of both the amount, and the kind, of information about players
which doctors and physiotherapists pass on to managers. This lack of a
common ethical code for dealing with confidential issues was especially striking
among physiotherapists, though a particularly striking example of unethical
behaviour on the part of a club doctor is cited later.

Most club doctors are general practitioners and many seek, insofar as it is
possible to do so, to apply the rules governing confidentiality in general practice
to their practice within the football club. Asked about how issues involving
patient confidentiality were best dealt with, one doctor replied:

> I find this one very difficult because coming from a background in general
> practice obviously anything between a patient and myself is confidential,
> unless it's an absolutely extreme case . . . Whereas inside a football club,
> it seems like everybody else thinks they have the right to know what's
> going on before the player does and when I have had disagreements with
> managers it's usually been around this issue.

Another doctor took a broadly similar view. Asked about the best way to deal
with a situation in which a player confided that he was drinking heavily, this
doctor replied:

> We would sit down and have a talk about it. I have a very strong feeling
> about confidentiality with the players. If I tell somebody that they're telling
> me something in confidence then it doesn't go any further, and I'm sure
> there are things that I'll probably carry to my grave that people have told
> me as players that I wouldn't say to anybody unless they said, 'Yes, OK,
> I'm happy to talk about it.' So I would try to sort out with them what to
> do, between the two of us.

Some physiotherapists expressed a similar view and emphasized their primary
responsibility towards the player-as-patient, though others saw their primary
responsibility as being towards the club. One physiotherapist, asked what information he passed on to the manager, explained, without any further prompting:
'Most physios know more about their staff than anybody in the club, and if it was
beneficial that the manager should know [something] – or essential that the
manager should know – then I would tell him.'

Asked whether he would inform the manager if a player was drinking heavily,
he replied:

> I'm employed by the football club. I'm employed by the manager and I'm
> supposed to be working with him and if I withhold information which he
> thinks he should have, then he would say that I wasn't working for the
> club or for him, so it puts me in a difficult position . . . if I didn't divulge
> what I knew and then it came out afterwards, we're in hot water . . . If

I thought it was beneficial to the club . . . that he should know, then I would say.

Another physiotherapist who placed particular emphasis on his responsibility to the club said:

I think if [a player's] breaking the law, i.e. taking drugs, whether performance-enhancing or whether they were just recreational, I think it's my duty to tell the football club. I work for the football club. And the players know where I sit. I'm not a player. I don't know who they've shagged, I don't know what they've drunk and I don't want to know what substances they're taking. They can do what the f*** they want. If they tell me, it will go back. And the players know that.

If they come to me confidentially and they're breaking the law, it will go back. If they're not breaking the law – I don't mind if they're out nightclubbing twice a week, I'm not judge and jury – but if the performance on the pitch . . . [if] they're not performing well or they're getting muscular irritations, and I know their lifestyle's all over the place . . . I would go to the manager and say, 'Look, his lifestyle is in a right mess.'

One ex-player, asked if confidential information about players was ever passed on by the physiotherapist, said:

I think maybe that happened at [the club] sometimes . . . if the physio is hearing that type of stuff it should be for his ears only and really shouldn't go any further. I mean . . . if he was a normal physio [and] he'd got a private practice, of course he wouldn't mention things his patients had said. It is a slightly different situation in a football club . . . because the manager's his boss and if the manager asks him something he might feel duty bound to tell him.

Given the considerable variation in terms of the way in which club medical staff deal with issues involving confidentiality, it is perhaps not surprising that some players expressed considerable reservations about revealing confidential information to club medical staff. One player, asked whether he would be happy to discuss a confidential matter with the club doctor or physiotherapist, answered with an emphatic 'No'. He explained:

Things get back. Things get back all the time. You can't say anything at a football club to anyone because basically they get back. There is no such thing as confidentiality at a football club. I found that out . . . something got back to a manager that I had said to a doctor . . . Well, it should be confidential . . . it was something [non-medical] I commented on . . . and it came straight back which I thought was a bit out of order . . . No, I wouldn't have confidence in anyone.

One player provided a striking example of a particularly serious breach of professional ethics on the part of his club doctor. In this incident the club doctor was clearly acting as an agent on behalf of the club, and used confidential medical information about a player to advance the interests of the club over and against those of the player. The player described what happened as follows:

> The club doctor, in my opinion, totally compromised his situation. I'd had [an operation] and my contract was up at the end of the season . . . I was approached by [three leading English clubs], Atletico Madrid and Lyon. Three or four weeks later, when I was talking to these clubs, I got summoned to the club doctor's . . . the club doctor called me and said would I go round to his house . . . I arrived there and he was there with the surgeon who did my operation . . . the surgeon wasn't particularly happy about being there. He [the club doctor] said, 'You're thinking about leaving the club this summer?' I said 'Yes'. He said, 'Well, the surgeon has told us that you've only got another year at the most to play football. If we make that common knowledge, no club in the world would pay millions of pounds for you.' I said, 'Well, what are you telling me?' He said, 'Well, if you're thinking of leaving the club and we made that common knowledge, then . . . no-one would buy you.' So . . . I ended up agreeing a new deal to stay.

The incident described by the player had taken place several years previously and, at the time of the interview, the player was still playing for the same club. The player said that he thought the club doctor was probably acting under great pressure, not in this case from the manager but from the club chairman, but he added that this did not excuse the doctor's behaviour: 'He was probably under great pressure to do that, but he's done wrong.'

Conclusion

Stephen Walk has suggested that one implication of Howard L. Nixon's work on pain and injury, outlined in Roderick's chapter in this volume, is that medicine is practised 'differently, more competently and/or more ethically in non-sports contexts' (Walk 1997: 24). In a not dissimilar vein, Dominic Malcolm, in Chapter 10 of this volume, raises the issue of whether sports medicine might be considered a 'very peculiar practice'. In this chapter, it has been argued that there are, indeed, some aspects of the work situation of club medical staff in professional football – and, by implication, in other sports settings – which are different from those that normally characterize the work situations of doctors in general medical practice or in hospital practice. In particular, attention has been focused on the dual obligations of club medical staff – to the club which employs them and to the individual player-as-patient – and to the ways in which these constraints on medical staff may be associated with ethical problems relating to the quality of care which is provided to players, and to issues concerning informed consent, return to play decisions and medical confidentiality.

Notwithstanding the practical difficulties which may confront medical staff with dual obligations, such as those employed by football clubs, there can be no doubt that many of the practices described in this chapter would be considered unacceptable in terms of the conventional understandings of medical ethics. For example, in the section on sports doctors in the British Medical Association's 2003 handbook, *Medical Ethics Today*, the advice is quite clear in relation to the ethical issues which have been the focus of this chapter. The Association says:

> Ethically, sports doctors need to be aware that their chief loyalty is to their patients, and that, contractual issues notwithstanding, the duty of medical confidentiality remains unchanged . . . Unless expressly indicated in the terms of the player's or athlete's contract, confidential information can be released only with the expressed consent of the patient, and breaches of confidentiality can be justified only when there is a risk of serious self harm or harm to a third party.

The handbook also notes that 'Individuals who have sustained injuries may come under pressure from managers to continue to play' and that this 'may be the case even when continuing to play may exacerbate injuries or incur risks of long term damage'. In this context, it notes that 'the doctor's chief obligation must be to the long term health and wellbeing of individual players. In such a situation, doctors must inform both player and manager of the risks involved so that both parties can make an informed decision about whether play should continue' (BMA 2003: 596).

The data reported in this chapter suggest that there is a need for a thoroughgoing re-examination of key aspects of the practice of sports medicine, with a view to ensuring that sports medicine is practised in accordance with the general ethical principles which underpin other forms of medical practice. Until such a critical review is undertaken and appropriate structural changes are made to ensure compliance with these general principles, then sports medicine will continue to be 'a very peculiar practice'.

Note

1 As Freidson (1960; 1970) noted in his seminal work on doctor–patient relationships, doctors are likely to be subject to a greater degree of client control in general practice (primary care) than in hospital practice.

Bibliography

British Medical Association (2003) *Medical Ethics Today: The BMA's handbook of ethics and law*, London: BMJ Books.

Crane, J. (1990) 'Association football: the team doctor' in S. D. W. Payne (ed.) *Medicine, Sport and the Law*, Oxford, Blackwell: 331–7.

Freidson, E. (1960) 'Client control and medical practice', *American Journal of Sociology*, 65: 374–82.

Freidson, E. (1970) *Profession of Medicine*, New York: Dodd, Mead and Company.

Graf-Baumann, T. (1997) 'The law and ethics of football injuries', *FIFA Magazine*, February: 31.

Herbert, D. L. and Herbert, W. G. (1991) 'Medico-legal issues' in R. C. Cantu and J. M. Lyle (eds) *ACSM's Guidelines for the Team Physician*, Philadelphia: Lea & Febiger: 118–25.

Newton, F. (1990) 'Medical hazards of water sports – and how to avoid them' in S. D. W. Payne (ed.), *Medicine, Sport and the Law*, Oxford: Blackwell: 299–309.

Mellion, M. B. and Walsh, W. (1994) 'The team physician' in M. B. Mellion (ed.) *Sports Medicine Secrets*, Philadelphia: Hamley & Belfus, pp. 1–4.

Nevin, P. and Sik, G. (1998) *In Ma Head, Son*, London: Headline.

Roy, S. and Irvin, R. (1983) *Sports Medicine: Prevention, Evaluation, Management and Rehabilitation*, Englewood Cliffs, NJ, Prentice Hall.

Sunday Times, 'Houlier's task hots up', 6 December 1998, Sports Section, p. 5.

Waddington, I. (2002) 'Jobs for the boys? A study of the employment of club doctors and physiotherapists in English professional football', *Soccer and Society*, 3: 51–64.

Waddington, I., Roderick, M. and Naik, R. (2001) 'Methods of appointment and qualifications of club doctors and physiotherapists in English professional football: some problems and issues', *British Journal of Sports Medicine*, 35, 1: 48–53.

Walk, S. R. (1997) 'Peers in pain: The experiences of Student Athletic Trainers', *Sociology of Sport Journal*, 14, 1: 22–56.

12 The ontology of sports injuries and professional medical ethics[1]

Yotam Lurie

Introduction: Ontology and meaning

The aim of this chapter is twofold: to disclose what I refer to as '*the ontology of sports injuries*' and to use the disclosure as an insightful perspective for dwelling on the ethics of sports medicine. To speak of the ontology of certain phenomena is to speak about the kind of 'being' they are. This may involve delineating the conceptual category under which they fall or noting the fundamental meaning they have for those who encounter them.

To note what is involved in disclosing either the ontology or the meaning of certain phenomena, and to see why this particular philosophical endeavour is so pertinent to the ethics of sports medicine, and why it should matter to the professional medical practitioner as well as to the athlete, consider a brief example. Consider an event with which most of us are fairly familiar: inserting a knife into the flesh of a certain creature and slashing the creature. This so-called biological or positivistic description of the event, though correct, is nonetheless missing something. It lacks the very essence of the event; it lacks a context that can provide it with meaning. There is a big ontological difference to be noted when this event involves an act on the part of a person who is dining on a well-cooked steak that is placed on a dinner plate, a butcher who is cutting pieces of meat from the flank of a slaughtered animal, a slaughterer who is using the knife to slaughter a cow, an assassin who is murdering another human being, a sadistic torturer who is bent on inflicting pain on a helpless prisoner, a surgeon who is operating on a patient who is under anaesthetic, a pathologist who is performing an autopsy on a cadaver, or a biologist who is vivisecting certain animals. In all these cases a knife is inserted into flesh. However, in each of these cases the meaning of the action performed is completely different. Indeed, it is so different that we might describe it in different terms, bringing the action under different conceptual categorizers. We might speak of killing, murdering, butchering, dissecting, operating and the like. As far as the instrument involved is concerned, we might use different terms such as a scalpel, knife or cleaver. We might describe the substance on which the action is performed as flesh, meat, carcasses, an animal, a living human being, a cadaver and the like, and the performer of the action as a butcher, doctor, biologist, murderer, diner and so on. All these concepts cater to our different conceptions of what is involved in each case. The concepts testify to the fact that, depending on the context, the action has different meanings to us, manifesting a different ontology in all the different cases described. Of course, what transforms the act of inserting a knife into flesh into so many different actions on the part of their practitioners is that they are more than simply acts of inserting a knife into flesh. They are embodied in different situations and are performed in different settings and different contexts. The philosophical dispute regarding the ontological question of whether these are different actions or different ways of regarding and conceiving of what is one and the same action seems to me to be a moot point. From an ethical point of view these are different actions, and they testify to the fact that they have different meanings, as they harbour a different ontology. A person who is unable to distinguish between them according to the different ontology and meanings they embody, a person who confuses one with the other, or a person who prefers one way of speaking and considering these different actions for all of them, would either be lacking crucial abilities for understanding different cultural ways of behaviour or would be implementing a constricted value-laden point of view on the multiplicity of value-laden ways of cultural behaviour. Without this ontology of meaning, the event remains vague and meaningless. The meaning of the event, and hence the ethical dimension of the event, has to do with its context.

Using the above discussion as a point of orientation, I would like to begin by commenting briefly on the phenomenon of pain in sports. Pain in the context of sports is a very different phenomenon from pain encountered in ordinary life, and particularly from how it has been regarded thus far in medicine. Pain, I propose, has a different ontology in these different contexts. Dr George Sheehan, who was both one of the great road-running gurus and a physician in his professional life, commented in one of his books about the issue at hand. As a physician, he claimed that he had learned to take pain as a warning sign. In contrast, as a runner entering a race he knew that 'the race *is* pain . . . We find that we must not merely accept pain, we must seek it' (Sheehan 1989: 57). For Sheehan, pain was a sign that he had given the race his utmost, which he strove to perform to the best of his ability. He saw it as a sign that he performed well in his sporting activity, and that all was well with him, sport wise. In other words, even with a primitive psychological sensation such as pain, the social and cultural context plays a significant role in determining what pain actually means and whether it should be embraced as a positive sign or rejected as a negative sign for something that should be mended or avoided.

Disclosing the ontology of sports injuries is insightful not only for gaining a better understanding of the professional ethics of sports medicine professionals, but also for understanding an important element as to the very nature of sport itself. The first part of the article is devoted to examining the professional ethics of specialists in sports medicine, within the special context of competitive sports. I discuss here some of the special responsibilities of the sports medicine specialist and the divided loyalties with which such specialists must grapple, given the complicated ontology of sports injuries. I ask whether the sports medi-cine specialist treats a *generic human being with an injury caused by sports,* in the same way that a medical specialist treats patients who have many other injuries that are brought about by many other causes and which require medical atten-tion, or, as an alternative, is the medical specialist treating an *injured athlete,* i.e., an ontologically special kind of creature who is first and foremost an athlete and who differs from the generic human being in certain important respects? The second part of the chapter offers insight into the meaning of sports injuries. Understanding their meaning is an important first step towards understanding how sports injuries should be treated. In this section I propose several models, which provide different conceptions of what constitutes a sports injury. If we could agree upon the proper model, then it would be much clearer how sports injuries should be handled. Consequently, I advocate a two-tier conclusion: first, a more negative conclusion that spells out the limitations of the medical model for understanding sports injuries. Following this, I offer a modest second-tier conclusion which suggests several possible perspectives through which the phenomena of sports injuries can be understood. Sports involve different types of athletes and, thus, various types of sports injuries. As a result, different answers exist as to the question of how to comprehend the meaning of sports injuries. On the basis of this understanding, different answers emerge as to how to attempt to treat sports injuries.

The medical point of view: Divided loyalties

Moving from the relatively unrelated analogies suggested above to a more concrete example, consider the case of Jerome Groopman. In a *New York Times* Op-Ed column (4 November 2000), Jerome Groopman, Professor of Medicine at Harvard, wrote about his short-lived marathon running days. Groopman testi-fied that he could now no longer run due to what he described as a 'ruptured lumbar disc and a spiral of operative catastrophes'. His injury in and of itself, however, is not what is interesting in the story he relates. The point to note is that even though he knew that he was probably injuring himself, and even though he knew that his injury would result in permanent damage, and despite the pain and agony that go along with pushing the body too hard and too far, Groopman (like thousands of other athletes) 'heard the voice of the sirens and let psychology trump over physiology'. Though he was not a professional athlete, and he had no chance of winning, he was more than willing to risk his health in an athletic competition.

When athletes like Groopman go to a physician, they put the sports medicine specialist in a difficult ethical dilemma. What exactly is a sports medicine specialist supposed to do for this particular (and somewhat peculiar) patient? The most straightforward and effortless answer is that the injury is a purely medical question, in which philosophers of sports obviously have no say, and which should be handled from a purely medical point of view. From a medical point of view, one's first intuition is that the best treatment one can prescribe for Groopman is to eliminate the cause of his ailment altogether, namely to stop him from running, and to do so immediately.[2] However, the medical point of view does not provide the only answer to Groopman's problems, nor does it necessarily provide the best answer. From Groopman's point of view, as an athlete striving for excellence as an end in and of itself, the only thing worse than to stop running right now, is never to run again. There is a great deal of controversy about what exactly constitutes a 'medical point of view' and whether, indeed there is only *one* medical point of view. The traditional paradigm of medicine assumes that health is a natural given depending on a body's intrinsic teleology and that medicine aims at restoring or preserving health, making a physician only an 'assistant to nature'. According to the traditional paradigm, the 'medical point of view' is concerned merely with biological/ physiological organisms. Others, taking a broader view, hold that it is the actual *person*, including both the patient's biological and psychological being, that must be considered under the guise of the medical point of view. The patient's psychological being has to do with the patient's views as to what constitutes the good life, the patient's aims, goals, ambitions and desires. Essentially, this is a controversy between those who maintain that the sports medicine specialist is a professional with a biologically defined area of expertise, namely to attend to sick and injured patients, and those who take a somewhat more holistic approach to the healing arts and try to focus on the human being. Some try to capture this difference by distinguishing between the notions of 'health' (having to do with medical wellbeing) in contrast to 'total wellbeing' (Veatch 2000). Clearly, the question being discussed will have a slightly different resonance for advocates of the more traditional notion of 'health' as the goal of the professional and those who focus on 'total wellbeing'.

To make this issue more concrete, consider the following very simple and common example: a sports medicine specialist is asked by a coach to administer first aid to a key elite player, who was injured halfway through the final game of the season. The coach wants the player treated so that the player, the patient, can continue to play in the game. Administering first aid in this particular case could potentially lead to permanent long-term damage to the athlete. But this final game is 'it', from both the athlete's and the coach's points of view. Hence, the athlete has at least formally given his consent to this treatment. One should, I believe, insert a restricting clause to this consent because it is not altogether clear whether an athlete has the ability to make such decisions freely and autonomously, given the intense peer pressure and significant financial incentives. Nevertheless, the athlete has formally consented to treatment. Should the sports medicine specialist comply with the coach's request and administer first aid, knowing that in the long run this might cause permanent damage?

The standard ethical prescriptions most commonly associated with medical ethics are of little use for the sports medicine specialist when treating these kinds of patients. For example, briefly consider the Hippocratic Oath. Hippocrates taught: 'Above all, do no harm.' What does it mean to do no harm in the context of the example provided above? Any physician who would have helped Jerome Groopman to continue running, as he requested, would have actually been assisting him to pursue a self-destructive path. On the other hand, as Groopman himself testifies, not running was the worst option available. Rabbi Moses ben-Maimon, the twelfth-century physician better known as Maimonides, asks God to help him see in the sufferer only the human being. In his plea to God, Maimonides was asking for the strength to treat patients according to their inherent merits as human beings and not according to the status granted to them by their social position. However, this ethical prescrip‧ tion is also of little use. What does it mean to see a patient like Groopman as a human being? Clearly, what is special about this and similar cases is that they have to do with athletes: most modern human beings, unless they are very serious about sports, do not intentionally inflict such pain and injury on them‧ selves. The generic notion of a human being is not what matters here. Rather, it is the unique circumstances and context of meaning that shape these particular human lives, and thus they are the parameters that must be evaluated.

In trying to situate the question of the professional ethics of sports medicine physicians, it is important to note that in a certain respect the question is not unique to sports medicine and might have broader applications. Essentially, the sports medicine physician is being asked to be party to the enabling of (will‧ ing) others to engage in activities that bring with them an unusually high risk of injury. The same can also be said of physicians who treat soldiers in the field, so that they may return to the front, or of physicians attending to circus perfor‧ mers, race car drivers, stuntmen and the like. From a professional ethics point of view, there are two central issues at stake. On the one hand, the physician is faced with a dilemma of professional responsibility and professional integrity. As a physician, i.e., as a person whose calling it is to aid the sick and injured, helping the person to get back to the very same activity that caused injury is counterproductive and does not really further the profession's calling. Is the professional responsible? Is it not overly paternalistic for the specialist not to allow consenting athletes back on the field? Related to this, the sports medicine specialist is faced with possible conflicts of interests and divided loyalties between: (i) caring for the health concerns of the athlete who is in his care as a patient (while allowing and actually helping the athlete to maximize athletic performance); (ii) the general welfare of the team and organization by whom the physician is employed; (iii) and, of course, the ideals of quality medicine, on the one hand, and fair competition and sportsmanship, on the other.

There is, however, something special about sports medicine physicians which distinguishes them from other physicians. Because of the significant role that physical skills play in contributing to success in sports and because of the physi‧ cian's in-depth understanding of our physical nature, the sports medicine pro‧ fessional is often asked to play, and can often play, a more significant role in preparing the athlete for competition/action than can physicians attending soldiers or race car drivers. The sports medicine physician can have a pro‧ active role in sports and does not intervene only when something goes wrong.

In principle, the sports medicine specialist often serves as an additional resource at the disposal of the coach and athlete to help improve the athlete's (or the team's) performance, similar to a trainer, psychologist and masseuse who also help the athlete excel. Ethically, this is potentially dangerous. If the physician is an agent of the team, the physician loses claim to professional independence and cannot 'save' the athlete from unwarranted pressure from team-mates, coaching staff, business and fans. In this respect the professional fails to maintain professional neutrality.

In spelling out the special ethical context of sports medicine, three distinctions are in place. The first distinction has to do with what in an everyday context we call the virtue of moderation and the vice of hubris. In sports the situation is different. Virtually all athletes need a certain degree of hubris – of passion and pride to exceed what seems normal and ordinary. Some amount of hubris is an athletic virtue and athletes who play it too safe will fail to excel. However, too much hubris and lack of moderation and self-knowledge are a sure path to injury. Hence, in treating athletes the sports medicine specialist must find the narrow ethical path between these two athletic virtues, hubris and moderation.

This is connected with risk taking. One of the most controversial dimensions of sports activities concerns the phenomenon of risk taking (Hyland 1990). Most sports involve risk taking, the most obvious being the risk of physical injury. The phenomenon of risk taking in sports is not one-dimensional, and a distinction should be made between two different senses in which we speak of risk taking. On the one hand, risk taking has to do with the statistical probability of injury. Various sports differ from one another in their probability of injury: football is probably riskier than volleyball, and maybe wrestling is riskier than swimming. In this respect the element of risk in sport is similar to the element of risk involved in the different jobs people hold or the probability of being involved in an accident under different driving conditions. But associating sports injuries merely with this type of risk is misleading. The risk involved in participating in a given sport is not like the risk involved in driving a car; it is more like the risk involved in falling in love. In sports, as in love, the more you are committed to a sport, the more you care about your particular sport. The more feeling and passions you invest, the higher the stakes and the greater the risk of getting hurt. People who are only casually engaged in sports – for example, people who practise intermittently and not too seriously – are like casual lovers. Their chances of getting hurt are much lower than those of the committed athlete.

Finally, a third distinction has to do with a difference between doctors who are agents of teams and doctors whose role is to help individual athletes. Supposedly, there is an important difference between a sports medicine specialist who injects the star of a professional soccer team with steroids in an attempt to help the team win the final game, and a specialist who injects a master division marathon runner with the same amount of steroids. In the first case, the player is supposedly treated as a means to the end of his team. In the second case it seems that at least *prima facie* the athlete is being treated as a moral agent. In some instances, however, the line between these two cases may be seriously blurred. On the one hand, there may be individual athletes, playing team sports, whose sense of success lies precisely in their contribution to the team effort. These are athletes for whom the cooperative team goal is tantamount to their own goal. In such cases, athletes who are members of sport teams are no less 'moral agents' than athletes who compete solely as individuals. Consequently, in such cases team physicians will not be treating these members *merely* as means to the goal of their team. On the other hand, when considering the master division marathon runner, serious thought has to be given to the sense in which we speak of this person as a moral agent: in many respects the runner is like a child who lacks the ability to make rational and autonomous decisions. This athlete is addicted to a favourite sport and, in behaviour that may appear somewhat childish, fails rationally to assess the activity.

To conclude this argument, each one of these three unique features of sports medicine – the virtue of hubris, the value of risk taking and the complexity of moral autonomy – is problematic because of the special meaning of sports injuries. Understanding what constitutes sports injuries requires that such issues be examined.

The ontology of an injury

In order to try to understand the nature of sports injuries, I propose several models, which provide different conceptions of what constitutes a sports injury. A model provides a perspective through which to consider how to act. Whereas earlier I spoke of different points of view – about the difference between Jerome Groopman's point of view and the medical point of view – I will now discuss different models. A model offers us a point of view on a given phenomenon by bringing a certain context to bear. In this respect a model for conceiving what constitutes a sports injury is like an interpretive theory about how to interpret the phenomenon. For example, advocates of total well-being, as a richer alternative than just health, with respect to the goal of the sports medicine specialist, actually suggest that the proper understanding of the phenomenon should develop as a result of what can be described as a hermeneutic dialogue between two world views, trying to come to a convergence: on the one hand, the perspective of the specialist and, on the other hand, the perspective of the injured athlete. The athlete–professional relationship need not be conceived as that of authority and control between a professional who has power and knowledge and a client who is in a position of need.

First and most straightforward is the *medical model*, which I introduced earlier. According to this model, a sports injury is a limiting condition, i.e. disease, injury or illness, on what is considered a healthy *normal human being*. Attempts to understand the nature of sports injuries can thus go in two directions: either a discussion of what constitutes 'normality' or, alternatively, a focus not on the definition of normality, but on the question of what constitutes 'disease' and 'illness'. If this model is adopted, the physician is to treat the limiting condition and restore the person to healthy, normal functioning (whatever that might mean). In this context the major ethical issues have to do with the effective application of notions such as autonomy, beneficence (if you can help, do good), malfeasance (first do no harm) and justice to the clinical treatment of injured athletes (Beauchamp and Childress 1994). As suggested earlier, the problematic issue here is that virtually no reference or attention is given to the special circumstances involving athletic competition.

The *normative model* refers to sports as a physical challenge performed within the context of *rule-governed practices*. In this model, a sports injury is an injury that hinders the athlete from meeting the challenge and excelling according to the rules of the game. The sports medicine doctor should therefore assist the athlete to meet the challenge as defined by the rules of the practice. In this context sports medicine specialists have to understand that they are treating athletes and not just ordinary human beings. There are differences between the two beings. Nonetheless, what seems problematic with this model is that it lacks a critical perspective for understanding the practice of sport. The *normative model* runs the risk of uncritically accepting the ideology of the sport-world (Morgan 1994). In other words, it is a model that accommodates to the conception of sports that is dominant within the world of elite professional sports with all the related ethical problems involved in this conception of sports.

The *liberal model* presents an alternative to the medical model. It challenges attempts to define 'normalcy' and 'illness' for a generic human being as such, without proper attention to the unique circumstances of any given individual. According to this model a sports injury is an injury that limits an autonomous individual, who in this particular case chose to be an athlete, from fulfilling his or her self-defined goals. The liberal model is a political model and asks about the athlete's personal goals and aspirations in order to prescribe a course of treatment that will help the athlete to fulfil these goals. The liberal (Kantian) principle of *respect for persons* can be evoked in this context. The athlete is an autonomous being and has the right to pursue his or her goals. As a physician one does not have the right to impose one's own goals, aspirations and notions of normalcy on the athlete.[3] The principle entails that the athlete's goals and aspirations are central to understanding the nature of the injury.

There are, however, drawbacks to the liberal model when bringing this to bear on the understanding of sports injuries. Athletes do not develop, aspire and set goals for themselves in a vacuum. An athlete is influenced and shaped within a certain athletic culture, composed of teachers and coaches, fellow athletes and fans, and finally a market that puts a price on performance and victory. Assessing (or in medical terms, diagnosing) a sports injury solely on the basis of an athlete's personal goals and aspirations is overly individualistic. It lacks critical attention to the sources of these goals and aspirations.

Finally, the *phenomenological model* tells us that when dealing with athletes we are dealing with people belonging to a culture that enables them to experience the world in a special way, similarly to the way in which a deaf person lives in a special world. I have adopted this model from research done in recent years on issues pertaining to the ethics of the disabled. If sports medicine specialists want to help athletes, they need to help them experience their life and world to its fullest on their own terms. The phenomenological approach explores the significance of sports in exercise and competition in terms of the ways in which athletes experience it. It examines what it means for the patient-athlete to have his or her life suddenly disrupted by a sports injury, what it means to have one's body, which is regularly catered to as a finely crafted tool, suddenly turn against oneself and become an adversary that challenges all previous assumptions about life and its possibilities. It examines what it means to have one's body suddenly open up questions about one's self-identity.[4]

Fundamentally, one might argue that this model is not radically different from the liberal model. The major difference is, however, that within the liberal model the so-called goals and athletic aspirations are dealt with in a political context, which requires respect and compromise. The liberal model is very keen on respecting the athlete's autonomous decisions regarding one's self-defined goals and aspirations. For the liberal sports medicine specialist, toleration of other people's goals is an important virtue. In contrast, the phenomenological model maintains that since being an athlete is a certain form of life in the sense that it has to do with a certain way of being in the world, the sports medicine specialist is required not only to respect and tolerate the athlete's goals, but also to understand and facilitate this way of experiencing the world. Being an athlete has to do with a certain way of relating to objects, practices and other people (including oneself); it is not merely a matter of making room for one's autonomous goals and aspirations. The point here is, as so eloquently expressed by John Bingham, that 'being an athlete is not about miles run, or times or personal records. Being an athlete is about how you encounter the world.' Bingham goes on to explain this idea by analogy to music:

> Being a musician is a way of encountering the world. It is a way of encountering sound. The difference between what I hear in a Mozart symphony and what a non-musician hears is not the notes. The notes are the same – the same frequencies, the same durations, the same decibel level. What separates my experience with music is that the sounds I hear are inside of my world, not outside. [. . .] The same transformation occurs when one becomes an athlete.
>
> (Bingham 1999: 70)

According to the phenomenological model, being an athlete has to do with a whole different way of encountering the world and, thus, a sports injury is not merely something that hinders an athlete from accomplishing a goal or fulfilling an aspiration, as suggested by the liberal model. A sports injury is liable to alter the way a patient-athlete encounters his or her world, often within the context of one's most significant and meaningful experiences.

In order to articulate further the phenomenological model, consider an example: in our capacity as athletes, a certain day of the week, Sunday for instance, can come to have a very special meaning for us as the day we always meet for our long-distance training run, or as the day of competition. It becomes not just another day of the week, but rather a day imbued with special meaning for the athlete. Being injured means that the athlete cannot experience Sunday in the same way as previously. In this respect a significant aspect of one's life is being eliminated. Similarly, according to the phenomenological model, an athlete is a person who has a very special relationship to other athletes with whom he or she shares this significant experience. Other athletes are not just other people; they are competitors, team members and training buddies. Team members, for example, are often people who devote themselves to the same affair in common; they become, in Heidegger's words, 'authentically bound together' (Heidegger 1962) They are partners with whom one shares not only goals and aspirations but also bodily and emotional experiences.

Though these models are not mutually exclusive, they do conflict with one another. Each of these four models offers unique advantages and disadvantages, and each has different implications for sports medicine and for the treatment of patients. Through them it is possible to clarify the concept of sports injuries in a way that can assist the professional to take the best course of action from an ethical point of view. They are each a manifestation of a different sport ethos and, consequently, each has different implications and relevance for a different type of athlete. If there is anything an ethics paper can add to the practitioner, it is the insight that some people engage in sports for health-related reasons and the *medical model* is most appropriate for diagnosing and treating their sports injuries. When treating professional athletes, the sports medicine professional will find the *normative model* most appropriate. People who come to understand that sports can affect their total well-being and not just their health, make the transformation into athletes whose sports injuries should be comprehended via the *liberal model*. Athletes such as Jerome Groopman, cited earlier, should be cared for through the spectrum of the *phenomenological model*. A sport medicine specialist who tries to negotiate a way of allowing athletes, in the best possible way, to fulfil their goals and aspirations is a liberal oriented specialist. In contrast, a sports physician who is concerned about enabling an athlete to continue to have those experiences and relationships that are important to him or her is a specialist who leans towards the *phenomenological model*. Ultimately, however, the model that should be adopted depends on choices that have to be made by both athlete and medical specialist regarding how they wish to regard both themselves and their different, but related, practices.

Notes

1 A version of this chapter was previously published as Y. Lurie (2002) 'The Ontology of Sports Injuries: Professional Ethics of Sports Medicine', *International Journal of Applied Philosophy* 16, 2: 265–79.

210   *Yotam Lurie*

2 Much has been written about this. See, for example, J. P. Bernstein, and A. R. Bartolozzi
   (2000) 'Ethics in Sports Medicine', *Clinical Orthopedics and Related Research* 378: 50–60;
   P. Berteau (1998) 'Medicine, Sports and Ethics', *Science and Sports* 13, 4: 188–92; P. Ford
   (1993) 'Ethics in Sports Medicine', *British Journal of Sports Medicine* 27, 2: 95–100;
   D. MacAuley (1999) 'Fair, Honest, Ethical and Last', *British Journal of Sports Medicine*
   33, 5: 293–4; B. J. Maron and S. Polsky (1998) 'Winning Medicine: Professional Sports
   Team Doctors' Conflicts of Interest', *Journal of Contemporary Health Law and Policy* 14,
   2: 189–223; J. Sim (1980) 'Sports Medicine: Some Ethical Issues', *British Journal of
   Sports Medicine* 14, 2/3: 90–1; P.N. Sperryn (1980) 'Ethics in Sports Medicine', *British
   Journal of Sports Medicine* 14, 2/3: 84–9.
3 It is, nevertheless, possible within certain versions of the liberal model to draw a line
   when professional considerations suggest that a person is operating against his or her
   best interests and actually endangering him or herself. Liberalism can allow for
   professional paternalism.
4 See, for example, Richard Zaner (1981) *The Concept of Self*, Athens: Ohio University
   Press; Gabriel Marcel (1952) *Metaphysical Journal*, trans. B. Wall, Chicago: Henry
   Regnery; Erwin Strauss (1966) *Phenomenological Psychology*, New York: Basic Books;
   D. M. Levin (1985) *The Body's Recollection of Being*, London: Routledge & Kegan
   Paul.

Bibliography

Beauchamp, T. L. and Childress, J. F. (1994) *Principles of Biomedical Ethics*, 4th edn,
   New York: Oxford University Press.
Bingham, J. (1999) *The Courage to Start*, New York: Simon and Schuster.
Heidegger, M. (1962) *Being and Time*, 7th edn, trans. J. Macquarrie and E. Robinson:
   New York: Harper and Row Publishers.
Hyland, D. (1990) *Philosophy of Sport*, St Paul, MN: Paragon House.
Morgan, W. J. (1994) *Leftist Theories of Sport: A Critique and Reconstruction*, Urbana:
   University of Illinois Press.
Sheehan, G. (1989) *Personal Best*, Emmaus, PA: Rodale Press: 57.
Veatch, R. (2000) 'Doctor Does Not Know Best: Why in the New Century Physicians
   Must Stop Trying to Benefit Patients', *The Journal of Medicine and Philosophy*, 25, 6:
   701–21.

13 The role of injury in the organization of Paralympic sport

P. David Howe

The socio-political implications of pain and injury as they relate to the organization of the Paralympic movement are the central concern of this chapter. After a brief look at Paralympic sport in the broadest sense the chapter will: (i) examine the management of injury among elite athletes with a disability; (ii) discuss issues surrounding the classification of disability in Paralympic sport; (iii) explore, by reference to the classification systems adopted in swimming and athletics, some alternative ways of organizing Paralympic sports, which may help to overcome some of the present problems associated with the disruption caused by injury; and (iv) discuss how the systems which are used to classify disability help to shape the socio-political environment within the Paralympic movement.

In the context of this chapter, injury is understood as a breakdown in the structure of the body, which may affect its function. Pain, on the other hand, can be understood as the marker of an injury and is an unpleasant sensory and emotional experience associated with actual or potential tissue damage, which may be divided into acute and chronic components (Howe 2004). The implications of the risk of pain and injury for the organization of elite sport for the disabled can have a profound effect upon the culture of the Paralympic movement. As this chapter is not concerned with the type and nature of injury, but rather with the organizational consequences of injury, it is sufficient to point the reader towards other accounts of pain and injury among disabled athletes. In this regard, Ferrara and Peterson (2000) have written a useful overview of injury patterns for athletes with a disability, and Howe (2004) provides some ethnographic insights related to injury and the Paralympic movement.

The ethnographic data on which this chapter is based were obtained through participant observation, collected over a period of 16 years and four Paralympic Games (1988–2000). The author was an athlete at all these Games and, from 1996 to 2003, also acted as a technical official for athletics on the International Paralympic Committee (IPC). In both these roles I was able to develop an understanding of pain and injury and observe the consequences of injury on participation levels at key events throughout the build-up to the Paralympic Games. As an athlete myself, I was from time to time confronted with pain and injury in the sporting context as part of the training regime that I undertook as an elite middle-distance runner. The mild cerebral palsy that has led to my impairment (muscle atrophy in the right hemisphere of my body) made me eligible for Paralympic sport in a category of my physical equals. Many of the athletes against whom I competed (who were also impaired by cerebral palsy on either the right or left side) also experienced pain and injury and these episodes shaped the discourse and therefore the world that we occupied at these events. This world was not, however, limited to those against whom I directly competed, but also included other eligible Paralympians with whom I socialized and trained in the lead up to, and during, major championships. It was in the environment around the major championships that are part of the quadrennial cycle of the Paralympics that I was able to develop an understanding of the important role that pain and injury can play in shaping the organization of the Paralympic movement. What follows should not be seen as a traditional ethnographic account of pain and injury related to the Paralympics (the limited space of a book chapter does not permit this); rather, it should be seen as a reflective account of that material.[1]

Paralympic sport

Since 1988 the major event of contemporary Paralympic sport – the Paralympic Games – has gone from being a pastime enjoyed by the performers to a spectacle that has attracted increasing media attention. The Paralympic Games are the most important sporting event in the calendar for people with disabilities. The Games receive a significant amount of media coverage, especially bearing in mind that little media attention is paid to sport for the disabled in between the quadrennial Games. Media attention is, however, still substantially less than that accorded to the Olympic Games (Schantz and Gilbert 2001; Schell and Rodriguez 2001).

The Paralympic Games which were held in Sydney, Australia, in 2000, attracted over 4000 athletes, from 125 nations, who competed in a variety of sports. Some events have the same rules as mainstream sports, some have adapted rules and yet others have been specifically developed to highlight the abilities of specific disability groups. At the moment, the Paralympics is the world's second biggest sporting event (after the Olympics[2]), but a recent agreement with the International Olympic Committee (IOC), related to financial assistance, means the Games will not get any larger in terms of the number of athletes involved (IPC 2001). Although this agreement will ease financial concerns for the IPC, it may force a restructuring of sport for the disabled. This is because, as we shall see, the history of sport for the disabled has left the IPC with a legacy of a cumbersome and complex classification system (DePauw and Gavron 1995; Steadward 1996; Vanlandewijck and Chappel 1996) which, it has been argued, detracts from the Paralympic Games as a sporting spectacle. As a result, in recent years sports such as swimming have established a new and simpler classification system which integrates swimmers with different kinds and levels of disability within the same race. This new system has met with a limited degree of success and many athletes and those scholars interested in classification do not feel that the system is ideal (Daly and Vanlandewijck 1999; Richter *et al.* 1992; Richter 1994). There has also been some preliminary discussion related to the development of an integrated system in athletics (Tweedy 2002).

At the Paralympic Games and other sporting events for disabled people, such as IPC sport-specific world championships, a classification system is used to divide participants not only by sex, but also by the level of ability that can be achieved within a specific impairment group. This is the system that has been inherited by the IPC from International Organisations for Sport for the Disabled (IOSDs), four of whom were the founding members of the IPC. These federations – Cerebral Palsy-International Sport and Recreation Association (CP ISRA), International Stoke Mandeville Wheelchair Sports Federation (ISMWSF), International Blind Sports Federation (IBSF), and International Sports Organisation for the Disabled (ISOD) – had all independently developed their own classification systems which, they felt, provided equitable competitive opportunities for their constituent members. Today these federations use their own systems based upon a tried and tested medical classification at their own regional and international championships.[3]

Increasingly, the IPC sports administrators are urging the adoption of integrated classification systems which will combine athletes from a number of specific impairment groups, and thus allow athletes with different disabilities to compete directly against each other. These athletes would be placed, regardless of impairment, in a distinct and equitable new system based on functional ability within their chosen sport. One of the problems with the traditional impairment specific classification system, which has more classes and fewer athletes in each category, is that if a number of competitors in the same class are injured, then this may lead to the cancellation of an event at the Paralympic Games. With so few competitors in some classes, the IPC might, quite wrongly, take the cancellation of the event as a sign of a lack of interest on the part of the athletes. With the existing classification system, therefore, injuries to a few athletes may have important implications for the cancellation of particular events, and possibly the disappearance of those events altogether in future Games.

The management of injury within Paralympic sport may initially be seen as a distinct and separate issue from the organizational implications of injury. However, the management of injury is directly tied to the professionalization of the Paralympics (Howe 2004) which has been a catalyst for reorganization within the Paralympic movement more generally. With limited numbers of competitors (in relation to mainstream sport) spread across a complex classification system, the organizational imperative of the IPC to streamline is driven by their desire for commercial success. Injuries that sideline elite athletes on a regular basis may increase the speed with which the rationalization of the classification system takes place. Therefore this chapter will consider issues related to the professionalization of the management of injuries, before turning to the organizational consequences of injuries in Paralympic sport.

Managing the risk of injury within the Paralympic movement

Since at least the 1988 Games in Seoul, the management of pain and injury have been concerns of all Western nations which send teams to the Paralympic Games. In many Western nations, the practice of sports medicine within disabled sport has become increasingly sophisticated and, in countries such as Britain and Canada, the provision for treatment of injury has improved dramatically both during the Games and, perhaps more importantly, while athletes are preparing for the Games. This shift in attitude towards pain and injury represents a 'coming of age' of disability sport. It is a result of the recognition of the need for a more professional attitude towards sport that is, in turn, a by-product of the new commercialism that has enveloped Paralympic sport and, in particular, the IPC in recent years (Howe 2004).

As noted earlier, this chapter is based on the collection of ethnographic data. By its very nature, the collection of data was sporadic or snapshot, because the best disabled athletes congregate in large numbers at most once a year during major events. It was on these occasions that the athletes' discourse about the trials and tribulations of the injuries they have endured, and the pain they have overcome, could best be documented.[4] Discussions of the chronology of pain and injury that athletes survived in order to get to that year's major event are key to understanding the importance of these concepts to the culture of Paralympic sport. These discussions, and the observation of those athletes receiving sports medicine support, suggest that as Paralympic sport has become more commercial, the medical provision has become more holistic in its approach. The adoption by many nations of massage therapy, osteopathy and acupuncture, among others, is now considered part of 'normal' provision for disabled athletes. Complementary medicine has been adopted to help effect a cure, or at least to return the athlete to competition, more rapidly than would have otherwise been possible by the exclusive use of traditional methods such as physiotherapy. There has also been a growing use of preventative measures.

The use of preventative medicine is important because it marks a shift in the role of the patient. Within general medicine, dentistry, a traditional medical sub-discipline, has employed a preventative paradigm for years (Nettleton 1992). Dutifully, most Westerners brush their teeth on at least a daily basis. This simple preventative action is designed to keep teeth and gums healthy and to keep away the pain associated with tooth decay. In the context of elite sport for the disabled, the preventative paradigm has been implemented through the establishment of personal stretching regimes before and after training and competitions, as well as regular 'check-ups' with massage therapists. The use of such preventative measures may alleviate the pressure on national team clinics that are set up on site to treat injuries at events such as the Paralympic Games. Yet although stretching techniques cost nothing, it is apparent that many athletes fail to use these simple practices. There would seem to be a need to improve awareness and education in relation to these practices.

The physical availability of sports medicine facilities at major events in the Paralympic calendar does generate its own difficulties. First, many athletes may not have access to affordable high-quality sports medicine treatment throughout the year, so they may, quite literally, come limping into major championships with minor injuries or, in some cases, a catalogue of injuries. One reason for this may be a lack of finance in their home nation which effectively blocks access to sports medicine, except during major events. The costs of providing high-quality care can be extremely expensive and, even in countries such as Canada and the United Kingdom, these costs are met only for performers with star potential that has been recognized in advance of the championships. If the athlete is not recognized as a Paralympic medal hopeful, such schemes may not be available.[5] Even if an athlete is deemed worthy of full medical support, the final intensive training period prior to competition may still leave the most careful, prevention-minded athlete with an injury. Therefore some athletes will present with injuries, even on the opening day of the clinic.

The second difficulty related to the provision of sports medicine is that some athletes may use the services even though they are not injured. Many athletes seeking treatments such as massage therapy do so only at major championships and never in between. This can have a number of consequences. First, the athlete's body takes time to get used to massage and immediately before a major competition may not be the most appropriate timing (at least in physiological terms) to get the benefit from this therapeutic intervention. Most massage therapists are aware of this issue and, as a result, will not adopt invasive treatments with patients who are not used to such treatment. One massage therapist who worked on elite disabled athletes prior to the 2002 IPC Athletics world championships commented:

> Often athletes who come to see me have not had a proper sport massage for over a year. It is difficult to know how to treat them. I think my treatment ends up being more a placebo than anything else.

Second, some athletes treated in clinics at the Games use those working in the clinic as a source of social support rather than for medical care *per se*. This behaviour may take place regardless of the age of the athlete, but it appears to be more common within certain impairment groups that have been more marginalized within society generally (see DePauw 1997). Thus athletes may come into the treatment room not for a medical reason, but because they may need the social support provided by the treatment staff. This is not, in and of itself, a problem unless there are athletes who need to be treated as a matter of urgency for 'real' injuries. The need to determine what is a 'real' treatment concern can create difficulties for treatment staff. The head of a national medical delegation stated:

> It gets really congested in the clinic at times. I think the clinic manager has a crucial role to play since they are the link between treatment staff and the

athlete/patient or in some cases the patient/athlete. It is important that the first group takes priority over the second. It is our belief that athlete/patients are our true clients.

The distinction between athlete/patient and patient/athlete is important, but whether it can be made accurately and effectively in the pressured atmosphere of a major championship is unclear. What is clear is that an important aspect of the role of the clinic manager is in screening clients at busy times.

In general, it appears that the manner in which Paralympic athletes cope with injury is not dissimilar to that of mainstream elite sporting performers (Ferrara and Peterson 2000; Howe 2004). However, due to the complex classification system used in sport for the disabled, injuries may have an important impact on the current organization and future direction of the Paralympic movement.

Classification and the nature of Paralympic injury

The rate of injury for athletes involved in Paralympic sport appears not to be significantly different from that in high-performance sport in able-bodied populations (Ferrara and Peterson 2000). What makes the management of injuries of particularly great importance within disability sport is the complex nature of the classification system used in sport for the disabled, which is continually evolving to allow for equitable and fair competition. As Sherrill suggests,

> A basic goal of classification is to ensure that winning or losing an event depends on talent, training, skill, fitness, and motivation rather than unevenness among competitors on disability-related variables (e.g., spasticity, paralysis, absence of limb segments).
>
> (Sherrill 1999: 210)

Given the nature of the classification systems generally used in disability sport, injury becomes an issue of considerable importance where there are only a small number of athletes in each classification.

In 1989, when the IPC was established, the IOSDs were on the front line offering expertise to the IPC. Many of the first officials of the new organization had earlier held posts within these founding federations. One of the legacies of this heritage is a complex classification system that many in the IPC now regard as too cumbersome and as a potential threat to the marketability of the games (Steadward 1996). For example, in athletics there are eight classes for athletes with cerebral palsy, three classes for the visually impaired, nine classes for amputees and four wheelchair classes for both track and field events, and this inevitably means that the organization of the Paralympic athletics programme is very complex.

It is argued by some within the Paralympic movement that the complexity of classification has made it difficult for the IPC to attract the media attention that it desires. According to Steadward, 'the potential benefit of decreasing classes by using a functional integrated classification system is that it may simplify the integration into the rest of the sports world' (1996: 36). This functional integrated classification system has been developed in some sports (such as swimming and winter sports) and it is held that this new system, by reducing the number of classes, leads to an increase in the number of viable events at major championships (Vanlandewijck and Chappel 1996: 70–1). Currently the IPC is eager to win control of the classification process for all its sports, which it is hoped will ultimately lead to the implementation of a code of practice by the end of 2006. The IPC suggests that the 'classification code will aim to synchronize all sport-specific classification processes and procedures, in much the same way that the world Anti-Doping Code has done for international anti-doping rules and regulations' (IPC 2004: 11).

At present there is a lack of agreement between the IPC and the IOSDs as to what is best for the athletes involved in various sports. Issues and debates surrounding classification are of perennial concern. As Wu and Williams suggest in relation to swimming, altering the classification system necessarily involves some tensions:

> One of the major difficulties in developing any classification system . . . is handling the assumption that all individuals in the same category demonstrate a similar performance standard. Decreasing the number of classes in a system increases the number of swimmers in each class. This is desirable when the goal is to increase the credibility of the whole swimming competition, but it is extremely problematic in single events because it increases the potential for differences between swimmers.
>
> (1999: 264)

The challenges involved in establishing an equitable classification system are numerous. The sport of swimming, which was one of the first to adopt the IPC's integrated functional classification system, will be contrasted with athletics which is in continual conflict about the most equitable system to employ in the classification process.

Swimming: Integrated functional classification

An integrated functional classification system has been part of the organization of IPC international swimming competitions since 1989 (Wu and Williams 1999). This system has greatly reduced the number of physical[6] impairment groups. The reduction in the number of classes is believed to have a number of benefits. 'Not only has the number of classes been reduced from 31 to 10, there has been a reduction in the cancellation of events and the number of races in which swimmers from several classes take part' (Wu and Williams 1999: 263). The second point here is key. The previous classification system, which as mentioned earlier was a product of disability-specific IOSDs, was hierarchical so that if two events needed to be combined then the athletes from the less impaired class were bound to dominate. By reducing the number of classes and focusing upon functional ability, the likelihood of having to combine classes has also been reduced; this does mean that events are usually able to go ahead as listed in the programme, thus making for greater predictability and allowing for the forward planning by athletes and coaches which is one of the hallmarks of high performance sport.

The IPC swimming classification system (Dummer 1999) includes what is known as a 'bench test' where the swimmers' range of motions of their various joints, muscular strength, and limb co-ordination are determined on a physio-therapy bench. This is followed by a swimming test where athletes show their ability to maintain horizontal body position and perform various technical skills, such as starts, strokes and turns, that are necessary in competitive swimming. Points are awarded for both the bench test and the swimming test and athletes are classified in one of three ways depending on the event in which they wish to compete: S class for freestyle, backstroke and butterfly; SB for breaststroke; and SM for individual medley. Swimmers can in fact compete is each swimming discipline in a different class and there is concern that as swimmers become more proficient they may be forced to move up a class although their impairment has not changed.

Whether the advent of this system is an improvement on the old impairment-specific classification is unclear. Critics of the integrated classification system suggest that some impairment groups may be at a systematic disadvantage and in some cases may no longer be able to compete (McCann 1994; Richter 1994). In addition, it may be more difficult to classify athletes within this system because of the need to consider a great number of impairments simultaneously. There is also a fear that some athletes will 'cheat' the system by fooling the classifiers because the classification tests have not been validated statistically (Richter *et al.* 1992). According to Wu and Williams,

> Misclassification is an interesting and perennial problem in disability sport. As with many others, it is the root cause of much frustration and anger (a) among swimmers who feel they have been disadvantaged by losing to a competitor who should be in a higher class and (b) among coaches and swimmers who may believe that they have been disadvantaged by being placed in a higher class than their impairment warrants.
>
> (1999: 262)

Perhaps most importantly, athletes may be penalized for enhancing their own performances. If athletes train and improve their technique in swimming (or any sport that adopts an integrated functional classification system) they may be reclassified into a higher class, based on their new ability. This is a key concern:

> The concept of athletic excellence can only be fully appreciated when the performance is related to the functional physical resources available to the

athlete in competition. These resources represent the athlete's performance potcntial. Whether such a potential is fully utilized by the athlete is one crucial determinant of excellence. An acceptable classification system would allow the definition and measurement of performance potential. The definition of *potential* in this way is the cornerstone of the classification process.

(Vanlandewijck and Chappel 1996: 73)

In practice, however, the determination of sporting potential is almost impossible to achieve through any of the current classification systems in place in Paralympic sport. Yet the aim of getting as fair a competition as possible is still the goal of the classification process. Wu and Williams (1999: 252) have suggested a number of criteria for fair swimming:

1 Swimming performance across classes should be different, with swimmers in higher classes outperforming those in lower ones.
2 Elite swimmers in the same class should demonstrate similar performances.
3 Elite swimmers with different types of impairment should have equal opportunities to advance to the finals and win medals in the Paralympic Games, World Championships, or comparable international competition.

While this does not eliminate the important issues regarding potential performances, advocates of the classification system currently in place in IPC swimming believe that the statistics show that competition is relatively fair (Daly and Vanlandewijck 1999). The system does allow for more spectacular competition, as well as viable races with a good number of competitors. The reduction in the number of classes is less confusing for the public and sponsors alike, and also means that events are unlikely to be cancelled or haphazardly combined at the last minute.

Athletics: Functional classification

While swimming has adopted an integrated functional classification system, political pressure and infighting within athletics have meant that the IOSDs classification systems are still currently used there. There has been considerable pressure placed upon the sport by the IPC to reorganize using some form of integrated system, but these pressures have largely been rebuffed. Athletics is arguably the flagship sport of the Paralympic Games and as such it has considerable influence within the Paralympic movement. Of all the athletes who competed in the Athens Paralympics in 2004, 25 per cent wcrc involved in athletics. Nevertheless, with the IPC pushing for an integrated functional classification code (IPC 2004), athletics may yet be required to adopt such a system.

In an effort to cope with the many classes eligible for participation in the Paralympics programme, the IPC introduced a rule that required an event to have at least six competitors from at least four nations to make it viable within the Games. Although such a rule would be unlikely to have a significant impact on mainstream sport, it has had a significant impact on the viability of some sports within the Paralympic programme. Sports such as swimming adopted an integrated functional classification system in large part as a response to the consequences of this rule change. In athletics, where there is disagreement as to how to achieve fairness in competition, this IPC rule has had a profound effect. Within some disability federations there may, as a result of the nature of IOSD classification systems, be insufficient competitors to meet these regulations. More recently, the IPC Athletics committee has ruled that there must be at least 10 athletes on its official ranking list for an event to be considered for the Paralympic or world championship programme, putting a further strain on events with few competitors.

This regulation has had a significant impact on the organization of Paralympic athletics. The cancellation of an event altogether or, in some cases, moving competitors up to a less impaired class in order to make the event viable, has an impact on future programmes. A competitor who is moved to a less impaired class is not competing on a level playing field. In an environment where medal tallies increasingly matter in terms of national prestige, athletes whose event is removed from the programme are unlikely to be selected by their National Paralympic Committee (NPC) for an event in which they are likely to perform less well. If several NPCs act in this way, a particular event may soon disappear from the Paralympic programme. It then becomes difficult, if not impossible, for the event to be reintroduced in future programmes because of the apparent disinterest by those in the relevant classification grouping. As mentioned earlier, the problem of low numbers of athletes competing is exacerbated by the onset of injury in even a small number of athletes.

There are a number of ways in which the sport of athletics has tried to address this issue of a low number of entries within particular events. For example, they have attempted to tackle the problem by combining wheelchair classes in track events. Both CP-ISRA and ISMWSF have athletes who compete from a sitting position in a wheelchair. However, at present elite male wheelchair CP-ISRA athletes are relatively few in number and, while there are sufficient to meet the IPC minimum requirement of six athletes from four countries for Paralympic eligibility, IPC Athletics has suggested that the class would not be competitive enough, so it has removed the last remaining men's cerebral palsy wheelchair classes from the Paralympic programme. In a bid to improve the quality of racing, IPC Athletics has combined the two impairment classifications of male wheelchair racers so that injury does not become an issue in the future for the relatively few CP-ISRA male athletes. Rather than trying to establish an equitable system where existing classes from both federations are the starting point for a new system, the authorities have merged classes of cerebral palsy athletes into the ISMWSF classification system. It had been proposed by the IPC that a combined system for athletics competitors in wheelchairs be in place before the 2002 World Championships but because there is lack of agreement between the individual sporting federations, progress has been relatively slow.

Many problems exist in attempting to combine all athletic competitors in wheelchairs. For example, the nature of the impairment in spinal injury means that wheelchair users differ in the degree of power they can generate while racing, as this varies with the location of the lesion on the spine. In the case of athletes with cerebral palsy in a wheelchair it is an issue of motor control while racing a chair (Richter 1999). Therefore combining all users of wheelchairs in athletics is problematic as it becomes an issue of giving points to athletes involved in the classification process based on two distinct components: power and control. During the 2002 IPC World Championships, three male athletes with cerebral palsy were good enough to qualify in their new class. These three men were all world record holders in their respective former classes but struggled to get beyond their heats in their new class. So the question remains: how can this system be considered equitable if there are two distinct forms of impairment with different implications for performance? For the Athens Paralympics only two of the men made the grade while the other retired, disenchanted with the sport. Fortunately CP-ISRA women's wheelchair events are still a viable part of the Paralympic programme[7] but at other IPC international events the combining of the male wheelchair classes has brought about the demise of elite male wheelchair racing for elite men with cerebral palsy, though it continues to be a part of the CP-ISRA World Championships.

In relation to field events, IPC Athletics has adopted a rather different approach to end the need to cancel events due to injury. Here the principle has been adopted of using tables to give an individual sporting performance a points value within each class. Events are staged using decathlon type tables, where the performances are ranked by turning each athlete's effort into points that can be compared across classes of disability. The winner is determined not by the furthest distance thrown or on length/height of jump but by the number of points each effort is worth. This system of tables could, in principle, also be used in track events, but this has been opposed by IPC Athletics.

Discussion

Although the IPC constitution states that the organization is athlete-centred, when the IPC was formed in 1989 a decision was made to follow the IOC structure which, it has been argued, is not always concerned with the welfare of athletes (Jennings and Simson 1992). Prior to the establishment of the IPC, some had argued for the integration of disabled athletes into the Olympic Games (Labanowich 1988). In recent years, impairment-specific federations have been concerned that decisions made about the programmes at both the Paralympics and IPC World Championships, particularly in athletics, are designed to streamline the classification system. The events that are being whittled away are those involving the more severely impaired, and also the female categories, which are already the most marginalized segments of the Paralympic community.

This pressure for change in the current classification system is a result of the desire of the IPC to move away from a system of medical classification in favour of an integrated functional classification system which allows athletes with different impairments to compete against each other (Steadward 1996). It is hoped that by contrasting the sports of swimming and athletics, this chapter may help to facilitate a broader discussion about what is equitable and fair with regard to the classification of impairment in sport. Swimming has adopted the integrated functional classification system which involves fewer but larger classes, and the larger number of competitors within each class has meant that events do not have to be cancelled as a result of injuries to competing swimmers. Athletics, on the other hand, has used a culturally specific technique (performance tables) in field events to reduce the likelihood of events being cancelled as a result of injuries to competing athletes. On the track however there has been resistance to adopting any system that is different from those developed independently from the IOSDs. Here injury continues to play a significant role. The merging of wheelchair track racing for men is a direct response to injuries to a few key competitors and this has been done in an attempt to fast forward the process of integration among classes without due consideration for all IOSDs concerned (Richter 1999).

The removal of several classes on the athletics programme of the Paralympic Games is not considered negatively by the IPC, in the light of their mandate to reduce the number of classes; rather, it is seen as necessary if the Games are to 'progress'. In spite of increased acceptance of sport for the disabled in society generally, the push to reduce the number of classification categories within sport for the disabled has had a dramatic effect on the people who should be central to its mission – the more severely impaired athletes. 'Progress', to the IPC, is not only about slimming down and simplifying the classification system they inherited from the IOSDs but also involves eliminating events involving the severely impaired athletes. These athletes are being forced out of sports such as track and field athletics that are considered the shop window of disability sport (Shogun 1998, 1999). For example in 1988 there were lower-class cerebral palsy athletes competing on the track but by the mid-1990s, athletes in this class were active only in field events, which are seldom the centre of attention (they are often staged in one corner of the infield while the track events take centre stage). Here the body, in a sense, disappears. On the track, where an event is centre stage, the aesthetics of the bodies can be vital to selling sponsorship and providing commercial opportunities.

The elimination of severely impaired bodies from the athletics track does not mean that these athletes have been left high and dry. In recent years, many competitors have begun to take up the sport of boccia, which is similar in some respects to lawn bowling. Boccia is a game that requires a high level of technical skill but because the type of training is less physically demanding than in many sports, pain and injury are minimized. From the perspective of the IPC, the development of boccia highlights the organization's commitment to severely impaired sportspeople, while removing them from the spotlight on the athletics track. The move from a demanding physical sport to one which is more tactical does reduce injury but it also sends the message that there are certain forms of physicality that are more acceptable than others within the Paralympic movement.

Conclusions

While countries such as Canada and the United Kingdom fund the training of their elite athletes, including their access to high-quality sports medicine, the system is not as comprehensive as that which is developed for mainstream high-performance athletes. The system caters for performers who have already achieved elite status and little is done for less established athletes. Because the system has little provision for up-and-coming competitors, it means that many future potential Paralympians may never achieve the performances required. The fact that some athletes may be forced to leave their sport through the onset of chronic injury before they can achieve elite status raises questions about the future of the Paralympic movement.

A serious injury to a handful of Paralympians, particularly in sports such as athletics that have yet to adopt an integrated functional classification process, can mean the cancellation of some events. It would seem important, therefore, to adopt a system of registration of injuries within the IPC in order that events which have low numbers of competitors (and these are often the events featuring the severely impaired or women) are given every opportunity to take place in the Paralympic Games. While it seems realistic to cancel international events with only a few entries, the elimination of one competitive opportunity, which may be the result of injury not to oneself but to others, may lead to serious consequences for the careers of the athletes involved in the event. The cancellation of an event means that it will be six to eight years before the event is back on the Paralympic programme. Because of this, and the importance of the role of pain and injury outlined above, there is a need for an International Injury Register for Potential Paralympians (IIRPP).

The establishment of such a policy initiative related to injury is of importance because injuries are on the increase within elite sport for the disabled. With only a limited number of high-profile sporting events, every injury for these athletes can have significant implications not only for their own participation but for the future of their sport. Financially, the sponsorship and government assistance programmes which are part of these athletes' livelihood in countries such as Canada and the United Kingdom are often performance-linked to success at sports-specific IPC events or the Paralympic Games and, as such, missing one of these events through injury can place added stress on an athlete. If a similar misfortune befalls several athletes in the same classification, particularly in the more severely impaired classes, then their event could be cancelled not because of lack of interest but because of the relationship between high-performance sport and injury.

Notes

1 For a more traditional ethnographic account see Howe (forthcoming).
2 The Paralympic Games is second in size to the Olympics in terms of an elite multi-sports event.
3 Follow the links from the IPC web site (www.paralympic.org) to get details of the individual federation's classification systems. For a good discussion of integration of classification systems see Vanlandewijck and Chappel (1996).
4 Of course in the age of email it is possible to continue real time discussions from the far corners of the world and an increasing amount of data is collected in this manner.
5 Provision for potential champions is far greater in mainstream sport.
6 Swimmers with visual impairment are not part of this system and compete using the IBSA classification system, details of which can be found at www.paralympic.org.
7 The rules on competitiveness that eliminated the cerebral palsy male wheelchair racers from the Paralympic programme are not as rigorously followed when it comes to female competitors. In an attempt to actively recruit more women to the sport for the disabled there are effective different rules for men and women.

Bibliography

Daly, D. J. and Vanlandewijck, Y. (1999) ' Some Criteria for Evaluating the "Fairness" of Swimming Classification', *Adapted Physical Activity Quarterly*, 16, 3: 271–89.

DePauw, K. and Gavron, S. (1995) *Disability and Sport,* Leeds: Human Kinetics.

DePauw, K. (1997) 'The (In)Visibility of DisAbility: Cultural Contexts and "Sporting Bodies"', *Quest*, 49: 416–30.

Dummer, G. M. (1999) 'Classification of Swimmers with Physical Disability', *Adapted Physical Activity Quarterly*, 16, 3: 216–18.

Ferrara, M. S. and Peterson, C. (2000) 'Injuries to Athletes with Disabilities: Identifying Injury Patterns', *Sports Medicine*, 30, 2: 137–43.

Howe, P. D. (2004) *Sport, Pain and Professionalism: Ethnographies of Injury and Risk,* London: Routledge.

Howe, P. D. (forthcoming) *The Cultural Politics of the Paralympic Movement: Through the Anthropological Lens*, London: Routledge.

IPC (2001) *The Paralympian: Official Newsletter of the International Paralympic Committee,* No. 1.

IPC (2004) *The Paralympian: Official Newsletter of the International Paralympic Committee,* No. 2.

Jennings, A. and Simson, V. (1992) *The Lords of the Rings: Power, Money and Drugs in the Modern Olympics,* London: Simon and Schuster.

Labanowich, S. (1988) 'A Case for the Integration of the Disabled into the Olympic Games', *Adapted Physical Activity Quarterly*, 5: 264–72.

McCann, B. C. (1994) 'The Medical Disability – Specific Classification System in Sport' in R. D. Steadward, E. R. Nelson and G. D. Wheeler (eds) *Vista '93: The Outlook. Proceedings of the International Conference on High Performance Sport for Athletes with Disabilities,* Jasper, Alberta: Rick Hansen Centre: 275–88.

Nettleton, S. (1992) *Power, Pain and Dentistry*, Milton Keynes: Open University Press.

Richter, K. J. (1994) 'Integrated Classification: An Analysis' in R. D. Steadward, E. R. Nelson and G. D. Wheeler (eds) *Vista '93: The Outlook. Proceedings of the International Conference on High Performance Sport for Athletes with Disabilities,* Jasper, Alberta: Rick Hansen Centre: 255–9.

Richter, K. J. (1999) *The Wheelchair Classification Debate*, Paper given at CP-ISRA STC, Ottawa, Canada, September 1999.

Richter, K. J., Adams-Mushett, C., Ferrara, M. S. and McCann, B. C. (1992) 'Integrated Swimming Classification: A Faulted System', *Adapted Physical Activity Quarterly*, 9: 5–13.

Schantz, O. J. and Gilbert, K. (2001) 'An Ideal Misconstrued: Newspaper Coverage of the Atlanta Paralympic Games in France and Germany', *Sociology of Sport*, 18, 1: 69–94.

Schell, L. A. and Rodriguez, S. (2001) 'Subverting Bodies/Ambivalent Representations: Media Analysis of Paralympian, Hope Lewellen', *Sociology of Sport*, 18, 1: 127–35.

Sherrill, C. (1999) 'Disability Sport and Classification Theory: A New Era', *Adapted Physical Activity Quarterly*, 16: 206–15.

Shogun, D. (1998) 'The Social Construction of Disability: The Impact of Statistics and Technology', *Adapted Physical Activity Quarterly*, 15: 269–77.

Shogun, D. (1999) *High-performance Athletes: Discipline, Diversity, and Ethics*, Toronto: University of Toronto Press.

Steadward, R. D. (1996) 'Integration and Sport in the Paralympic Movement', *Sport Science Review*, 5, 1: 26–41.

Tweedy, S. M. (2002) 'Taxonomic Theory and the ICF: Disability Athletics Classification', *Adapted Physical Activity Quarterly*, 19: 220–37.

Vanlandewijck, Y. C. and Chappel, R. J. (1996) 'Integration and Classification Issues in Competitive Sports for Athletes with Disabilities', *Sport Science Review*, 5, 1: 65–88.

Wu, S. K. and Williams, T. (1999) 'Paralympic Swimming Performance, Impairment, and the Functional Classification System', *Adapted Physical Activity Quarterly*, 16, 3: 251–70.

Section V

The meaning of pain and injury

14 Suffering in and for sport

Some philosophical remarks on a painful emotion

Mike McNamee

Think of the countless times when sports commentators have made reference to the emotions in sport. Arrogance, anger and anxiety are known to playground sports just as they populate Olympic hearts, minds and stadia. The sheer variety of emotions, however, makes them difficult to pin down. Compare the tears of Mary Decker Slaney, the hot favourite who was tripped in the women's 5000 metres final of the 1984 Olympics at Los Angeles, with the uncontrolled weeping of Matthew Pinsent on the podium in Athens in 2004, as he won his fourth consecutive Olympic Gold medal in rowing. These extreme examples of intense emotions in sport should warn us against simple classifications of the emotions. In this chapter I want to make sense of how we can best understand emotions generally and the emotionally saturated concept of suffering in particular. I do this by first discussing some opposing philosophical analyses of the emotions. I then show the need to distinguish carefully between pain and suffering more carefully than is typically done in sports medicine or sports anthropology, which often conceive of them as synonymous with private or subjective feelings. I go on to present critically some philosophical accounts of the concept of suffering in medical ethics. Finally, I sketch a picture of human suffering in sport from an ethical point of view. I articulate and exemplify a range of issues that arise from thinking of suffering in sport as an extended emotional experience, inherently linked to the projects which we care about, are committed to, and which partly constitute our identities as sportspersons.

Philosophers and the emotions

The thought that emotions are irrational has a long philosophical history reaching back to Plato, who writes in the *Republic* (1974: 440a) of 'reason and its civil war with desire'. In the picture that emerges, rationality wins by a knockout. Emotions, it is said, must be allowed neither to cloud our judgement nor to give us grounds for partiality or bias. This conception remained dominant in philosophy and religion into modernity where the German philosopher Immanuel Kant gave it particular prominence. Kant is frequently credited with denying the rationality of the emotions and viewing them as obstacles to rational moral action.[1] One part of that picture, which is commonly held, is that we experience emotions passively and therefore that we are not responsible for them.[2] This latter point is worth dwelling on. Ought we to excuse people who, for example, react violently to a rough challenge in football, by simply saying that it was done 'in the heat of the moment' – that it was merely an emotional outburst? Surely we should not use feelings and emotions as objects to excuse our moral responsibility. Typically in sport, however, emotional excuses are employed in precisely such a vein: 'he made me angry and I retaliated without thinking'; or 'I just could not get out of the depressed slump in order to pick myself out and pull out one last jump' (dive, shot, putt, throw, etc.). It is in these contexts that we often hear that X's judgement was 'clouded by emotion'.

Where has this got us? To understand concepts such as 'suffering' we need in part to understand the philosophical ethical traditions that give them their general shape as an emotion. Most sports ethicists celebrate a Kantian picture of impersonal rational morality in which emotion is to be mastered. This issues in a view of sports ethics as the observance of universal rules conceived of as duties or obligations. It is from this foundation that the deontological conception of ethics is built.[3] Other recent writings[4] have tended to focus on virtue theoretical accounts of character development where being the right kind of sportsperson entails acting out of the right feelings and emotions in accord with rational perception of the situations in which we find ourselves. The good life in Aristotelian thought is always a complex of thought, feeling and action in harmonious coalition.

Critics of an Aristotelian view of the role of emotion in moral judgement and action will point typically to the lack of impartiality in our emotional attachments and experiences. More strongly it could be argued that capriciousness arises precisely because of the biased commitments of an ethics based on the emotions. Surely one would want from sports administrators and officials such as judges and referees precisely the kind of impartiality that deontology offers and that an emotion-laden ethics undermines? Citing a list of duties and rights to guide our actions, choices and emotions might be thought necessary. This, it could be argued, is needed in order to avoid the kind of biases seen in so many judged sports, or even in the selection of high-school teams or extra-curricular sports where considerations extraneous to athletic merit wrongly influence roster decisions. Perhaps then, the leap to a neo-Aristotelian position, which I advocate, is too swift and too open to subjectivity?

One of the reasons for favouring an Aristotelian position over a Kantian one would be rooted in the role that biological aspects of emotions play in their understandings of ethics and the emotions. Kant's writings have much in common with biological theories of emotions which are grounded empirically (and therefore contingently) in human nature or our biological endowment. So feelings of basic emotions (the list, of course, varies from researcher to researcher) of anger, grief, shame, joy, interest should obtain across cultures (see Ekman 1999).

Characterizing emotions as merely subjective feelings – as biological theorists typically do – ignores two important aspects: first, that emotions entail judgements and, second, that they are to a considerable degree influenced by space and time. Early philosophical analyses of the emotions have been inspired by Wittgenstein's anti-essentialism idea. That is to say, there is no essence to the concept of 'emotions' (as there is in other complex ideas such as art, democracy, education, and so on). Instead it is better to think of the different meanings of the term as illustrating a family of resemblances. Just as family members share certain traits but not others, so there is neither an essence nor a unifying set of properties to the concept of emotion. Some are voluntary, some involuntary; some are passive, yet others are active. Likewise, their intensity, though typically greater than felt moods, can vary too; compare a punch in anger at an opponent for a late tackle, to the studied resentment of an opponent where one stews in one's own juices. Even allowing for their biological basis, Amelie Rorty's remark seems precise: 'the emotions do not form a natural kind' (1988: 1). Moreover, certain emotions such as panic are experienced as self-referring while other emotions have a very significant interpersonal role in preserving boundaries of conduct by reinforcing norms of the acceptable and unacceptable. Emotions such as guilt, remorse, regret, Schadenfreude and shame all have a negative power that we typically seek to avoid or to work off.[5] Sometimes the emotions are felt in anticipation of action; at other times they succeed it. Sometimes they are directly motivational, at other times they are not.

To elicit the ethical import of the emotion of suffering (or any of its close cousins in the emotional field – anguish, despair, desolation, to name a few[6]) is to attribute the fact that the sportsperson him- or herself responds in part to a judgement or an interpretation of their situation. This point alone allows us to deny the description 'irrational' to the emotions.[7] Moreover, the emotions can be allowed a much more positive role in our identification of what matters to us in both fleeting and more considered ways. While it is easy to recall instances when emotions have got in the way of good judgement, or indeed been obstacles to right action, we can also think of examples where our emotional (though still cognitively based) responses are salient. Let me use a sports-emotion example which arose at the time of writing this chapter: the news of the death of one of the most celebrated and controversial British football managers, Brian Clough.

The manner in which Clough positively affected the lives of the inhabitants of a provincial English town, on the way to achieving successive European Cup football victories, is nothing short of remarkable. In listening to the supporters' grief and their sense of admiration, one gets an idea of what Clough achieved and how his coaching and managerial philosophy in the late 1980s touched their lives. Of course one can go overboard here. One can sentimentalize inappropriately: this is precisely the Kantian warning. Not for nothing did Clough refer to himself as 'Old Bighead'. Notoriously, he struck a fan who ran on to the pitch at the end of a game. Perhaps this is precisely the point at which a Kantian will want a strong role to be given to a controlling rationality distinct from the emotions. Yet the grieving spectators' emotional responses properly register their estimation of the part Clough played in more memorable days of their lives and the life of the town. To conceive of the emotions more generously then can open a conceptual space in which we can consider more broadly the roles they play in our lives beyond exculpation and the denial of responsibility.

Nancy Sherman captures this point beautifully:

> We can think of them [emotions] as modes of attention enabling us to notice what is morally salient, important, or urgent in ourselves and our surroundings. They help us to track the morally relevant 'news'. They are a medium by which we discern the particulars . . . In addition to their role as modes of attention, emotion plays a role in communicating information to others. They are modes of responding. Putting the two together, emotions become modes both for receiving information and signalling it. Through the emotions we both track and convey what we care about.
>
> (2000: 40)

It is precisely the spirit of these remarks, inspired by Aristotle's idea of the harmony of thought, feeling and action in ethically admirable persons, that drives my thoughts about the painful emotion of suffering in sport. I shall attempt to show how suffering is an emotional response to deleterious events in our lives, to harms or losses in relation to the things which matter to us in an enduring way.

On suffering and pain: Some initial conceptual geography

There is not a developed philosophical literature on pain and suffering in sport. Jeff Fry (2002) has published a very insightful overview of the theodicy of pain and suffering as it applies (and does not apply) to sport. In sports anthropology, David Howe has catalogued the habitus of injury-acceptance as part and parcel of what is variously called the social field (after Bourdieu) or practice (after MacIntyre) of elite sport.[8] Neither Fry nor Howe, however, directs attention significantly to the relations between the two concepts. What I shall do in this section is to set out some analytical remarks concerning the two concepts – and only hint at the theological similarities and dissimilarities in an attempt to enquire as to whether a consideration of suffering might have something interesting to say about the nature and purposes of sport, and the sportspersons' emotional components seen as part of the living of a good life.

There is often conceptual confusion in sports talk surrounding these thorny concepts. Typically suffering and pain are conflated. One is thought to be suffering when in pain, and when pained, to be suffering. One of the ways of dealing with the complexity of the conceptual connections of pain and suffering is crudely to dualize them in the aspect of the person. Under such a dualism, pain is physical, suffering is mental. Thus Howe writes: 'Pain is a highly subjective phenomenon, and this has led to its exclusion from much discussion of injury, which may be seen as more objective' (2004: 74).

Despite disavowals to the contrary throughout the book, it is difficult to read passages in Howe's book in any way other than dualistically.[9] After Descartes, and dominating Western philosophy until Gilbert Ryle's brilliant debunking in *The Concept of Mind*, people were thought to consist of separate parts – minds and bodies – whose natures were distinct. Howe's writings, like those of many other social scientists (especially with the rise of the sociology of the body, with authors who are not naturally inclined to a phenomenological mien) and even sports psychologists (who really should know better), has difficulty in escaping the language that separates mind and body as distinct entities. So in Howe's fine book, it is perhaps not surprising that 'mental' concepts such as 'anguish' or 'suffering' do not appear in the index. It seems clear that physical pain is the paradigmatic object of discussion. And there is of course nothing necessarily wrong with this. What is problematic, and what is found in many places elsewhere, is a particular set of relations between pain and suffering. On the one hand there is an apparently non-dualistic position where writers casually refer to 'bodily suffering' as a sensation 'usually' in the body. On the other hand there is the dualistic one: suffering is supposed to be the felt marker: pain indicates suffering.[10]

A further, less frequently observed, aspect of suffering and pain is brought out by Ivan Illich[11] (1987):

> The Old Testament is very rich in words that express a deep, deep sense of suffering: anguish, fear, bitterness, the experience of being lost, forlorn, beaten up, exposed to the wrath of the Lord. It was only very much later, during the Christian epoch, that rabbis felt the need to assign a specific word for that which we moderns now call pain. When these same rabbis had to talk about physical pain they used the word that designated punishments which I inflict. The English word pain comes from the Latin poena, from being punished. The concept of a physical pain, one specifically physical, comes from the experience of being chastised by another. In our language pain does not come from the inside; it is imposed on us from outside.

In what follows I will assume that the concepts of suffering and pain are closely related and will develop some ideas more concerned with suffering that is not driven by pain. To do this I shall draw upon analyses of suffering from the medical ethics literature.

Concepts of 'suffering' in medical ethics

In a well-known medical ethics text, Cassell (1991: 33) offers the following definition of suffering:

> Suffering occurs when an impending destruction of the person is perceived; it continues until the threat of disintegration has occurred or until the

integrity of the person can be restored in some other manner. [. . .] suffering extends beyond the physical.

And later: 'suffering can be defined as the state of severe distress associated with events that threaten the intactness of person' (Cassell 1991: 33).

The two features of this definition might be called the (i) feeling and (ii) integrity criteria.[12] It is worth observing how these criteria relate to aspects of privacy and subjectivity. There can be times when there seems to be a simple causal relationship between pain and suffering – though it must be noted that Cassell avoids the simple dualism of caused in the body, suffered in the mind. In such cases one suffers because one is in pain. Cassell refers (pp. 25–36) to situations 'when the pain is so severe it is virtually overwhelming', 'when the patient believes the pain cannot be controlled' and also to 'pain that is not over-whelming but continues for a very long time'. It is not difficult to find sporting examples for these instances of suffering because of pain. They represent, perhaps, a kind of paradigm for sporting suffering in that they are at least the most obvious of cases of sporting suffering.

Cassell, however, makes a couple of further conceptual remarks that are interesting for our purposes. Like Howe, he writes dualistically in the vein of an essentially private character of suffering: 'Suffering is ultimately a personal matter – something whose presence can only be known by the sufferer' (1991: 35).

This privatization of suffering runs counter to the view that I shall adopt and adapt later. In that account, suffering can indeed be attributed by another. Indeed, our predication of empathy as sports spectators rests on this point. As I watch the gymnast fall on the last movement of her routine my heart goes out to her. I can appreciate at least sufficient of her misery to see how and why she suffers. In later remarks, however, Cassell captures at least some of what I take to be the inherent sociality of suffering:

> Suffering must be distinguished from its uses. In some theologies, especially the Christian, suffering has been seen as presenting the opportunity of bringing the sufferer closer to God. This 'function' of suffering is at once its glorification and relief. If, through great pain or deprivation, someone is brought closer to a cherished goal, that person may have no sense of having suffered but, instead, may feel enormous triumph. To an observer, the only thing apparent may be the deprivation. This cautionary note is especially important because people are often said to have suffered greatly, in a religious context, when we know only that they were injured, tortured or in pain, not whether they suffered.
>
> (1991: 35)

He summarizes: 'Although pain and suffering are closely identified in the minds of most people and in the medical literature, they are phenomenologically distinct' (1991: 35).

Given that the concepts are so frequently run together, we should ask: precisely what does it mean to say that pain and suffering are conceptually distinct? One could think of minor ailments, when one is in pain but not suffering. One could think of fleeting twinges – for example, the type which, in my early middle age, I encounter in my knee, back and ankles when I run – where it would be a piece of gross conceptual inflation to say that I was suffering. Finally, one could imagine cases of minor injuries; knocks, bumps, soreness, that are inherent in contact sport. When we experience minor injury or dysfunction it is no more than the consequence of the graft and grind of any sporting life. These simple remarks serve to establish the point that pain and suffering are not synonymous. We may often be in pain but it does not follow that we should speak of ourselves as suffering.

One further idea which might cut through the simplistic body–mind pain/ suffering complex is the idea of significance. It can be argued that what the integrity criterion attempts to secure is a quality of 'depth' in our experience. Suffering under such a description necessarily draws on both significance (extent or duration) and psychological distress. It would be odd to speak of one who suffered momentarily or in the blinking of an eye. In what follows below I consider Edwards's critique of the 'feeling' and 'integrity' criteria of Cassell's account and his own analysis of the concept.

Edwards bases his criticisms of the concepts of suffering proposed by Cassell, among others, upon a more cautious appropriation of the concept. His leading point is a rejection of the essentialism entailed in the necessary and sufficient conditions they propose; that is to say, he rejects their method on Wittgensteinian grounds. Edwards says that we should attend to the uses of the concept 'suffering' in order to establish its meaning. And following our appreciation of that heterogeneity we shall find no crystallized essence but rather a family of meanings that criss-cross and overlap without containing any indisputable linguistic essence. Suffering is the kind of experience that must be felt. To suffer is to be in a state that is necessarily felt by the agent. In this respect, it is like pain. He says: 'Would it make sense to say of a person "You're in pain" if this came as a complete surprise to them?'(2003: 65). Of course, stories are legion of sportspersons who are injured without consciousness of it as they perform heroic deeds – only later to collapse in agony. One image which springs to mind is that of the bandaged American gymnast Kelly Strug as she prepared to risk even more serious injury lining up for the vault which won the American team the gold medal at the 1996 Olympic Games. However, although one may be injured without being in pain, one cannot be said to suffer without the cognitive aspect of the emotion registered at some conscious level. This condition seems indisputable for human suffering. Put formally we might say that it – the awareness of some seriously negative happening – is a necessary condition of suffering but not a sufficient one. Well, for the moment we may say that. I think there are good grounds for denying even that much, as we shall see.

Second, Edwards argues that suffering must be extended in time. Something as fleeting as a pinprick, or stepping on a sharp stone, cannot count. Moreover, though this seems a separate point, he argues that pain is not a necessary condition of suffering, for we may grieve deeply while experiencing no pain – where this is taken to be the unpleasant sensation produced by physical causes. Third, he argues that one cannot be happy and suffer. To suffer is to have a shadow cast – for that time – over one's enjoyment of life. He does note that in theological accounts of suffering – martyrdom is the extreme – the suffering is a central part of one's conception of the good life but he argues that here one merely has a stronger preference for the suffering.[13] Edwards summarizes his threefold account thus:

> The first is a 'self' component; the sufferer must realise that it is he or she that is suffering, that the experiences are his or her own. Second, the phenomenological component, the distinct way or ways it feels to suffer. And third, a temporal component; this will signal the duration of the experience of suffering. Schematically we might express such experiences thus: [S, p, t]. Where the components are the self component S, the phenomenological component p, and the temporal component t, respectively.
>
> (2003: 65)

We can conclude that there is at least a generic meaning here; a conceptual core but nothing as strong as an essence conceived of as a set of necessary and sufficient conditions. That general sense of 'suffering' means little more than experiencing something significantly deleterious to our well-being. In relation to human suffering we typically qualify the nature of that suffering in an adverbial way by drawing out the qualities of mind and character that attend the suffering. In addition, I want to draw attention to a specific dimension – the emotionally saturated idea of suffering. It seems to me that much suffering in sport is merely the experience of distressing pain – and this is surely worthy of explanation. But I shall not address it below, preferring instead to highlight a few remarks about the emotionality of suffering in sport. By way of summary, let us agree for the moment that suffering in sport is an extended emotional response to events that are significantly deleterious to our well-being. Where will that take us?

Conceptualizing human suffering as emotion

Let us say that we can articulate human suffering as a felt emotion. This point arises from Edwards's first two conditions, though he does not employ the description of suffering as an emotion as such. The idea that suffering is an emotion is denied by some. Consider Meyerfeld (1999: 50) who argues that one may suffer without cognisance. He asserts that one may be stunned, inarticulate or confused. Yet it seems that here he is presupposing that for which he must argue. For while it is true of certain moods ('distress' being one candidate) that they are to a certain extent diffused or inchoate, I cannot see what conceptual advantage there is in thinking that the epistemological condition is not necessary.

In my discussion of emotion above, I included the cognitive element of emotion which is typically in the form of a judgement. Imagine being told by someone who looked desolate that they are suffering but they did not know why. We might think, quite reasonably, that they had taken leave of their senses. Of course they might be experiencing a sense of foreboding, anticipating some bad event, or simply be feeling melancholic. If this were the case, though, we would have moved away from emotion-talk and back into the territory of moods which have a lower cognitive threshold and no specific intentional object. Moreover, that someone is inarticulate or stunned or confused is a psychological condition – one that need not impinge upon our conceptualization of suffering as an emotion. So let me assume here that to suffer is to experience an emotion with an intentional object: we suffer because of our perceptions of something significantly bad about our condition. Nevertheless, this alone is insufficient to make sense of suffering. In the light of the foregoing we should say that to suffer is to undergo some unpleasant emotion for some significant duration. Now what is to count as 'significant duration' cannot be pre-specified in some abstract way. The particularity of the phenomenology of suffering means that what counts as extended in one context may be brief in another. But that does not open the door to subjectivity of meaning. Consider the intensity of effort of the 400 metre runner as (s)he comes down the final straight, paradoxically trying to produce and remove lactates from her/his legs. I want to maintain that to use the word 'suffering' here, as commentators do, is inappropriate. Contrast the use of the word 'suffering' to describe the efforts of marathon runners in the last mile, or Tour de France cyclists going for the last climb of a mountain stage. Here the use of the word has a more natural home. Edwards does not develop this point and so I shall say a little by way of justification for the position.

For us to speak of emotionally saturated suffering, we must at least have time to dwell (should we so desire) on our misfortune in order for us to suffer. In this sense we could contrast suffering with more episodic emotions – such as the joy of scoring a goal. This is brief, however much we recall, re-describe and relish it on later occasions. Now if we were to evaluate the benefit or disbenefit of an emotion we might well be required to consider its duration as well as its extent. Ought we to opt for a few years of adulation, status and wealth at the expense of a lifetime's suffering, as many elite sportspersons do? Typically, the experience of the emotion in sport does not last in time in the same way as the caring love of a parent or child. Equally, though pain can range from mild to excruciating, it seems to make little sense to say that suffering could be mild. This is not to say that suffering is all or nothing. We do not need to be absolutist about this. But it makes sense to say that there is a certain threshold before we meaningfully apply the concept.

By coalescing pain and suffering, by failing to keep them analytically distinct, Meyerfeld denies this attribution. He draws on the *locus classicus* of the pain register (Melzack and Torgerson 1971) which describes pain as ranging from mild to discomforting, and then to distressing, horrible and, finally, excruciating.

Meyerfeld goes further by saying: 'These words recognisably refer to the intensity of suffering not just pain' (1999: 39).

I do not see the coherence of this application. And Meyerfeld offers no argument for it. In order that one may be said to suffer, one must experience a certain intensity or one cannot say one suffered. To suffer mildly makes little sense, *pace* Meyerfeld, though to describe a pain as mild does make sense. Cassell is much clearer here. He says that we suffer – in relation to pain – 'when the pain is so severe it is virtually overwhelming' (1991: 36) and later 'when the patient believes the pain cannot be controlled' or 'in relation to pain that is not overwhelming but continues for a very long time' (1991: 36). It is not an accident that in the biomedical literature, where pain and suffering co-mingle, we find that chronic pain is the paradigmatic example. Extension in time, and a certain intensity, are all present in Cassell's examples. They are part of the condition of suffering. But an articulation of that condition is not complete without the articulation of a sense of meaning that attaches inherently to it.

In addition, it seems reasonable to say that we cannot suffer in relation to things to which we are indifferent. Whereof one does not care, thereof one cannot suffer. That for which we suffer we must, in some fairly strong sense, be committed to, or care for, or identify with. There must be some sense of both attachment and value. This is the direction in which Cassell's 'intactness' condition aims, but it sets too high a threshold. Equally, Edwards holds that suffering 'must have a fairly central place in the mental life of the subject'. But this condition does not have direction; it does not specify the inherent negativity of the concept. Here Cassell merely asserts that the religious martyr suffers yet experiences the suffering positively. This seems to be too open-ended. Can we not hold that the negativity is, logically speaking, internal to the concept of human suffering? Where one embraces a painful death, in what sense can one be said to suffer? It strikes me that that would be contradictory. It is a mistake founded on the generalizability of experience – yes, you and I might suffer in such circumstances but our *Weltanschauungen* are radically different.

What is at stake in suffering, as I have said, is something that is not a matter of indifference to us – it is something that is part of our 'horizon of significance', to use Charles Taylor's apt phrase. As Cassell observes, we can only see the Christian sufferer in pain. Perhaps we can put it more strongly by saying that martyrs do not suffer the pains of fire, rather they rejoice in it. Now a chief question will be whether sportspersons, like religious martyrs, find the depths of meaning in sport that their forebears found in Christianity.

Having only hinted at the features that I consider critical to capture our emotional sense of human suffering, I will merely point to aspects of sports suffering that would bear further analysis and note certain social and theological parameters that might serve to deepen our understanding of suffering – especially for those such as physicians or physiotherapists or sports coaches who necessarily deal with the equally necessary sense of the inevitably tragic in sport.

Suffering in and for sport: Three possibilities

As I have said, the paradigmatic cases of suffering in sport relate closely to those cases wherein pain drives the suffering over time in relation to something of importance to the sufferer. There are three categories where this could usefully be explored in sports-related literatures. They help to point to what I think of as the inherent tragedy of sport. Forget the myth of continual progress so dear to global capitalism and crystallized in sports marketing. The point is simply that sport careers (however humble or exalted) are not best represented in a linear fashion. Rather they are cruelly, inescapably, elliptical. They rise, they peak and then, necessarily, they fall. The simple fact can be seen in three categories of sportspersons to whom we might look naturally for suffering: (i) the elite athlete; (ii) the ageing athlete; (iii) the retired athlete. In each of these cases the meaning of the suffering will be coloured in distinct ways; the manner in which the sport informs the life of the elite athlete – who may be almost suffocating in its exclusivity and intensity – will be quite distinct from the more chronic experiences of the ageing athlete and the desolation of the retired athlete who may wallow in a post-sport world devoid of emotional peaks and troughs (along with other lacunae).

If we were to agree that suffering in sport (as elsewhere) is best thought of as an emotional experience, then we should be able to point to the intentional objects involved. What might 'cause' such suffering? Some potential precursors might be (i) the anticipation of loss or the infliction of a defeat; (ii) the recognition of consequences of injury; (iii) distress of possible termination of career, perhaps most strongly for elite athletes; and (iv) sports 'death' as it were: the loss of economic and social identity. Of course the list is not exhaustive and merely attempts to suggest where one might toil for more interesting phenomenological investigations. In these cases one could ask whether sportspersons, *contra* Huizinga, take their sports too seriously. Here the status of the sportsperson is all important. For professional players, sports may well be 'everything' – the phrase 'it's only a game' is a banal utterance in this context. The rest of us, however, need to find a place for the sports activities we care for, love and value, in ways that are not as totalizing. It also opens up at least one significant normative question: ought we really to suffer for sport?

Having merely hinted at the meaning-driven facets of sports suffering, it might be worth thinking how the duration element might draw us to look for central cases in sport. Where might we find suffering in the performance of sport – as opposed to the preparation for sport? The obvious point to look at is those endurance sports where performance is not merely extended over time – a round of golf after all takes three to four hours – but also those where there is a limited array of performance factors. Typically, sports where the production of power is not dominated by technical or aesthetic concerns seem rich candidates for sites of suffering. We find not merely temporal extension in marathon running, biathlon, triathlon, in cycle races such as the Tour de France, but a quality of extension where one has time and space for a welter of factors to impinge upon one's consciousness in the experience of the activity.

A recent incident may go some way to pointing up this interesting aspect in a literal way. At the 2004 Olympics the British runner Paula Radcliffe was the favourite for the marathon. She had posted the year's fastest times for 10,000 metres on the track and had recently smashed the world record for the marathon. Having struggled to control the pace, in heat that made even some African athletes retire earlier in the race, Radcliffe withdrew with only three miles to go to the finish, apparently in the knowledge that she would not win a medal. Clearly she suffered over the difficult, hilly, terrain in exhausting heat. Mile after mile her face grew more contorted, more anguished. What were her thoughts over those miles, those hours and minutes as she considered personal failure, in the certain knowledge that she had 'blown' her last and best chance to gain an Olympic gold? What contents of scathing introspection occupied her every stride? And just as one can experience emotion after the fact, what emotions fuelled her anticipation of the savage British sports press in the aftermath of what would be written as a national tragedy? Or as it was later written up, even in some of the most thoughtful quarters of the British media, not so much a national disgrace as a moment of personal egoism and cowardice. Robert Philip's (2004) article, entitled 'Radcliffe was a sore loser', was as critical of the national press that supported Radcliffe as a heroine as he was of the athlete herself:

> The Tears of a Hero proclaimed one headline alongside a picture of Paula Radcliffe. Well, if it's heroes you want, then I'll give you heroes: Japan's Mizuki Noguchi, who won the Olympic marathon, was a hero. So, too, was Briton Liz Yelling, who produced a late sprint to overtake Maria Abel, of Spain, in a photo-finish for 25th place.
>
> Nor should we forget her team-mate Tracey Morris, who ran in the same heat and up the same hills as Radcliffe to finish 29th only to be totally ignored by Fleet Street. And was there anyone more heroic than Mongolian Lursan Ikhundeg Otgonbayar, the 66th and last competitor across the line in the Panathanaiko Stadium, a full 30 minutes behind the woman in front and almost 1½ hours adrift of Noguchi?
>
> But no, it is poor, distraught, anguished, heroic (I could go on but you get the drift) Radcliffe sitting in a gutter by the side of the road on whom we are expected to bestow the laurel leaf for Olympic gallantry.
>
> Call me a cynic, but the way I see it is that unless the medics in Athens can come up with a physical reason why she quit just over three miles from the finish, Radcliffe stopped running and started blubbing for the simple reason that she had just seen gold, silver and bronze medals disappear into the distance. [. . .]
>
> What most observers appear to have overlooked is that, yes, while there are only three medals on offer, every runner who completes any marathon course is a winner. Radcliffe – as brave, heroic, and dedicated as she might

have proved herself to be in the past – was a loser on Sunday night and, judging by her reaction when she opted out of the race having conceded third place, a pretty sore loser at that.

What is striking in this appraisal is the adverbial quality that Philip imports to the appraisal of the athlete's character. Without knowing it, Philip has charged Radcliffe and held her to account for her suffering. He has judged her character through an emotional evaluation. Yet he has captured only a small part of the aetiology of her suffering – the anticipated failure. It might be argued that he himself has failed (on a monumental scale) to empathize with the athlete in her suffering before moving to his strong critique. The significance of the goal, the preparation of a lifetime, the realization of a lost dream, the estimation of one's fall from esteem (and then from grace) all seem to meet our criteria for suffering to the point that make her devastation comprehensible. For Philip, all that is perceived is a wallowing, egoistic, pity. Now it might be held by others, properly, that Radcliffe's response lacked courage, that it was weak in some meaningful sense – but then that is not the position before us. It is clear that she experiences herself as suffering as she ran and eventually gave up. Ought she to have had this emotion? Is she entitled to the empathetic responses that are proper to the perception of a suffering one? These are the questions Philip fails to ask. Instead, he arrives too quickly at his conclusion: she is a shallow loser. For my own part, and based upon the analysis of suffering above, I think it makes every sense to see Radcliffe as suffering and worthy of an aptly felt empathy. I do not say that this makes her a model of good character; one to be admired or envied, but simply one for whom we may feel, with justification, some considerable sadness.

To explore such suffering further – and our ethically responsible responses to it – we would need to evaluate the adverbial character of the emotion in a more compassionate manner. Precisely how does one suffer here? Is it wallowing in the failure to achieve one's expected goal? Is it more intense as one battles to dislocate one's sensory experiences, to dull the pain of chronic injuries or heat-driven distress? Again these are only suggestions as to where we might meaningfully further explore suffering in sport.

A set of interesting questions remains that is located beyond the individualized phenomenological conception that we are naturally drawn to in the West. I take my cue here from the socio-theological writings of the Catholic intellectual and polymath Ivan Illich. Illich (1987) writes of 'communities of suffering'. It is an idea rich in possibilities for understanding the places of suffering in sport. Of course this could refer to the suffering that is closely related to intense pain: the gym, weights room, the track, the pool. Commentators frequently remark on the camaraderie wrought by the masochistic mutuality of boxing, or the tacit acknowledgement of chronic neck and back pain suffered by front row players in rugby, or American footballers on the line of scrimmage, at the tight end, protecting the quarterback at the risk of life and limb.

If we eschew a model of emotion that is pejoratively characterized as mere moods, or as uncognitive – as feelings that visit rather like a thief in the night – it makes sense to ask questions regarding the history of suffering in sport. From whom do we learn to suffer? In what ways are we initiated to it? Do we embrace it as a friend or as an enemy? What coping strategies are authentic? Are such strategies for anti-suffering (such as withdrawal) somehow inauthentic? In what sense can coaches or team-mates or indeed opponents share in the suffering of others?

Suffering, sports medicine and the ethics of sport

Finally, there is a further set of Aristotelian-inspired ethical questions that we can ask in respect to the non-theological ethical significance of suffering under the physical and emotional aspects of the concept. Might there be virtuous responses to suffering? Could we think of the boxer, humiliated by his opponent, as acting courageously while he suffers? Or ought we to think of it as courage gone awry, as rash or reckless suffering? Is the boxer's suffering (especially where self-inflicted) in some sense wrenched from virtuous ends – and means? For virtue, if Aristotle is right, is always in the service of good ends. No amount of courage is to be thought of as bravery – a point that Philip might have borne in mind during his verbal laceration of Radcliffe. Should we think differently of Stoic suffering in the face of unbearable pain forced on us by another – a model of passive suffering? Lance Armstrong talks of precisely such a disposition in his account of cycling in the Tour de France, of making the other endure suffering. To what point do we admire the forbearance? At what point does it become pathological? Is the quality of suffering conceptually relevant when that person is ourselves, pushing through the 'pain barrier', when we are active in the construction of our own suffering?

It seems best to think of suffering in sport in a teleological way. In medicine we suffer in rehabilitation. In Christian thought we suffer for redemption. What ends are served by suffering in and for sport? There will be no global answers here, only particular ones. But we are minded as philosophers to ask of coaches, players and physicians, especially in elite sports, a question put by Plato long ago: What limits should we observe in our efforts to improve our bodily performance and remove causes of suffering? (1974: 407a)

In asking such a question, though not answering it, we would begin to challenge many myths in modern sport and sports medicine. There is a pressing need to understand the moral topography of sports medicine. Key to that challenge is the need to understand sports as well as sports medicine as social practices and, in particular, to uncover that which is often latent – the idea that medicine is merely a technical, unproblematic, means to unquestioned (and unquestionably valuable) ends.[15] So when we talk of medical professionals and professionalization of sports, we need to ask: whose ethics? Surely there is no necessarily shared ethic between the doctors' cure, the physiotherapists' care, in relation to the players' career. How this is both gendered and loaded – or not – with emotional content will be worthy of exploration and explanation.

Rather than asking whether the pain is positive or negative we might ask: 'What qualities attend the suffering?' In what ways specifically do we suffer in sports? This requires us necessarily to arrange and argue about the adverbial qualities of our selves and our sufferings. These questions force us to deny the hegemony of physicalized, biomedically explainable, pain as the paradigm of negative experiences in sport. They force us to take the social and emotional aspects of the emotion of suffering more seriously than hitherto has been the case. As Illich (1987) concluded:

> I am taking the liberty of speaking of suffering as the culturally shaped way of dealing with the shadow side of life rather than with its lighted, sunny side. I shall use the term suffering to indicate a particular socially and culturally acquired art of dealing with that shadow side, of bearing burdens which come with living. I'm speaking about the art of suffering. Pain is only one narrow, but very special, kind of condition in which one would properly need the art of suffering.

I hope, in the vein of these words, that I have at least offered a framework in which to consider suffering as an emotion loaded with ethical significance, and a minor agenda item for sports philosophers, physicians and practitioners alike.

Notes

1 On which see Williams' (1973) classic essay on the emotions.
2 According to Baron this position is not based on an accurate reading of Kant and should instead be called 'Kantian' but this is not the place for scholastic technicism.
3 I have argued against this conception elsewhere and elaborated the value of such virtues as trust and not mere rule-responsibility. See McNamee (1998).
4 I have attempted elsewhere to say more about the ethical significance of the emotions, and their place in a virtue-based ethics of sport (McNamee 2002; 2003).
5 Specifically in the rationality of subjective guilt caused by the unintentional infliction of an injury to an opponent, see McNamee (2002a).
6 The point may be put more generally that the emotions, like virtues and vices, come in clusters. On which see Rorty (1988).
7 I have developed this point, and given a fuller account of the centrality in the concept of personhood in the contexts of sport and physical education in McNamee (1992).
8 See also Fry's chapter *passim*.
9 Of course, the mistake was made by philosophers for centuries so this should not be thought of as a particularly damning criticism.
10 It is worth observing that so many people mistakenly believe that pain is somehow an inescapably private event that, in so far as it happens, can only be accessed and understood by the person in pain. This position was philosophically demolished in part by Ryle's famous attack on Cartesian dualism but also by Wittgenstein's private

language argument about the social and learning contexts which demand a non-private reading of these types of experiences.

11 I am grateful to Martin Lipscombe for drawing my attention to this essay.

12 I am grateful to Steve Edwards for sharing with me his thoughts on suffering and also for alerting me to his critique of Cassell's account of suffering *inter alia* with which I am in general agreement. I merely revise his analysis in a minor way in what follows. I note that he refers to Cassell's criteria as the phenomenological and intactness conditions.

13 One might say here that Edwards has not embraced theodicy from the inside. But this is not the place to argue this point.

14 I am mindful that this is 'grist to the mill' of anthropologists of sports medicine such as Howe and Waddington – part of their everyday discourses. Nevertheless, the ideas are typically ignored or pejoratively dismissed by biomedical scientists in sports.

Bibliography

Baron, M. (1995) *Kantian Ethics Almost Without Apology*, London: Cornell University Press.

Cassell E. J. (1991) *The Nature of Suffering*, Oxford: Oxford University Press.

Edwards, S. D. (2003) 'Three concepts of Suffering', *Medicine, Health Care and Philosophy*, 6: 59–66.

Ekman, P. (ed.) (1999) *The Expression of Emotion in Man and Animals*, Oxford: Oxford University Press.

Fry, J. (2002) 'Coaches' accountability for pain and suffering in the athletic body', *Professional Ethics*, 9, 1 and 2: 5–14.

Howe, P. D. (2004) *Sport, Professionalism and Pain*, London: Routledge.

Huizinga, J. (1970) *Homo Ludens: A Study of the Play Element in Culture*, London: Paladin.

Illich, I. (1987) *Some Theological Perspectives on Pain and Suffering: The Meaning and Management of Pain*, Institute for Theological Encounter with Science and Technology. Online. Available HTTP: <http://itest.slu.edu/dloads/80s/suffer.txt> (accessed 13.11.2003).

McNamee, M. J. (1992) 'Physical Education and the development of personhood', *Physical Education Review*, 15, 1: 13–28.

McNamee, M. J. (1998) 'Celebrating trust; virtues and rules in the ethical conduct of sports coaches' in M. J. McNamee and S. J. Parry (eds) *Ethics and Sport*, London: Routledge: 148–68.

McNamee, M. J. (2002) 'Is guilt a proper emotional response to the causing of an unintentional injury?', *European Journal of Sport Science*, 2, 1: 1–10.

McNamee, M. J. (2002a) 'Hubris, humility and humiliation: vice and virtue in sporting communities', *Journal of the Philosophy of Sport*, 29, 1: 38–53.

McNamee, M. J. (2003) 'Schadenfreude in sport: envy, justice and self-esteem', *Journal of the Philosophy of Sport*, 30, 1: 1–16.

Melzack, R. and Torgerson, W. S. (1971) 'On the language of pain', *Anaesthesiology*, 34: 50–59.

Meyerfeld, J. (1999) *Suffering and Moral Responsibility*, Oxford: Oxford University Press.

Philip, R. (2004) 'Radcliffe was a sore loser'. Online. Available HTTP: <http://www.telegraph.co.uk/sport/main.jhtml?xml=/sport/2004/08/25/sorp25.xml> (accessed 25 August 2004).

Plato (1974) *Republic*, 2nd edn, trans. D. Lee, London: Penguin.

Rorty, A. O. (1980) *Explaining Emotion*, Berkeley: University of California Press.
Rorty, A.O. (1988) *Mind in Action*, Boston: Beacon Press.
Ryle, G. (1949) *The Concept of Mind*, London: Hutchinson.
Sherman, N. (2000) *Making a Virtue of Necessity*, Oxford: Clarendon Press.
Williams, B. A. O. (1973) *Problems of the Self*, Cambridge: Cambridge University Press.
Wittgenstein. L. (1967) *Philosophical Investigations*, 3rd edn, trans. G. E. M. Anscombe, Oxford: Blackwell.

15 Pain, suffering and paradox in sport and religion

Jeffrey P. Fry

According to numerous scholars, the perception that pain and suffering are bad is widespread. Daniel Callahan, noted bio-ethicist and co-founder of the Hastings Center in the State of New York, writes:

> What can be said about human suffering? This much at least. No one wants to suffer . . . Suffering not only brings pain, physical and mental (just as pain can bring suffering), it can in its extreme form seem to rob people altogether of their humanity.
>
> (Callahan 1997: 201)

In her book, *Regarding the Pain of Others*, Susan Sontag (2003: 99) writes of 'a modern sensibility, which regards suffering as something that is a mistake or an accident or a crime. Something to be fixed. Something to be refused. Something that makes one feel powerless.' Elaine Scarry (1985) argues in her influential book, *The Body in Pain: The Making and Unmaking of the World*, that pain constricts experience, destroys language, and 'unmakes' the world. Ariel Glucklich (2001) suggests in his book, *Sacred Pain: Hurting the Body for the Sake of the Soul*, that pain is widely perceived as a medical problem.[1] He writes: 'One hundred fifty years of this bourgeois medical psychology have all but erased the memory of pain as an experience that signifies something other than personal disintegration' (Glucklich 2001: 7).

These claims may indeed capture widespread sensibilities. But pain and suffering are polyvalent. I argue in this chapter that experiences of pain and suffering present an ambiguous picture. In doing so, I focus on discourses and practices in sport and religion that shed light on experiences of pain and suffering. Devotees of both sport and religion bear witness to an ambiguous and even paradoxical relationship to these experiences. On the one hand, it is true that among practitioners of both religion and sport, one encounters protests against pain and suffering. Within religion this protest may be registered in a demand for theodicy and in sport in laments over career-threatening injuries.[2] But the picture is complicated for, on the other hand, as Glucklich (2001: 7) notes, religion and sport also represent two arenas where one can still find positive appraisals of pain. Both religion and sport bear witness to a willingness among some adherents to accept pain and suffering and even, at times, to embrace them. Pain and suffering may even be viewed as empowering. Further, the meanings which devotees of religion and sport employ in assigning a positive sense to these experiences are similar in intriguing ways. Indeed, one finds a cross-fertilization of interpretive frameworks. Do the religious voices contribute to our understanding of pain and suffering in sport? I argue that they do; moreover, sport reciprocates by contributing to religious understanding.

In what ways do these testimonies illuminate experiences of pain and suffering? In particular, do these testimonies helpfully illuminate our assessments of the moral significance of pain and suffering in sport? While the ambiguous and even paradoxical nature of the accounts complicates matters, this complexity need not lead to moral paralysis. By holding the multiplicity of views together, we can allow them to inform and perhaps expand our moral imaginations.

In the first section of this chapter I survey various approaches to understanding pain and suffering, culminating in the nomic structures invoked in sport and religion.[3] As noted above, one finds an intriguing interplay of ideas employed in sport and religion. In the second section I highlight the fact that both sport and religion exhibit testimonies that underscore a paradoxical relationship to pain and suffering. In the third I examine the contributions and limitations of these testimonies with respect to their potential for informing and even expanding our moral imaginations when we engage in ethical reflection. In this part of the analysis, I also look at the sometimes uneasy relationship between, on the one hand, pain and suffering in sport and, on the other, moral responsibility.

Meanings of pain and suffering

Some important distinctions

As pain researcher David Morris (1996: 152) states in a chapter title in his book, *The Culture of Pain*, 'Pain is always in your head'. To see the relevance of this claim, one need only consider the fact that anxiety and fear are widely recognized as intensifiers of pain. The view that perceptions shape experiences of pain is related to the further claim that pain and suffering should not be conflated. Glucklich (2001: 11) claims that pain is a 'sensation', while suffering involves 'an emotional and evaluative reaction'. Mayerfeld (1999: 3, 11) distinguishes between 'psychological' and 'objectivist' accounts of suffering. In his account, the former refers to an 'affliction of feeling' and the latter points to circumstances such as calamities that may befall an individual. On this view, pain is not to be equated even with a psychological account of suffering (Mayerfeld 1999: 25–6). Indeed, Glucklich (2001: 11) notes that pain may even alleviate psychological suffering. For example, in some cases pain may reduce suffering by assuaging a sense of guilt or depression. The distinction between pain and suffering is by no means a novel idea. It is a tenet of Buddhist doctrine, in which attachments, born of ignorance, lead to suffering.[4] To mitigate one's suffering, one must dampen the desires that fuel it, including the desire to be free from physical pain.[5] The widely acknowledged separability of pain from suffering does not, however, negate the fact that in our common experience pain often leads to suffering, and that, in experiences of agony, pain and suffering seem to fuse.

Pain may warn us of imminent injury. But pain does not always indicate injury. Thus, one should not simply discount an individual's claim to be in a state of pain when no tissue damage is detectable. Nor does injury always occasion pain and suffering. In times of war, some wounded soldiers appear impervious to pain and suffering.[6] These are important facts to bear in mind when considering athletes' and others' initially puzzling stances towards their own pain, suffering and injury.[7]

Still, given human vulnerability to injury, pain can play an important positive function by sending us warning signals. The importance of this function is pointed out by Paul Brand (Yancey and Brand 1997), physician and medical pioneer, who for decades worked with leprosy patients who could not feel pain in their hands and feet because they had suffered neurological damage. As a result of their insensitivity to pain, patients were prone to serious injuries. In the world of modern sports, athletes with lucrative contracts are highly sensitive to the fact that pain can signal a career-threatening injury. Even so, many athletes will play while in pain, especially if they are given reassurances that they can do so without causing further damage to injured tissue. Thus, medical personnel at times find themselves faced with difficult decisions regarding injured athletes' availability to participate. On the one hand, the participation of an injured athlete may be of immense short-term value to the team; on the other hand, taking the long view, participation could jeopardize both an athlete's and a team's future.

According to some accounts, pain may also have benefits beyond the function of signalling physical injury. Andrew Miller's (1998) acclaimed novel, *Ingenious Pain*, set in eighteenth-century England, tells the story of a mysterious individual who is born with an insensibility to pain. His 'faculty of suffering is frozen' (Miller 1998: 134). Later, he becomes a skilled surgeon, but his anomalous condition renders him bereft of sympathy for his patients. An encounter with a witch-like woman draws him into the world of pain, which comes to him like a burning within. His history is revealed to him in this pain which also, in an ironic twist, softens and humanizes him. Can pain function in a similar way in the real world and, in particular, in the world of sport? As I will show, some individuals claim that it can.

For most of us pain is a familiar experience. But is our pain similar in character and meaningfully communicable? Pain can take on multiple personae. The McGill Pain Questionnaire, which has appeared in numerous incarnations, was developed to help people articulate the quality of their pain by supplying words for sensory and affective qualities of pain, as well as evaluative words to describe the overall intensity of the experience. Thus, pain may be described in terms such as gnawing, crushing, pinching, wrenching, punishing, fearful, gruelling and wretched (Melzack 1973: 41–7; Melzack and Wall 1983: 56–67).[8] Pain may also be acute or chronic, and experiences of acute pain may differ greatly from those of chronic pain (Morris 1996: Ch. 3).

At a complementary level of analysis, David Morris (1996: 6) reminds us of the historical nature of pain. He writes of 'Victorian hysterical pain', 'Nazi Holocaust pain', 'pagan Stoic pain', and 'Medieval Christian pain'. By categorizing pain in these ways, Morris reinforces the notion that there may be important similarities across pain experiences, thus lending credence to the previously discussed claim that there is a widespread modern sensibility, negative in outlook, with respect to pain. But Morris's account of the historicity of pain also leaves room for considerable relativity and individuation of pain experiences. Morris (1996: 6) writes: 'My argument that pain is always historical – always shaped by a particular time, culture, and individual psyche – cannot finally be historical enough.'

Meanings in religious discourse

Where can individuals go to find help in interpreting their pain and suffering? Religion has been one important locus of meaning for these experiences. According to sociologist Peter Berger (1969), religion provides a 'sacred canopy' of meaning. Religion even spreads its 'canopy' over experiences such as pain, suffering and death, which at times defy our sense-making capacities. In this regard, Berger (1969: 28) writes that 'religion is the audacious attempt to conceive of the entire universe as being humanly significant'.

The literature of theodicy, broadly understood, attempts to deal with pain and suffering both as intellectual and existential problems. In Eastern religions the notions of attachment and karma play pivotal explanatory roles. The philosopher John Hick (1978) explores two prominent routes in Christian theodicy. The Augustinian approach views pain and suffering as punishment for humanity's fallen nature. In contrast, an approach that Hick associates with Irenaeus focuses on the contributions to 'soul-making' made by pain and suffering. Common to both Eastern and Western perspectives is the fact that religion provides nomic structures for interpreting these experiences. The meanings assigned to these experiences help to make them bearable for some people. As Judith Perkins (1995: 183) writes in her book, *The Suffering Self: Pain and Narrative Representation in Early Christianity*, 'Pain is always easier to bear if a nomic structure can be provided for it.'

Religion testifies at times to struggles against pain and suffering, both on one's own account and on behalf of others. But religious contexts also point to an acceptance of pain and suffering that is made easier by assigning certain meanings to the experiences. Of particular interest is the fact that some devotees of religion are depicted as *embracing* these experiences. Voluntary and even involuntary experiences of pain and suffering are sometimes portrayed as empowering and even ecstatic experiences. Early Christian martyrs were represented as rejoicing in the opportunity to be sacrifices for their religious faith. Perkins (1995: 32, 33) writes that suffering figures were typically represented by Christian documents of the second century as 'heroic athletes, warriors, victors', and that the martyrs confirmed a 'central belief that to be a Christian was to suffer, and that suffering itself was potent'.

Glucklich (2001: 3) cites a wide variety of types of religious discourses and practices that suggest a positive appraisal of voluntary physical pain or 'self-hurting'. This list includes pilgrimages, funerals, initiations, mystical disciplines, annual celebrations of various sorts, sermons, religious biographies, authoritative pronouncements and poetry. Glucklich (2001: 16–31) finds a number of transcultural models at work in interpretations of pain. These models provide numerous ways of assigning a positive significance to pain. It is noteworthy that he mentions the athletic model as one of these transcultural models, alongside juridical, medical, military, magical, educational, psychotropic and shared or communal models. Thus, pain conceived in terms of a medical model can be viewed as having a preventive or curative function. Even when pain is viewed as punishment, it can be given a positive twist. This can be seen in cases where the pain is assigned an educational role, or when it functions in a penitential mode, whereby the pain may pre-empt yet worse punishments in the future.

With respect to the 'shared' or communal model, Glucklich (2001: 28–9) points out the perception of pain as a 'transitive experience'. One can suffer on behalf of others, who are 'deeply affected by [one's] pain'. In a related vein, solidarity may emerge out of a sense of suffering together. Perkins (1995) documents how early Christians, for whom belief in the redemptive suffering of Jesus was at the heart of their theology, carved out over the first two centuries of the Common Era an identity as a community of willing sufferers. According to Perkins, 'Christian narrative representation':

> Functioned to construct Christians as a community of sufferers . . . Christian discourse relentlessly repeated this message and Christian subjects enacted it to the point that in the early centuries even pagan contemporaries who knew almost nothing about Christianity knew that Christians were sufferers.
> (Perkins 1995: 40)

While it may be tempting to explain away the significance of religious suffering in the light of a unitary psychological explanation, one should be wary of simplistic reductions. As Perkins (1995) notes, nomic structures have provided powerful validations of such experiences. Furthermore, as William James ([1902] 1985: 4–5) pointed out over a century ago in his classic treatment of the psychology of religion, *The Varieties of Religious Experience*, an 'existential judgment' about the origins of a religious experience is separable from a 'spiritual judgment' regarding the value of that experience. The same holds true with respect to experiences of pain and suffering in sport.

Meanings in sports discourse

When we shift our attention to sport, we find testimonies regarding pain and suffering that are similar in nature to those encountered in religious contexts. These testimonies include laments over the disabling features of pain and suffering. But we also find acceptance of, and even attraction to, these experiences. The mantra 'no pain no gain' has a strong foothold in athletic culture. Pain and suffering are often seen as means to desired ends. Cyclist Lance Armstrong states:

> The experience of suffering is like the experience of exploring, of finding something unexpected and revelatory. When you find the outermost thresholds of pain, or fear, or uncertainty, what you experience afterward is an expansive feeling, a widening of your capacities.
>
> Pain is good because it teaches your body to improve. It's almost as if part of your unconscious says, 'I'm going to remember this, remember how it hurt, and I'll increase my capacities so that next time, it doesn't hurt as much.' The body literally builds on your experiences, and a physique and temperament that have gone through a Tour de France one year will be better the next year, because it has the memory to build on. Maybe the same is true of living too.
>
> (Armstrong and Jenkins 2003: 222–3)

Recalling thoughts he had entertained before a planned attempt to reach the summit of Mount Everest, climber Jim Wickwire (Wickwire and Bullitt 1998) suggests that arduousness can be linked both to the purity of sport and to a sense of personal well-being. Wickwire states that:

> Ludicrous as it sounds – my strong desire to reach the summit without oxygen was fundamental to my search for a fuller meaning to my life. I wanted to achieve something special. To climb without oxygen would be unusually demanding and dangerous, but I felt prepared to make the sacrifice; what mattered to me was *how* I made the ascent.[9]
>
> (Wickwire and Bullitt 1998: 264–5)

As in religious contexts, so too in the world of sport we encounter claims that pain and suffering are efficacious for 'soul-making' purposes. Lance Armstrong (Armstrong and Jenkins 2003) reports that after the 2000 Tour de France his view of suffering was transformed. He came to view suffering in sport not only as a means to improved performance, but also as possessing redemptive qualities for him as a person. He states:

> Suffering, I was beginning to think, was essential to a good life, and as inextricable from such a life as bliss. It's a great enhancer. It might last a minute, or a month, but eventually it subsides, and when it does, something else

takes its place, and maybe that thing is a greater space. For happiness. Each time that I encountered suffering, I believed that I grew, and further defined my capacities – not just my physical ones, but my interior ones as well, for contentment, friendship, or any other human experience. The real reward for pain is this: self-knowledge.

(Armstrong and Jenkins 2003: 57–8)

During the Tour de France in 2000, Armstrong intimated in an interview with *Sports Illustrated* that the suffering he endures in cycling has an intrinsically satisfying quality for him.[10] In his words, 'You suffer a little during a training ride, you suffer during a race. I like that. I would really be upset if I never had the opportunity to suffer' (Thomsen 2000: 48).

Elsewhere pain and suffering in sport are embraced with a quasi-theological halo. John Krakauer's (1997) book, *Into Thin Air*, recounts Krakauer's first-hand experience of the disastrous 1996 climbing season at Mount Everest. Of his ascent of Mount Everest, Krakauer writes:

Above the comforts of Base Camp . . . the expedition in fact becomes an almost Calvinistic undertaking . . . I quickly came to understand that climbing Everest was primarily about enduring pain. And in subjecting ourselves to week after week of toil, tedium, and suffering, it struck me that most of us were probably seeking, above all, something like a state of grace.

(Quoted in Ackerman 1999: 136)

The story of American football star Jim Otto (1999), former center for the Oakland Raiders, and a member of the Pro Football Hall of Fame, provides another case where suffering for sport takes on a quasi-religious dimension. Over a period of 15 years, Otto played in 210 consecutive professional football games before retiring in the 1970s. Although durable, Otto has paid a price for his devotion to football. At the time of the publication of his book, *The Pain of Glory*, in 1999, he had undergone 38 major surgical operations, including 28 operations on his knees. Otto had received six artificial left knees, two artificial right knees and two artificial shoulders. He had endured a broken back and, on 20 occasions, a broken nose. Otto had nearly died on three occasions from what he takes to be football-related conditions.

Still, Otto holds no grudge against football, which was his ticket out of poverty. Instead, he states: 'You must understand one thing about me, an important point that puts my life in clearer perspective. I didn't want to be saved from football. That's because football saved me' (Otto 1999: 16). Otto thus reveals himself to be a willing martyr for football.

As in the case of religion, endurance of pain in sport at times has a transferable potency. Before the seventh and decisive game of the 1970 National Basketball Association championship series, it appeared that the New York Knicks' star center Willis Reed would be sidelined with a knee injury. Not even Reed's team-mates knew whether he would be able to play. But just prior to the game Reed limped on to the court in front of a roaring crowd. Reed won the opening tip-off against Wilt Chamberlain of the Los Angeles Lakers, then scored New York's first two baskets. After that, he did not score again. But that was enough. Inspired by Reed's presence and courage, the Knicks defeated the Los Angeles Lakers in what became an epic game.[11]

As with religion, sport also has its communities of sufferers. Lance Armstrong (Armstrong and Jenkins 2003: 4) calls the Tour de France a 'festival of suffering'.[12] A similar community identity exists among endurance athletes in other sports. In the mountain-climbing community, solidarity is sometimes demonstrated in the act of placing at the summit of a mountain a personal possession of a fellow climber who has died while climbing.[13] Sometimes solidarity also extends to those outside the sporting community, such as when participants dedicate their athletic performances to those who suffer from various afflictions, or to loved ones who have died.[14] This is often the case in mass participation events such as races and other athletic contests that are staged to raise money for cancer research or other causes.

Thus far I have focused on parallels between discourses and practices in sport and religion. In summary, while it is the case that both religious and sporting accounts reveal an ambiguous relationship to pain and suffering, it is noteworthy that there are adherents in both realms who embrace these experiences for their perceived beneficial effects. In the case of sport, the benefits are cast in terms of improved performance, and, as in religious discourse, as occasions propitious for soul-making. In turn, in religious contexts the suffering of devotees is sometimes viewed in terms of athletic heroism. In both sporting and religious contexts, we also find some individuals who suggest that pain and suffering have intrinsically positive features. Both sport and religion have their willing martyrs. Both have communities of sufferers.

But one can find even closer unions. For example, athleticism and spirituality are fused in the practices of the so-called 'marathon monks of mount Hiei'. These Buddhist monks, who reside in the area of Kyoto, Japan, undertake feats of athletic endurance as part of their quest to achieve Enlightenment. The athletic aspect of this discipline reaches its apex when, over a period of one hundred consecutive days, the monks daily traverse the equivalent of two marathons (Stevens 1998).

This comparative analysis of perceptions of pain and suffering in religion and sport leaves us with an ambiguous picture. I will now show that testimony to the paradoxical character of pain and suffering further complicates any appraisal of the significance, and especially the moral significance, of these experiences.

Pain, suffering and paradox

With respect to the pain of religious devotees, Glucklich (2001: 17) writes of a 'puzzling' paradox. He states: 'On the one hand, the martyrs and ascetics regard pain as the phenomenal face of a divine mechanism – retributive and just, while on the other hand, their certainty produces a strange insensitivity to pain.'

Indeed, as we have seen, some devotees find joy not only in spite of, but in the midst of, pain and suffering.

In sport, we find similar paradoxes. During the early stages of the 2003 Tour de France, American rider Tyler Hamilton fell and broke his collar bone. In spite of the injury and resultant pain, Hamilton went on to win a mountain stage and to complete the Tour de France. He had already forged a reputation for toughness. The previous year, while riding in the Giro d'Italia with a broken shoulder, he had ground down several teeth due to the pain he was experiencing. As a result, he had to have his teeth capped.[15] The 2003 Tour de France merely confirmed Hamilton's ability to endure pain. His comments on his participation in the 2003 Tour de France reveal the somewhat paradoxical nature of his pain experience. In a radio interview he explained, in Buddhist fashion, how his acceptance of the pain had made it bearable.[16]

Perhaps an attitude of acceptance accounts, in part, for a notable feature of mountain-climbing accidents observed by the legendary climber, Reinhold Messner. When Messner interviewed individuals who had survived falls while climbing, they indicated that they had not felt fear when falling. Instead, they had experienced a sense of well-being (Wickwire and Bullitt 1998: 250).

Joe Simpson, author of the classic mountaineering book, *Touching the Void* (1998), contends that mountain climbing presents some further paradoxes. Writing of his devotion to mountain climbing, Simpson states:

> It was, after all, a passion for me, something I loved fiercely, and yet it had hurt and unnerved me so much and killed so many of my friends. I tried without success to understand the conflict between pleasure and attrition.
>
> (Simpson 2003: 65)

Elsewhere, Simpson explicitly acknowledges the paradoxical nature of climbing. He states:

> It is a paradox. It can be at once idiotic to the point of insanity and one of the coolest, calmest, most lucidly controlled, and vivid things you will ever do. It is so stupid as to be wonderful.
>
> (Simpson 2003: 106)

He continues:

> The paradox and incongruity lie in the fact that we willingly choose such risks when we want so much to stay alive. Why? Perhaps it all boils down to sensation – what we feel is all we really know; all we can accurately say we are. Yet others may not feel the same way. That isolates us.
>
> (Simpson 2003: 129)

In another passage, Simpson again elaborates on his willingness to assume the risks associated with mountain climbing. Perhaps this poignant insight, which jolted him like a revelation after he was nearly killed, gets near the heart of the matter. While Simpson was climbing in the Bolivian Andes, a collapsing ice cliff sent an avalanche of debris in his direction. He pressed himself hard against a boulder for protection. Finally, the roar subsided. Simpson recalls:

> There was for a moment an immense self-satisfied pleasure at being there. The stars moved. I could hear again. I listened to my heart beating. It was a wonderful comfort, a balm soothing the ebbing terror. Breathing was good. I heard my companions breathe and I felt the living warmth of their backs as I released the protective pressure of my arms. The aliveness made me quiver. I realized with a start that I was never more alive than when I was almost dead.
>
> (Simpson 2003: 41)

Simpson's claim elicits a comparison with the paradoxical statement in the Christian Gospels in which Jesus proclaims: 'He who finds his life will lose it, and he who loses his life for my sake will find it' (Matthew 10: 39).[17] In both cases, we find a dialectical movement of thesis, negation and higher synthesis. Interesting parallels can also be found in other traditions. For example, even in Buddhist doctrine, where the self is a problematic notion, the dampening of desire leads to a more highly realized state of the empirical self.

In sport and religion we encounter varying responses to pain and suffering among different individuals. We have also observed testimony that a para-doxical relationship to these experiences can exist within a single person at a given point in time. Given these ambiguities and paradoxes, how can we reach clarity with respect to the significance, including the moral significance, of pain and suffering in sport? The approach I shall outline features the notion of responsibility.

Pain, suffering and the moral imagination

In his book, *Suffering and Moral Responsibility*, Jamie Mayerfeld (1999: 1) offers a normative assessment of psychological suffering, which he refers to as an 'afflic-tion of feeling'. According to his account, suffering is bad for the individual experiencing it, and bad from an impersonal standpoint. Further, suffering is intrinsically bad for the individual who undergoes it, although it may have posi-tive instrumental value. From this construal of suffering, Mayerfeld derives a *prima facie* duty to relieve suffering (1999: 85; see Chs. 4, 5).

But is there, in fact, such a *prima facie* duty? The testimonies drawn from religious and sporting contexts suggest that a claim to such a duty over-generalizes. Indeed, our obligations to relieve pain and suffering appear to be fairly context specific.[18] Although there may be a widespread modern sensibility that pain and suffering are bad, this sensibility reflects a social construction of these experiences, in which the medicalization of pain has played a significant role (Glucklich 2001: Ch. 8). As we have seen, however, this construction is one that is not universally shared. Depictions of pain and suffering from the worlds of both sport and religion suggest that these experiences can have not only instrumental value, but perhaps also intrinsic value. How might such accounts inform and perhaps expand our moral imaginations with respect to sport?

We should not reject these accounts out of hand or subject them to simplistic reductions.[19] Still, we must acknowledge the possibility that self-deception and faulty memory may play roles in individuals' interpretations of their experiencing of pain and suffering. One's self-estimation of moral growth as a result of pain and suffering may be skewed. Self-knowledge is not easy to come by. Further, those who claim that pain and suffering have an intrinsically satisfying character may do so because, after the fact, they can no longer accurately recall or recreate the feelings and sensations they previously experienced (Mayerfeld 1999: 101). But while these factors may complicate an assessment of any one individual's account of his or her experiences, they do not justify wholesale rejection of positive appraisals of pain and suffering. These testimonies have a cumulative weight. If we adapt William James's ([1902] 1985) receptive, pluralistically minded approach to religious experiences to the world of sport, we will grant a fair hearing to positive appraisals of pain and suffering in sport.

This is not to say that executing proper assessments of pain and suffering in sport is a simple matter.[20] The challenge before us is to be responsible in a way that is helpfully illuminated by the theologian H. Richard Niebuhr. In *The Responsible Self: An Essay in Christian Moral Philosophy* Niebuhr writes:

> The idea or pattern of responsibility, then, may summarily and abstractly be defined as the idea of an agent's action as response to an action upon him in accordance with his interpretation of the latter action and with his expectation of response to his response; and all of this in a continuing community of agents.
>
> (Niebuhr 1978: 65)

An important, and perhaps largely overlooked, aspect of pain and suffering in sport concerns the sufferer's responsibilities to others, and especially to those who are dependent on the sufferer. For example, mountain-climbing expeditions can last several months and may involve missing anniversaries, birthdays, illnesses and deaths of loved ones, as well as other significant events in the lives of those who remain behind. Thus, an individual's suffering for sport can be a luxury that comes at others' expense.[21] This is especially true when the sport in question is inherently dangerous. When individuals die in pursuit of their love of sport, or are left severely disabled, others too must live with the consequences.[22] This raises the question: what is responsible action on the part of the sufferer?

While these may be surmountable obstacles, other important considerations remain with respect to assessing the significance of pain and suffering in sport. For example, while we can distinguish conceptually between voluntary and involuntary experiences of pain and suffering, in reality the line of demarcation is sometimes blurry. To illustrate this point, consider the roles played by coaches and athletes. Subtle or not so subtle influences from coaches raise questions about what constitutes undue pressure and a violation of proper player autonomy. Coaches may be tempted to impose their own medical and juridical models of pain and suffering on athletes, whether from paternalistic or more sinister motives.

Pain thresholds may also vary considerably from one team member to another. Thus, a demand placed on a team does not produce uniform experiences. Debilitating injuries and even death can result from such mismatches. These factors underscore the moral responsibility of coaches, expedition leaders and others whose charge is the well-being of athletes, to be attentive and *responsive* to differences among participants. Elsewhere, it has been argued (Fry 2001) that coaches and athletes should work cooperatively in terms of what expectations are placed upon athletes. Indeed, a kind of theodicy is required for coaches' expectations, and coaches should not add unnecessary or gratuitous suffering to athletes' pain.

Nonetheless, this does not nullify the fact that for many athletes pain and suffering are integral parts of the challenge of sport. For some athletes, they are even viewed as expansive and deepening experiences. They are not just means to ends, but rather challenges to be faced as part of the sporting experience. Therefore, assuming that an athlete is acting responsibly towards others, any duty to attempt to mitigate the athlete's pain and suffering must outweigh not only the instrumental value of such pain and suffering, but also their potentially intrinsic value for the athlete. In the present climate, a perception of the instrumental value of pain and suffering in sport plays a significant role in validating these experiences. That being said, persons who have responsibility for athletes' welfare should be wary of imposing their own interpretive models on athletes' pain and suffering, whether to validate or to invalidate those experiences.

Conclusion

There is a widespread assumption that pain and suffering are bad. However, this view is not held universally. Even the view that pain and suffering are at least *intrinsically* bad, though they perhaps possess positive instrumental value, lacks universal assent. This pluralism should be given its due, particularly in cases where the experiences are voluntarily endured.[23] There is no automatic correlation between having these experiences and a higher state of self-realization. Pain and suffering can be disintegrative, can 'unmake' worlds and leave behind shattered individuals. But that is not the whole story. Some individuals, at least, claim that these experiences are not merely negative in character, but rather vehicles to a higher synthesis. These responses call for further and careful exploration, rather than simplistic reductions. Thus, in our attempts to understand and assess pain and suffering in sport we do well to acknowledge, to recast the words of William James, the varieties of suffering and pain experiences.

Acknowledgments

I would like to thank my colleagues Elizabeth N. Agnew and David B. Annis for their helpful comments on earlier drafts of this chapter. Some of the ideas presented here are also discussed in Fry 2001.

Notes

1   See Glucklich (2001), especially Ch. 8, 'Anesthetics and the End of Good Pain'.
2   The word 'theodicy' is derived from the Greek words *theos* ('god') and *dike* ('justice'). A theodicy is an attempt to defend divine justice in the face of the existence of evil. More broadly considered, 'theodicy' refers to religious 'legitimations' of experiences such as suffering, evil, and death (Berger 1969: 53).
3   Viewing our experiences in terms of 'nomic structures' refers to the meaningful ordering of our experiences.
4   For example, Roshi Philip Kapleau (1980: 18) of the Rochester, New York Zen Center states: '[Z]azen makes . . . plain that what we term "suffering" is our evaluation of pain from which we stand apart, that pain courageously accepted is a means to liberation in that it frees our natural sympathies and compassion even as it enables us to experience pleasure and joy in a new depth and purity'.
5   I am indebted to Elizabeth N. Agnew for this insight.
6   Mayerfeld (1999: 27) notes two studies of soldiers wounded in battle who experienced an 'analgesic reaction' rather than pain after being injured. Researchers attributed this effect to the fact that the wounded soldiers knew that they were leaving the danger of combat to receive treatment in a safe area.
7   Speaking of an injured player, former Major League Baseball manager George ('Sparky') Anderson once remarked that 'pain don't hurt' (Glucklich 2001: 209).
8   Glucklich (2001: 47) points out that the use of metaphors to describe pain can be complicated. For example, one may describe a pain in a tooth as a 'shooting pain', However, according to Glucklich, 'the sensation of being shot is not "shooting" at all, it is more of a blow followed by heat'. Such complications, however, do not nullify the importance of giving people a voice for their pain.
9   Given his condition, Wickwire later wavered on this commitment and probably would have used supplemental oxygen. It became a moot point since the attempt to summit was aborted.
10 Perhaps this import can be read into Armstrong's (Armstrong and Jenkins 2000: 220) claim elsewhere that the Tour de France involves 'purposeless suffering'. Although Armstrong seems more recently to have come to the view that the suffering he endures in cycling is not purposeless, his earlier claim may perhaps be interpreted to indicate that there is something intrinsic to this suffering that is attractive to Armstrong.
11 To read an account of the game online, see *NBA History*, http://www.nba.com/history/players/reed_bio.html.
12 After the Prologue race of the 2000 Tour de France, while sitting in the team hotel, Armstrong posed a question to his son. 'What does daddy do?' the elder Armstrong asked. Thus prompted, the child replied that 'Daddy makes 'em suffer in the mountains' (Armstrong and Jenkins 2003: 176).
13 See climber Jim Wickwire's personal account (Wickwire and Bullitt 1998) for an example of this.
14 See, for example, the account of the Australian ultra runner Pat Farmer, who dedicated his 14,986 kilometre Centenary of Federation Run around Australia in 1999 to

his deceased wife. Farmer accomplished the feat in 195 days on the road (Eckersley 2000).

15 This was discussed in a piece on Hamilton which aired on National Public Radio's 'All Things Considered', 11 July 2003.

16 Hamilton stated this in an interview broadcast on National Public Radio's 'All Things Considered', 29 July 2003.

17 The translation is from the Revised Standard Version (May and Metzger 1993).

18 I am indebted to Mike McNamee and David B. Annis for sharing important insights with respect to these issues. On limitations on obligations, see Fishkin (1982).

19 Glucklich argues that one must go beyond a functional analysis of 'sacred pain' in order to understand it adequately. He writes: 'A successful explanation of sacred pain needs to account for the subjective phenomena, that is, the experiential contours of pain. A good theory also needs to explain how hurting contributes to a sense of the sacred in a way that is not reducible either to pathology or social determinism' (2001: 41–2). Glucklich draws on a number of disciplines, including neuropsychology and neurology, to help illuminate the self-transformation undergone in experiences of sacred pain.

20 According to William James, both insiders and outsiders face obstacles when evaluating experiences of religious conversion. He writes: 'Neither an outside observer nor the Subject who undergoes the process can explain fully how particular experiences are able to change one's center of energy so decisively, or why they so often bide their hour to do so . . . And our explanations then get so vague and general that one realizes all the more the intense individuality of the whole phenomenon' (James [1902] 1985: 196–7). Perhaps similar thoughts apply to experiences of pain and suffering.

21 See Wickwire and Bullitt (1998).

22 There seems to be a difference in expectations of fathers and mothers. Mothers who pursue dangerous sports are perhaps subjected to a higher degree of scrutiny than are fathers. See the account of the climbing career of Allison Hargreaves, who was killed while climbing K2 (Rose and Douglas 2000).

23 Again, the words of William James serve us well when he writes that 'nothing can be more stupid than to bar out phenomena from our notice, merely because we are incapable of taking part in anything like them ourselves' ([1902] 1985: 109).

Bibliography

Ackerman, D. (1999) *Deep Play*, New York: Vintage Books.

Armstrong, L. and Jenkins, S. (2000) *It's Not About the Bike: My Journey Back to Life*, New York: G.P. Putnam's Sons.

Armstrong, L. and Jenkins, S. (2003) *Every Second Counts*, New York: Broadway Books.

Berger, P. (1969) *The Sacred Canopy: Elements of a Sociological Theory of Religion*, New York: Anchor Books.

Callahan, D. (1997) 'The immorality of assisted suicide', reprinted in R. Abelson and M.-L. Friquenon (eds) (2003) *Ethics for Modern Life*, 6th edn, Boston and New York: Bedford/St. Martin's.

Eckersley, I. (2000) *Running on a Dream: The Pat Farmer Story*, St Leonard's, NSW, Australia: Allen & Unwin.

Fishkin, J. S. (1982) *The Limits of Obligation*, New Haven, CT and London: Yale University Press.

Fry, J. P. (2001) 'Coaches' accountability for pain and suffering in the athletic body', *Professional Ethics*, 9: 9–26.

Glucklich, A. (2001) *Sacred Pain: Hurting the Body for the Sake of the Soul*, Oxford: Oxford University Press.

Hick, J. (1978) *Evil and the God of Love*, New York: Harper & Row.

James, W. (1902/1985) *The Varieties of Religious Experience: A Study in Human Nature*, New York: Penguin Books.

Kapleau, R. P. (1980) *The Three Pillars of Zen: Teaching, Practice, and Enlightenment*. New York: Doubleday.

Krakauer, J. (1997) *Into Thin Air: A Personal Account of the Mount Everest Disaster*, New York: Villard Books.

May, H. G. and Metzger, B. M. (1973) *The New Oxford Annotated Bible with the Apocrypha: Revised Standard Version*, New York: Oxford University Press.

Mayerfeld, J. (1999) *Suffering and Moral Responsibility*, Oxford and New York: Oxford University Press.

Melzack, R. (1973) *The Puzzle of Pain*, New York: Basic Books.

Melzack, R. and Wall, P. (1983) *The Challenge of Pain*, New York: Basic Books.

Miller, A. (1998) *Ingenious Pain*, San Diego, CA and New York: Harcourt Brace & Company.

Morris, D. (1996) *The Culture of Pain*, Berkeley, CA; University of California Press.

NBA History (2004). Online. Available HTTP: <http://www.nba.com/history/players/reed_bio.html> (accessed 8 June 2004).

Niebuhr, H. R. (1978) *The Responsible Self: An Essay in Christian Moral Philosophy*, San Francisco: Harper & Row.

Otto, J. with Newhouse, D. (1999) *The Pain of Glory*, Sports Publishing Inc.

Perkins, J. (1995) *The Suffering Self: Pain and Narrative Representation in the Early Christian Era*, London and New York: Routledge.

Rose, D. and Douglas, E. (2000) *Regions of the Heart: The Triumph and Tragedy of Allison Hargreaves*, Washington, DC: Adventure Press/National Geographic.

Scarry, E. (1985) *The Body in Pain: The Making and Unmaking of the World*, New York and Oxford: Oxford University Press.

Simpson, J. (1998) *Touching the Void*, New York: Harper Periennial.

Simpson, J. (2003) *The Beckoning Silence*, Seattle, WA: The Mountaineers Books.

Sontag, S. (2003) *Regarding the Pain of Others*, New York: Farrer, Straus, and Giroux.

Stevens, J. (1998) *The Marathon Monks of Mount Hiei*, Boston: Shambhala.

Thomsen, I. (2000) 'Heavenly ascent', *Sports Illustrated*, 24 July: 40–8.

Wickwire, J. and Bullitt, D. (1998) *Addicted to Danger*, New York: Pocket Books.

Yancey, P. and Brand, P. (1997) *The Gift of Pain: Why We Hurt and What We Can Do About It*, Grand Rapids, MI: Zondervan Publishing House.

Index

Page references including figure are given in **bold**. Notes are indicated by 'n' followed by the note number.

Elliott, H. 68
emotional pain 19, 70–4, 113, 229;
 anguish 146; in polar exploration 78–9,
 81, 83; running 70–4
emotions: and biology 230–1; and ethics
 229–32; as 'family of resmblances' 231;
 as feelings 230–1; and judgement 231,
 237; and philosophy 229–32; and
 psychology of pain 35; and suffering
 236–8
enforced competition 116–18
enjoyment of pain 67–70
Enlightenment 52
ethics: autonomy 153, 155–6, 207;
 beneficence 154, 157, 207; biomedical
 ethical principles 152–4; boxing 129,
 132–7, 149–51; deliberate infliction of
 pain 144–61; double effect 153, 156–7;
 and emotions 229–32; German
 Democratic Republic (GDR):
 mandatory doping 154–5, 156; ignoring
 pain/injury 198; informed consent 153,
 154–5, 187–9, 204; and medical
 confidentiality 194–7; non-maleficence
 153–4, 156, 203–4; parentalism 153,
 155, 204; and rights 152, 153; of self-
 inflicted pain 157–61; sports medicine
 and other medical practice 204–5; and
 suffering 230, 233–6, 242–3; violence
 148–9
European Boxing Union 140
Ewald, Manfred 111, 118
exercise and health 5, 20
exhaustion 68
experience of pain 18, 19, 22, 23;
 individual factors 37;
 phenomenological study of pain 55–8;
 and women athletes 25–6, *see also*
 suffering
expressions of pain 95–7, 99–100

Farmer, Pat 258n14
fatigue 69
Fédération International de Football
 Association (FIFA) 183
femininity 100–2
feminism 22
Ferrara, M.S. 211
Fiennes, Sir Ranulf 77
football: attitudes to injury 185–9;
 conflicting loyalties in medical care
 183–4; costs of injury 7; doctors 165,
 167, 182–3; doping in the GDR 112;

ignoring pain/injury 185–9; medical
 care survey methods 184; medical
 confidentiality 183–4, 194–7; medical
 staff and managers 191–4; overuse
 injuries 6; physiotherapists 173,
 189–90; return to play after injury
 189–94; risks of injury 8
Foucault, M. 54
Freidson, E. 198n1
Freud, S. 35, 36
Fry, J. 232
Fuller, C.W. 8
function of pain 51, 248

Gad, Rose 43, 44
Galileo 53
Gallwey, T. 56
Gate Control Theory 36–7
Gautvik, Willy 85
Gebauer, G. 74
gender 22, 23, 86–7, 98–105, *see also*
 women athletes
German Democratic Republic (GDR)
 109–24, 154–5; defection 118–19;
 detraining 121; discipline through pain
 114–16, 119–22; and ethical principles
 154–5; ignoring pain 122; organization
 of doping 110–12; pain: case studies
 113–19; recruitment of athletes
 109–10, **111**; relationships in the sport
 system 122–4, **123**; side effects 112–13;
 Stasi-volunteers in Olympic teams **111**
Giddens, A. 28
Giro d'Italia 254
Glucklich, A. 246, 247, 250, 253, 258n8,
 259n19
Goldman, R. 160
'good' pain 41–2, 43, 67–70
Graf-Baumann, T. 183–4
Gratton, C. 6
Greenland 79, 82, 84, 87n2
Groopman, Jerome 202–3, 204
Guttmann, A. 20, 69

habitus (Bourdieu) 27, 232
Hamilton, Tyler 254
happiness 236
Harris, D.V. 101
health: biomedical/social theories 1–3, 18;
 holistic view 203; and the medical
 model of injuries 206–7; and sport 4–5,
 20, 202–3
Heinilä, K. 66–7